STORYTRACKING

STORYTRACKING

Texts, Stories, & Histories in Central Australia

SAM D. GILL

New York • Oxford

Oxford University Press

1998

Oxford University Press

Oxford New York
Athens Auckland Bangkok Bogota Bombay Buenos Aires
Calcutta Cape Town Dar es Salaam Delhi Florence Hong Kong
Istanbul Karachi Kuala Lumpur Madras Madrid Melbourne
Mexico City Nairobi Paris Singapore Taipei Tokyo Toronto Warsaw

and associated companies in
Berlin Ibadan

Published by Oxford University Press, Inc.
198 Madison Avenue, New York, New York 10016

Library of Congress Cataloging-in-Publication Data
Gill, Sam D., 1943–
Storytracking : texts, stories, and histories
in Central Australia / Sam D. Gill.
p. cm.
Includes bibliographical references and index.
ISBN 0-19-511587-2; ISBN 0-19-511588-0 (pbk.)
1. Australian aborigines—Australia—Central Australia—Folklore.
2. Tales—Australia—Central Australia—History and criticism.
3. Mythology, Australian aboriginal—Australia—Central Australia.
I. Title.
GR366.A87G56 1998
96-51727

1 2 3 4 5 6 7 8 9

Printed in the United States of America
on acid-free paper

In memory of

Harry F. Corbin
1917–1990

and my relatives

Ralph Fulton Gill
1902–1996

Howard Ellis Gill
1897–1987

Bernice Mae Gill Hilts
1904–1994

Preface and Acknowledgments

I wrote this book primarily for myself, because I wanted to, but also because I was compelled to. Realizing that the "Numbakulla and the Sacred Pole" example that I had "borrowed" from Eliade may well not have much of anything to do with the Arrernte, I became abducted (I won't say obsessed, though readers may disagree) by the effort to trace it to its aboriginal source. After exhausting published sources, I found myself in Australian archives and libraries ferreting out field journals and notebooks. By then I had also come to be abducted by Australia, especially the history of the development of Central Australia. I found myself in Central Australia, walking the tracks of the main players in this skein of entangled stories. In this setting it is fashionable to be critically hostile toward missionaries and pastoralists (actually any Australians of European heritage), accusing them of harm done to aborigines and their land. They are easy targets who do not talk back. But after learning their stories, I find them all, in light of their own intentions, nothing short of heroic. I doubt that I would have wanted to be close personal friends with the Hermannsburg missionaries, or they with me, but they gave their lives selflessly to what they considered the greatest cause. John Stuart, the great explorer, was a man of remarkable passion and perseverance. William Willshire, the mounted constable, despite a certain buffoonery and counter to the infamy with which he is usually remembered, gained my respect and sympathies because of his dedication and his self-transcendence. Among the aborigines of this history, I came most to know Moses and Charlie Cooper, both fascinating men who bear with intelligence and dignity the peculiar new lifeways made necessary by radical change.

But then the implications of the issues that first motivated the task never disappeared. What was I to do about the cold, hard fact that I and my teachers before me had manipulated cultural materials beyond the constraint of my sources to make them fit my views, my theories? I realized that this was more than a momentary slip, an embarrassing but nonetheless isolated instance of bad scholarship. I suspected (actually, I felt almost certain) that this incident represents the profession, the academic enterprise, and beyond that, it reflects "Western man's" way of being in the world—colonist and imperialist, arrogant and insensitive, professing great humane causes but accomplishing the opposite. I began to fear that this tiny incident in my academic practice characterized not only my work but also the work of my profession and my cultural and intellectual heritage. Not wanting to face this way of spending (a grave term in this context) my life, the research and reflections that have become this book were self-examination in service to self-justification: my efforts to rationalize why I am doing with my life what I am. Stated more constructively, it has been an effort to prescribe what I must strive to do to avoid concocting what Jean Baudrillard calls a "precession of simulacra," the generation by models of a real without reality.

In some sense this book is a also about fathers and sons. Both Mircea Eliade and Jonathan Smith were my teachers at Chicago. I have been influenced by both, though more powerfully and pervasively by Smith. Wanting to honor and embrace them both, although critically (which in my mind is the greatest honor one can pay another), while finding my own way has doubtless strongly shaped this work. I have had a strange relationship with the University of Chicago, much like my relationship with the field known as religious studies. I have often felt and have wanted to feel on the outside, on the margin, the stranger within. I have wanted to retain my connection to the farmlands of Kansas, to physical labor, and to the daily experience of the activities of the "minded body." I have wanted my personal identity to be independent of but in some ways inclusive of the aspects of identity I gain from my alma mater, my place of employment, my subjects of study, and my academic methods. Perhaps in doing this work I have begun to understand more deeply this desire. While it may appear to remove my stake in what I do, I believe that the effect is to guard against the false notion that one's stake is only in one's own academic works—that is, what one makes—rather than in the reality that is one's subject. In short, being in some respects an outsider gives me distance and the perspective to be self-conscious and self-critical. I deeply care about the reality of the Arrernte, the explorers, the pastoralists, the ethnographers, my own mentors, and all the rest. I care about the culturally and historically other, if for no other reason than to avoid narcissistic self-indulgence.

Apart from, or as a part of, these more personal matters, this book is about academic processes. It depends on, is engaged by, and strives to contribute to the academic fields of anthropology, history, philosophy, psychology, and religion, yet I do not see any of these areas as particularly focal or most important. It is about Australia and Australian aborigines (the Arrernte in particular), yet I am not Australian and I have studied this area for only a few years. I will be curious to see how the book is classified by publisher and cataloguer.

THERE ARE MANY to thank for the invaluable assistance they gave me during this project. In Australia, Diane Austin-Broos and Tony Swain at Sydney University offered support and suggestions for my visit to Central Australia. Tony's book *A Place for Strangers* has been a major inspiration. Hans D. Oberscheidt was extraordinarily generous in permitting me to use his meticulous translation of Carl Strehlow's massive *Die Aranda-Und Loritja-Stämme in Zentral-Australien*. Diane Austin-Broos helped me to connect with Oberscheidt and the actual translation manuscript. Consistently gracious and helpful were the staff members of several Australian research facilities: the Museum of Victoria in Melbourne, the Barr Smith Library at the University of Adelaide, the Australian Institute for Aboriginal and Torres Strait Studies in Canberra, and the Strehlow Research Centre and the Finke River Mission in Alice Springs. I want to sincerely thank the University of Colorado at Boulder for its generous support, without which I would not have been able either to visit Australia or to have had the time to do this work. I was awarded a faculty fellowship and research grant by the Council on Research and Creative Work and a travel grant by the Graduate Committee on the Arts and Humanities. I am also grateful to the dean of the College of Arts and Sciences for providing substantial research assistance.

A number of friends read the manuscript and offered important reflections and suggestions. I was not only guided and corrected by them but also moved by the care and thoughtfulness of their readings. I want to thank Edmund Gilday, Richard Hecht, Jim Jeffries, Jonathan Smith, Tony Swain and Michael Zogry. My students have always been among my most insightful critics; they are my daily colleagues in learning. Several groups of students have read and heard portions of this study, and many have offered their criticism and insights. Though too numerous to name, they all need to know that I am honored and vitalized by their ongoing interest, questions, and comments.

I want to thank Kimberly Christen, a graduate student who spent time in the Tennant Creek area studying with Warumungu women, for sharing her considerable knowledge of Australian aborigines and for her work as my research assistant. Thanks also to Angela Farone for her encouragement and research assistance and to Jason Gilbreath for his wonderful cover design.

Cynthia A. Read, executive editor at Oxford University Press, receives my gratitude for her interest in the book, as does MaryBeth Branigan, production editor, for helping through the production process.

Many years ago, while working toward a master of science in business at Wichita State University, I had the opportunity to take a course in world religion from Harry F. Corbin. When I was an undergraduate, he was president of the university, but in the meantime had returned to teaching. Corbin's course had nothing to do with my graduate program in business. My attraction was more to the man than to the subject because I had come to see him as the epitome of the gentleman scholar—gentle and humane yet strong-minded, incisive, and critical. He was a man of passion and a great inspiration. Even before I had completed his course, I had made plans to study religion at the University of Chicago. Inspired and guided by Corbin, that decision put me on the road I am still trekking.

Through the years I often thought of Harry Corbin, but I had no contact with him. More than twenty years slipped by. One evening I received an unexpected telephone call from him, and we visited as though no time had passed. He was filled with hopes and dreams for the both of us, but especially for me. I was shocked to learn that he had read much of my work. Over the following months we corresponded and occasionally spoke by telephone. He asked for manuscripts of unpublished works. Though he did not tell me, I learned that he was dying of cancer. Those conversations and exchanges are among my most treasured experiences. Corbin had shown such confidence in me decades earlier that I had found the courage to risk change, to try something entirely new, and to attempt to always live and work diligently and with passion.

I dedicate this book to the memory of Harry F. Corbin because I believe that the issues I raise and attempt to deal with here are ones that he would have found interesting and important, ones on which he would have supported my struggles. Corbin asked the difficult questions and, being toughly critical and relentless in his pursuits, he was never satisfied by easy answers. After all these years I am still attempting to live up to the confidence he showed in me; I am still driven by the excitement and aspirations he awakened.

Over a decade ago I dedicated a book to the memory of my grandparents on my father's side and my great aunts—my mother's aunts—all of whom lived to a ripe old age. Other family elders who mean much to me have since died, and I want to remember them and their influence, which complements that of Harry Corbin's.

During my youth I did farm work that brought me close to my father's family, especially two of his brothers and one of his sisters. They all had tiny Kansas farms clustered in the same neighborhood. When I was eight, my Uncle Ralph allowed me to drive tractor during the haying season. When I was older, in the late summers I helped fill his silo. My job was to enter the silo and walk round and round tramping down the silage as it was blown through a tube up and over the rim of the cylindrical structure. Those of us doing this tramping job would rise higher and higher, with our shoes growing greener and greener, as the silo filled. Sometime during the second day, we would arrive at the top. The glorious reward for our labor was the view of rolling farm country from the rim of the silo and the thrill of continuing to tramp until it was brimming full. I worked with my Uncle Howard preparing the soil, harvesting grain, and taking in the hay. Uncle Howard was also superintendent of schools in my home town, Cherryvale. He had been my father's teacher, and I always knew that he had a watchful eye directed my way, making sure I not only kept out of trouble but that I also excelled in academics, athletics, and activities.

Many were the occasions when a large group of working men sat down together midday for "dinner" to consume enormous quantities of delicious mid-western fare: meat, potatoes, gravy, fresh vegetables, and pies. I earned a place at the table by being one of the workers. My father's sister, Aunt Bernice, as well as my grandma, my mother, and the wives of my uncles, were always on hand, having labored the morning together to prepare the meal. These were great times for me. This was my family, my community.

I learned so much from these wonderful people. There were no lectures, no specific advice given; never a walk in the fields to reveal some special wisdom to a nephew in need. Teaching was done by example. Together we worked and ate and went to church. The lessons were in the salt-of-the-earth style of life: family, honesty, neighborliness, integrity, belief in God, responsibility, service to community, tenacity, and, above all, work. The lessons imparted good values. I find myself living in a world different in important respects from the world of these elders. Unlike their world, most everything in mine seems problematic and deeply complex, making it difficult for me to find the solid ground that they never questioned. But lessons learned in the way these elders taught them really can never be unlearned. They are bone deep. Perhaps it is the nostalgia for their world, the world I knew as a child, that has been a driving force in my writing this book.

Uncle Ralph, Uncle Howard, and Aunt Bea would perhaps have thought it strange that I would have liked to have acknowledged the depth of my gratitude to them face to face. They didn't do any of these things for any reason other than to be who they were. Of course, I didn't know until I was much older what they had done for me, and before I got around to saying anything to them it was too late. I know telling them would have felt good. While they won't read this dedication, I will, and so will my kids, Corbin and Jenny, and maybe we'll remember these old ones from time to time. Would that we live our lives as they did theirs.

September 1997 S. G.

Storytracking depends heavily on systematic detailed comparison done often at the level of word and even alphabetic character. These comparative studies are equivalent to the data and calculations in a scientific report. Although they would be out of place in a book of this kind, any reader who wishes to consult them can find them on the World Wide Web at http://www.oup-usa.org/authors/gill/

Contents

STORYTRACKING

1

Storytracking the Arrernte through the Academic Bush

A Gaping Chasm

The academy exists because there is a gaping chasm between the reality of our world and our understanding of it.[1] It is the academic's job to imagine how one might span this chasm, even attempt to do so, yet knowing full well that whatever efforts are made one must never nullify, deny, or forget that the chasm exists. The chasm is to be honored for it is in this nothingness that we academics realize our being.

We have come to realize that the quotidian action of perceiving reality, a reality that we posit as independent of us, is an active process that affects reality, making at least our understanding of it dependent on us. That is, although we know that reality must be independent of our understanding of it—that reality exists independently of the mind—to attempt to understand it makes it in some measure dependent on us. This paradox pertains at all levels, from perception, in which individual human senses are active processes, to signification and reference and to scientific paradigms as analyzed, for example, by Thomas Kuhn.[2]

The responses to this paradox swing in a pendulum arc between a retrenched denial of the implications of this paradox[3] and a kind of nihilism painted either in the dark makeup of gloom or the gaudy makeup of the clown. Being convinced that there is no firm, safe, unchangeable, final place on which to stand to do our work, we are uncomfortable and nervous wherever we find ourselves standing; for we must stand somewhere. We are caught between objectivism and subjectivism as between a rock and a hard place. Fleeing solipsism, we run smack into essentialism and vice versa. Most commonly we carry out our work in vagueness, awaiting some clarifying insights or the revelation of an entirely new approach. Occasionally we may buck up our courage and enter the world of the tricky, abstract philosophical discourses that are designed to self-destruct or self-deconstruct, yet doing so often leaves us as fearful as though in the presence of trigger-happy terrorists.

Most of the time we go about our work as "normal scientists,"[4] snug in the reigning paradigm and trying to keep sufficiently busy to distract ourselves from the disconcerting suspicion that what we do is more groundless than we care to know, more a mirror of our personal, cultural, and historical peculiarities than we care to imagine. One of the conventions by which human and social scientists carry on this normal science is the interpretation of text. A discussion of text may present more concretely the academic issues I have attempted to suggest by the chasm metaphor. The word *text*,[5] particularly when it designates what is more properly termed *primary text*, is widely used to designate an object, usually a language object, that is a given, that exists outside of the academic enterprise and outside of the domain of the historian. Texts are found, chosen, recorded, translated, deciphered, presented, and used. Their existence, though not necessarily their content, is factual. Texts are the historian's counterpart to what the natural sciences call facts. Perhaps the principal defining characteristic of a primary text, even more than its denoted literary form,[6] is that it exists in its own right. Its existence, independent of its readers, and its givenness can be depended on.

That a text has independent existence does not mean that its meaning is evident. It is almost always the opaqueness or suggestiveness that makes a text interesting. Traditionally understood, it is the work of the historian to discern, to discover, or to decipher the meaning or meanings of tantalizingly opaque texts.

Texts embody evidence from the subjects studied. They have the form of scriptures, books, documents, records, journals, diaries, letters, and so forth, and with the rise of ethnography they are ethnographic recordings of oral narratives and descriptions of cultural performances.[7] Put simply, what historians do is to select, present, explain, and interpret texts.

Often the end toward which such interpretations[8] are made surpasses the texts and the cultures or temporal frames they represent in striving to make general statements: broadly applicable hypotheses, theories, and principles. The study of history and culture is always an interpretive endeavor, for the meanings of texts are never self-evident or singular. Texts can and do mean different things at different times and to different people. It is the job of the historian to interpret texts in various contexts. Still, no matter what kind of glory or mess a historian makes of interpreting a text, the interpretation never replaces the text. According to this common view, the text survives both good and bad interpretations of it.

Texts also function to bring closure. They are the basis for settling arguments and differences of opinion. It is to texts that one makes final appeal. They illustrate, test, or otherwise ground written history, culture studies, and academic theory. They anchor legitimate academic constructs in a nontheoretical, nonacademic reality in the world of subject, in the "real" world. To cite text in service to a history, a culture study, or an interpretation is to cross between interpretation and that which is interpreted, thus bringing closure, even if temporary. The interpretive enterprise is the anchor rope, the bridge, the connecting force between the given—the subject—that is terra firma and a rendering of its meaning. Interpretation bridges the chasm between us, that is, our understanding, and the reality of our subject.

To consider this view of texts from another angle, the human and social sciences (the enterprise that interprets texts) are secondary endeavors; thus academic writings are secondary texts. Historians and students of culture do not make history; they do not engage in actions that have an immediate effect on the world except, of course, the far corner of reality that is itself academia. At best, it would seem, scholars respond to what has happened, what is given, and their interpretive responses thereby may enrich our understanding of the past; of others; and it is hoped, even of ourselves. Thus, academic work may be felt in the world as a second-order effect, the effect of actions performed by those who are enriched by knowledge and understanding.

This discussion of text is intended only to remind us of the obvious, to articulate widely held assumptions. But of course these notions of text are undergoing challenge and transformation as one of the forefronts of the discussion of how there is an inevitable interdependence between scholar (or looker) and subject (object looked at) of study. While according to a reigning paradigm the independence of the text is fundamental, it is difficult to demonstrate that independence. Even as we present text it undergoes transformation, again revealing the paradox with which we began.

I am interested in this paradox and believe that some satisfactory position in its regard must be reached. I want to begin with an example of the presentation of a text and inquire and reflect on the sort of bridging that occurs in the interpretive operations that serve to join the presenter of this text with its reported subjects. Using an approach I call storytracking, which will be given a more thorough and technical description in chapter 2, I will attempt to follow the track from the report of a culture as presented in a recent academic study to the independent reality of the subject for the purpose of revealing and analyzing how the academic bridgework to the reality of the subject is built.

Storytracking, in this first use, is the simple method of comparing a text version as presented in an academic report with the text version as it appears as that report's cited source. The comparison helps reveal the motivations and extent to which the text is transformed through its presentation. I simply follow the chain of citations, comparing presentation versions with source versions to approach as closely as possible the independent subject. This method will produce the story—or as I call it, the storytrack—that interconnects the scholar with the scholar-independent subject. The storytrack will tell the story of the various academic operations conducted to build a bridge connecting subject and scholarly report. An account of these operations will reveal the character of the relationship between subject and scholar.

"Numbakulla and the Sacred Pole"

Mircea Eliade's Text

The cultural example I have chosen is from the Arrernte culture, an aboriginal people of Central Australia, as presented by the late, eminent student of religion Mircea Eliade.[9] Eliade, who shaped much of the present academic and popular understanding of religion, held that space is not homogeneous, that some places are held to be more important, of higher value, than other places. His position can scarcely be denied—it seems obvious, as does his assertion that the most important place is the one designated as the center. The center, to Eliade's understanding, is synonymous with the religious. Key to his argument, Eliade used to dramatic effect an Arrernte[10] example, which, following Eliade,[11] I call "Numbakulla and the Sacred Pole":

> Numbakulla arose "out of nothing" and traveled to the north, making mountains, rivers, and all sorts of animals and plants. He also created the "spirit children" (*kuruna*), a very large number of whom were concealed inside his body. Eventually he made a cave or storehouse, [in which] to hide the *tjuringas* that he was producing. At that time men did not yet exist. He inserted a *kuruna* into a *tjuringa*, and thus there arose the first Achilpa (mythical) Ancestor. Numbakulla then implanted a large number of *kuruna* in different *tjuringa*, producing other mythical Ancestors. He taught the first Achilpa how to perform the many ceremonies connected with the various totems.
>
> Now, Numbakulla had planted a pole called *kauwa-auwa* in the middle of a sacred ground. . . . After anointing it with blood, he began to climb it. He told the first Achilpa Ancestor to follow him; but the blood made the pole too slippery, and the man slid down. "Numbakulla went on alone, drew up the pole after him and was never seen again."
>
> One day an incident befell one of these mythical groups: while pulling up the *kauwa-auwa*, which was very deeply implanted, the old chief broke it just above the ground. They carried the broken pole until they met another group. They were so tired and sad that they did not even try to erect their own *kauwa-auwa* "but, lying down together, died where they lay. A large hill, covered with big stones, arose to mark the spot."[12]

Eliade recognizes the pole as marking the center place and as functioning to maintain a channel of communication with the creator god, withdrawn into the sky. The break in communication is a loss of center and meaning for the Achilpa. In recounting these events, Eliade illustrates and gives dramatic ethnographic grounding to his understanding of the religious character of the center place: "Seldom do we find a more pathetic avowal that man cannot live without a 'sacred center' which permits him both to 'cosmicize' space and to communicate with the transhuman world of heaven. As long as they had their *kauwa-auwa*, the Achilpa Ancestors were never lost in the surrounding 'chaos.' Moreover, the sacred pole was for them the proof par excellence of Numbakulla's existence and activity."[13]

Furthermore, as is incumbent upon historians, Eliade's presentation of the Numbakulla text renders meaningful the otherwise enigmatic and incredulous act of people voluntarily dying because they break a pole. Eliade used this example on several occasions. It first appeared in his *The Sacred and the Profane*,[14] where it is presented as though it were an ethnographic account, an event that had been physically observed by the ethnographers Baldwin Spencer and Francis Gillen in the late nineteenth century in Australia.[15] In his *Australian Religions* (1967) Eliade changed the event from an ethnographic observation to a recorded account of a myth, that is, a story collected from the Arrernte by Spencer and Gillen. Only an outline of the process and results is presented here.

"Numbakulla and the Sacred Pole" is a minor ethnographic text. Although Eliade used it several times and it appears occasionally in the work of others, it is not a text widely debated or interpreted. Eliade makes a semiformal presentation of the text. He cites his source as Baldwin Spencer and Francis Gillen, *The Arunta: The Story of a Stone Age People* (1927). He provides brief quotations, designated by quotation marks, from his source. The portions of the text not directly quoted must be assumed by the reader to be close approximations of the materials presented in the source. Thus Eliade presents material from Arrernte culture with all of the authority that accompanies the designation "text." The convention by which Eliade presents the Arrernte example, that is, a referenced ethnographic account of an identified culture, denotes that it is independent of Eliade and his use or interpretation of it. As presented, the Arrernte example is not of Eliade's making and the attribute of independence appears to be essential to the effectiveness of his presentation. As factual material, independent of Eliade and his theories and interpretations, the Arrernte example serves as exemplification, grounding, and closure to Eliade's theoretical position.

Spencer and Gillen's *The Arunta* (1927)

To begin now to storytrack this presentation of the Arrernte to the actual Arrernte people in Central Australia, I simply compare Eliade's "Numbakulla and the Sacred Pole" text to the text in his cited source. The storytrack begins with a detailed comparison of Eliade's text with the passages he cites from Spencer and Gillen's *The Arunta* (1927). This comparison shows how Eliade selected, organized, and presented the materials from his source. Eliade presents the Arrernte example in the span of five paragraphs of thirty-seven sentences. The information is taken principally from six pages in Spencer and Gillen, although those pages are selected from a span of twenty-eight pages that are an integral part of a forty-five-page section. While virtually every word in Eliade's account can be found in his source,[16] it is remarkable how, through his selection, ordering, and presentation, the resulting cultural event drastically differs. Further, of the thirty-seven sentences, fully seventeen are devoted to Eliade's interpretational comments, a fact that, while obvious if known, is perhaps not so obvious if not known.

In his first paragraph Eliade draws heavily on a five-page section (pp. 355–60) in Spencer and Gillen to establish that the Arrernte believe in a primordial figure named Numbakulla, who after performing his acts of creation planted a pole in the center of a ceremonial ground and then climbed up it to the sky. An ancestral figure was unable to follow him up the blood-anointed pole. Eliade then summarizes twenty-eight pages in Spencer and Gillen as "seemingly endless detail of wanderings of the first Achilpa Ancestors after the disappearance of Numbakulla" and then he leaps to an incident (Spencer and Gillen, p. 388) of only one of the several groups of Tjilpa,[17] or wildcat people, to recount the breaking of the pole and the radical response to this event. Given that this is an incident of only one Tjilpa group, given that most groups of ancestors die at the end of their journey and only one of four groups is connected with a pole at all, and given the many variances from Spencer and Gillen of Eliade's presentation, the conclusion cannot be avoided that although most of the words and phrases in Eliade's account can be traced to his source, the events or cultural elements that Eliade presents as primary are—by virtue of his selection, organization, and presentation—almost entirely concocted by him. The account resembles its source in that it contains many of the same words and phrases, but the account is different in structure and composition. The term *concoct* effectively portrays this relationship. *Concoct*, in a basic sense, means "to boil together, to prepare by cooking." Thus, the relationship of Eliade's Numbakulla text to its source is on the order of boiled potato soup to a vegetable garden. It is clear that Eliade's constructions are directly motivated by the necessity of supporting the principle he wished to establish, that is, that the center place is synonymous with the religious.

If the five paragraphs presented in Eliade as "Numbakulla and the Sacred Pole" are thought to be a primary text, which not only Eliade but also others have believed,[18] there is a breach in the essential criteria for a primary text. This text is not solely evidence from the Arrernte; it is a product of Mircea Eliade's reading, selecting, organizing, and presenting materials from Spencer and Gillen's *The Arunta*. The text is the scholar's making. It is at best tertiary but presented in the guise of primary. While there appears to be a realm beyond academia, by virtue of Eliade's citation of an ethnographic source, Eliade's presentation smudges the boundary between primary and secondary and violates the principle of the independence of the primary.

Rather than confirming academic closure, comparison of Eliade with his cited source opens questions about his approach. Importantly, the comparison shows that while Eliade's theoretical position is confirmed by his example, the confirmation seems to be achieved at the expense of the Arrernte, who thus recede from Eliade's readers. While there may be some trace of Arrernte experience and culture that survives in Eliade's "Numbakulla and the Sacred Pole" text, it appears to be less, both in quantity and accuracy, than it is in Spencer and Gillen. More radically, the Arrernte, at least as they are known to the large readership of Eliade's works, become a creation of the scholar, proceeding from his understanding of religion, rather than a culture with an existence independent of the academic. Rather than Eliade's work being dependent on the Arrernte, the Arrernte are dependent on Eliade.

In *The Sacred and the Profane*, Eliade presents broad patterns within religion as he understands it throughout the history of human existence. His citation of an Arrernte example, along with examples from other cultures, is illustrative of a pattern. The Arrernte example as Eliade presents it could be defended as correct, even if at odds with ethnographic sources, since for the Arrernte to be religious, as Eliade understands religion, they must have patterns consistent with those he described. It could be suggested that ethnographers did not record what must have been present. It could be argued that while this particular Arrernte example might not support Eliade's position, other examples from the Arrernte could doubtless be found that would very well do so.[19] But this argument turns around the interpretive enterprise; it holds that the scholar's understanding of the generic is more primary than the cultural specific. In time I will return to this possibility.

Eliade's *Australian Religions* is a work seemingly directed toward the presentation of specific religions in their specific historical and cultural contexts. In his preface to the book, Eliade describes his task as presenting "the understanding of the meaning of a particular culture, as it is understood and assumed by its own members."[20] This is one of the few comprehensive books on Australian religions.[21] Nonetheless even a cursory review of Eliade's treatment of his sources makes it entirely clear that even in this work he was more interested and confident in the universal religious patterns he brings to the study than he was in Australian aboriginal religions.

The comparison of Eliade's "Numbakulla and the Sacred Pole" with its source raises basic questions. Is it possible to approach the Arrernte point of view? Can the people be presented accurately and in their terms? Do history and culture studies necessarily take us further from their subjects? If so, how do we justify these studies? Are texts actually independent of interpretation? Is history independent of the writing of history? Are cultures independent of students of culture? Are texts presented as primary actually considered more primary than academic constructions of the generic?

Spencer and Gillen's *Native Tribes* (1899)

To storytrack this Arrernte example from Eliade to Spencer and Gillen's *The Arunta* (1927) goes only part way. It is important to inquire about Spencer and Gillen's presentation of the Arrernte. This storytracking work, that is, an attempt to get as close as possible to the Arrernte, is done to more properly ground my proposed approach and to more fully establish the comprehension and appreciation of the Arrernte.

By beginning with Eliade's "Numbakulla and the Sacred Pole" text, it is possible to trace the trail of texts and records backward, source upon source, toward the Arrernte, comparing each document (text) with its source, as I did with Eliade's text. The effect, while moving progressively toward the Arrernte, is also to reveal, as it has done with Eliade, how various presenters of the Arrernte have influenced their presentations, that is, how the Arrernte, at least as known to the non-Australian world, have been dependent on those who have studied them.

The preface to *The Arunta*, written by Baldwin Spencer, states that this two-volume work is a revision of an earlier work, *The Native Tribes in Central Australia*, published in 1899. Gillen died in 1912, and Spencer returned to the field in 1926 to check the accuracy of the 1899 work and to collect additional information. Eliade did not cite the earlier edition.

The next storytracking task is to compare the sections relevant to the "Numbakulla and the Sacred Pole" text in the first edition with those in the revised edition to determine what, if any, information was added or changed by Spencer, based on his 1926 field study. This comparison shows that the entire section about Numbakulla as the creator and his climb up the pole does not exist in the earlier version. In both the 1899 and 1927 editions, there is a creation story in which sky beings come to earth, create people from embryolike forms, and then turn into lizards. Thus the part of Eliade's account in which Numbakulla creates things, then climbs up the pole into the sky, was added by Spencer as chapter XIII to the revised edition, based, as it will soon be shown, on his 1926 field study. However, the part of Eliade's story about people lying down to die when their pole is broken appears much the same in both editions. Eliade's conjunction of materials, which in Spencer and Gillen are separated by thirty pages, is also the conjunction of materials whose recording from the Arrernte was separated by thirty years.

Rather than two texts, Eliade and his source, there are now three: Eliade's, Spencer's of 1927, and Spencer and Gillen's of 1899. Is the 1927 version a correction and completion of the 1899 version? Does the 1927 version reflect historical changes that had occurred since 1899? Are there more texts? What did the Arrernte say? Who were Spencer and Gillen? Which Arrernte talked with Spencer and Gillen? Did Spencer talk with the same Arrernte in 1926 as he and Gillen did in 1896? These questions demand attention. Perhaps at this point it is more effective to turn the story around and tell some of it as it unfolded.

Spencer and Gillen's Early Field Studies

From his position as biologist at the University of Melbourne, Baldwin Spencer agreed to accompany the Horn expedition into Central Australia. The expedition, which lasted eleven weeks and covered 2,000 miles, began on May 3, 1894. While Spencer sketched and described many plants and animals and served as photographer for this expedition, he also became interested in the aboriginal peoples. When the expedition arrived at Alice Springs, Spencer met the postmaster, Francis Gillen, who shared Spencer's interest in the aborigines and had begun collecting information about Arrernte culture, that of the aboriginal people who lived near Alice Springs. Gillen knew little of the Arrernte language,[22] communicating with the people mostly in aboriginal English. When, after three days, the Horn expedition moved beyond Alice Springs, Spencer remained behind for a time. Gillen sent aborigines to get biological specimens for Spencer's study, and the two men continued their conversations about aborigines.[23]

With Spencer back in Melbourne following the Horn expedition, his conversations with Gillen about aborigines continued, now by mail and telegraph. Spencer began to realize that Gillen's collections of aboriginal stories and customs deserved publication. He agreed to go to Alice Springs in November 1896 to observe a major ritual. Upon his return to Melbourne, loaded with field notes, he immediately began to prepare the manuscript. Sir James George Frazer, in London, learned of Spencer and Gillen's field studies and encouraged the publication of the work with Macmillan and suggested the title, *The Native Tribes of Central Australia*. Frazer, along with E. B. Tylor, edited the manuscript for an early 1899 publication.

Given the general history of the field studies behind the publications of the Arrernte ethnographies of Spencer and Gillen, it is possible to trace to the field sources the various elements that contribute to Eliade's "Numbakulla and the Sacred Pole" account. In the 1899 edition of *Native Tribes* the relevant passages are (1) a human creation account and (2) a series of so-called totem group stories in which the Tjilpa ancestors traveled about the landscape and performed ceremonies. These accounts are revised in minor ways for the 1927 edition and supplemented by another: the Numbakulla creation story.

The portion of Eliade's Numbakulla account that is the same in both the 1899 and 1927 editions of Spencer and Gillen's work is the section of the Tjilpa story in which the pole is broken and, in response, the Tjilpa ancestors lie down and die. Arrernte stories, as reported in these sources, commonly depict ancestral beings who are traveling across the land. Typically the ancestors emerge from the ground; go to a location that is sometimes identified by a distinctive geological or even biological feature; and there perform an act, commonly a set of rites. They may encounter other people who reside at the camping place. They often leave someone behind when they go on to the next camping place. The stories can be traced by the Arrernte across the physical land. The stories begin by indicating that the ancestors "jump up of themselves," which means that they are uncreated beings. The stories usually end with the death or transformation into *tjurungas* (stone or wooden emblems, to be discussed in chapter 6) of the ancestral figure(s). Commonly the ancestral figure is considered to still reside at this final location or as a *tjurunga* in the local storehouse for these ritual objects. The Tjilpa—the wildcat group that Eliade identified simply as one of the Arrernte groups—stories depict several groups of ancestors who are traveling different routes across the landscape. The incident of the broken pole appears in the accounts of only one group of Tjilpa ancestors. All of the extant accounts of the Tjilpa stories were recorded by Gillen. The story that contains the broken pole incident was recorded in April or May 1897, identified as Column III, or the Eastern group of Tjilpa. He recorded other versions of this story, those not including the incident of the broken pole, on November 12, 18, and 26, 1896.

The seven sentences in *Native Tribes* that describe the broken pole incident closely match Gillen's journal account. The only notable variation is that Gillen's concluding sentence is clearer and simpler: "Their bodies [i.e., the bodies of the deceased ancestors] became Churinga [*tjurunga*] many large & long & which are now in the possession of local Achilpa." In editing the journal for publication, Spencer constructs two sentences and blurs Gillen's clarity: "Their [i.e., the deceased ancestors] Churinga, each with its associated spirit individual, remained behind. Many of them are very large and long, and now in the *ertnatulunga* or storehouse at Unjiacherta."

Human Creation Account

The account of human creation in *Native Tribes* underwent minor revision for the 1927 edition and, importantly, was supplemented by the Numbakulla creation story in a chapter entitled "The Achilpa Tradition. I. The Earlier Wanderings; the Tradition of Numbakulla and of the Origin of Churinga and Kuruna."

Although the human creation account in *Native Tribes* (pp. 387–89), repeated in *The Arunta* (pp. 307–9), was not considered by Eliade, it is nonetheless relevant. A study of how this account relates to its field sources reveals both Gillen's and Spencer's presumptions about religion and culture, what they expected and assumed in their field studies, and what ideas guided the preparation of their publications. The story recounts how, in the days before there were men and women, two beings who dwelt in the western sky saw some rudimentary or incomplete human beings. These beings came down from their dwelling place, taking as their mission the transformation of the rudimentary beings into men and women, accomplished by cutting with their stone knives the arms, fingers, legs, toes, and so forth to release and complete them. The tale explains that these rudimentary creatures were stages in the transformation of animals and plants into human beings, thus accounting for the identification of groups of human beings with plants and animals—an explanation for the origin of totems. The story ends with the statement that after completing their mission, the sky beings transformed themselves into little lizards. In the preparation of this story of human origins, Spencer drew on two of Gillen's journal entries: the first, "Traditions of Origin," was recorded by Gillen in 1894; the other was recorded in June 1897 and identified as "Amunga-quinyirquinya, Flycatching lizard, Earliest alchiringa."

In 1894, when Gillen began keeping a journal about the Arrernte, one of the first things he recorded was an account he titled "Traditions of Origin." It tells how primordial ancestors of the aborigines were transformed into human beings by a spirit man who came from the east and used a magic knife to release their arms, legs, and so on. This spirit man gave them speech, instructed them on gender roles and social divisions, and circumcised the men. Gillen identified these figures as belonging to a giant species of porcupine (or Echidna), apparently both because of the similarity of their appearance with Echidnas and because they were called "Inaapwerta,"[24] which he rendered as *Echidna*. This account was published in 1896 in the *Report on the Work of the Horn Scientific Expedition to Central Australia* in a section authored by Gillen. The 1899 published account, though more refined, is in substance not at variance with the journal account.[25]

In June 1897 Gillen collected information linked, at least in Spencer's mind, to his "Traditions of Origin" by the common reference to what in the earlier account he had identified as "Inaapwerta." In the 1897 account, Gillen revealed the discovery of his error in understanding and translating this term. The term reported as "Inaapwerta" in the Horn expedition report, Gillen now believed, should be "Inaapertwa," meaning "rudimentary men or men unable to walk."[26] Gillen noted this correction in his journal in the midst (sentence 5) of his account of the "Flycatching Lizard," which he identified as the "earliest alcheringa," meaning the earliest of the heroic or mythic ancestors. This story tells of two men, identified as flycatching lizards, who were Ungambikulla; that is, they came "out of nothing or [were] enough in themselves"[27] and living in the western sky. They saw the Inaapertwa, who dwelt in various places. After the saltwaters were withdrawn, these men came down and used their knives to circumcise and subincise these rudimentary men, thus making them fully initiated men. In this way the flycatching lizard men made numerous groups[28] of initiated people. These groups were, however, threatened by "Oruncha devils,"[29] who attacked and ate many of them. A defense was prepared in which the peoples armed themselves with spears and awaited the Oruncha attack. When it occurred, all of the Oruncha were killed. Their dead bodies turned to stone, accounting for the great jumble of stones at the mouth of Simpson's Gap, west of Alice Springs. In a postscript, Gillen explains that the flycatching lizard men made some initiated groups while little hawk made others, both accomplished by performing the rites of circumcision and subincision. With their mission accomplished, "these men of the heavens turned themselves into little lizards." This is a story of the origin of some totem groups and accounts for the origin of the circumcision and subincision initiatory practices in which youths, "rudimentary men," are transformed into fully initiated men.

Spencer combined and edited sections of Gillen's 1894 and 1897 journals in preparation for the account entitled "Origin of the Alcheringa Ancestors" in *Native Tribes* and "The Alchera and Alchera Ancestors" in *The Arunta*. Importantly, Spencer begins by stating that "in reality the traditions of the tribe recognize four more or less distinct eras in the Alcheringa." The earliest of these eras must, according to Spencer's understanding, account for origins. Spencer's construction of this chronology guided his reading of Gillen's two accounts, linked only in their common reference to the rudimentary by the term *Inaapertwa*. Spencer first draws on the beginning of the 1897 account, which as a biologist he found remarkable because it describes the land as once being covered with saltwater.[30] Against this setting, which certainly can appear primordial, Spencer places the two sky-dwelling figures. Although Gillen identifies them from the outset as flycatching lizard ancestors, Spencer does not. Rather he allows the adjective[31] *ungambikula*, which simply identifies figures that were themselves not created (i.e., they "jump up of themselves" or "out of nothing" or are "self existing"), to become their proper names. Unsupported by Gillen's journals, Spencer adds that "in those days there were no men and women." Having drawn only on the first five of the nineteen sentences in Gillen's 1897 account, Spencer turns to Gillen's 1894 "Traditions of Origin." He ignores the fact that the protagonists of this story are clearly different from those of the 1897 story and draws on the part of the 1894 story in which redimentary figures are transformed into human beings. With several interesting variances, such as omitting the creation of genitals,[32] Spencer holds closely to Gillen's 1894 account. But at the end Spencer seems to have remembered the 1897 account and concludes the text with "after having performed their mission, the *Ungambikula* transformed themselves into little lizards called *Amunga-quiniaquinia*. . . . There is no reason given for this, and in no other tradition do we meet with either the *Ungambikula* or the special kind of lizard into which they changed."

By combining sections of two accounts recorded by Gillen, Spencer meets the need he has created for himself through his temporal classification of Arrernte stories. He needed evidence of the "earliest wanderings," that is, stories about creation. Finding no stories for this era, he concocted one. Spencer's motivation seems clear in the editorial choices he made. He had to ignore any reference to the initiatory elements in Gillen's 1897 account because these would require the stories to be classified in Spencer's middle period. Yet he wanted to pick up the beginning of the 1897 account to establish a primordial setting not provided in Gillen's 1894 account. Spencer construed the knife-cutting operations of the 1897 account, which are definitely operations of circumcision, in terms of the transformations of prehuman, rudimentary forms. Perhaps the most curious and inexplicable part of Spencer's text is his concluding reference to lizards. In the last sentence, it seems that Spencer looked back at the story, ignoring or forgetting that it is of his own construction, and was genuinely puzzled by the unexplained transformation of creators into lizards.[33]

Spencer's 1926 Field Studies

Spencer's 1927 account of the same "earliest tradition" has some curious changes from the 1899 account. He begins the chapter in which the account appears with a discussion of the term *Alchera*, including some phrases he had his aboriginal informants render into Arrernte to support his interruption of the term. Then he discusses "the earliest tradition" and makes two important points in this comparative inquiry. First, he writes that for most local groups of Arrernte, "the creation of men and women is ascribed to the action of certain superhuman Beings called Numbakulla—self-existing or self-originating—who appeared upon the scene, completed their work of creation, or transformation, and then disappeared and were never seen again."[34] In a footnote (p. 307, n.1) Spencer holds that Numbakulla had been called Ungambikula in *Native Tribes*. Second, Spencer continues to support his periodization, despite denouncing it all the while: "Certain of the traditions seem to recognize a division of the Alchera times into three or four periods, which are not, however, by any means sharply defined, and in others, such as the great Achilpa [Tjilpa] tradition, are not, or at most, only vaguely, indicated."[35] In a footnote to this sentence, Spencer rejects even more emphatically the temporal categorizations he had made in *Native Tribes*: "We previously described the traditions as recognizing four more or less distinct periods in the Alchera. . . . The general sequence of events thus indicated holds good, but further information shows that the periods overlap and merge into one another, and are not sufficiently distinctly marked off to make their retention serve any useful purpose."[36] But in the next sentence in the body of the work, Spencer begins the account of the creation of people from rudimentary forms with "the earliest tradition. . . . "

Thus, there are two significant changes in the 1927 account from the 1899 account. The term *Numbakulla* replaces in every case the term *Ungambikula,* and the final sentence, revealing Spencer's confusion about the creators turning into lizards, is omitted.

The effect of this account in *Native Tribes* and *The Arunta* is that it satisfies both Spencer's and Gillen's expectations that the Arrernte have stories that explain the creation of human beings, if not also the cosmos. Logic would demand that these stories relate to the "earliest" period. There are no such stories in all the field records. Further, Spencer's simple conversion of *Ungambikula* from an adjective to a noun gives a proper-name identity to sky-dwelling creator figures, establishing a precedent to be followed in his revisions for *The Arunta*. Here this Tjilpa story presents the creator Numbakulla and prepares for the account presented in his following chapter in *The Arunta* (on which Eliade drew), broadly depicting Numbakulla as a creator figure. A further effect of this identification of creator figures by name is that it facilitates the conflation of figures having different identities, having different domiciles, and appearing in different stories.

Gillen, I believe, shared Spencer's expectations that creation stories of some sort should exist. That Gillen's "Traditions of Origin" appears early[37] in his first field journal, following entries such as "Spiritual Beings," indicates that his inquiries about creation were among his earliest.

Spencer's 1927 Creation Story

The last link in this story is the source for the creation account that identifies Numbakulla as a cosmic creator figure. This part of the story did not appear, as shown above, until the revised version of *Native Tribes* was published as *The Arunta* in 1927. Its source is Spencer's field research in 1926. When Spencer went to the Alice Springs area in 1926, thirty years after seeing the rites performed for him and Gillen, he discovered that not a single person in that community had survived. However, Spencer found a man he had worked with in 1896 who was from Owen Springs, south of Alice Springs. Spencer was pleased to learn that this man had, in the meantime, learned better English.[38] His English name was Charlie Cooper, and he served as Spencer's principal source of information in 1926. For the creation account, Spencer worked from information he recorded from Cooper on June 11 and July 23, 1926. Field notes, the apparent basis for fuller narrative journal accounts, bear the same dates.

The June 11 story, identified as a Tjilpa tale of the origin of various Arrernte groups, is about an Alcheringa being who is called Numbakulla. He made a ritual drawing in a cave that served as a *tjurunga* storehouse and put boughs all around it. He made a *tjurunga* and placed it on the painting, and from the *tjurunga* arose the first Tjilpa man. Numbakulla made many *tjurungas* for other totem groups. He showed the first Tjilpa man how to make ritual objects and perform ceremonies. Numbakulla made a second ritual painting outside the storehouse cave, and in the middle of this painting he planted a large ritual pole, *kauwa-auwa*, which he painted with blood to help him climb up it. He told the first Tjilpa man that the Tjilpa man had been given everything, that is, the ritual implements and ritual knowledge. Numbakulla told the Tjilpa man to follow, and he climbed up the pole. The Tjilpa man tried to climb the pole but slipped down. Numbakulla drew the pole up after him and was never seen again.

The July 23 account is summarized as follows: Numbakulla originated at Lamburkna. He made a Tjilpa *tjurunga*, with which he associated a *kuruna* (the spirit part of every person), thereby creating the first Tjilpa man. Numbakulla made a group of *kuruna*. He made many stone *tjurungas*, split them into pairs, and in between the halves of each pair placed a *kuruna*. He put all these in a ritual storehouse. Following Numbakulla's instructions, the first Tjilpa man walked all over the country, settling on all the spots identified with groups and leaving ground paintings and "marks" at all of them. Then the first Tjilpa man returned to Numbakulla. Numbakulla told the man how to make all the ritual objects and perform the rites. Numbakulla climbed up his pole, telling the Tjilpa man to follow him. The man slipped down. Numbakulla drew the pole up after him. The first Tjilpa man then went to the ritual storehouse, where he found the *tjurungas* with the *kurunas* in them. He walked about the country and threw out the *tjurungas* at the places associated with the various totem groups. At a place called Wairidja, a figure (Inkata Tjilpa *oknirra*) came out of the *tjurunga*. This figure went back to Lamburkna, and the first Tjilpa man gave him two *tjurungas* to take with him and instructed him about everything. Out of these *tjurungas* arose two more people—a man, *kupitcha*, which means "small" or "little," and a woman, *illapurinja*, which means "the changed one" and refers to the first woman made by the first Tjilpa man. The man was given ritual objects and taught the rites. This man and woman camped together. A number of *kurunas* entered the woman and come out of her as people. The couple walked to a second camp, and other *kurunas* entered the woman and came out of her as men. They traveled to a third camp, although the actions there are unclear.

Moving beyond any support from his field notes, Spencer's journal at this point returns to Numbakulla, who is speaking to the first Tjilpa man. Spencer provides the Arrernte language text without a literal translation and then freely renders the story. The first Tjilpa man goes out and settles at all the group places. When Numbakulla was about to go up his *kauwa auwa* (pole), he said (in good aboriginal English) to the first Tjilpa man, "We two go up see camp." Numbakulla climbs the pole. Nothing is said about the first Tjilpa man attempting or failing to follow Numbakulla up the pole or about it being painted with blood. The story ends with the first Tjilpa man finding the *tjurungas* made by Numbakulla in a ritual storehouse.

Spencer draws extensively but highly selectively on both these accounts in preparing the creation story for chapter XIII in *The Arunta*. The most significant variance from the journals is the shift of Numbakulla's role from the ritualist who originates the first Tjilpa man, who then becomes the principal ritualist, to Numbakulla's role as a cosmic creator. Spencer makes Numbakulla into the one who travels "all over the country." During these travels, "He created many of the features of the country and decided upon the location of the central places now associated with all the *Knanjas* [totems]." He creates by the actions of placing his foot and speaking: "At every place he put his foot down, saying. . . . " Rather than Numbakulla being the creator of the Tjilpa ancestor, as in the journals, Spencer makes him be the one who leaves marks on the land associated with group places. Though completely unsupported by the journals, Spencer has Numbakulla create everything: "While traversing the country he not only created mountains, rivers, flats and sand-hills, but also brought into existence all kinds of animals and plants." Many of the other variances from the journals are of interest, but this broad recasting of the story is the most significant.

Spencer's editorial management of his field sources for "The Earlier Wanderings" in *The Arunta* is consistent with his motivation for preparing the "Origin of Alcheringa Ancestors" in *Native Tribes*. Even though in a footnote Spencer indicates the uselessness of his periodization, he retains these periods as his principal organizational scheme. It is clear that his expectations and periodization of mythology demand an era of cosmic creation in which a sky-dwelling figure creates the earth and human beings. Though none of the field resources support such an account, Spencer's selections, interpretations, contextualizations, embellishments, interpolations, conflation, and organizations transform the field sources into what his expectations demand. Stories that clearly recount group origins—that focus on the ritual acts of circumcision to transform the uninitiated into fully initiated men—and that would necessarily fit into the "middle wanderings" era of Spencer's classification are transformed into tales of cosmic and human creation. Group ancestors, such as the flycatching lizard, are called Ungambikula or Numbakulla, terms that are allowed to appear as proper names, by converting an adjective, which indicates that they were uncreated beings, to a noun.

"Numbakalla and the Sacred Pole" Summary

The results of storytracking the "Numbakulla and the Sacred Pole" text that appears in Eliade's *Australian Religions* will now be summarized. Eliade based his account on a section in Spencer and Gillen's *The Arunta*. The twenty sentences of Eliade's concocted account present what in Spencer and Gillen cover forty-five pages. His text is inspired most directly by two passages separated by thirty pages in Spencer and Gillen. One passage of *The Arunta* relevant to Eliade's Numbakulla account is based on Spencer's concoction of a creation account based on two accounts he recorded from Charlie Cooper in 1926. The other passage Eliade uses is the product of Baldwin Spencer's editing and conflation of two of Francis Gillen's field reports, reports recorded at a three-year interval. Thus the two relevant passages were separated not only by thirty pages but also by thirty years. Spencer constructed a chronology for Arrernte mythology and then performed creative and heavy-handed editing to provide materials for the earliest creation period. In preparation for the 1899 edition (slightly revised in the 1927 edition), Spencer conflates two of Gillen's field reports to almost wholly concoct a creation account, one that clearly contradicts the Gillen field sources. In the 1927 edition, Spencer complements this account with one based on two of his own field reports. Spencer's editorial choices are based on eliminating elements that would have placed these materials in a period other than his "early wanderings" designation. Spencer wanted an Arrernte creation story, and he created two of them. While field notes are not available for Gillen's journals, they are for Spencer's. A comparison of Spencer's journals and his field notes indicates the further extent of his creative role in interpreting what Charlie Cooper told him. Neither Spencer nor Gillen was fluent in Arrernte. Both relied extensively on aboriginal English.

The Arrernte Sources

The name of at least one Arrernte man has emerged as an actual Arrernte source of information for Spencer, and thus for Eliade and many others. The question is, Who were the Arrernte on whom Spencer and Gillen depended and what was the extent of their knowledge of their culture?

The significance of Spencer's and Gillen's lack of knowledge of the Arrernte language cannot be overstated. The limitations of aboriginal English are fully evident in Spencer's field notes. Theodor Strehlow, who knew Arrernte from childhood, had long listened to court proceedings in Alice Springs, where aborigines communicated through aboriginal English interpreters.[39] Strehlow concludes that "rarely, if ever, did an interpreter to whom I listened pass on a literal rendering of the original question; and even his summary of the answer was sometimes coloured by his own ideas. The person who had posed the first question remained at the mercy of his interpreter throughout."[40] Spencer noted in the preface to *The Arunta* that Charlie Cooper had been old enough in 1896 to be one of the leaders of the rites that he and Gillen had observed, but the implication is that at that time he did not speak aboriginal English: "He had since [i.e., since 1896] learnt to speak English well. . . . "[41] Cooper then might have been a source of information for Spencer and Gillen in 1896, but he would have had to have spoken with them through aboriginal interpreters. The knowledge and identities of these interpreters, or how influential their role was in "translation," is not known. There is no question, however, whether these "interpreters" played a huge role in what Spencer and Gillen heard.

Which Arrernte knew aboriginal English in 1896? The motivation for learning it was primarily to communicate with English-speaking Australians. Those who needed to do so were mostly young men[42] who had left the full practice of their traditional cultures to work for wages for Australians of European descent as police boys, trackers, and stock boys. These were the Arrernte on whom Gillen relied as interpreters so that he might speak to all other Arrernte, and these were the interpreters employed by Spencer and Gillen in 1896 to speak with the leaders of the rites. These young men were, effectively, Spencer's and Gillen's principal sources of information for Arrernte culture.

But there is Charlie Cooper, reportedly a leader in the 1896 rites. By 1926 he had learned aboriginal English and could speak for himself in response to Spencer's enquiries. In the preface to *The Arunta*, Spencer identifies him as "a Purula man of the Irriakura (a plant bulb) totem."[43] In his description of the "local organization associated with totemic groups," Spencer indicates that his information came from "a Purula man named Rera-knilliga of the Irriakura totem."[44] According to Strehlow, who also knew Cooper, he was

> a Purula man, from Ultunta (Owen Springs), whose ordinary name was Iriakura or Ireakura. His secret name was Reralautnulaka, which means "where the hair-roots bit each other", i.e., "where the hair-roots intersected." The ereakura plants grow in dense stands, and the thin hair-roots of the individual plants cross and intertwine. It is allegedly at these crossing points that the ereakura bulbs form in the ground. Reralautnalaka

was corrupted by Spencer into "Rera-knillinga." Ireakura, under the name of Charlie Cooper, became, some time after 1911, the head tracker of Sergeant Robert Stott, of Alice Springs.[45]

There are issues regarding Cooper's significance as a source of information. He came from Owen Springs and, therefore, would not have been fully knowledgeable of the rites being performed in 1896 by people from Inteera, Imanda, and Tjoritja local groups.[46] He had been a police tracker for perhaps fifteen years by the time he spoke with Spencer in 1926, thus growing accustomed to European-Australian interests and probably knowing well the information desired by them. Further, Theodor Strehlow reported that Cooper told him that he contrived the information he gave Spencer as a creation story.[47] As will be presented more fully later, Strehlow frequently criticized Spencer. The criticism was part of Strehlow's defense of his missionary father, Carl Strehlow, whose work on the Arrernte was frequently attacked by Spencer.

Only Bush

Beginning with Mircea Eliade's presentations of a specific Arrernte example, "Numbakulla and the Sacred Pole," I have, through a detailed comparative analysis (one aspect of a technique I call storytracking), attempted to trace the example to actual Arrernte sources, that is, to the other side of the chasm, to Arrernte reality, a reality independent of academics. As the Arrernte sources of Arrernte information are approached, the ground quakes with the heaviness of nonaboriginal feet. The chasm seems to have disappeared in that there appears to be only one side, the side on which the scholar stands. Although one Arrernte can be named, he seems to be a pawn in the nonaboriginal game of claiming authority for recording and presenting the Arrernte. Gillen often seems to be the pawn of Spencer in this game. But we will see that even Baldwin Spencer and Carl Strehlow were pawns in the larger game being played by James G. Frazer, Andrew Lang, and others over the nature of religion and culture. There are no clear Arrernte voices. There are no Arrernte texts independent of nonaborigines.

The task of storytracking the Arrernte through the academic bush has failed to find an independent Arrernte reality (at least in any clear sense), but it has revealed much about the character of the academic bush. At every stop along the itinerary of this storytrack, the academic operation revealed has been one of concocting a description of the Arrernte, presented to the reader in more or less primary terms, drawing freely on content elements found in source materials. These concoctions are invariably heavily influenced by the generic perspectives held by the presenter.

Storytracking powerfully illustrates the paradox of the necessity, yet seeming impossibility, of the subject of study being a reality independent of the scholar. While to all surface appearances the textual presentations considered are descriptions of a real and independent culture, storytracking has shown that in these text presentations the scholar and subject become enmeshed and the subject is finally extensively dependent on the scholar's presentation. Further analysis is necessary.

2

Storytracking Toward Theory

> The world we know is not this ultimately simple configuration where events are reduced to accentuate their essential fruits, their final meaning, or their initial and final value. On the contrary, it is a profusion of entangled events.
>
> Michel Foucault

> Today abstraction is no longer that of the map, the double, the mirror, or the concept. Simulation is no longer that of a territory, a referential being, or a substance. It is the generation of models of a real without origin or reality: a hyperreal. The territory no longer precedes the map, nor does it survive it. It is nevertheless the map that precedes the territory—*precession of simulacra*—that engenders the territory.
>
> Jean Baudrillard

Although clearly many other objectives and interests exist, the principal academic objective of the human sciences is the extension of knowledge of the world, particularly of the human beings inhabiting the world. The academic business, in its main concern, is cognitive. What a reader of, say, Eliade's *Australian Religions* seeks is knowledge—knowledge of Australian aboriginal religions, knowledge of religions of small-scale cultures, or knowledge of human religiousness. Given that knowing and knowledge are central, it is beneficial to place the analysis of the Numbakulla example in the context of cognitive theory.

Cognition and Interpretation

The problem of knowing is that cognition is a process in which the subject to be known is affected by the knower. The knower is an active agent whose concepts do not perfectly reflect some preexisting structure in the mind-independent reality. Rather, concepts play a role in the creation of some aspects of the reality known. Minimally, concepts give reality meaning. Though broadly accepted, this view of cognition struggles to supplant the still commonly held, more traditional view that meaning is a given residing within reality and awaiting discovery. In this view, language and signs function as conduits that carry meanings from reality into the mind. The most radical rejection of the traditional view holds that cognition is the sole factor in creating reality, that is, that there is no reality independent of mind. Neither of these positions, taken to their extreme of operating independently, is acceptable. One leads to solipsism, the other to essentialism. One leads to pure subjectivism, the other to pure objectivism. Both truncate the powers of human cognition and both eventually are caught in insurmountable problems. It is interesting that both positions leave human beings impotent with regard to acquiring knowledge.

The interactionist view of cognition attempts to resolve these problems and provides a more satisfying description of the cognitive process. This view continues to posit that the cognitive agent plays a role in creating the structure of reality as experienced by giving it meaning, yet there is a mind-independent reality with its own structure that at least constrains the cognitive agent's conceptual organization of it. Rather than a reality that bears some essence, some meaning, reality is understood as a matrix that can tolerate a range of meaningful structures applied to it but not any structure at all. Alternatively stated, reality has many possible profiles it can show relative to the perspective or stance of the cognitive agent.[1] But for any reality these profiles are limited. The interactionist view of cognition retains the belief that meaning is the creation of the cognitive agent without giving up the view that a mind-external reality plays a role in what meanings it will legitimately support.

The philosophical heritage of the interactionist view was initiated by Kant,[2] matured by Cassirer,[3] with contemporary work done by Nelson Goodman[4] and Bipin Indurkhya.[5] The view was advanced in important ways by Piaget[6] regarding the accommodative and assimilative strategies of human interaction with the world. The view was advanced by Lakoff and Johnson's work[7] on metaphor theory, a theory further advanced by Indurkhya. Lakoff's work on category theory is also relevant.[8]

Beginning in the late nineteenth century, the gestalt movement in psychology produced evidence that the human perceptual and cognitive apparatus is not a passive objective receptor of sensory stimuli, but rather it asserts a shaping influence on the sense data.[9] This kind of finding was supplemented by the demonstration by such scholars as Benjamin Lee Whorf[10] that cultures that bear different concepts of the world cognize it differently. The persuasiveness of these findings opposed the objectivist view of the world (though it remains alive and healthy in many areas of academic study), but it left unanswered the problem of how the world is cognized if, at least, one wishes to avoid the pitfalls and consequences of the view that concepts simply organize the world arbitrarily. Such a view would obviate any critical discourse, any notion of legitimacy, even the notion of simple mistake, and it would eventually result in a world in which mind is the only reality.[11] Interactionist views of cognition attempt to resolve these problems.

A number of terms and relationships need to be defined and explored.[12] The *cognitive agent* is the one performing the cognitive operation. The cognitive agent has a *concept network*, a symbolic system having an operational structure. External to the cognitive agent, the other side of the interaction, is *reality*. Reality is made available for cognition through the cognitive agent's sensorimotor apparatus, which produces a *sensorimotor data set*. The ontology of this data set is determined by the cognitive agent's perceptual apparatus.[13] The interactionist view depends on the structure of the data set being determined, or at least constrained, by reality. Though the cognitive agent cannot directly access this data set—that is, one cannot "see" the retinal image—there is nonetheless a mapping of reality onto the sensorimotor data set. This data set is linked to concepts in the concept network by *cognitive relations*, which provide the cognitive agent with an experiential ontology, that is, an *environment*. Cognitive relations are what bring reality within the grasp of the cognitive agent and what make the cognitive network *meaningful*. While the ontology of the environment is given by the cognitive agent, the structure of the environment with respect to this ontology is determined by reality as mapped onto the sensorimotor data set of the cognitive agent.

Given this model of the interactionist view of cognition, there are then two autonomous structures: the concept network and the environment (i.e., the experience of reality). The cognitive agent's goal is to manipulate and negotiate the constituents of the situation of cognition to produce *coherency*, which can be achieved in limited ways. For any given ontology, the structure of the environment cannot be changed. Any change to the environment would violate the autonomy of the structure of reality as present in the sensorimotor data set. What can be changed are only the structure of the concept network, that is, one's concepts, and the ontology of the environment, that is, how the concept networks are instantiated on the environment by cognitive relations. The latter is accomplished by drawing different cognitive relationships to the sensorimotor data set to produce a different environment. Following Piaget, the first strategy—changing the structure of the concept network—is called *accommodation*. The second strategy—keeping the structure of the concept network invariant while modifying the cognitive relations to change the experiential ontology of the environment—is termed *projection*.[14] While these strategies can theoretically be employed separately, and our analysis demands that they be considered separately, they are both engaged to achieve the negotiation that is common to cognition.[15]

Particularly since notions of "place" and mapping strategies are common metaphors for methods of the academic study of religion and culture, Indurkhya's mapping examples are clarifying.[16] Mapping a given terrain is an example of an accommodative strategy. Although the cognitive agent determines what such things as "land" and "water" mean, once determined these concepts are unchanged; however, the relations between these concepts are altered to reflect the state of affairs in the environment. An example of projection used in mapping may be illustrated by lines of longitude and latitude. There are many ways in which systems might be designed and applied for establishing mapping coordinates, but once a convention is adopted all others are ruled out. Holding the concept network fixed, instantiating it on the sensorimotor data set, creates a particular environment. This illustration shows how the projective operation is constrained by the structure of reality. For example, while latitude might be conceived in many ways, a city in each of the states of Colorado, New York, and Florida cannot all be assigned the same latitude. Further, once the system of reference is put in place, there is no occasion for arbitrary decisions; it is a matter of objective verification.

From an interactionist perspective, academic interpretation may be described as an external counterpart to the internal cognitive process. Interpretation, as a formal academic method, is not simply a cognitive act. It is a cognitive act that is formalized and externalized, that is, made public by displaying the interpretive components as well as the interpretive operations. The work of "reading,"[17] that is, interpreting, requires three components: (1) academic theories and hypotheses, the counterpart of the concept network. This is a formal statement of academic perspective, but it is based on the academics' network of concepts developed throughout their life of experience; (2) the focal subject to be interpreted, the counterpart of the environment for the cognitive agent. The designated subject must have a reality independent of the interpreter; (3) argumentation and explanation, the counterpart of the cognitive relations drawn between the concept network and the environment. Argumentation and explanation document and justify the negotiation and manipulation of the theories and hypotheses, on the one hand, and the subject, on the other. It is incumbent upon argumentation to ensure that the manipulation of the subject is legitimate, that is, properly constrained by the independent reality of the subject.

The interpreter's objective is to obtain "coherence"[18] as a characterization of the correspondence, achieved through the negotiation (justified by argumentation and explanation) between theory and subject. The initial correspondence will not be adequately coherent because theory and subject are two different orders of reality. The operations of interpretation, presented as formal argumentation and explanation, parallel the interactionist view of cognition, that is, they may be analyzed as being either "accommodative" or "projective" or some combination of the two. Unlike cognition, where both strategies are always jointly operative, in interpretation it is customary, particularly at specific stages in the process, for one or the other strategy to be prominent.

Analysis of the Numbakulla Case

With these concepts and terms in place, Eliade's work with the "Numbakulla and the Sacred Pole" example can be reconsidered, though any of the episodes in the storytrack would serve as well. For Eliade's writing to be considered an interpretation, according to the theory framing this analysis, the three components described above must be present: theory, subject, and argument.

1. *Theory.* Briefly, Eliade held that religion is synonymous with the symbolic temporal designation of the origin, the time of creation, and spatially with the cen-

ter of the world, the *axis mundi*, which in this example he called "the sacred center." This synonymy is based on Eliade's view that reality is established by the gods through their originating actions, which occurred in the beginning, and that their actions established a point of orientation, "the sacred center," which also remains as the channel by which human beings continue to communicate with the creators in the period following their departure to the sky realm.[19]

2. *Subject.* Eliade formally identifies his subject as "Numbakulla and the Sacred Pole." He identifies his source as the ethnographic document *The Arunta*, by Spencer and Gillen (1927). Eliade fostered the presumption that his description of the Arrernte example and his source, that is, Spencer and Gillen, are transparent mediations of the cultural source, the Arrernte culture of Central Australia. From the analysis in the first chapter, it is clear that Eliade did not present an Arrernte subject that was adequately constrained by the sources he cited. The perplexing issues raised by this incongruity are important, but in order to raise other significant issues they will be briefly postponed.

3. *Argumentation.* There is remarkable coherence between the reported aboriginal actions regarding the pole and Eliade's theory of religion as focused on the concept of the sacred center. Rather than argumentation, Eliade's method appears to be illustration or exemplification.

Granted, temporarily at least, the presence of the three components necessary for an interpretation to exist, the question is, What interpretive strategies, though tacit to his readers, did Eliade employ? Did he engage accommodative, projective, or a combination of both interpretive methods? Accommodation would require that he keep the correspondence invariant and alter his theory to obtain coherence. Eliade clearly maintained complete invariance of his understanding of religion. Projection would require that he keep his view invariant but present a particular profile of his subject as revealed from the perspective of his theory. This would amount to a reontologization limited by the independent structure of the reality of his subject. In other words, in using this strategy Eliade would have had to project the structure of his theory of religion onto his subject to restructure it in such a way as to reveal a compatible profile. Since at the level of presentation there is no evidence of instantiating his theory on the subject, Eliade does not appear to have used projection.

What is most interesting and curious is that Eliade's presentation seems to require neither interpretive nor cognitive operation. He appears to simply present a description of a cultural reality that is in full concert with his generic conception of reality. Rather than interpretation, it appears that Eliade engaged in a style of rhetoric that produces illustration or exemplification in support of a conclusion that depends largely on his authority or the authority of his former work. Even when his description of the Arrernte material is disentangled from his remarks about the example in order to identify the three components necessary to an interpretation, the correspondence between his theory and the subject is so highly coherent as to require no interpretation. While, on the surface, projection is not apparent, the storytracking method used in the first chapter revealed that Eliade obtained the Arrernte materials he presented by selecting and reorganizing elements from his source. Despite appearances, Eliade engaged in interpretation, using a projective strategy in the operation of obtaining what he presents as an objective description of his subject. In this way he constructed a profile of the Arrernte coherent with his general theory of religion.

While the analysis of Eliade's interpretive method indicates that the structure of operations is consistent with the projective method, two issues are raised. First, are the actual projective actions Eliade performed legitimate? To be legitimate, Eliade's presentation of the Arrernte must adequately correspond both to the text sources on which he relied and to the subject reality he purports to present. In other words, does Eliade's resulting "Numbakulla and the Sacred Pole" text correspond with the Spencer and Gillen texts on which he relied? And does it correspond with some Arrernte reality? Second, is it appropriate that Eliade, in effect, hid his interpretive operations from his readers by presenting the interpretation as an illustrative description of reality?

Evaluating Legitimacy of Interpretation

To be considered successful and legitimate, an interpretation must accurately present the sources on which it depends and the actual subject it purports to present.[20] Both are necessary to ensure that an interpretation is adequately constrained by its subject reality. The satisfactory demonstration of constraint exerted by reality is necessary to the interactionist view of cognition. If the structure of the interpreter-independent reality does not assert constraint, there is no interaction. The interactionist view of cognition describes internal cognitive processes in which the structures of reality play a "natural" constraining role on the cognitive agent's operations. If they do not, the cognitive agent would be considered pathological. The interactionist view of academic interpretation describes external operations that parallel internal cognitive operations. Because interpretation involves both internal and external operations, the complexity of interpretive argumentation and explanation is compounded. Whereas cognition is an internal process, the cognitive agent's experience of coherency marks a successful cognition. However, since interpretation is external and public, successful interpretation is not simply measured by the cognitive agent's internal experience of coherence but also by the interpreter's ability, independently testable and subject to critical analysis, to externalize, as explanation, the manipulative operations performed to achieve coherency. Interpretation requires making the usually tacit cognitive operations formal and public.

By understanding interpretation as being parallel to cognition, the legitimacy of interpretation can be more clearly evaluated. Certainly the identification of interpretive strategy—accommodative, projective, or a combination of both—provides the foundation for criticism. This analytical distinction gives focus to the critical task by pointing either to the change in theory or to the restructuring of the subject. The success or failure of interpretation is based on the explanation and argumentation, which must include the demonstration of the legitimacy of the manipulations and negotiations of the interpretative operation. Where pathology can be designated in cognitive failure, something akin to pathology ought to be possible in the realm of academic interpretation. Such a condition would pertain when the uncontested structures of reality are ignored or somehow unaccounted for in an interpretive operation. Probably a whole range of academic pathologies might be identified.

The evaluation of the legitimacy of the interpretation, whether accommodative or projective, including the argumentation, raises fascinating issues. On what basis can one evaluate another's interpretation? Where can one stand to say that the profile of a reality seen by another does or does not surpass the constraints of that reality? In other words, when it is acknowledged that all interactions with a subject affect what is seen as the subject, the stance of the evaluator is as creative and as precarious as is the stance of the interpreter whose interpretation is being evaluated. Rules and principles for evaluating legitimacy must be addressed. First, to evaluate a projective restructuring of a source of reality, one must assume the perspective of the interpreter; that is, one must internalize, or indwell,[21] the theories and assumptions of the interpreter. Second, the profile of the focal reality that results from the interpretation must be compared with the source from which the profile is drawn. In the case in question, Eliade's interpretation of Spencer and Gillen that produced his "Numbakulla and the Sacred Pole" text must be compared with his source, Spencer and Gillen's *The Arunta*. Third, ideally a comparison of an academic report with its sources will reveal differences, all of which must be explained in terms of logical and supportable argumentation. However, since all views of the sources involve some level of interpretation (tacit, if not explicit), how can evaluation lead to anything other than endless argumentation over theory?

It must be recognized that many assumptions are operating within the interpretive process. These assumptions are often not explicitly chosen or acknowledged but are features of the perspective indwelt. For example, Spencer and Gillen wrote in English, which by convention is based on a specific alphabet, vocabulary, and grammar. Spencer and Gillen share with their readers a modern Western view of the world, based on many assumptions about humanity, culture, nature, geography, and so on. Any of these indwelt sets of assumptions may be chosen to frame the comparison performed to evaluate legitimacy. The frame chosen must be one that is held in common by both interpreter and critic, by both source and resulting interpretation. Generally, the more conventional, pervasive, and uncontentious the assumed frame of comparison, the more convincing the critical evaluation. For example, when comparing Eliade's "Numbakulla and the Sacred Pole" with passages from Spencer and Gillen's *The Arunta*, to show variance at the level of alphabetic character, syllable, and word is more convincing in identifying fallaciousness than to show variance of the meanings of broad passages. If an interpreter presents a term in the singular whereas a source presents the same term in the plural, because of the broadly held conventions of English language, to say that the interpreter's resulting profile of the subject is fallacious in number is, other things remaining equal, convincing. At the level of language conventions, the determination of validity approaches objectivity. At this level a noun is objectively either singular or plural; a given word is either present or absent.

In the case of Eliade's interpretation, it is more objective and less contentious to evaluate the interpretation by comparing the text that resulted from his projective interpretation to its source at the level of alphabetical character and word. This rule is practiced in the evaluations in the first chapter. A text that results from an interpretation is compared at the level of the word with the text interpreted. By operating within a conceptual frame of a given language system, such highly significant values as gender, time, number, positivity or negativity, and place are objectively designated by so little as a word, a syllable, or an alphabetic character. To alter (including adding and deleting material) without explanation any of these designations in the process of interpretation signals the possibility that the projective operation of the interpreter has violated the structure of the source. In the strict sense, any variance between the source and the resulting interpretation requires explanation. This is the burden of interpretation, that is, to explain why a source should be seen in a particular way or how the source shows a particular profile. The absence of explanation signals a failed interpretation or a fallacious presentation.

At more general levels, contextualization is another principle. If two or more interpreters engage independent interpretations of a common subject from a common perspective, it is arguable that while they may interpret a specific item quite differently out of context, this interpretive difference diminishes as the specific item is seen in the light of, and in relation to, wider and wider contexts. Thus, if an interpretation of a term or a statement in isolation from its context in the environment presents a meaning in significant variance from the meaning it appears to have when considered in the light of its context, there is an increase in the potential for failed interpretation or fallacious presentation.

I have attempted to indicate a number of ways in which one might formulate principles for evaluating the legitimacy of interpretations. Such principles are important both to evaluate interpretive explanation and, the more difficult task, to ensure that the subject interpreted has asserted proper constraint on the interpretation, that is, to be assured that the interpretation is not arbitrary with respect to the subject.

Using these principles and criteria for evaluation, I determined that Eliade's and most of Spencer's interpretations examined in chapter 1 are illegitimate; that is, the results of their interpretations were not adequately constrained by their disclosed and undisclosed sources.

The correspondence of the interpretive results with the subject reality must also be evaluated. In this case, is the information presented as Arrernten actually about some Arrernte reality? I call the method employed in the first chapter storytracking. In that application, storytracking amounted to the serial evaluation of the legitimacy of covert interpretations in which a projective operation was used to restructure source texts to reveal new, though often illegitimate, profiles, or new texts. Storytracking is a method that facilitates this kind of evaluation. Eliade presents his "Numbakulla and the Sacred Pole" account as identified with the Arrernte, a people who live in Central Australia. It is vital to verify that the account indeed legitimately presents some Arrernten reality.

The storytracking method tracked the Arrernte through the academic bush formed by a series of texts, each one a creation on a former one achieved by methods of selection and reconstruction. The results of storytracking, beginning with Eliade and leading backward through Baldwin Spencer and Francis Gillen to specific Arrernte persons, were conclusive in showing that demonstrably Arrernte sources played a remarkably small role in the processes of interpreting them either by constraining or legitimating anything in the stream of texts flowing from Arrernte encounters with Gillen and Spencer. Storytracking revealed further that the Arrernte individuals in contact with Gillen and Spencer may well have presented themselves to these outsiders to accommodate what was expected of them in deference to Spencer and Gillen's lack of proficiency in the Arrernte language and limited by the capacities of aboriginal English.

Thus the question is no longer, Did Eliade misread the text? but rather, Is there any authentic text to be misread? And the answer is that, at least in these terms, there is no clearly authentic Arrernte text. Initially this may seem a small matter. One might argue that even if Eliade's theory of religion loses this particular Arrernten example entirely, it would surely have little effect on the status of his theory. A similar argument might be made for the entire Arrernte subject were it not for the sobering statement made in 1913 by Bronislaw Malinowski that "since the publication of their first volume [Spencer and Gillen's *Native Tribes*], half of the total production in anthropological theory has been based upon their work, and nine-tenths affected or modified by it."[22] The eagerness to advance such a wish suggests a clue to our fuller analysis. The scale of this problem increases when it is recognized that what may be in question is not only an ethnographic example but also the legitimacy of a pervasive academic method.

When an academic study of history and culture is based on an interpretation of Arrernte culture, if that interpretation is determined to be illegitimate or unauthentic, that is, not an authentic presentation of the Arrernte, it would seem the whole process slides into a form of academic solipsism. Without the Arrernte reality, there is nothing to interpret. Without the Arrernte, all of the conclusions drawn are called into question. Furthermore, an especially interesting implication for essentialist views such as Eliade's is that the loss of the independent reality of the Arrernte means that the reality presented is wholly constructed by the academic method, thus exposing a hidden relativism to this position.[23] Without some reality external to the interpreter, the entire academic enterprise of interpretation would tumble like a house of cards. It becomes deceptive, even self-deceptive, in that it presents itself as the study of human histories and cultures when such histories and cultures have only a tenuous connection with the studies.

Hidden Interpretation

Now the second issue, hopefully not forgotten, has to do with the appropriateness of the transparency of the interpretive method, what in negative terms amounts to hiding the interpretive process. Storytracking the Numbakulla text revealed that some forms of interpretation are hidden behind what appears to be the straightforward presentation of text. Such tacit interpretations are presented in the guise of artifact somehow attachable to the world outside of the interpretive process.[24] Interpretation presented as primary text is a powerfully persuasive form because, while it is theory driven, the theory remains tacit, as does the interpretive process. For example, Eliade so tightly interweaves "facts" (though revealed as fallacious) identified as "Arrernte" with his theoretical statements that only a close reading, as well as comparison with his source, which is unavailable in Eliade's work, can even begin to unravel subject from interpretation. The theories that drive Spencer's interpretations are even more transparent, although I would argue that, as with Eliade's presentation, once it is known that Spencer is presenting an interpretation rather than cultural facts, even the imprint of his interpretive hand becomes visible. When interpreting by the method of text presentation, even what is being interpreted remains hidden among an array of false fronts. Eliade appears to be interpreting an Arrernte historical act (*The Sacred and the Profane* version) or a myth (*Australian Religions* version), but what appears cannot be real since both the act and the myth attributed to the Arrernte are of his own construction; that is, they do not have demonstrably authentic Arrernte sources. Rather he is (to present my own interpretation) determining by the tacit assertion of his theory the details of specific religions and, consequently, through this self-circulating process, the structure of all religions. This process will be considered more fully below.

Spencer is faced with the awesome task, given his time and place in history, of rendering Arrernte culture sensible to a European readership and, more broadly, all Australian aborigines in light of the history of human existence. Spencer's theory, tacit to his presentation, was that all human beings need some explanation, some description, of their origins. His theory insisted that there be some chronology based on a logical sequence of events: creation of the world must precede creation of humans, which in turn precedes the creation of group identities, and so on. Spencer constructed Arrernte texts to fit his expectations. In doing so, he created an Arrernte culture for his readers and provided what have been understood as primary examples for the constructions of dozens of culture and religion theorists who have used his and Gillen's books as a primary ethnographic source. What appears to be ethnographic fact in both Spencer's work and Eliade's writings is academic artifact (thing made).

From the perspective of style and persuasiveness, there may be arguments for leaving the explicit interpretive process hidden from the reader. The detailed valuative process exemplified in chapter 1 risks overwhelming the results of the interpretation with the complexities of a fully presented, self-consciously conducted interpretation. Further, the extent to which judgments and assumptions are made as necessary to any interpretation are much more apparent when the full interpretive process is explicitly and formally presented. Explicit interpretation may suffer a loss of persuasiveness because of the exposure of the cognitive operations and the subjectivity inherent in interpretation. However, covert interpretation runs the risk of being deceptive. The issue hinges on the distinction between rhetorical style and improper interpretive methods. To consciously hide an interpretation in the presentation of a restructured subject raises an ethical issue since the restructured subject may actually replace the preinterpreted subject. In other words, if Eliade's readers are unaware that his presentation of the Arrernte is the result of an interpretation, they may consider his description a legitimate, factual presentation of the subject, usable as a primary source for their own studies of the Arrernte. Particularly when this unwitting deception is an accepted academic method and when it is an operation that is performed through a lineage of scholarship, whole fields of study become simply groundless; their connection with a reality external to the academic process becomes increasingly tenuous.

While I do not intend to suggest that Eliade or any other scholar has been consciously deceptive, good academic intentions do not suspend the ethical implications of this academic operation. It is common academic practice to present highly selective cultural and historical examples to illustrate and exemplify theories. While this is a rhetorical style,[25] it may hide projective interpretive operations. What all too rarely occurs is an explicit accounting of the projective operation, that is, one showing how an original environment is reconstructed and how the structures of the subject's reality were encountered and permitted to interact with, as well as expressing constraint on, the new construction. The crux of this issue is the confusion of rhetoric with responsible method. There is a clear difference between the rhetorical device of illustration and exemplification and the academic methods of interpretation and explanation. Illustration and exemplification are appropriate primarily when a theory has been established and enjoys broad consensual acceptance and when the purpose of illustrating theory is not to gain its establishment.

Preceding Simulation

I have proceeded under the assumption that Spencer's and Eliade's studies of the Arrernte were primarily interpretative enterprises. I have stated the ground rules and criteria for such an academic operation and criticized their works accordingly. The problem that has persistently arisen in this comparative and critical analysis, following the technique of storytracking, has been that the gap between scholar and subject has seemed often, in some respect, absent because the scholars constructed some of their own primary sources. No interpretation, no attempt to bridge the gap, therefore, seemed necessary to these scholars. I found their "tacit" interpretations to be illegitimate in that what sources they used did not exert adequate constraint, and more seriously, the cultural reality of their stated subject of study was scarcely present.

This storytracking analysis suggests a number of clues that need to be explored more fully. I had to work hard to place Eliade and Spencer in the framework of interpretation, and neither fit well. I do not believe that they are, as scholars, exceptional in this regard. The attempt to place their work in the frame of this academic operation invariably revealed that they did not consider their views of culture, religion, and humankind theoretical, that is, in any way negotiable. It is also clear that they felt limited constraint by available cultural sources.

When I reflect on these accumulating clues, I think that to some extent I have had it backward. These scholars have not considered their cultural human subjects to be the reality studied; indeed, the aboriginal cultural reality is not the most fundamental reality to them. While they present their studies as concerned with their subjects—they entitle their books in reference to these cultures—the storytracking analysis reveals that the cultural materials are often seen to be secondary, in an important sense, rather than primary. We must also recall that Spencer could study the Arrernte without learning their language and Eliade could study Australian religions without even going to Australia. Something other than academic interpretation of a cultural reality is going on here. What is primary, in the sense of being most fundamentally reliable, to these scholars is their generic ideas about nature, culture, and humankind.

Inspired by Jean Baudrillard's essays on simulacra and simulation,[26] I suggest that, rather than an interpretation of Arrernte culture and religion, these scholars have presented preceding simulations, that is, academic simulations based on ideas that they firmly held before their contact with their subject cultures. Spencer's simulations were based on a hybrid of morphological and evolutionary comparative theories established by the natural sciences, which he applied to culture; Eliade's, on his views of religion. What has issued forth in the modern period (most clearly arising from an attempt at broadly encompassing comparative studies) is the establishment of universally applicable generic realities, ways of seeing as whole the otherwise diverse and incoherent world. Postmodernity is marked by self-consciousness regarding the implications of this way of approaching the world.

The process that gives rise to academic simulation is rather simple in its broad outline. Based on foundational studies of specific materials, a general theory is constructed. In this formative stage, interpretation probably engages a rich interplay of accommodation and projection. This new general theory may be tested on other sets of specific natural or cultural materials. In this stage of development, projection begins to outweigh accommodation. Eventually, confidence in the theory attains such heights that the theory is no longer seen as a map of reality but rather as the plan manifest in various cultural and natural forms. Finally, the abstract generic theory is seen as universal and real in a primary sense. Rather than a map of reality, it has become the structure, plan, or essence that is more reliable, more real than any instance in a cultural, historical setting. Confidence is demonstrated by using the theory (though no longer strictly theoretical) to simulate rather than to interpret.

There is a parallel to scientific method. To be useful, theories should be capable of prediction, which is often achieved by the technique of simulation. Given conditions at a specific time and place, the theory should support the simulation of conditions at any other specifiable time and place. The demonstration of the accuracy of simulation, through the later comparison with observation, helps demonstrate the usefulness of the theory. Simulation serves the interpretative and scientific methods; it continues to hold that reality is outside theory. Despite the parallel to scientific method, Spencer and Eliade (and I do not believe their approach in this regard is highly exceptional in social scientific and humanities scholarship during the last century) do not present their views as theoretical but rather as ontological.

From this perspective, what I see taking place in Spencer's and Eliade's studies is a shift in the location of reality from the subject to the scholar's operative theory (I retain the term gratuitously). This shift allows Australian cultures to be studied in terms of preceding simulations without a need to compare the results of simulations to any scholar-independent reality. For example, Eliade prepared himself to study Australian religions by studying aspects of other traditions throughout the world. The result for him was an understanding of religion in which he believed so firmly that it was simply unthinkable that it would not apply to Australian aborigines. Consequently, Australian aborigines need not be studied in the sense of attempting to comprehend them in their own terms (though recall that this is exactly what Eliade claimed as his goal) or even in terms of testing or modifying his theory of religion. The theory of religion was no longer theory; it was reality and felt to be so real as to be more primary than the actual cultural examples. Consequently, the published sources of Australian religions had to be only casually consulted to provide Australian terms to the resulting simulacrum.

It is not difficult to see that Spencer—though presenting and attending much more fully to materials independent of him than did Eliade—held the temporally sequenced morphological stages of development that constituted cultural evolution as a higher order of reality than the field data he and Gillen collected from the Arrernte.

Simulation is akin to exemplification (discussed in the analysis of interpretation above) but different in one very crucial respect. Exemplification still requires that the presentation of the culturally specific example be adequately constrained by the independent reality. Simulation, however, is burdened little, if at all, by the cultural reality; indeed, it is the absence of what, according to the theory, should be present in the culture that is the strength and contribution of simulation. Simulation provides what is not found. The idea of simulation thus helps us understand why Spencer and Eliade were not faced with issues of legitimacy when they concocted cultural "facts." They were simply aligning what they knew of the culture with their understanding of reality and filling in the blanks with their own informed concoctions. The fact that these specific works of both scholars have been widely used by other scholars without criticism[27] on this point suggests that preceding simulation is acceptable academic practice.

The break with the scientific method of comparing simulation with observed simulator-independent reality is, of course, the remaining problem. It seems that there are a number of reasons why this problem has never surfaced. The first, doubtless, is the shift in primary reality, the shift from cultural realities (territory) as primary to the theories or generic views (maps). Once this transformation has taken place, any challenge to these beliefs amounts to a threat, to these scholars, to the real world of experience. Through their academic studies, they live their views through their academic work rather than tentatively positing them. The second reason, just as strong, is that once made a concoction is difficult to detect as a simulation. Making an absence present has the effect of grasping the real. The labor of storytracking, as exemplified in the first chapter, is a measure of what is required to detect simulation, to separate interpretation from academic artifact. Even in situations of greatest disclosure,[28] once a simulation has been set forth, it is almost impossible to continue to qualify it as a simulation. Often, as is usually the case in the study of Australian aborigines, nothing exists other than preceding simulacra. Simulacra are provided often because it is impractical to do otherwise.

Preceding simulation characterizes the modern period.[29] In the most pragmatic sense, it is a product of the necessity of comprehending a multitude of differences with little time and patience to consider the specific, the individual. But it destroys even the possibility of difference as a result. In the construction of generic terms such as *evolution*, *culture*, and *religion* and the subsequent bestowal on the generic of the designation of the real, all observations become, in part, preceding simulations. The results are not always pretty and suggest a broad pathology, a kind of academic narcissism. Our human studies are hardly humane in that they contribute to the destruction of our stated subjects of study. If they are not actually physically destroyed, as they so often are, they are invariably destroyed by the force exerted by the claims to reality of our simulations, what Baudrillard calls the production of the "hyperreal."[30] Our presentations of cultures, developed as preceding simulations, become greater, more forceful, and more authoritative than simple cultural reality. These presentations, after all, cohere and make sense, in contrast to the confusing hodgepodge we directly experience as our subject. Our human studies often force our "deceased" subjects, if they even remain physically alive, to act out parodies of themselves in imitation of our simulations.

There is the possibility of another stage, a fourth stage, in this process as I am imagining it. I alluded to it previously. Once preceding simulation becomes the primary reality, the whole system, as Baudrillard says, "becomes weightless, it is no longer itself anything but a giant simulacrum—not unreal, but a simulacrum, that is to say never exchanged for the real, but exchanged for itself, in an uninterrupted circuit without reference or circumference."[31] This exchange of simulacrum for itself, this orbital recurrence, occurs concretely when field scholars confirm the simulacra of former scholars by observing members of a culture acting out simulations in their attempt to gain some participation in reality (or hyperreality). This may well have occurred as early as Gillen's 1894 recording of his "Traditions of Origin" and most certainly was a significant factor in Spencer's 1926 interviews with Charlie Cooper.

The hyperreal of simulation implodes the distinction between theory and subject, between map and territory. It collapses the gap that underlies the necessity of interpretation and the possibility of representation. As Baudrillard found, "Simulation stems from the utopia of the principle of equivalence, *from the radical negation of the sign as value*, from the sign as the reversion and death sentence of every reference."[32] Thus, simulation, academic or not (yet as presented and practiced by academics), threatens to transform scholarship by implosion into the manufacture of the hyperreal—pure simulacra, on the one hand, and, on the other, products of the nostalgia for reference, for a stake in reality, for history, for the imaginary, and for the theoretical.

Storytracking

What has become increasingly evident in the effort to approach the Arrernte in this particular example is that we can know and see the Arrernte, or any other subject of study, only through particular eyes and words, usually the eyes and words of others, as well as our own. We must accept that we can never know any Arrernte reality free of these often invisible interpretations, whether they are the interpretations from the point of view of others or the invisible conditioning of our own views of the world.[33] Furthermore, it may well be that the Arrernte we think we are coming to know amount to the hyperreal, products of preceding simulation by which scholars effect their abstract views as cultural realities. The Arrernte—or any label by which we designate a subject in the sense of specifying some set of facts, some essences, some cultural givens that are free of academic imprint—is a fiction created to make humanistic scholarship appear, on the one hand, to be about something and, on the other hand, to appear grounded, scientific, and based on fact. The texts that present, represent, or simulate our subjects are not found or given and are not wholly independent of us. Texts are not somehow kernels that bear essences or hidden meanings. Texts may reflect history or culture, but they are also products of trying to discern history and culture. They may be the hyperreality of preceding simulation. Interpretation is not a process of revealing meanings that are somehow *in* the text, somehow *true* although hidden from view. It is not that interpretation somehow reveals the truths about a culture, a people, or a religion. Indeed, even categories such as culture and religion are as much our creation as is Eliade's equation of the religious with "the sacred center" and Spencer's morphological- and evolutionary-based temporal periodization of Arrernte mythology. The categories we use to interpret our subject in some measure shape all that we see and understand.[34]

What impact do these observations have on academic methods? Simply put, texts cannot be studied without also studying their histories. Texts are not given facts, free from academic or other interpretive imprint. Texts may be, and often are, disguised interpretations or simulacra. Certainly this insistence seems at first to invite a wallowing in academic histories, giving up the goal of learning anything about anything outside of academia, but entering some mire is not my intention. I simply want to insist that once these probabilities are known to exist, ignoring them—avoiding the histories and interpretations and simulations inseparable from the presentation of texts—amounts to ethically questionable and willful misrepresentation. If it is never known that Eliade concocted his Arrernte example from Spencer and Gillen; if it is never known that Spencer concocted his Arrernte example from Gillen's journals and his own Arrernte informants; if it is never known that the Arrernte themselves may have responded to Spencer's and Gillen's inquiries, already prepared by Christian missionaries for just such questions, then "the Arrernte" can be described with the confidence, although decidedly unfounded, that the descriptions are based on information that came from the horse's mouth instead of from some other part of its anatomy. The results are specious and almost certainly an unwitting fall in the direction of narcissism—the descriptions are mere reflections of the describers.

Academic traditions operate extensively on trust. It is common to believe that reputable histories and culture studies maintain a strict separation between text and interpretation. Based on this trust, it is common practice to extract primary texts from academic works. Often these extractions and the way they are presented in different contexts for different purposes re-create texts to fit new needs and other theories. This process can form a tradition of divergence from the supposed subjects, or a tradition of weightless simulacra. The designation of canon in some academic traditions is intended to foil this loss of grounding. For exclusively oral traditions, a body of accepted ethnographies, such as Spencer and Gillen's works, makes up an informal canon. The problem here is that the acceptance of canon tends to produce the view that a specific body of texts actually and adequately presents a culture, a religion, or a tradition and that the meanings are *in* the canonized texts, as though hidden there, rather than made in the act of reading or the act of interpretation.

The creative and constructive response to the awareness of academic methods opens the way to seeing anew what academics do. Once we see that there is no hidden truth or goal, we can begin to see that the academic enterprise is a network of tracks, intersecting an academic, cultural, and historical landscape, even if that landscape is imagined. While none of these tracks is destined to reach "the truth," the end of the academic line, all of them come from somewhere and, in heading along their destined line, intersect and thus encounter others. The analysis of any of these lines of inquiry can be understood as storytracking (as I have termed the idea), that is, one's investigation, comprehension, and presentation (as storytrack) of the ways of others. Once we see the multiplicity of storytracks, it is no longer possible to pursue "the truth"; to attempt to find "the meaning"; to construct the final, ultimately satisfying explanation for any culture or history or religion. From a given perspective, some histories and some culture studies are decidedly superior to others. Furthermore, the perspective from which this judgment is made may be so widely accepted that the studies deemed superior may appear to contain truth and finality. Such has been the case in the Arrernte materials presented by Spencer and Gillen and even by Eliade. What storytracking reveals is that even this determination of apparent truth and final meaning is a judgment based in or created by some one perspective among potentially many perspectives. Thus, in principle at least, histories and culture studies differ from one another and, from a variety of perspectives, can be ranked relative to one another, but apart from determinations of legitimacy and the distinction between interpretation and preceding simulation no one may be ultimately superior to others. Storytracking, as applied to academic methods, is a way of gauging the legitimacy of interpretation and the extent of preceding simulation. Though it may be laborious, its yield can be significant.

What seems increasingly clear is that even the pursuit of such goals as truth and essence is destined to disappoint. But without these goals, what motivates history and culture studies? What makes these activities satisfying? I suggest that the storytracks of the study of history and culture are tracks with no final goal, no ultimate destination. Though there may be many hypotheses, many theories, and many temporary goals, none are final. These academic approaches are tracks of both discovery and construction, along which we both discover and create ourselves as we create and discover others. The places we find sufficiently important to cause us to pause are the intersections of our storytrack with the storytracks of others. At these crossing points we perform the academic rites of negotiating and manipulating the intersecting sets of values so that they might more fully and meaningfully interact with others. Through these interactions, which are the occasions for interpretation, we are refueled for our journey. We travel not to get anywhere but because our identity, our being, is inseparable from the track along which we travel, and to journey along our track is how we enact who we are.[35]

There is an Arrernten counterpart to storytracking; indeed it has served as an inspiring metaphor for the development of storytracking. Arrernte society, as the story goes, is divided into totem groups, distinguished from one another by identity with their mythic ancestors.[36] The ancestors, identified as various animals, plants, or natural forms, traveled along specific tracks in the Australian landscape. The country through which they traveled is the country with which the people in the totem group identify themselves. The ancestral itineraries trace an ancestral track. At the geographic places that make up this itinerary, the Arrernte people sometimes camp, where they sing the songs and perform the dances of the ancestors in order to vitalize, initiate, and increase the people, plants, and animals of their country and their group. Over a period of years these groups trace the ancestral journeys. There are many Arrernte groups, each identified by track. Each group is also designated by an emblem, by rituals and songs inseparable from geography. For Arrernte society, these many tracks crisscross the landscape, overlaying one another, with no one more fundamental, more important, or more real or true than any other. Most Arrernte rites are identified by totem group and specific geographic location. Associated rituals are conducted at specific geographic locations. When any group performs totem-locality rites, the people of other groups whose track crosses at the same ritual location are required to attend and participate in the ritual dance-dramas. This is a common way in which knowledge is shared and peoples interrelate.[37]

Drawing on this model of Arrernte ancestral tracks—which, of course, is the product of my interpretation—history and culture studies, indeed all humanistic studies and all history, may be seen as a network of storytracks that unfold across various spatial, temporal, and imagined landscapes. As a student of religion, Eliade's work blazed a storytrack that was followed by many. This track is a major thoroughfare through the history of religions. Importantly, to the extent to which Eliade identified the religious with the center place, he not only established a road but also determined the territory others would see or construct as religious. In the case of religion, that landscape is the history of religions, itself the construction of story. Like the Arrernte, we, too, have our heroes, like Eliade, who arose for a time from the landscape to shape the way we now see and imagine the world. It is difficult to comprehend the world at all except as such heroic figures have revealed it. We feel something of their presence as we stop to ponder what they have done. An important insight that we may gain from the Arrernte or this storytrack of the Arrernte, a major difference from the views we probably hold, is that no storytrack leads us to some greater or more fundamental reality. Any number of storytracks may exist. No one of them, in any ultimate sense, is truer or more real than any other, though, of course, travelers often see their own track as more important, more relevant, and more useful than any of the others they encounter. We may gain further insight from the Arrernte by recognizing that while no track or country is more important to them than any other, the existence of territory is always fundamentally important. Religion, culture, and life itself is unthinkable apart from concrete reference to territory. It is through the symbolical, social, and physical interaction with territory that Arrernte life finds its poetry and its meaning. The hyperreal of simulation amounts to deterritorialization.

Scholars, then, are not necessarily only interpreters of events given in history (though from more than one storytrack the sight is so limited); they can and should be seen also as makers of history and culture by virtue of their interpretive and simulative powers, often enacted through the presentation of cultural artifacts that they construct. Storytracking is not simply a way of accounting for that small segment of makers of history known as academics; it is also a way of viewing all of history. To study history is not to look at the past to discern the truth or to find its inherent meanings, it is an interactive creative process, just as is history itself. History is made up of storytracks, as is the study of history, culture, and religion. Storytracks can be isolated in the telling, but they are most interesting where they intersect.

The development of Central Australia in the late nineteenth and early twentieth centuries provides an excellent landscape in which to demonstrate this storytrack view of history. The aborigines had occupied the landscape for upward of 40,000 years when, suddenly, groups of nonaboriginal Australians entered the huge landscape to build a telegraph line, to establish a cattle industry, to mine the riches from the soil, to bring Christ, to build a railroad, and to make ethnographic records. Then, although using different kinds of vehicles, the landscape was traversed by dozens of scholars, who never set physical foot on Australian soil, whose theories and preceding simulations, seemingly anchored in aboriginal Australia, have shaped much of the social scientific and humanistic theory fundamental to twentieth-century Western views of the world.

The notion of storytracking corresponds with Jonathan Smith's statement that the historian has "no place on which to stand."[38] In other words, there is no final correct position, no single position of objectivity, no position free of the subjectivities of the observer, or no way to get free of one's own cultural and historical skin[39] (or eyes). The strongest statement of this would be solipsism, that the world is entirely of our own making, the world being exclusively hyperreal, or a simulacrum. In this sense there are no Australians, no other scholars, no books, and so on. Holding to this radical view stifles the motivation for paying any attention to anything so exasperating as the construction of an idea that there are people that we call Arrernte to use as images through which to consider the self. For me, solipsism is not an attractive choice.

Another, much more subtle approach, which, following Baudrillard, I have called preceding simulation, constructs the cultural specific to the extent necessary to correspond with generic models that precede and direct studies of the culturally specific. This approach ultimately supplants reality with hyperreality, deterritorializes, eliminates difference, and stifles reference. For me, though it may characterize our time, preceding simulation is not an attractive choice.

I hold that there is some real world outside the self, outside one's own concoctions, but that it does not have meanings, essences, or identities inherent in it. The world does not await us or someone who has the right or correct approach or sensitivity or theory for its meanings to be discovered, expressed, or experienced.[40] I hold that meaning and experience exist only in encounter, in relating, or in interacting. When I or anyone else encounters some Arrernte reality,[41] either physically in Central Australia or by how it is presented in print, interactions and relations necessarily exist as attributes of the encounter. But the encounter is not like two hard rocks colliding, for who I am and who the Arrernte are are as much products of the encounter as some condition prior to the encounter. Certainly I have an identity prior to this encounter, as do the Arrernte. These identities are not unchangeable essences. Identity is an ongoing, constantly changing program. Through my encounter with others, through every interaction or interrelationship, I enact my being; I "be" who I am in that moment. And, I would hold, that so do the Arrernte I encounter, individually and also collectively, if as a group, culture, or subject presented by others in print they can be thought of as having existence. All have being only in relationship to others that they are not.

Storytracking, as I am presenting it, is the construction of a narrative of coherence (a storytrack). Storytracking constructs meanings (i.e., the elements of coherence) on the relationships, encounters, and experiences of self and other. The term *story* suggests plot, development, and sequence, and it allows for a sense of construction or concoction—thus a narrative of coherence. The classical Greek *istorias*, from which derive our words *story* and *history,* meant "trackings." The modern Greek *istoria* means both "story" and "exciting event."[42] In the common folk sense, *story* denotes the engaging or exciting narrative. *Track* suggests direction or orientation, a path traveled. The notion of track can be rooted in either or both spatial and temporal ontologies. It suggests a series of connected past moments and an intention toward the future. It suggests an orientation, a tendency, or an intention. Track may be blazed or followed, that is, constructed or repeated. Track also suggests a concrete grounding in a territory that may be geographical, ideological, or both. But these orientations, intentions, and connections are not *in* the subject of the storytrack or its past but are the *product* of the storytracking, a product of encounter. Though presently storytracks are understood as sequentially structured narrative, it is possible to envision a more imaginative construction not limited to the standard conventions of biography or history, that is, not constrained by a logical temporally ordered cause-and-effect account or even a written account. I see no necessity to give such reigning power to time and to literacy. I also recognize that my sense of urgency for scholarship to be grounded in reference to the historical and cultural is probably, to some extent, a nostalgic reaction to the perceived threat of pure simulacra.

Storytrack also implies journey or travel, which suggests the importance not only of the visual but also of the other senses that make up the sensorium. Our visual domination of the sensorium tends to limit our experience of others to merely a view. Storytrack should account for more than worldview and perspective. It should be more broadly informed by the experiences of all of the senses.[43]

One important reason for storytracking is to provide—though fully subject to criticism, modification, and reconstruction—some temporary perspective, that is, the appearance of grounding, the suggestion of objectivity, or a place on which to stand momentarily.[44] To call this narrative of coherence storytrack rather than history or data or fact is to remind us that it is a product, often even a byproduct, of encounters with others. A storytrack is someone's story. It is a hedge against relativism while embracing the necessity of a kind of relativism in the absence of strict objectivism.[45] It is to embrace Michael Polanyi's notion that all knowledge is personal[46] without abandoning the necessity and importance of criticism, academic convention, theory construction, scientific method, and the constraining power of our subject realities. Storytracking holds that there are many, even limitless, perspectives on every subject and that the most satisfying manner of comprehending the world is to pursue multiperspectivality by constructing storytracks, yet knowing that such an approach is always a product of one's own unfolding story.

The storytracking approach is a creatively descriptive method, but it is more; it is also a comparative method. As an academic method, one approaches one's subject always within two logical frames. Comparison involves the juxtaposition of two or more perspectives that are similar in some respects but different in others. Comparison is, of course, the operation that is inevitably conducted from each indwelt storytrack perspective. From the perspective of any given storytrack, one "sees" the rest of the world. The operations of comparison in this local logical frame are largely concrete and historical, that is, of a type that is based on self/other, we/they distinctions with regard to some shared historical or cultural concern. This particular framing of comparison is always relative, primarily to the particular perspectives taken.[47]

Complementing this "on the ground" type of comparison is the academic type of comparison, no longer operating from one or another of the perspectives within the subject but from an abstract, more theoretically framed perspective.[48] Academic comparison operates in and defines a different logical frame. It operates concurrently with, and as a complement to, the comparisons that occur within the multiperspectival subject. The academic perspective corresponds with the gestalt as being different from the sum of the views from specific perspectives. It is that double-minded frame in which the scholar is self-consciously moving among subject perspectives guided by her or his own academic agenda, which is not part of the landscape of the subject. The terms of this comparison are set by academic theories and hypotheses that are, and must be, unrelated to the subject. In other words, it must be acknowledged that since they belong to the storytrack of the interpreter, theories are always entirely separate from the subject that is being interpreted. This is only an insistence on the distinction between map and territory, between sign and signified. This distinction of logical levels is parallel to the distinction of the study of histories or cultures or religions (all plural) from the study of history, culture, or religion (all singular).[49] Comparison in both senses is the principal medium of our encounter with the subjects of our study.

History, religion, and culture, then, may be envisioned as grids of intersecting storytracks. Events, movements, and practices should be seen from multiple perspectives. These are always located at the crossing point of several storytracks that can be independently traced. While it is crucial to acknowledge that every one of these storytracks is the result of an interactive interpretive process, each one provides a perspective from which to value the intersecting situation.

The tracing of a storytrack is the attempt to comprehend a perspective (or more broadly, "world sense"), its vocabularies, behaviors, and rules of transformation. Any storytrack is always under revision and criticism as it is used in explanation. By tracing several intersecting storytracks it is possible to appreciate conflict, difference, and acts of violence without the necessity of resolving differences or devaluing perspectives. The result of this comparative process is a more interesting and satisfyingly complex interpretive description and discussion of events and processes. Furthermore, in that every storytracking is self-consciously conducted as a comparative operation, not only among a number of perspectives but also between two independent logical frames, the storytracking approach offers a powerful academic method. Storytracking is, in the sense of being a self-consciously used technique, assisting in the protection against the dissolution of the function of sign, that is, the power of the sign to represent. It gives weight to the academic enterprise, thus avoiding the lapse into pure simulacra, by grounding interpretation in its stated subject reality.[50]

Relentless Self-consciousness

Acknowledging that this complex paradoxical process of knowing is never free of perspective, I must follow Jonathan Smith's dictum to be "relentlessly self-conscious."[51] This presentation of storytracking as method and theory, including the following presentation of Australian storytracks, is to some degree the product of my storytrack. Who I am and what tracks I am forging and following influence this work in significant ways.

This is no occasion for a midlife memoir, and I believe that even when dedicated to self-reflection, one's own perspective on the self is usually less interesting and less revealing than are evaluations of others. Nonetheless, this is the occasion for appropriate self-disclosure. I am interested in the cultural and religious diversity of the world from an academic and decidedly Western perspective that holds that this diversity coheres and informs within constructed categories. I am interested in the peculiar position—distinct, I believe, in some respects in human history—of this academic agenda. Because, to my frequent surprise and dismay, this agenda seems to foster and encourage the opposite of what it proclaims, I find it especially challenging. That is, in all of the attempts to understand others—peoples, cultures, and histories—we seem bound to a narcissism that forces us to see all others only in terms of ourselves. As we try to comprehend others, we somehow place ourselves in positions of superiority to them, thus subverting or inverting our motivating intent. I believe that we must depend on the otherness of our subject (seeing it or them on the other side of the chasm), yet at the same time acknowledge that neither our subjects nor ourselves exist to the other except in relationship. I believe in the gap and abhor pure simulacra.

Thus, since we often accomplish the opposite of our stated intent, we must be not only relentlessly self-conscious but also relentlessly self-critical as individuals and as communities that share common academic storytracks. We must constantly acknowledge that as we reveal, construct, or create meanings and conclusions (what in the local terms of our storytrack might be called truths), these are in part the products of our perspective and our pursuit. It seems all that can be claimed to distinguish the self-consciously pursued storytrack of storytracking is a certain relentless doublemindedness (or a multiple one), but then this frame of mind rests on the human capacity to laugh at jokes, to enjoy irony, to engage in play, and to embrace tolerance. It is in celebration of this human capability that I pursue this work.

Looking Forward

In the following several chapters I intend to at once exemplify, illustrate, clarify, and establish storytracking as a comparative academic method of encountering a subject historically and culturally. As the method has been developed in the context of the academic study of Australian aborigines, Central Australia will remain the setting for and the leitmotif that interconnects these several studies.

The character of Central Australia—its land, its people, and its history—is fundamental as background. Chapter 3 demonstrates how this broad area of land may be appreciated if seen as the crossroads for many distinct storytracks, such as those of the aborigines, the explorers, the pastoralists, the miners, and the missionaries. To narrow the focus geographically, a single geographic location known as Irbmangkara—Running Waters in English—is considered in chapter 4 as the intersection for a number of distinct storytracks. The ramifications of the interactions at Irbmangkara echo throughout the history of encounter, the history of the study of Australian aborigines. In chapter 5, I turn from the landscape to a more abstract point of encounter: the Arrernte word *altjira,* which has been interpreted and used by so many in so many different ways, from the early missionary effort to find a native term to translate the idea of God to the broadly used rendering of the word as "dreamtime" and "the dreaming." Whole cultures, conceptualized as distinct and named entities, are the common intersection for ethnography. The Arrernte is a classic ethnographic focus. In chapter 6 I show that this culture has been the common concern of four major ethnographic efforts—Baldwin Spencer and Francis Gillen, Carl

Strehlow, Géza Róheim, and Theodor Strehlow—each constructing the culture in terms that are relevant to and compatible with his own distinctive storytrack. The academic issues so energetically fought among these ethnographers are determined by the distinct encounters from their respective ethnographic perspectives. Although encounters with aborigines have often been mediated through the ethnographic texts, in chapter 7 I return to the academic context of my opening concern with Eliade's use of the "Numbakulla and the Sacred Pole" text. The encounter here is again this text, but my concern is to show that the interaction among two important scholars—Mircea Eliade and Jonathan Smith—on this single text illuminates key issues in the academic study of religion.

Having held myself above all these storytrack encounters throughout this work, I must in the final chapter evaluate this stance, to acknowledge that it serves only the current needs of my own storytrack, which may or may not be shared by others. While I find this endeavor or this method presently meaningful to me, I must in the end see it as transitory, limited, and restricted.

3

Central Australia

> Things separate from their stories have no meaning. They are only shapes. Of a certain size and color. A certain weight. When their meaning has become lost to us they no longer have even a name. The story on the other hand can never be lost from its place in the world for it is that place.
>
> Cormac McCarthy

History is the kind of storytrack that stretches across a landscape of time. The storytracks recognized as histories are interconnected, temporal series of events. Although histories may correlate with movements across spatial landscapes, their plotting of some sort of meaningful geographical journey is nonessential and always secondary to the temporal dimension. History is a kind of storytrack that is given priority and distinction by some cultures, certainly by those with a Western intellectual heritage. To make sense of things we Westerners write histories. We need history to frame and contextualize much that we encounter. We root things in history. We honor those who make or shape history. Even the fact of our mortality is somehow easier to bear if we contribute to history, if we leave something that will endure—works or progeny—beyond our mortal bodies.

While we must remain in continuity with the prejudices of our culture, we must also acknowledge and attempt to imagine that not all cultures give such sovereignty to time. Aboriginal cultures in Central Australian are such cultures. At present there is a whole industry selling the idea of aboriginal "dreamtime." This romanticized concoction is the product of a perhaps unavoidable disenchantment with oppressive aspects of giving time such reining power. When, with an iron hand, chronology rules so many aspects of modern life in the West, it is little wonder that there is such attraction to the idea that there are people somewhere whose lives are directed by dreams, mythology, and spirituality. Such ideas, attributed to Australian aborigines, are constructed by Westerners (later joined by enterprising aborigines) as commodities to meet primarily Western needs.[1] Conceptions indicated by such aboriginal terms as *altjiringa* and *jukurrpa* are rendered for English-speaking audiences as a kind of time, that is, a "dreamtime." Even in seeking an alternative to the oppressive aspects of Western temporal sovereignty, the imagination has been unable to grasp anything other than time. W. E. H. Stanner caught something of a more striking alternative by rendering these terms "everywhen,"[2] though time still reigns.

It cannot be argued that any aboriginal peoples or persons have no experience or interest in time, but space is the reigning dimension of their human experience. Events are significant and related to other events not because they occurred in some temporally interconnected stream but because they occurred in some spatially interconnected network or track. If it is correct that aboriginal peoples have occupied the landscape for as much as 40,000 years—to reassert a temporal frame in order to help build bridges to Australian views—what do they have available to mark temporal changes over either the long or short duration? In the landscape of Central Australia, its people following the lifeways that have endured throughout much of this period, no human works last for long. There are no buildings, no monuments, no earthworks, no technological innovations, no ruins. Within a short time of its abandonment, no trace will remain of an aboriginal camp. Rock paintings may last for generations; however, they are attributed to the ancestors rather than to human achievement, and the paintings do not change—they endure. Although seasons change, they change in oscillating cycles. Individual human acts are remembered and chronicled, but without writing the nature and limitation of human memory suggest that only the most immediately relevant of these acts are long retained. In aboriginal languages there are few concrete temporal markers—no year numbers, no years of age, and so on—by which to sequence and keep temporal track of events. The Arrernte language has only two ordinals.[3] There are no named months.

What endures is the landscape, its shape and distinctive features. What occurred at a specific place is how aboriginal peoples shape their storytracks, how they give meaning to the interconnectedness of the forces that shape their lives. Further, the physical landscape is not simply objectively presented to all people alike. Every person is born with connections to specific country. This is not an area designated by a distinctive perimeter—a bordered territory—but a series of named places interconnected by an itinerary recountable in story, at which occurred what Tony Swain terms "abiding events."[4] Distinct countries, so designated, may crisscross one another within the same geographic territory. These are events located more importantly in space than in time. If required to refer to the occurrence of these events in a strictly temporal dimension, contemporary aborigines use vague terms like "the long ago." Using the Arrernte language, one simply could not reply more precisely. I suspect that this temporal frame of reference would have been alien to aboriginal people prior to significant Western contact. However, in contrast to the paucity of temporal terms and numbers in the Arrernte language—both of which are required for developing elaborate temporal markers—it is unlimited in its capabilities to designate geographical locations. Thousands of Arrernte place names have been recorded.[5]

The storytracks that occupy my present concern permit time to reign; they are histories. Adding to their interest are the traces they have left on the physical Australian landscape. The long duration of the aboriginal peoples is a story that when traced seems a vast interwoven network of tracks with scarcely any significance that correlates with time. The enormity of the temporal duration is mocked by how completely insignificant time is in this frame of reckoning. Further, the whole notion of history seems ridiculed by the fact that despite Australian habitation for 40,000 years, aborigines have left almost no physical traces. The explorers were the first non-aborigines to enter this vast desert region. They are heroes of Australian history. While they left few marks on the physical landscape—abandoned equipment and survey markers—the marks they made on paper, their maps and journals, transformed the unknown into the known and demonstrated the potential for wealth and opportunity to be gained from the land. Miners and pastoralists quickly made more permanent marks and transformations on the land, as did the builders of telegraphs, roads, railroads, and finally cities. At least the outlines of these stories must be told here to establish the context for the more detailed examples of intersecting storytracks that are to follow. In the great sandy desert these storytracks meet and interact, forming an era of Australian history. Being mindful that history is only one kind of storytrack, I proceed.

Aborigines

Evidence found on shores of long extinct lakes in present-day western New South Wales dates human habitation in Australia to 38,000 years ago. At that time, because of the depth of the ocean, Australia was perhaps 10% larger than it currently is, with Tasmania and New Guinea joined to it by land. Asia via Indonesia would have been within reach of Australia by canoe. This route of migration is one of the principal theories for explaining the ancient habitation of Australia. Through much of the ensuing period, the ancestors of those presently called aborigines lived everywhere in Australia. As hunters and gatherers, they lived in small groups. Throughout Australia are found the occasional chipped stone tools they made. In Northern Australia, they made ground stone axes. Shaped bone points barbed their spears. Boomerangs of many varieties were used for hunting. Rock surfaces in caves were often painted with designs. As the climate gradually changed over this long period, accompanying changes occurred in the diet because of the change in available foods, as did slight changes in the style of tools. For example, fishhooks fashioned from shells appeared along the coastal regions of New South Wales 2,000 to 3,000 years ago.

While change and adaptation were undoubtedly a constant in the aboriginal way of life throughout the period of habitation in Australia, these changes were not of the sort that accumulated evidence either to be found by archaeologists (although Australian archaeology is continually progressing) or to be inferred from postcontact ethnography (although linguistic and physical anthropologists are able to draw some conclusions). In some respects, it is believed, the aborigines encountered by Cook in 1788 were living a life-style rather similar to their own ancient ancestors, spanning 2,000 generations. When Cook landed, aborigines throughout Australia lived in small groups of from ten to fifty persons, and they sustained themselves by hunting animals and by gathering plants, insects, honey, and shellfish. Their social structure and relationship to the land, so closely integrated with their way of life, probably had ancient roots.[6]

Explorers

The spatial ontology of the aborigines in Central Australia suffered a jolt in the mid-nineteenth century as groups of explorers raced to earn the £2,000 reward offered in 1859 by the South Australian government to the first person to cross Australia. The effort was mounted principally from south to north. From the perspective of these storytracks, aborigines play no role at all except for the occasional hindrance they caused explorers because of threats or acts of violence. Aborigines were members of many of the expeditions. The part they played in these parties is rarely mentioned. Explorers made few references even to the aborigines who occupied the land they crossed. Never a word is mentioned that would indicate contemplation of the inevitable impact on aboriginal peoples and their cultures, except that of John McDouall Stuart; on the occasion of planting the British flag on top of a mountain that marks the center of Australia, he wrote: "May it be a sign to the natives that the dawn of liberty, civilization, and Christianity is about to break upon them."

As early as 1839, Edward John Eyre, a New South Welshman, led an expedition northward from Port Augusta to determine the pastoral and mining potential of the region. He had dreamed of an inland sea and fertile highlands in the unexplored region. From atop Mt. Arden, he saw barren mountains to the east and north and to the west he saw only sandy desert. The next year he led another party north to investigate a body of water he had seen the year before. He skirted Lake Torrens, a boggy salt lake. From a hill he named Mount Hopeless, Eyre reported salt lakes, barring farther northward progress.[7]

Coincidentally, far to the north, the *H.M.S. Beagle*, the ship on which Charles Darwin had traveled for six years—1830 to 1836—to South America and across the Pacific to Australia, was surveying the northern shores of Australia. The encounter, on September 9, 1839, of a "magnificent harbour" afforded the *Beagle's* Commander Wickham the "appropriate opportunity of convincing an old shipmate and friend that he still lived in our memory." Thus, Port Darwin was named. The survey ship recorded many other significant finds, notably the Adelaide River and a river so magnificent that is was named in honor of Queen Victoria.[8]

In the south a few years later, 1844–1845, Charles Sturt traveled beyond Eyre's farthest point, but he returned with the pessimistic report that his travels were blocked by a great stony desert, perhaps impassible. Thus, accounts of great salt lakes and a great stony desert left an atmosphere of pessimism about exploiting lands in and beyond the South Australian northern borders.[9]

Explorations were conducted from other directions as well. Thomas Livingstone Mitchell left New South Wales in 1845, heading northwesterly. He reasoned that by following the tributaries of the Darling River to its source in the Great Dividing

Range and upon crossing the divide, he would find the headwaters of the Victoria River, which he could then follow across Australia to the sea. All seemed to go well, and he found a north-flowing river, but after nine months, with supplies running low, he turned back. An exploring party the following year deflated Mitchell's brief moment of glory by discerning that the river he believed was the Victoria was actually Cooper's Creek, already named by Sturt.[10]

In 1845, Ludwig Leichhardt initiated a massive effort to make an east-to-west crossing of Australia. To support an expected two-year journey, his party drove herds of goats, sheep, and bullocks, as well as carts and wagons loaded with provisions. The first attempt failed when they lost most of the livestock and supplies in unexpected floods. A second attempt was made in 1848, following Mitchell's discovery of the "Victoria." After posting a letter to the *Sydney Morning Herald* from the farthest outpost, Leichhardt and his impressively equipped party headed west and vanished. Never has a trace of the party ever been found. The vastness of the great desert simply swallowed them.[11]

In the late 1840s several other official parties, not to mention the attempts of many private groups, mounted explorations. The discovery of gold in New South Wales in the 1850s led many to believe that gold might be found elsewhere in Australia. This spurred exploration, as did the growing interest in pastoral lands needed as cattle-breeding grounds to provide beef for the rapidly growing population concentrated in Southeastern Australia.

In 1855, Augustus Charles Gregory led the North Australian Exploring Expedition to explore the Victoria River area from the north coast. The party followed the Victoria about 200 miles to its source, disproving a long-standing theory that the Victoria was a major river, draining all of Australia to the north and west of the Great Dividing Range. Mitchell's and Leichhard's theories were not correct.[12] Returning to Sydney after other explorations in the north, Gregory was funded by the government of New South Wales to lead an expedition to determine the fate of Leichhardt, whose disappearance had occurred ten years earlier. Though he found no trace of the lost expedition, Gregory did find an overland route to Adelaide. His style, in contrast to many expeditions, was to travel light, unencumbered by herds and heavy equipment. His success proved the wisdom of this approach.[13]

John McDouall Stuart,[14] who had traveled with Sturt's party in 1844, was equipped by William Finke to look for new grazing country north and west of Lake Torrens. The year was 1858. Stuart was to become the most famous and accomplished of Australian explorers. His approach, like Gregory's, was practical. Accompanied by only two men—one an aboriginal—he reached farther north than anyone else and revealed that contrary to Eyre's report, there was no great salt lake barrier. Stuart traveled 1,000 miles in four months at very little expense. He proved himself an explorer, and the journal of his first expedition was published as a Parliamentary Paper.[15]

By the late 1850s the possibility of connecting the populated southern regions of Australia with the rest of the world by telegraph was being actively considered. Colonial Governor Sir Richard MacDonnell was the first to see the real possibility of an overland route.[16] Charles Todd, superintendent of telegraphs for South Australia, established overland telegraph communications with Melbourne in 1858. This connected Adelaide with Sydney through Melbourne. Francis Gisbourne was at this time proposing an undersea cable to connect Australia to Europe through Asia. The possibility of joining Australia to the rest of the world via telegraph communications instigated a flurry of efforts among competing interests to gain control of the communications industry. The likelihood of a sea cable that linked Asia to Australia's north coast increased the incentive to find a south-to-north route across the country, especially for the ambitious South Australians. Seeking pastoral land, gold, and a telegraph route, Stuart embarked upon his second exploration, in 1859, financed privately by James Chambers and by William Finke, who made a fortune buying and selling Glenelg.[17] As land speculators they leased land and later sold their rights to it.[18] Stuart experienced intense physical suffering during this trip, which crossed the northern border of South Australia, reaching present-day Oodnadatta and Hergott Springs (named for the artist David Hergott, who accompanied Stuart, although the springs was renamed Marree during the German-hating days of World War I). He surveyed cattle runs for his patrons, reported indications of gold, and extended yet again the northward penetration, charting a chain of water sources that permitted further advances. He opened the gateway to the north. Charles Todd was, understandably, elated.[19]

The Victorians refused to cooperate with South Australia because they had become inspired to make their own explorations. They approached the task in grandiose style. Dr. Ferdinand von Mueller, who had accompanied Gregory on his explorations in the far north, returned to Melbourne and began raising funds for the Victorian Exploring Expedition to Central Australia. The spirit of adventure, the competition with a rival colony, even the off-chance of discovering the fate of Leichhardt caught on, and Victorians contributed generously to the expedition fund. Not to pass up any possible advantage, more than two dozen camels were purchased from a supplier in India, as were the services of Afghan drivers. The South Australian government's offer of £2,000 reward to the first person to cross the continent only increased the competitive fervor.

Meanwhile, in 1859 Finke and Chambers funded a third expedition for Stuart to survey pastoral runs west of the lake that now bore the name of the early explorer John Eyre. Stuart suffered excruciating eye pains and near blindness from exposure to the sun on this trip. He did not attempt to push his northern reaches but explored the lands on both sides of his northern route. On this trip, he learned the worth of his companions, Bill Kekwick and Ben Head, the team that would serve with him on future expeditions.[20]

After little more than a month to recuperate from the return of this expedition, the trio once again set their faces northward. These three, on Stuart's fourth expedition in 1860, were the first nonaborigines to enter the most interior region of the continent. Stuart provided names for land forms and waterways, filling in the vacant spaces on Australian maps. Suffering eye pain and sun blindness all along, he found rich grasslands (it was winter), abundant creeks, and large trees where Sturt had previously indicated there should be a great stony desert. He followed northward the river that turned out to be the largest in Central Australia and that he named for his patron, William Finke. Stuart discovered the unusual sandstone pillar that he named Chambers Pillar to honor his other patron. He pressed onward to a location he believed to be the very center of Australia, which he calculated to be near a prominent mountain. On April 21, 1860, he climbed the mountain, planted the British flag, and left a message in a bottle. The mountain was named Mt. Sturt in honor of the leader of the 1844 expedition on which Stuart had served as draftsman. Appropriately, the mountain was later renamed to honor Stuart.

Being so far north, Stuart was eager to attempt the crossing that would earn him the reward offered by the South Australian government. He calculated that the headwaters of the Victoria should be 360 miles northwest of his location. Suffering constant pain now from masses of sores that covered his body (the symptom of scurvy), as well as his eye affliction, Stuart traveled onward and tried repeatedly in several directions to make his way through. He rode his horses to their limits, pushed his companions to their limits, and pushed his own body far beyond any reasonable limit. Despite these heroic efforts he fell short of his goal. Yet the only thing to stop the doggedness of this man was the presence of hostile aborigines. Fearing the loss of the whole party to an aboriginal attack, Stuart finally turned back at a place he named Attack Creek.[21] In four months the three men had crossed Central Australia, penetrating 700 miles into the Northern Territory and 800 miles through unexplored areas, reaching a point 1,500 miles north of Adelaide and only 300 miles from the Elsey River country explored by Gregory.[22]

Meanwhile in Melbourne, Robert O'Hara Burke had been chosen to lead the Victorian Exploring Expedition and preparations were complete. Before Stuart returned from his fourth expedition, the Victorian group departed under the most gala circumstances imaginable. Grand gatherings were held, with speeches offered by dignitaries. On the day of departure, August 20, 1860, 10,000 people gathered at Royal Park to cheer on the expedition, which included twenty-eight camels, twenty-eight horses, and eighteen men. For the first 100 miles, people lined the roads and hundreds even walked along with the party, celebrating this remarkable event.

The route followed by the Victorian expedition was to follow Cooper's Creek to its source, cross the Great Dividing Range, and then head north to the Gulf of Carpentaria. By the time Stuart returned, Burke's party had advanced too far to be reached and informed of Stuart's findings. But Stuart soon learned of the Victorian expedition and feared that it would claim the victory and reward for being the first to cross Australia. Knowing that with such a large party it would travel slowly, Stuart believed he still had a chance; he immediately applied to the government and received a grant to equip a new expedition, which he prepared at Chamber's Moolooloo station. On January 1, 1861, he departed in summer heat with a party of a dozen men and forty-nine horses. The race was on.

Neither party obviously had any way to know of the other's progress. By the time of Stuart's departure, Burke and his companions William John Wills, John King, and Charley Grey had arrived at a river, later to be named Diamentina, that would lead them to the Gulf of Carpentaria. The four men took five camels and a horse and made the dash to the gulf. Burke and Wills left their companions behind and traveled alone the last twenty-five miles, arriving on February 11, 1861.

As Stuart continued northward, Burke's party of four headed back home, the two groups going in opposite directions on parallel courses about 300 miles apart. Burke's party was by this time suffering from dwindling supplies and exhaustion. Grey died at Andagini Lake, 70 miles from the depot camp at Cooper's Creek, where the balance of the party was waiting. Burke arrived at Cooper's Creek on April 21, only nine hours after the remainder of his party had departed, giving Burke up for lost after waiting there for four months. Burke's decision was to hurry ahead, following Cooper's Creek to Mount Hopeless in South Australia. His two remaining camels did not have sufficient reserves to make the trip and died, leaving Burke, Wills, and King stranded without any means of crossing the arid areas that stood before them. Burke and Wills died of slow starvation. King survived by living with aborigines and was eventually rescued to tell the story.

To the far north, Stuart was again attempting to find a way through to the coast. Again and again he prodded the area without success, turning back after advancing beyond his previous achievements by only 150 miles. When Stuart arrived back in the south, he learned that Burke had not returned but that several search parties had been sent to look for him. It was the party led by Alfred Howitt, noted student of aboriginal cultures and later friend of Baldwin Spencer, that found Burke's camp on Cooper's Creek and its survivor, King. John McKinlay, leading another search party, began from Adelaide, passed near Mount Hopeless, and headed northeastward. By interrogating aborigines along the way, McKinlay was led to the grave of Charley Grey. McKinlay misunderstood the aborigines to say that they had killed and eaten Burke, Wills, and King. Unnecessarily fearful of the aborigines, McKinlay ordered shots to be fired at them. He then sent a messenger back to Adelaide with the story that he had discovered the fate of the Victoria expedition. Having achieved the goal of his mission, McKinlay transformed his search party into an exploring expedition and headed northward for the Gulf of Carpentaria. Since Burke and Wills had perished, they could not claim the reward; McKinlay sought this honor for himself.

Stuart's report, delivered in September 1861, encouraged the South Australian government to believe that an overland telegraph route was still possible. The government approached Stuart to lead yet another expedition north, with the strategy this time to continue northward to the Elsey River, explored by Gregory in 1856, and to follow this river system to the coast at Escape Cliffs, charted in 1839 by the *H.M.S. Beagle*. Stuart knew that McKinlay and Howitt were leading expeditions northward, but he believed that he knew his route so thoroughly he still had a chance to claim the £2,000 prize. Only twenty-nine days after Stuart's return, he embarked with a new party for his sixth effort. The date was October 21, 1861. Stuart moved quickly, as was his usual pace, and soon overtook McKinlay's latitude. If only latitude were the measure, Stuart would have won. But his chosen path, west of the Gulf of Carpentaria, required traveling hundreds of miles farther north to reach the sea. Furthermore, Stuart was driven once again to make efforts—as before, unsuccessful—to gain access to the headwaters of the Victoria. In the meantime, McKinlay arrived at the Gulf of Carpentaria by following the Leichhardt River, arriving on May 22, 1862. McKinlay, who herded sheep and traveled by camel, horse, and bullock, proved that such a passage was possible. His party returned by traveling east through Queensland to Port Denison.

Stuart continued his trek northward, finally connecting with Gregory's track, whereupon he followed the river courses to the sea, arriving on July 24, 1862. The landing place was about 20 miles east of the mouth of the Adelaide River. The return journey of over 2,000 miles proved enormously difficult for Stuart. Having lived almost constantly with pain, he had yet another personal test to endure. Hardly before they started the return journey, Stuart was so ill he could not ride. A dose of laudanum helped for a while, but before they arrived at Mount Stuart he was unable to travel. The party camped for eighteen days, awaiting his recovery. With Stuart's feet and legs swollen and black, his body having to be lifted to and from his saddle, the party pressed on. Ten days later Stuart turned worse and believed he was dying. Again the party camped and killed a horse for food. Stuart gained a bit of strength but could not travel. As a last resort, a stretcher was made and suspended between two horses on which Stuart traveled for thirty-nine days over 600 miles to Chamber's Creek. From there, Stuart was strong enough to ride to Port Augusta and travel by sea to Adelaide, leaving Bill Kekwick to lead the others overland. When the party arrived on January 21, 1863, Stuart was well enough to ride with them in a public entry to the city. They were greeted as returning heroes by streets lined with cheering crowds. In all of his expeditions, Stuart never lost a man. The route to the north had been opened, and it had been proven that it was passable.[23] However, time would reveal that Stuart was overly optimistic about the potential of Central Australia.[24] After the drama of forging a route across the continent closed, exploration shifted to the land that lay east and west of the known south-north route. Certainly further exploration was necessary to complete the overland telegraph line. This exploration took place virtually simultaneously with construction of the line. Other exploration through much of the decade of the 1870s facilitated settlement.[25]

Overland Telegraph

John Stuart's return to South Australia in December 1862 marks a turning point in Australian history. For the colony of South Australia, Stuart's crossing had made it clear that there was a rich future to the north, and the possibility of building an overland telegraph had been demonstrated. The South Australian government immediately saw the importance of gaining control over the Northern Territory and began the necessary political maneuvering to bring it about. Control of the Northern Territory was conferred on South Australia in July 1863.[26]

But for some time crossing the great nation overland must have remained a task few wanted to attempt. The development of the north was accomplished by an approach from the sea, a voyage from South Australia of nearly two months, rather than overland. With increasing talk about connecting Australia to an undersea telegraph cable, South Australia plotted a course that would provide the capital to compete with her sister colonies in this enterprise. The South Australian plan was to sell plots of land in the north even before they were surveyed. Purchasers had to put one-third down, the money used as working capital for the government, and were promised that within five years they could take their choice of surveyed sites, which they could occupy upon paying the balance. Ignorance of the impact of the rainy season on surveying and establishing pastoral districts and town sites was the cause of much misfortune. It took more than the planned five years to prepare for settlement,[27] but by the late 1860s settlement on the north coast had begun. The city of Darwin, at Port Darwin, originally named Palmerstown, was founded in February 1869.[28]

Through the decade, negotiations continued with cable-laying companies. Numerous plans were proposed to link Australia at many different locations. Cable technology was rapidly developing as well, although several undersea cables had failed because of the corrosion or damage of the rubber-encased cable. A multistrand steel-and-rubber-encased cable was developed, but this only presented the new problem of finding a ship capable of carrying the resulting tonnage. This problem was solved by the *Great Eastern*, which had been built as a commercial luxury liner. Though it had failed commercially, it had proven its seaworthiness. It was the only ship in the world capable of laying the cable, and it was converted to do so.[29]

The way cleared, South Australia won the contract to connect with the sea cable to be brought ashore at Darwin. However, the South Australian government had to guarantee that the overland line would be completed and ready for use by the first of the year 1872. The South Australian government approved the project on April 29, 1870, surely one of the most ambitious acts of any modern government. The task that lay before it, to be accomplished in little more than a year and a half, was to build an 1,800-mile-long telegraph line from coast to coast across lands that for 1,200 miles were known only by Stuart's journals.[30]

Charles Todd, who was put in charge, divided the task geographically into three large sections. The northern and southern sections were to be completed by private contractors, the center section by government workers. The center section was divided further into five work parties, each to build 100 to 120 miles of line. Survey parties were sent out immediately to determine the major course. Wire, insulators, and poles were ordered from England. A massive effort of cartage—using bullocks, horses, and camels—was organized to haul men, provisions, tools, wire, poles, insulators, and equipment into Central Australia.

The surveying parties that worked in advance of the construction crews explored numerous uncharted areas and named many land features. Though almost a minor incident, yet part of the effort to find passage across the MacDonnell Ranges, a survey party discovered what later became known as Heavitree Gap and a spring-fed pool of clear water several miles to the north. The springs was named Alice Springs in honor of Alice Todd, the wife of the superintendent of telegraphs.[31] Alice Springs was chosen as the site for a repeater station, and its proximity to the center of the line destined it to play an important role in the development of Central Australia.

Before long, a town sprouted in the area a couple of miles south of Alice Springs. Not surprisingly it was called Stuart, later changed to Alice Springs. It is said that when the post office at the telegraph station was moved to the village, the postmaster simply continued to use the Alice Springs postmark to frank the mail. In time the name Stuart was forgotten.[32]

The southern section, largely within South Australia and crossing well-known territory, offered little difficulty to construction work. Even the five work parties of the center section made excellent progress, all finishing by the deadline. It was the northern section that caused all the difficulty. Again, lack of familiarity with the tropical rainy season underlay mistakes in timing the delivery of supplies and materials to the construction areas. The crews were isolated by the rains without adequate provision or equipment. With little work accomplished at the end of the first year, the project was abandoned, the contract declared in default, and everyone returned to Adelaide to try to reorganize. The dry season was spent in negotiation rather than construction so that by the time the workers returned, the rainy season was again soon upon them. The deadline of January 1, 1872, slipped by with little work in the north. What progress was made was done by government crews from the south, supplied by the foresight of Todd, trying to link with the effort from the north.

The line was connected finally on August 22, 1872, though shortly thereafter the oceanic cable went dead. The problem was finally solved in October. Australia was now in communication with the world. In the early days of the colony, the late eighteenth century, it had taken four to six months to travel from Sydney to London. This time was shortened in the 1850s with the advent of clipper ships, which made the voyage in sixty to eighty days. Steamers were introduced by the late 1860s, but passage time remained at two months. With the telegraph in operation, messages could be sent and received between Australia and England in a matter of minutes. The construction of the overland telegraph line was hailed as Australia's greatest technological event of the nineteenth century. Charles Todd was knighted.

After 40,000 years of the reign of a spatial ontology in Central Australia, as suddenly as the instant the electricity first coursed through the single steel wire, time asserted its undeniable power. Though rickety and fragile in appearance, the telegraph line virtually stands for the temporal domination of space. Every exertion of every muscle of every man who explored the territory and who built the line was an exertion to achieve the conquest of space and the enthronement of time.

Although Stuart had shown the way, few entered the territory until the overland telegraph line had been established. Perhaps it remained empty of Australians of European ancestry simply because time held no power in the face of such spatial vastness. Perhaps the telegraph line provided comfort to adventurous Australians: they were not alone; space would not overwhelm them. The telegraph repeater stations that were necessary at intervals along the line served naturally as government outposts: as post offices, police headquarters, and liaison points. Pastoralists entered and occupied huge areas of land. Miners came to search for mineral wealth. Missionaries entered to bring Christianity. Ethnographers entered to collect and write down information about the aborigines.

Until modern cities like Alice Springs arose—cities whose success is connected with a disguise that masks the enduring spatial qualities of Central Australia—few entered the area with the intent of permanent residence. The relationship of the aborigines and the land was replaced by a situation in which all comers wanted to take something from or bring something to the land. The land was related to only in terms of how it could serve faraway interests, at first in Australian cities to the southeast and far north but eventually interests in Europe and around the world. This relationship to the land must have been, and perhaps remains, an enormous puzzlement to aboriginal peoples.

Pastoralists

As an extension of the pastoral development of South Australia, the pastoral development of Central Australia is interconnected with the history of this colony. South Australia was settled in 1836 as a utopian community. It soundly rejected the convict colony status of New South Wales and declared its eagerness to remain distinct from all other Australian colonies.[33] Pastoral concerns were strong from the beginning. By 1843 pastoral occupation of land had stretched 100 miles north of Adelaide and 50 miles farther by 1846. Exploration of Central Australia, funded and motivated largely by pastoral interests, reported extensive potential for the industry. On the grounds that the future Northern Territory would provide inexpensive squatting, South Australia persuaded the federal government to annex the territory to South Australia. Thus in July 1863, South Australia controlled from coast to coast the area between the 129th and the 138th meridians.[34] The severe drought that lasted from 1864 to 1866 slowed the northward progress and expansion into Central Australia.

Pastoral expansion was controlled by the government, which leased land to entrepreneurs with the provision that it be stocked to a stated level within a specified period of time. A small lease fee was levied per square mile. The Foundation Act of South Australia declared that the lands in the province were "waste and unoccupied." Aborigines, obvious occupants of the land, were offered protection under British law, but because they could show no proof of ownership, they were never considered to be owners. South Australia never made any payments to aborigines for the land that included the entire middle longitudes from the south shore to the north coast. Aboriginal welfare was overseen by a protector of aborigines, a position created in 1836, but it remained unoccupied until 1838 because no one could be found to fill it.[35] Although assimilation of the aborigines was attempted, by midcentury this policy had been replaced by one of "assimilation after segregation." The government established "feeding stations" for the infirm and elderly. By 1876 there were fifty-four of these stations. Throughout the nineteenth century, the policy toward aborigines was to civilize and Christianize them. Yet with the growing experience of contact, certainly by 1860, the attitude of contempt toward them arose, as well as the conviction that aborigines were doomed to extinction.[36]

Pastoral expansion into Central Australia did not follow the successful explorations in the early 1860s; however, it did expand immediately upon the complete construction of the overland telegraph line in 1872,[37] doubtless because of the growing population of construction workers and those who staffed the repeater stations. In 1872, before the line was complete, William Gilbert was driving a herd of cattle and horses to the MacDonnell Ranges for Joseph Gilbert, William's father, and E. M. Bagot to stock runs near Alice Springs and Owen Springs.[38] Through the balance of the decade, the pastoral lands along the Finke and Hugh rivers and in the MacDonnell Ranges were stocked primarily by established pastoralists in South Australia. New interest in exploration on both sides of the telegraph line were conducted through the 1870s and 1880s, largely motivated by the desire to find the best pastoral lands.

Weather good for pastoralists endured through the decade, and many runs were successfully stocked. The annual increase in livestock is estimated to have been 25%. By 1880, 3,000 square miles of land were declared stocked. But success in growth was offset by other problems, problems that would persist until the collapse of the industry. Costs for cartage of supplies from the south were high, and marketing the cattle, essential to the realization of profit, was difficult because of the great distance from markets, either in South Australia or the Top End, and the harsh terrain over which the cattle had to be driven. Through the decade, the nearest railhead was Port Augusta. The local market, mainly sales to the telegraph stations, was inconsequential.

Beef prices held up in the first years of the 1880s, and explorers' reports of good pastoral country added interest in the industry's expansion. Another attraction was a great deal of talk about the potential of cattle markets in Java, India, and even Japan.[39] By the end of 1881, every square mile of Central Australia had been leased or held under application. Since so little was known about the actual lands being leased, the situation invited speculation. Speculation required one only to apply for a lease to a parcel of land, make the payment of small lease fees, and have the patience to see how nearby leases turned out. If a lease showed promise, a speculator could sell it at a large profit to someone willing to attempt to stock it. Most of these speculators had failed by the mid-1880s.[40]

By the mid-1880s, overstocking had begun to occur, soon reflected in the deteriorating condition of the fragile land. Adding to the problems of the costs of cartage and the delivery of stock to market was the growing incidence of cattle killed by aborigines. The aborigines' response of fear and avoidance of Europeans upon early contact had, by the 1880s, become one of active resistance. Quickly overpowered even by the small number of settlers, having their water and food supplies threatened by Europeans and their ever-increasing herds of livestock, aborigines faced major crises. Perhaps the only recourse they could identify was to kill cattle and to occasionally threaten and injure the settlers. Because of aboriginal lifeways, a small population spread widely over a huge land, no organized mass physical resistance was practical. Much simpler was the spearing of cattle easily found in a landscape where aborigines lived. The scale of cattle killing, which some years reached a thousand head, clearly indicated the motivation of resistance rather than an occasional easy meal.

The pastoralists encouraged the government to establish a police force to protect the settlers and to punish aboriginal cattle killers. Into the early 1890s, the police were a significant presence in achieving the balance of interests. Pastoralists, missionaries, aborigines, and government workers often had conflicting interests. Because the area was so far from the Australian court system—Port Augusta was the closest—it was considered too inconvenient and costly to conduct justice in the strict terms of the law. The mounted constable in Central Australia commonly represented the entire justice system, such as it was, having to bear the praise or wrath of those whose interests he affected.

Because of drought (from 1889 to 1894), overgrazing, cartage costs, plummeting beef prices, inaccessible markets, and inefficient management practices, the pastoral industry collapsed. Competition from Queensland pastoralists had grown steadily from the late 1880s and soon overwhelmed the South Australian market, especially with the development of overland routes between Queensland and South Australia.[41]

The cattle stations established in Central Australia in the 1880s had generally been large operations that covered thousands of square miles. Barrow Creek Pastoral Company, for example, held 20,000 square miles of land. On these large stations, cost-effective aboriginal help was rarely used and few gardens were planted to supply pastoralists with food. When the large stations collapsed, some smaller operations took their places. These small-scale enterprises were often run by a rugged individual of European descent whose entire livelihood was tied up in this single effort.[42] These pastoralists hired aborigines as helpers, and many of the men had enduring relationships with aboriginal women,[43] although the children of such couples were usually not recognized by their father.[44] Gardens supplemented their food, and they economized on everything. These pastoralists endured in Central Australia, known for their work-or-bust attitude, their rugged individualism, their enormous hospitality, and their willingness to help and serve one another in times of need.

The first census records for Central Australia are for the year 1881. Between the north border of South Australia and Barrow Creek, 150 miles north of Alice Springs, there were 79 males and 3 females. Aborigines obviously were not counted. In 1886 the population had exploded to 290, with 150 more who were described as "floating," that is, temporary residents. In 1891 there were 313 males and 37 females. Except for periods in the late 1880s, the number of miners fluctuated between 30 and 50. Before 1894, there were never more than 6 police officers in the area, and the employees of the telegraph stations never exceeded 36.[45] These figures suggest that in the 1880s and early 1890s, there were never many more than 200 pastoralists in Central Australia, with perhaps fewer than that number floating. The professions of the floaters are interesting. Doubtless some were prospectors and temporary laborers, but others were dodgers, sly-grogsters (illegal sellers of liquor), cattle thieves, and spelers (gamblers).[46]

Missionaries

Friedrich Adolph Hermann Kempe and Wilhelm Friedrich Schwarz, trained as Lutheran missionaries[47] at Hermannsburg Mission Institute in Germany, arrived at Glenelg in September 1875. To prepare for the 1,500-mile journey to their assigned post in the heart of Australia, they went to the Lutheran community in the Barossa Valley northeast of Adelaide. When they departed with thousands of sheep and hundreds of other livestock, neither man knew anything about the physical demands of living in Central Australia and neither was prepared for what he was about to experience. The trip alone proved almost more than they could endure, but after nearly two years, they arrived (in June 1877) at the 900 square miles of land leased to them by the government. They chose a site for the mission station and got to work.

Rather than immediately seeking contact with aborigines, they first had to tend to their livestock, building pens and establishing water supplies. Housing came next. Needing physical more than spiritual labor, the missionaries requested another missionary and some capable lay workers. Louis Gustav Schulze was assigned to the new mission, as well as four lay workers. Soon all of these men were joined by women who became their wives. The first child of European-Australian parents was born to the Schwarz's in March 1879. The presence of European Australians on this station was growing rapidly, reaching thirteen adults and seventeen children by 1887.

The missionaries stationed in Central Australia accepted their posting with the understanding that they would make it their permanent home. Kempe wrote: "We want to live, to die, and to work here until . . . we enter our true home."[48] Following the example of the Lutheran settlers in the Barossa Valley and in Germany, the missionaries turned immediately to agriculture to supplement their livelihood, key, they believed, for the mission to achieve self-sufficiency. They also believed that agricultural labor would soon provide employment opportunities for aborigines. In their first year they prepared and planted small plots of cereal grains and vegetables. They had only modest success from gardening until 1879, when their gardens succeeded beyond all expectation. But despite modest success the following years, by the late 1880s drought set in, and they never again succeeded in their agricultural efforts despite working with the experimental botanist Baron Ferdinand von Mueller, trying to breed and select plant strains that would thrive in desert conditions. Failure was probably due to exhausting the land, as well as ruining it by irrigating with brackish water.

The mission station was also a pastoral station. The early emphasis was on sheep. The hope was that the labor intensity of producing wool would provide employment for aborigines while moving the station toward self-sufficiency. Suffering from the poor quality of wool, as well as the high cost of transporting the wool to southern markets, the missionaries soon began to turn to cattle. Attempts at employing aborigines met with little success.

The purpose of the mission was, of course, to convert aborigines to Christianity and to prepare them for assimilation into the nonmission community by education and segregation from their former cultural ways. At Hermannsburg these goals were approached through several methods and objectives. The missionaries were charged with placing the station on a sound economic footing, which they attempted to do by establishing local industries—agricultural and pastoral. Along with helping them meet this economic goal, these industries would provide employment for aborigines, which in turn would, they hoped, advance the religious goal of the mission by establishing a stable aboriginal community at Hermannsburg. To stabilize the community, so that the people could be educated and proselytized, the missionaries attempted to convert nomadic hunter-gatherers to farmer-pastoralists. Language was recognized as a key to this process. It was held to be more efficient for the missionaries to learn aboriginal languages and to introduce aborigines to literacy in their own languages than to attempt to introduce European languages (including literacy), cultural practices, and religious ideas all at once.

The missionaries engaged in limited anthropological endeavors, seeking to understand aspects of aboriginal cultures to be better able to address the issues of conversion. The missionaries of the first decade denied that aborigines had anything at all like a religion. In 1885 Kempe wrote that "even the rudest fetish worshipers of West Africa stand much higher than these heathen. The only trace of religion still with them is fear."[49] Kempe's statement reflects the Christian position that all humans were created and given knowledge by the same god, with some cultures slipping from this state over time. This position contrasts markedly with the cultural evolutionism widely embraced among European anthropologists at the time.

The mission station was a location for the distribution of rations to aborigines. The missionaries used the rations to attract aborigines to school and church services, essentially trading rations for attendance. But the aboriginal languages were difficult to learn, and aborigines became less cooperative when they began to learn that knowledge of their language could be used against them.

With little development of labor-intensive industries, the mission became overstaffed and there was little for aborigines to do, and certainly no means by which to compensate them. What success the mission realized toward its goal of Christianizing and assimilating aborigines came largely with the children, most of them orphans. Adults were often attracted to the mission during hard times such as protracted drought or for short periods corresponding with the arrival of rations, but when the weather would break or the rations were gone, the adults soon returned to their nomadic hunter-gatherer life-style. Even among the children, when the girls approached adulthood many were enticed away from the mission by opportunities offered by pastoralists. In time the hopes of the missionaries rested almost wholly on the orphan boys who grew up on the mission station. The first converts in 1887 were all orphans, none older than seventeen.

The first mission era at Hermannsburg, that of Kempe, Schwarz, and Schulze, was a long succession of discouragements. Although the mission was nearly self-sufficient, at times this was largely because the missionaries did without a salary and lived the most frugal of lives. The mission eventually began baptizing aborigines, but the hopes of Christianizing aborigines were severely scaled back and the plans to prepare aborigines for assimilation were virtually abandoned. While the missionaries at first did not share other Australians' assessment that aborigines were doomed to extinction, in time they began to embrace this position.[50] Further, the missionaries were highly critical of their European-Australian neighbors, as scarce as they were. They objected to pastoralists having sex with aboriginal women. They complained of the unnecessary brutality of pastoral and police methods in the effort to stop aboriginal cattle killing. In turn, the missionaries were accused by pastoralists and police of harboring aboriginal criminals, of harshly punishing aborigines, and of keeping aboriginal children essentially captive in inadequate facilities. The charges and countercharges flew, precipitating a number of formal investigations, though none resulted in much change. The missionaries suffered constant health problems—dysentery, pulmonary infections, eye inflammation, colds, and physical exhaustion. By the early 1890s the missionaries realized that they could no longer continue to survive in this place they had chosen as their permanent home. They requested replacement. Politically the synods of the Lutheran church were widely divided at the time, and the continuance of the mission itself was in doubt. Without replacement, the missionaries finally departed, leaving it in lay hands, both European-Australian and aboriginal. A group attached to the Horn scientific expedition passed through Hermannsburg in 1894 and found little evidence—other than a few aborigines who were wearing scraps of clothing and had a predominance of scriptural names among them—that the mission had ever existed.

Carl Strehlow was assigned the post as missionary at Hermannsburg in late 1894 and began the arduous work of recovery, setting the mission back on the track of its former goals. Strehlow spent twenty-eight years at Hermannsburg and established enough of a Christian aboriginal community that it has survived to the present day. Strehlow's story and that of the mission during his era will be told in greater detail in chapter 5.

Miners

In 1886 the explorer David Lindsay followed the directions of an aboriginal to Glen Annie Gorge,[51] eighty miles east of Alice Springs. In the gorge he found red stones strewn on the ground, which he believed to be rubies. Lindsay headed north to carry out his survey task, planning to return to Glen Annie to stake a claim and collect rubies to take with him on his return to Adelaide. Impatient members of his party slipped away to return to the ruby fields to stake claims and collect rubies. When passing Emily Gap, near Alice Springs, one of this party could not resist showing a ruby to a water-drawer. The information leak inspired a mad dash from Alice Springs to Glen Annie, resulting in an explosion of mining activity in Central Australia.[52]

Richard Pearson, one of the impatient members of Lindsay's party, rushed to Adelaide to register his claim. Lindsay, realizing that his discovery was about to be lost to him, rushed to register his claims, which he accomplished a few days after Pearson. Although from the beginning there was some doubt that the red stones were indeed rubies, some gem experts confirmed that they were. Even more important was the news that arrived from London, where Pearson had directly gone with 50,000 carats of rubies. He wired a report that the rubies were bringing a high price in London, £6 to £20 per carat. Within months 800 claims had been filed and 22 ruby companies formed, most of them in Adelaide. In December 1887, 60 men were gathering rubies; by March 1888, there were 150 to 200 men.[53]

Mineral wealth in Central Australia was welcome news in South Australia. While the other colonies had enjoyed considerable mineral wealth,[54] South Australians had opened, worked, and exhausted hundreds of mines during the 1880s without realizing significant wealth. By 1886 South Australia was also experiencing a depression. South Australians were eager to put their remaining funds into mineral speculation, especially for minerals in their own territory. For the first time since the 1872 construction of the overland telegraph line, the attention of South Australia turned back to Central Australia. Reports on life in the ruby fields and the promise of other mineral wealth were important news. Pearson, still in London, was attempting to induce a syndicate to purchase his MacDonnell Range Ruby Company for £200,000. Meanwhile some ten tons of rubies were sent from the fields.

In May 1888, experts began to agree more consistently that the rubies were, in fact, high-quality garnets, news met by plummeting prices of ruby shares on the Adelaide Stock Exchange, the failure of Pearson's efforts in London, and the immediate abandonment of all mining claims. However, some of the miners in the area remained, seeking their fortune in other minerals, most notably gold, which at the time appeared promising.[55] Stuart had indicated there was gold near Tennant Creek; the explorers Ross and Lindsay had reported gold-bearing quartz near the ruby fields; the explorers for the overland telegraph line had reported the promise of gold. South Australian prospectors were so unskilled and inexperienced that they were ineffectual in finding gold deposits. However, prospectors from the Top End and the Kimberleys areas were skillful veterans. In 1887, one of them, Alec Paterson, located a gold-bearing reef near Paddy's Hole,[56] some seventy miles east-northeast of Alice Springs. This area, known as Arltunga, was to become the first settlement in Central Australia distinguished by its own post office, which opened in January 1891. Gold fever struck, and by December 1887, twenty men were prospecting or working claims. A group of wealthy South Australians formed the Wheal Fortune Gold Mining Company and sent a mill to Paddy's Hole in 1889.

Mounted Constable William Willshire,[57] stationed at Heavitree Gap in 1887, was appointed warden in charge of issuing mining permits. The job came without pay, and his complaints about it led to his transfer to Boggy Hole. He was replaced by W. G. South. Arltunga struggled along from year to year, passing from hand to hand, but it never realized the expectations many had for it.[58]

In 1891, high-quality mica was discovered on the south side of Harts Range. Billy Benstead—who later built the first hotel, the Stuart Arms, in Alice Springs—reported high prices for mica in the London market. The report spawned a rush for mica claims. But the first efforts revealed the difficulty of this industry: mica did not survive the camel trip to the coast and the sea transport to London. Only 5% of the mica on the first shipment to London arrived in salable condition. The mica miners soon drifted back to the gold fields.[59]

The excitement of the wealth of mineral fields in Central Australia produced more than mineral wealth. It also produced its share of colorful characters.[60] Perhaps those most successful were the sly-grogsters (bootleggers) and gamblers. There was little law enforcement at the time, and the laws were easily skirted; for example, merchants sold glasses of water while giving away free glasses of beer to go with them.[61] Lewis Harold Bell Lasseter was a sailor aboard ship when he learned of the ruby wealth in Central Australia. He jumped ship at Cairns to seek his fortune. Though he found only garnets, he claimed to have discovered a gold-studded reef in the Petermanns Range. Many believe it to be a story concocted by Lasseter, but others spent years looking unsuccessfully (so far) for the reef.[62]

By 1888 Heavitree Gap had become a common camping place for those moving through Central Australia. Men camped all along the Todd River, from the gap to the telegraph station several miles to the north. The government decided to make this a town site and sent David Lindsay to survey it on his way to his ruby fields. The town site of Stuart, later to be known as Alice Springs, was proclaimed in November 1888. A couple of stores and a hotel sprang up. A local court was established in 1892, the same year that the few residents of Central Australia asserted their political influence by electing a man named Griffiths as representative of the Northern Territory to the South Australian government. They believed him to be familiar with Central Australia.[63]

Also 1888 was the year that saw restriction on the entry of Chinese into Australia and more severe restrictions on their travel to Central Australia and the ruby fields. Reports that 50,000 to 100,000 Chinese were expected to enter the territory at Port Darwin before midyear galvanized anti-Chinese sentiments. It was believed that they intended to head directly to the ruby and gold fields. It was feared that once there the Chinese would spread throughout all the provinces. Pressure was brought to bear on the South Australian government to place severe restrictions on the Chinese.[64]

By the end of the 1880s, many recognized that the development of mining in Central Australia, as well as other industries, was dependent on the construction of a transcontinental railroad. The South Australian government was divided on how to finance the construction—public, private, or land grants. Although the line was extended as far north as Oodnadatta, hard economic times and growing interest payments on existing railway loans led to the defeat of all railroad building proposals. The expansion of the railroad to Alice Springs would have to wait decades.[65]

With attention drawn again to Central Australia, scientific expeditions were formed to systematically explore and document it. Among the most noted was an expedition sponsored by W. A. Horn, a South Australian who had made his wealth in copper mines and gold shares in Broken Hill in western New South Wales.[66] Some of the most noted scientists in Australia were gathered for this 1894 expedition. Although it reported no new pastoral lands, it did find the geological composition of the MacDonnell Ranges favorable to minerals. The expedition documented many new biological and zoological species and advanced the knowledge of aboriginal cultures. The expedition's report was disappointing to many because, unlike so many of its predecessors, it did not overstate its findings—perhaps because the expedition was conducted during a dry season, perhaps because the observations were made by trained scientists. It was during this expedition that a University of Melbourne biologist, Baldwin Spencer, made the acquaintance of the Alice Springs postmaster and telegraph officer, Francis Gillen, forming an important anthropological collaboration.[67]

As the large pastoral operations were replaced in the mid-1890s by rugged individuals operating on a small scale, so too were mining companies. Many of these individuals combined mining and small-scale pastoral enterprises. The colorful reputation of Central Australia is almost synonymous with the character of these men. They were hard-working, hard-drinking, hard-riding, rugged individuals who created among themselves a powerful solidarity in support of their life-style, which often included living with aboriginal women. Many of the miners formed a working partnership with their female aboriginal companions. Whereas the earlier settlers had seen aborigines as rivals—for cattle, land, and jobs—these men saw aborigines as important partners with whom they shared the land and their way of life.

Observations and Reflections

This brief history of Central Australia through roughly the turn of the twentieth century shows some extraordinary features and hints at what, though largely undocumented, must have been remarkable. From the aboriginals' perspective this period must have been a whirlwind of unprecedented change, change that assaulted their ontological roots. Though they did not think in terms of the long duration of 40,000 years, it is amazing that within one generation these cultures experienced the transformation from an ontology based almost entirely on space to one in which time would eventually reign supreme. For them nothing would ever again be the same, nothing would ever again seem to endure, to be characterized, as had the land and their ancestors' actions, by abidingness.

Although every imaginable feature of the landscape of Central Australia bore aboriginal names, almost none of them were retained by the European explorers and cartographers. They saw the landscape as a huge tablet, a tabula rasa, on which to inscribe the names of European-Australians of note, most of whom would never even see the land. Sometimes the inscribing of names was literal, as at Chambers Pillar (named for James Chambers by Stuart), where many a traveler scratched his name in the soft rock along with the date of his passage.

Reflection on the naming practices of these European-Australians is revealing. The names suggest that the explorers reflected little, if any, on the character or shape of the landscape. Almost none of the names reflect the physical character of the landscape (Horseshoe Bend is an exception) or even the experiences of the explorers (Attack Creek is an exception). Though aboriginal names existed for every land feature, the dearth of these names reflects the absence of contact explorers (often the namers) had with aborigines, who were mostly seen at a distance. It may also reflect the European attitude toward aborigines as brute primitives doomed to extinction.[68]

The names given to rivers, mountains, and other distinctive features are almost wholly of two groups: (1) contemporary Australian men, either the explorers themselves or men of economic or political significance,[69] and (2) contemporary Australian women, invariably the spouses or daughters of this group of men. The naming rule was to give the surname (sometimes both Christian and surname) to the features named for men—Finke River, Todd River, Krichauff Range, George Gill Range, MacDonnell Range, Ayers Rock, Mount Stuart, and so on—and only the Christian name to features named for women—Alice Well, Alice Springs, Emily Gap, Charlotte Waters, and Glen Helen. Notable is the difference in naming practices of other Australian colonies, who looked to England, as well as to aborigines, for sources of names. South Australia proclaimed its distinctiveness from the other colonies and declared its independence from England through the naming practices used in Central Australia.[70] Perhaps the use of Christian names when honoring women continued the custom of naming places after British queens, but it must also reflect the highly gendered character of this history. While the naming practices that have indelibly marked the great heart of Australia record the distinctiveness of the South Australian venture; while it, in a sense, distinguishes this region as truly Australian; while it has inscribed the who's who of a formative period of Australian history—it also reveals the depth of ignorance about and shallowness of contact with the actual Australian landscape (these same practices were used in assigning names to plants and animals unknown to European scientific classification) and the aboriginal peoples who inhabited it.

The history of the European-Australian development of Central Australia was almost exclusively male. All of the explorers, the missionaries, the pastoralists, the miners, the surveyors, and the telegraph line construction workers were men. Almost no women accompanied these men when they entered the territory. Some few women eventually joined their husbands, most notably the wives of the missionaries. Women were always secondary. What they did remains almost unrecorded. Most certainly there must have been some remarkable women, both of aboriginal and European ancestry, whose lives made their impact on this history, but whose stories remain untold. To name a land feature after a woman may have been motivated by a romantic fondness for women not present, but it was as likely motivated by an extension of the desire to further honor politically powerful men; by using only the Christian names of their spouses or daughters the men received the greater recognition.[71]

This was a history of South Australian and, to an extent, Australian national politics, directed to not only a British but also a growing worldwide audience. It was played out on the stage of the great heart of Australia, seen by Australians as both mysterious and empty. Central Australia, so far from South Australia, was the land of challenge and opportunity, almost invariably seen as a land to pass through or at most a temporary residence. It was to be crossed and explored, its features named, its flora and fauna documented, and its people described. Central Australia provided an opportunity for speculation, for quick wealth, and for adventure. During the first thirty years, only the missionaries entered the area expecting to live out their lives there, and their plans were defeated by the landscape. Not until the 1890s did rugged individuals consider the land their permanent home and were able to come to terms with what that demanded of them. Certainly no nonaboriginal peoples other than these rare individuals, embraced the land and lived on its remarkably demanding terms. They all came for the short term to harvest, reap, build, explore, mine, proselytize, or otherwise take advantage of the land. The peoples on the land, the aborigines, were rarely seen as much different from a zoological or biological feature to be controlled or used if possible, to be minimized or ignored if not. The European-Australian temporary inhabitants of Central Australia demanded that their terms should prevail. These terms were the product of European economic, political, and religious history. It can be suggested that because of the narrow and demanding perspective (storytrack) of these history makers, much in the landscape went unseen and unacknowledged; much remains to be discovered. The sheer size and power of the land have served to test all human perspectives tried on it. In this great landscape, any human perspective, human existence itself, seems somehow absurd. Perhaps the heroism of these Australians is marked by their courage and creativity in the face of such absurdity.

4

Irbmangkara

Irbmangkara[1] is a four-mile stretch of pools fed by a spring bubbling out of the Finke riverbed thirty miles south of the old mission station at Hermannsburg. Because of the dependable supply of water; the surrounding lush vegetation; and the abundance of fish, animals, and birds, Irbmangkara is well suited to support the extensive activities of a major ceremonial center, which it probably has been for a very long time. European-Australians know this area as Running Waters. Irbmangkara is the intersection of many storytracks.

Irbmangkara is located on the south side of the Krichauff Range at the intersection of Western, Southern, and Central Arrernte territories and a short distance from Matuntara[2] territory. The journeys across the landscape of the ancestors, with which several contemporary Arrernte groups identify themselves, intersect at Irbmangkara. It is the home of the duck (*ibiljakua*) ancestors. Groups of duck ancestors traveled in several directions from Irbmangkara. One group followed an ancestral leader named Remala (crane) to Nunta, his home to the north. They traveled through Rubula, Lalkarintinerama, Pmaletnama, Ntarea, Jikala, Rama, Ulbmantaljerra, and Erulba.[3] Another group of duck ancestors was led by Ankebera, a cormorant ancestor, to Tnauutatara, which is located on the middle Palmer River.[4] Irbmangkara was linked to Walbmara (known also as Tempe Downs) in the Matuntara area by a cormorant ancestor from Irbmangkara who stole mulga[5] seeds from ancestors at Walbmara. The snake ancestor at Walbmara pursued the cormorant back to Irbmangkara and decided to stay there forever. Traveling in a flood, the fish ancestors came from Ankurowunga to the south. They passed through Irbmangkara and broke through a fish weir set to catch them. This broken weir came to be a section of the Krichauff Range. The gap through which the fish escaped is called Iltjanmalitnjaka ("where the crayfish had dug"), also known as Parke's Pass.[6] The Upper Southern Arrernte tell stories about *nditja tara* ("two young men") who hunted kangaroo near Irbmangkara. One of the curlew ancestors of Ilkakngara (Northern Arrernte) died but attempted to rise from his grave. This angered a magpie ancestor from Urburakana (in the Central Arrernte territory) who stamped the curlew back into his grave. Seeing this, the other curlew ancestors fled to Irbmangkara.[7]

Groups of Arrernte identify themselves with groups of ancestors and travel these storytracks to perform rites at the places where the ancestors stopped and camped. The people of each of these groups belong to the country traversed by their ancestors, and they own the songs, rites, and stories of their ancestors. When rites are performed at a ceremonial center by any of these groups, all other groups who share this ceremonial center have the right to come as visitors. Thus Irbmangkara, located at the intersection of storytracks from every direction, is a place where Western Arrernte, Northern Arrernte, Central Arrernte, Upper Southern Arrernte, and the Matuntara people have encountered one another, probably for centuries.[8]

Irbmangkara is the physical setting of another story, this one with a specific historical setting. It is a story of murder, revenge, and counterrevenge. It was accompanied by gossip, complaint, and official report. It involved the encounter—the intersection of the storytracks—of aborigines from several regions, missionaries, mounted constables, cattle ranchers, and a justice of the peace. The following account is drawn from Theodor Strehlow.[9] It intends to present Strehlow's point of view.

Trouble at Irbmangkara

In 1875,[10] before European-Australians had come to this area of Central Australia,[11] Kalejika, a middle-aged Central Arrernte man, reported to groups surrounding Irbmangkara a serious ritual crime. He said that while visiting Irbmangkara he saw the ceremonial leader, Ltjabakuka, giving uninitiated boys blood to drink from a ceremonial shield.[12] This act was part of a rite reserved for the fully initiated. Because of the secrecy of the rite and its importance, the ritual crime was most odious and called for the severest punishment, death. This punishment had to be administered by members of a group story-linked (perhaps dream-linked) to Irbmangkara.

The people at Tnauutatara[13] refused to take action against the Irbmangkara group because they were too closely related. The people at Kularata found Kalejika's story "an empty fabrication of malicious lies." But the Matuntara people, linked to Irbmangkara by their snake ancestor, agreed to punish the Irbmangkara community.[14]

Led by Tjinawariti (which means "Eagle Foot"),[15] fifty to sixty Matuntara warriors, supplemented by a few men from the Upper South Arrernte area, headed for Irbmangkara. They found the people camped at Urualbukara, the southernmost pool of Irbmangkara. The avengers divided into three groups; two took positions on the hill slopes above the encampment, and the third hid in the underbrush in the river below the camp. At dusk, when they believed that all the people had returned from hunting and gathering, they swarmed the camp, killing everyone encountered. They broke the limbs of the infants to let them die a natural death. With their spears they prodded the 80 to 100 people killed to make certain there would be no survivors to identify them.

During the attack, one of Ltjabakuka's wives, Laparintja, in the effort to save herself and her baby, fell across her baby, feigning death.[16] She was able to remain silent when prodded. When the camp grew silent, she escaped with her infant north to Arbanta, where other Irbmangkara were camped.

As the warriors were leaving the camp, they encountered two hunters, Nameia and Ilbalta, returning late to camp. The warriors pursued them to eliminate the chance of being identified. Suffering an old wound that slowed his flight, Ilbalta was soon brought down. Nameia managed to escape, though wounded, even resorting to picking up and returning spears thrown at him that had missed. Most of the avengers were well known to Nameia. Their effort at anonymity had failed.

Upon hearing the story of the massacre, broadcast by Laparintja and Nameia to nearby camps, mourning ceremonies commenced and soon acts of revenge were planned. It was decided[17] that to avenge this massacre a small, highly select party lead by Nameia would take as their task the killing of every man identified. Knowing that they would have to travel singly through the territories of these enemy peoples, the task not only would be difficult but also would probably take years to accomplish. Rites were performed for this group to make them impervious to enemy spears and to endow them with stealth. This revenge party did not return until 1878, having completed their task without a single casualty. They even managed to kill Tjinawariti and Kapaluru, both important Matuntara leaders.

The Matuntara wanted to counteravenge these killings, but they were hampered by the growing presence of European-Australians. The Hermannsburg missionaries had arrived in 1877, and in 1878 cattle were being introduced to the Finke and Palmer river valleys. The Matuntara decided that at least one Irbmangkara death was necessary, and they chose as the victim Nameia. They were patient and awaited the opportunity to take action.

Twelve years later—in 1890—a police outstation had been established at Alitera a few miles north of Irbmangkara on the Finke River. It is also known as Boggy Waterhole or Boggy Hole. Mounted Constable William H. Willshire was in charge. The police station had been established to protect the cattle industry from aboriginal poaching, an act commonly called "cattle spearing." To be effective, the constables hired aboriginal trackers to help them survive in the severity of the landscape and to help them find and punish poachers. Among the trackers hired by Willshire was Aremala, Nameia's eldest son, who had survived the massacre years before because he had been in Arbanta at the time. In January 1890, Nameia came to Alitera to visit his son. He planned to stay for some time.

The Matuntara soon learned that Nameia was at Alitera. They took advantage of Alitera's proximity to Matuntara territory to gain their final act of revenge. Stealing to the Alitera camp by moonlight, several Matuntara awaited Nameia to arise and tend the fire. When he did they killed him and disappeared into the night. Willshire recorded in his police journal that the "old man Naimi" had been murdered at his camp "at midnight on 9th January, 1890," by a party of "Tempe Downs blacks."[18]

The Hermannsburg missionaries disapproved of Willshire, while the cattle ranchers were grateful for his presence. Complaints lodged with the authorities in South Australia by the missionaries reported that Willshire used brutal and unnecessary force to discourage cattle spearing. They accused him of responding to reports of cattle spearing by killing every aborigine he could find in the area. The complaints spawned an official inquiry of Willshire that was scheduled to take place in July 1890.

When Nameia was killed at the Boggy Waterhole police camp, Willshire was incensed, believing the killing offensive to his trackers. He wanted to go to Tempe Downs in pursuit of the murderers, but under the heat of the upcoming investigation he bided his time. The July enquiry found no wrongdoings committed by Willshire, but it recommended that the police station be moved farther down the Finke River from Hermannsburg.

The following January, when the manager of the Tempe Downs cattle station complained of cattle spearing in his area, Willshire got his chance to get in on this long history of violence. He armed four of his trackers with rifles and led them to Tempe Downs. On the morning of February 22, under his direction, the trackers attacked the aboriginal camp near Tempe Downs and killed a man as he arose from sleep. Others escaped before another man was also killed. Willshire and his trackers had breakfast at Tempe Downs before they took the bodies to separate locations and burned them, with the help of a local station hand, William H. Abbot.

The news of this killing soon reached Francis J. Gillen, the justice of the peace in Alice Springs. Believing that these senseless killings of aboriginal people had gone on long enough, Gillen, accompanied by Mounted Constable William G. South, went to Boggy Waterhole and took Willshire with them to Tempe Downs to investigate. Believing he had sufficient evidence, Gillen committed Willshire for trial in Port Augusta on the charge of murder. Willshire spent seventeen days in jail before the northern cattlemen could raise his bail. During his trial, he was supported by friends, among them Sir John Downer, Q.C., who had been premier of South Australia from 1885 to 1887 and would be premier again in 1892 and 1893. Willshire was acquitted, but he was not reassigned to the same region.

The Arrernte were impressed with Gillen's courage in acting on their behalf against Willshire. Years later, in 1896, the Arrernte were able to express their gratitude by holding a ceremonial—the secret cycle of Imanda—at Alice Springs, allowing Gillen and his friend Baldwin Spencer to be the first nonaborigines to witness these rites.

At this juncture the Irbmangkara storytrack crosses the Numbakulla and the Sacred Pole storytrack. Were it not for the Irbmangkara track, Spencer and Gillen probably would not have witnessed any aboriginal rites in 1896, and consequently their *Native Tribes* and its revision, *The Arunta*, might never have existed.

Aboriginal Story Genre

Time and again, Irbmangkara is the intersection of storytracks. Two types of aboriginal storytracks are engaged in the first incident. The initial action that motivated the clash of communities was not the objective act of uninitiated youth who were drinking blood from a shield; it was the story that this act had occurred. Kalejika told the story abroad to various communities in the Irbmangkara region. How they received the story of the ritual crime correlated with their relationship with the Irbmangkara community and with the storytrack they occupied. The story is more or less irrelevant to any aboriginal groups other than those whose ancestral stories—that is, the itineraries of the journeys of their ancestors—cross at Irbmangkara. Only these groups would have the right or the responsibility to punish a ritual crime. Of these groups, one was too closely related to the people at Irbmangkara, whatever they thought of Kalejika's story; another rejected the story as incredulous; but another, the Matuntara, seized on it, perhaps, as Theodor Strehlow suggests, as an opportunity to act on an existing grudge.

To summarize, Kalejika presented an oral narrative to several aboriginal groups. Each group heard it and reconstructed it according to the perspectives, values, and needs of its own storytrack and how it intersected with the subject—the supposed Irbmangkara ritual crime. How Kalejika's story was heard and acted on or not acted on is a matter of perspective.

This storytrack intersection is similar to the complaints lodged against William H. Willshire, accused of unnecessary brutality and murder in his capacity as mounted constable. The complaints were made by the missionaries at Hermannsburg who—although their own methods and practices were commonly subject to criticism—were attempting to "civilize" and "Christianize" the aborigines. Opposition to police brutality and settlers' immorality were common themes of their storytrack. Encouraging the aborigines to tell stories about mission opposition to police and ranchers was a means by which missionaries established their identity and reputation. An example of this kind of story is told by Theodor Strehlow of his father, Carl Strehlow. The event was supposed to have occurred during his first months at Hermannsburg:

> In Strehlow's time there were still many families living at Hermannsburg who mourned the loss of relatives shot by Wurmbrand and his ruthless trackers. The chief monument to his memory in Central Australia was a place known as Wurmbrand's Rockhole—a large, deep rockhole on the side of Ilorara saltlake. Here Wurmbrand had come upon a peaceful camp of men, women, and children; and he and his party had shot all those who had not been fast enough to escape from their bullets. At Hermannsburg it was claimed that soon after Strehlow's arrival Wurmbrand had paid his last visit to the station. He had rounded up a group of men, women, and children in the station camp, and then got ready to take them away and shoot them some miles out in the bush. Their terrified relatives had run screaming for help to Strehlow, and the latter had rushed in blazing fury to Wurmbrand's camp, where the police party were still saddling their horses. Strehlow had allegedly shouted angrily at Wurmbrand, and told him to release his prisoners and get out of the place himself. "And don't ever let me catch you hunting people again at Hermannsburg," he had added, in menacing tones. To everyone's amazement, Wurmbrand had been so taken aback by Strehlow's fury that he had released his prisoners, kicked his own tins, billies, and buckets in all directions, yelled at his trackers to hurry on with the saddling and the packing of the

> horses, and finally ridden off like a madman, cracking his whip and digging his spurs into his mount till it reared and plunged madly with pain. Nor had he and his trackers ever returned to Hermannsburg.[19]

Carl Strehlow had arrived at Hermannsburg in 1894; Theodor Strehlow, Carl's son, was born in 1908 and remained there until 1922, when his ailing father was carried by wagon toward medical help, dying in Horseshoe Bend. Probably Theodor would have heard this story as a youth while still at Hermannsburg, meaning that it was extant more than a decade after its historical setting. Apparently such stories were fundamental to the missionaries' reputation among the Arrernte. Theodor Strehlow notes: "The stories of his courage in standing up for the rights of the dark man were numerous and varied, and some of them could well have become embroidered with legendary trappings during the passage of the years. But they were firmly believed, and helped to confirm the Aranda folk in their unshakable conviction that all would be well at Hermannsburg as long as Strehlow was their ingkata."[20]

During the decade of telling and retelling, the son suspected some embroidery of the story of his father's encounter with Wurmbrand. According to personnel records, Wurmbrand left the area in 1892, two years before Strehlow's arrival.[21] Recognizing the incongruity, Theodor Strehlow writes of the story: "It was more than likely that the police officer thus checked had not been Wurmbrand at all, but one of Willshire's successors, and that the image of the latter had become confused in later aboriginal memory with that of his hated and dreaded predecessor. However, whether authentic or not, this story fitted in excellently with Strehlow's character. . . . Strehlow could be as tough as any other man, as long as he felt that he was acting in the interests of law, order, and justice, and in accord with the ordinances of the Almighty."[22]

The story of Carl Strehlow's courage against the police on behalf of the Arrernte seems one of a genre, joined by stories of Gillen's similar actions, a type of tale told among aborigines to establish the character and allegiance of certain European-Australians in Central Australia. The description of Wurmbrand's brutality suggests a parallel genre, that is, a group of stories that attested to the infamy of another group of nonaborigines. The meaning and importance of all these stories probably had far less to do with any historical events than with establishing and portraying the character of European-Australians among aboriginal peoples. For these stories of European-Australian figures, as consistent with the tradition of the stories of the Arrernte ancestors, the identification of specific places—Wurmbrand's Rockhole and Hermannsburg—was surely more important than the accurate identification of year and historical personages.

Perhaps the strongest action taken by the missionaries against the police was to lodge complaints with the authorities of the South Australian government. Their mission track, their objective, found that killing aborigines was criminal whatever the motivation. The cattle ranchers in the region, in contrast, found police tactics, whatever they were, acceptable. The police were there to defend the cattle herds against aboriginal poaching. When Willshire was taken to Port Augusta to stand trial for murder, it was the cattlemen who raised Willshire's bail bond. Gillen, although his friend Spencer was a persistent critic of Hermannsburg, was subprotector of the aborigines and justice of the peace. From Gillen's track, Willshire's supposed actions were considered criminal.

What really happened at Irbmangkara, at Boggy Hole, at Tempe Downs? Were the ritualists at Irbmangkara ritual criminals? Were Wurmbrand and Willshire and their trackers murderers? These are important questions. Lives hung in the balance, as did history. Can there be certainty about what occurred? Who was dealt justice and who not?

Theodor Strehlow's Account Analyzed

The only existing published accounts of this aboriginal punishment of a ritual crime, revenge, and counterrevenge at Irbmangkara are those written by Theodor Strehlow. The fullest account is presented in his *Journey to Horseshoe Bend*, first published in 1969. This book chronicles the 1922 trip from Hermannsburg to Horseshoe Bend, a desperate effort to get Strehlow's dying father to medical help. The route of the journey followed the camel trail along the Finke River, the shortest, though not the easiest, way. As the journey unfolds along the Finke, Strehlow describes the features in the landscape and tells the aboriginal stories he knows that are relevant to each place. Some are the stories of mythical ancestors associated with the places in the landscape; others are stories of human events set within history. The stories associated with Irbmangkara are of both types.

Historical markers must be noted. The ritual crime at Irbmangkara reportedly took place around 1875. This was 2 years before the arrival of the first missionaries at Hermannsburg, 3 years before cattle ranching was introduced to the area between the Finke and Palmer rivers, 19 years before Carl Strehlow arrived at Hermannsburg, 33 years before Theodor Strehlow was born, 95 years before the story was first published, and 120 years before I was assured by residents at Hermannsburg (Ntaria) that these Irbmangkara events remain today a shaping factor in the politics in the area.

Though the story was summarized above, it is valuable to look more closely at the "text" of the story as Theodor Strehlow presents it. Consider the following passage:

> The sun had sunk very low in the western sky before the waiting warriors could be reasonably certain that all members of the Irbmangkara camp had returned. Keeping under the cover of bushes and trees, the armed men crept forward with the relentless and uncanny skill of hunters used to stalking suspicious game animals. As soon as the clearing around the camp had been reached, they rushed in, like swift dingoes upon a flock of unsuspecting emus. Spears and boomerangs flew with deadly aim. Within a matter of minutes Ltjabakuka and his men were lying lifeless in their blood at their brush shelters. Then the warriors turned their murderous attention to the women and older children, and either speared or clubbed them to death.[23]

Most immediately the literary character of the story must be acknowledged. Strehlow embellishes the details of the events with many a literary trope, such as "like swift dingoes upon a flock of unsuspecting emus." He adds a method of reckoning time ("within a matter of minutes") completely alien to nineteenth-century aborigines. A very large portion of the story is Strehlow's literary development.

What are the "facts" of the story? What witnesses could have provided the details of this attack? The Matuntara warriors were the only ones who could have reported the maneuvers and stealth of the attackers. The same warriors and Laparintja, the surviving Irbmangkara woman, could have reported the order and character of the attack and killing. However, all of the Matuntara warriors were supposed to have been killed in the succeeding two or three years by the Irbmangkara revenge party. One possible source of these elements of the event would have been some existing story tradition told by the Arrernte that was built on circumstantial evidence. Consider the passage in Strehlow's account on the flight of Nameia:

> Nameia, though hurt by a spear-thrust in one leg, proved unexpectedly fleet-footed. When his pursuers drew uncomfortably close to him, he stopped, picked up some of the spears that had missed him, and threw them back at his attackers. The latter paused for a few minutes, and the break enabled Nameia to continue his flight. Since rising clouds of smoke in the distance showed that there were other camps of people located up-stream from Irbmangkara, the warriors did not dare to pursue him too far, lest they should encounter additional late-returning hunters. Tjinawariti called off the chase.[24]

Strehlow combines detailed descriptions of the flight and escape with statements of motivation, such as why Tjinawariti called off the pursuit.

Consider one other passage from Strehlow's account. It is the description of the Matuntara killing of Nameia:

> One night in January, a few days after the time of full moon, a number of dark figures stole over the ranges as soon as complete darkness had fallen over the narrow, closed-in Finke valley. They had several hours in which to move into position behind clumps of bushes; for the moon, according to local Central Australian time, was not due to rise til about nine-thirty that night. Although it was summer, the proximity of the great waterhole, whose waves were lapping the black rock walls of the gorge on the left side of the river, soon brought a delicious coolness to the campsite; and all the Aranda men made up their night fires from substantial logs, in readiness for the chilly midnight air. When the moon rose, sharp eyes began to watch the sleepers in the Alitera camp from behind the nearby bushes—eyes that were eager to identify the campfire of Nameia. The watchers were very tense, but managed to curb their impatience. A mistake had to be avoided at all costs: Nameia had to be killed, not wounded, and no other person harmed. The night grew colder with the passing hours; and, with the increasing chill in the air, one sleeper after the other began to stir and to stoke afresh the fires that were burning at his side.[25]

Here Strehlow presents information known only to the attackers, whom he does not name.

Strehlow's description of the killings at Tempe Downs contains information that could have been known only to Willshire and his trackers, information that if revealed would have incriminated them. Furthermore, in so clearly identifying Willshire as directing the trackers to kill the Matuntara men at Tempe Downs,

Strehlow ignores the evidence presented in trial, which convinced a jury that Willshire did not direct the murderous actions.

Where did this story of Irbmangkara come from? How could Theodor Strehlow obtain such a detailed account, representing so many private and opposing perspectives? Several conclusions seem likely. Though I know of no physical evidence that anything at all occurred at Irbmangkara in 1875, it seems likely that at least something occurred there on a scale to be considered important by peoples throughout this region. Supported by the evidence that people who are now living at Hermannsburg acknowledged these events as still politically important—though it is entirely possible that they first heard the story in the mid-twentieth century from Theodor Strehlow—it is quite likely that an aboriginal story tradition has long recounted these acts. There is evidence independent of Strehlow's account that a man named Nameia was killed at Boggy Waterhole (Alitera) on January 9, 1890, and that Willshire and his trackers were involved in the killing of aborigines at Tempe Downs in 1891. Beyond these scant traces of independent evidence, the story of these events is not simply reported by Strehlow but also imaginatively concocted by him. His confidence, authority, and motivations for such a construction are not difficult to identify.

Strehlow identified with the aborigines. Throughout his career, he took advantage of the experience of his early years, growing up among aborigines at Hermannsburg. He learned the Arrernte language as a mother tongue along with German. His childhood companions were Arrernte children. He often reported that the Arrernte considered his father to be an *ingkata,* or ceremonial chief.[26] Bearing the lineage of his father, Strehlow believed that he knew the Arrernte so well and was sufficiently like-minded that he could think and speak for them. This presumptuousness was to bring criticism and embarrassment to Strehlow in 1978, just months before his death. He had sold photographs of secret aboriginal rites to the German magazine *Stern*, who sold secondary publication rites to the Australian magazine *People*. A huge controversy erupted. Ronald Berndt, who had been appointed chairman of the soon to open Strehlow Research Foundation, asked Strehlow to make a public statement to calm the furor. Berndt told Strehlow's biographer, Ward McNally, "I am not sure whether he did this [i.e., make a public statement]. However, he also attempted to justify his action to me by stating that he alone had the right to make such material available: that the old men in the photographs were now dead, and that he was the true owner; moreover, that present-day Arandas had no knowledge of the traditional material. . . . He also saw himself as custodian and owner of that knowledge. And in his statement to me he named certain Aborigines as not knowing about their background."[27]

As evident in his account of the Irbmangkara events, Strehlow's storytrack is a peculiar hybrid. Unabashedly he speaks with authority of aboriginal motives and actions that could not be directly known to him. Yet he surpasses all aboriginal senses of boundaries by presuming knowledge from any and all culture areas, social classes, and groups. He speaks as easily from the perspectives of the Arrernte of Irbmangkara as of the Matuntara. He presumes to be more aboriginal than would any aborigine;

yet he writes as literary figure and academic to a principally, one could say, exclusively, nonaboriginal audience. The text set at Irbmangkara as presented by Strehlow in *Journey to Horseshoe Bend* is a rich product of the confluence of several storytracks—missionary, aboriginal, academic, literary figure—that characterize the odd and enigmatic track of Strehlow's life.[28] Seen only in the light of the intersection of storytracks can this story of conflict at Irbmangkara be critically appreciated and responsibly used.

Irbmangkara plays another role in Strehlow's personal storytrack. His biographer writes that he told him: "I recall listening intently to the Aborigines telling me about one area we went over [i.e., during the journey to Horseshoe Bend] called Irbmangkara. . . . They were wonderful stories, and they started me on my search for more."[29] It seems that when Strehlow crossed this place and encountered the many storytracks that intersected there, it initiated his lifelong study of Australian aborigines.

William H. Willshire

Leaving an imprint at Irbmangkara, the storytrack of Theodor Strehlow is not the only one identified with an individual who reflects the multiperspectivality of this place and this time. Another storytrack is that of the Mounted Constable William H. Willshire, who wrote three books about his experience with the aboriginal people. The books, published near the end of the nineteenth century, are rarely cited.

Willshire was the son of James Doughty Willshire, a British schoolteacher who arrived in Sydney around 1845 and soon moved to Darlington in South Australia, where he set up a private school. William was born to James and Amalia, from Dresden, on March 5, 1852. The extensive literary and anthropological references in his books reflect the kind of education he received in his father's school.[30]

William listed his occupation as drover when he joined the South Australian police force in 1878. After several short-term appointments he was, in August 1882, posted briefly as a relieving officer at Alice Springs; later that year, beginning October 10, he was promoted to mounted constable, first class, and given a regular assignment at Alice Springs. At that time Alice Springs referred to the telegraph and police station located three kilometers north of the present city of Alice Springs. The town developed after 1882 and was called Stuart until it was officially named Alice Springs in 1933.[31] Willshire served in various locations other than Alice Springs in Central Australia, including a post near Heavitree Gap, a few kilometers south of the Alice Springs station, and Boggy Hole, on the Finke River a few kilometers north of Irbmangkara.

Important aspects of Willshire's perspective on many subjects can be discerned from his three books. The first book, *The Aborigines of Central Australia*, was published in 1888 and revised for republication in 1891.[32] *A Thrilling Tale of Real Life in the Wilds of Australia* followed in 1895.[33] The last work, completed at Victoria River Downs in the far north,[34] was *The Land of the Dawning: Being Facts Gleaned from Cannibals in the Australian Stone Age*, published in 1896.[35] Central Australia is the exclusive subject of the first two books, whereas the final book is principally about Willshire's Victoria River experience, with occasional reflections, delivered with considerable bitterness, about his work in Central Australia. Willshire identifies ethnography as his motivation for writing the books.[36] Given the historical setting and Willshire's background, his ethnographic contribution was significant, although I do not know a single reference that acknowledges Willshire as an ethnographic source.

A comparison of Willshire with his contemporaries—Baldwin Spencer, Francis Gillen, and Carl Strehlow—is illuminating. Willshire arrived at Alice Springs in 1882, years before either Gillen or Carl Strehlow. Spencer traveled through Central Australia on many occasions between 1894 (with the Horn expedition) and 1926 (when he returned to Alice Springs to collect material to revise *Native Tribes*) but never for more than two or three months—except for the year's work with Gillen in 1901 and 1902. Willshire traveled extensively throughout Central Australia for more than eight years and was an active student of aboriginal languages, primarily facilitated by keeping word lists. He noted that he had filled "nine pocket-books" with words at the time of publishing *The Aborigines of Central Australia*. Gillen's access to Arrernte culture was primarily through the aboriginal-English-speaking Arrernte, who worked at the Alice Springs Telegraph Station. Aboriginal culture was more or less brought to him and Spencer. Carl Strehlow, as a missionary, did not travel among aboriginal peoples, nor did he observe the cultures as they were lived. His Arrernte informants came to Hermannsburg to respond to his inquiries. Strehlow's approach to the study of aboriginal languages was more systematic than Willshire's word lists, but Strehlow's motivation for language study was primarily to serve his Christian mission work, which was the preaching to and teaching the people Christianity in their own languages and translating Christian scripture. Thus Willshire not only encountered a much broader spectrum of aboriginal peoples than the others and more in situ, but also his communication with them was far less dependent than Spencer's and Gillen's on aboriginal English.

Willshire's ethnography was not systematic, nor was it intended to be. He reports what he came upon, the observations incidental to his travels as a police officer, supplemented by the inquiries that time permitted and motivated by his own considerable interests. Of his own work he wrote: "The Mounted Police Force of South Australia, entrusted with the supervision and regulation of the affairs of an enormous tract of unsettled country, apparently afforded him favorable opportunities of studying the mode of life and condition of the aboriginal natives, in reality it threw serious obstacles in the way of a systematic investigation of the facts at which he desired to arrive."[37] The obstacles were, of course, the demands of being a policeman.

Willshire's ethnography dealt extensively with cultural and ritual practices: social structure (including reporting on the existence of matriliny and a "caste" system), marriage rules, circumcision and subincision rites as part of male initiatory practices, "superstitions," "taboos," death and burial customs, rock paintings and their cultural and ritual correlates, infanticide, names and naming practices, the abandonment of the elderly, sucking shamanism, and (perhaps his favorite topic) cannibalism. Willshire often describes specific situations he observed supplemented by his comments on or explanations of these practices. Unlike Spencer, Gillen, and Strehlow, Willshire reports not a single story, not a single reference to Alcheringa or the ancient ancestors. Importantly, this suggests that these topics and genre did not arise naturally among aborigines but were more likely to be how aborigines responded when asked questions by outsiders who were probing their cultures by formal inquiry of select individuals apart from the practice of their cultures. It may indicate the more esoteric nature of this knowledge.

Interestingly, Willshire identifies what he observed among aborigines as "religious,"[38] whereas *religion* is a term rarely used by Spencer and Gillen, probably because of the influence on Spencer's evolutionist theory, which identified the *ab original* as prereligious. For Willshire, whose religious background is not known to me,[39] religion is closely synonymous with superstition.

During the first decade in which the missionaries and settlers shared the Finke River region, it would seem that since there were so few nonaboriginal people in such a vast landscape, they would have welcomed one another's presence, but this was not the case. Through the 1880s, complaints flowed from the Northern Territory to South Australia from both missionaries and cattle ranchers about each other. The missionaries complained that the ranchers and the government police were unnecessarily killing aborigines to punish them for cattle spearing and that they were committing immoral acts by taking aboriginal women as sexual partners. The ranchers complained that the missionaries were harboring aborigines known to be cattle-poaching criminals, that they were physically restraining aborigines in order to Christianize them, and that they were cruel in their punishment of aboriginal wrongdoings. In 1886 Willshire conducted a preliminary investigation of the missionaries at Hermannsburg as part of an official investigation.

Throughout his *Aborigines of Central Australia*, Willshire compliments and supports the Hermannsburg missionaries, acknowledging them as "kind and hospitable in the highest degree to strangers and others who come in their way."[40] He describes how he helped convince a runaway aboriginal woman to return to Hermannsburg: "It was a matter of duty on the part of the police to assist the missionaries as much as possible."[41] But he thought that the missionaries were unnecessarily gullible: "The blacks are extremely cunning in the way in which they enlist the sympathies of the inhabitants of the mission stations. If a white man happened to be out shooting emus or kangaroos, and blacks happened to be in the near vicinity, they would be likely to go to the missionaries and say that they had been shot at. . . . Too much reliance is often placed on the assertions of the blacks."[42]

Willshire defends the practice of pastoralists and aboriginal women as sexual partners on the same grounds it was supported by the official report. Though the practice was found to be common, it was not restricted or discouraged because it appeared that aboriginal women joined into these relationships voluntarily.[43] Willshire believed that the missionaries' influence was harmful. In opposing their approach, he formulated his aboriginal policy, which was that it is best "to leave them alone. They are far better off if they are allowed to come and go to and from the stations as they feel inclined."[44]

By the time Willshire wrote *A Thrilling Tale*, he had stood trial for murder and he felt less sympathetic toward the missionaries: "It is the impious villain—the missionary—who contaminates the innocent, and, hitherto, unwary blacks, and I know that the natives from their innate hatred would, if they could, expel them ruthlessly from their land."[45] Willshire reported that he often gave aborigines extensive amounts of food and goods from his own resources.[46] He spoke with pride at the happiness of the aborigines who were part of his police camp.[47] In contrast, he found the missionary service sorely wanting: "If I were provided with the means I could raise them all [the aborigines] to a better condition by diplomacy and kindness. But no, the government would rather give a thousand miles of country to imprudent missionaries, who violate the popular rites of the aborigines. Reader, think me not uncharitable, if I denounce the mission work in Central Australia. What I mean, is, they do not possess the necessary tact to deal successfully with the aborigines,—they do not do the right thing at the right time."[48]

Willshire had no systematic policy toward aboriginal peoples. He believed that the missionaries were far too intrusive and that the aborigines would be better off left alone. As the organizer and leader of a native police force, Willshire spent most of his time in the exclusive company of aborigines. His statements about them cover a considerable range, from disgust and disdain to admiration and appreciation. He thought them brutish and ignorant; deceitful and deceptive; and, a point he often mentioned, unappreciative. Apparently the aborigines who so willingly took the gifts Willshire offered never thanked him for them.

Willshire's attitude toward aborigines differed markedly according to their gender. He wrote in *Land of the Dawning*: "Women are good but men are bad."[49] Although all his native police were male, Willshire valued aboriginal men far less highly than women. In his works, there are few accounts of the acts and contributions of his male trackers, but there are many romanticized descriptions of aboriginal women. This aspect of Willshire's storytrack is most fully developed in *A Thrilling Tale of Real Life*, which he dedicated, in a highly romantic tribute, to a female aboriginal guide and helper. The dedication reads:

> A light-hearted girl, who loved the free air of the ranges and the excitement of the chase. When dark clouds overshadowed our trackless way, the sunbeams of her heart dispelled adversity; when surrounded by scenes of the deepest historical interest, and scenes of desolate wildness, I was assisted to record items of Aboriginal lore, that will be handed down to posterity. When apprehensive of native hostility by my whilom foes, in the mighty centre of a mighty realm, she did not desert me, but returned to my party into civilization on the Finke river, and died as she lived. Chaste as the morning dew, she has now gone to that undiscovered country from whence no traveler returned.

It appears that Willshire intended *A Thrilling Tale* to read like one. He begins the work by focusing on the relationship between a European-Australian male traveler and his young aboriginal female guide. The girl's name is Chillberta, and she affectionately calls the man Oleara.[50] Willshire describes her: "Chillberta had a face of unaffected simplicity; sixteen years of age, budding into womanhood, the admiration of the whole tribe, especially the young men, who thought her comely and amiable, which, undoubtedly, she was."[51] Willshire describes the travels of the innocent—they both remained chaste—Oleara and Chillberta. Oleara's intentions were only to learn about Chillberta's people. Within only a few pages, Willshire begins to occasionally use the first person. A few pages further, Willshire tires altogether of the third person and assumes the first person, with a very occasional return to the third. It is his story, and he wants to tell it as directly as possible.

His admiration for Chillberta is constant, as is his pride in his influence on her: "Chillberta was fast adopting the habits of a refined white woman, using a comb and looking-glass with, no doubt, as much vanity and self approbation as her fairer sisters."[52] Once Chillberta was "well clothed, fat and happy, [she] went off into a rhapsody of song, wild and rambling . . .

We have the life so free from care,
O'er hill and valley everywhere,
  No matter where we roam;
We go to water, fresh and clear,
Of one another have no fear,
  And anywhere's our home.

Mid' desert oaks and sandhills high,
Beneath a hot and sultry sky,
  We hunt our daily food;
Returning when the sun is low,
To water and our camp we go,
  And cook what we pursued.

We grease our limbs and body, too,
With emu fat and kangaroo,
  And come shining to the play;
The lubras smile, with looks they steal,
And reckon us their beau-ideal,
  And heroes of the day.[53]

Willshire admitted to the difficulty of the translation task, perhaps impossible were it not for the help given him by "the lovely and pure-souled Chillberta." He also acknowledged that this "uncontaminated dusky virgin . . . did all in her power to assist Oleara to observe, preserve, and record, the customs and habits of her own race, which are strange beyond description."[54]

A Pocahontas theme appears frequently in Willshire's writings.[55] In June 1894, Willshire was stationed on the Victoria River in the far north. Chasing a group of aboriginal men, Willshire and his friend, James Ledgerwood, found themselves trapped when the men suddenly scattered in every direction and set fire to the dry grass all around them. However, an aboriginal "beauty" came to their rescue:

> The mountain was swathed in a regal robe of fiery grandeur, and its ominous roar was close upon us. The weird, awful beauty of the scene held us spellbound for a few seconds. Out from between the rocks came a strapping young girl, with the agility of a mountain creature. She jumped from rock to rock, straight to the grey horse that I was sitting upon, took hold of my stirrup-iron, and ran alongside until we were out of danger. She was arrayed in her native modesty, and I may state this was the prettiest black girl I ever saw. She would not leave us, but when we camped sat down on our swags and smiled at the horses, all the time trying to tell us something, while a couple of imprisoned sunbeams seemed to be basking around her dimpled cheeks, and the grass beneath her feet shed tears of newly fallen dew. She was remarkably handsome, and every lineament of her face indicated a good disposition.[56]

Willshire describes his (Oleara's) visit to a kind of aboriginal harem, occupying a cave forbidden to most. He exercised much persuasion to be permitted to enter. "On entering the cave he [Oleara] was met by a young woman, perfectly nude; around her head she wore a wreath of orange and lilac blossoms, from her neck hung a unique necklace of quondong stones, through her nose stuck a snow white bone, and her ribs and thighs were adorned with stripes of red ochre, bordered with pipe-clay and charcoal. She was called the Duenna of the Harem."[57] He explored the rooms of the cave, finding among the many young women one who recognized him because of his relationship with Chillberta. To please Oleara, the women adorned themselves with flower garlands and shell necklaces and sang for him.

Willshire repeatedly espoused his chasteness, despite the many offers he claimed to have received to cohabit with aboriginal women.[58] Although he was usually the observer and recorder, he describes his occasional participation:

> On some occasions I discarded my habiliments, painted my bread-basket with red ochre and charcoal, just to be in the fashion, and to please the natives. At the special request of some male aborigines, on one occasion, I stripped, and they painted me all over with red ochre and charcoal, and stuck feathers and down on my chest, and then marched me to the corrobboree.
>
> I did not expect to see such a large audience present, but, when it came to my turn to stamp down the race to where the black beauties were sitting, I blushed beautifully, I must have appeared supremely attractive. I noticed the ladies could scarcely restrain their genuine admiration.[59]

There are many examples in Willshire's writings of his fascination with and admiration of aboriginal women. Even in his post on the Victoria River he had a female guide named Narlen.[60]

Occasionally Willshire makes literary references in his writing, quoting Tennyson, Poe, Byron, Sladen, Shakespeare, Pope, and the Bible, among many others. He wrote poetry, such as the tribute he wrote "In loving memory of Police Trooper Shirley who died of thirst in the Northern Territory, November 7, 1883, aged 30 years." The poem tells the story of a search party of six sent after the attacker of a man named

Harry Redford. When the party failed to return in time, Willshire searched for them. He found only A. M. Giles alive, and he buried his friend Shirley.[61]

The Strehlow-Willshire Storytrack Crossing

With this sketch of Willshire's storytrack, the focus turns to the crossing points that began with Theodor Strehlow's story, which started at Irbmangkara and continued on to Tempe Downs, where two aboriginal men were killed, and then to Port Augusta, where Willshire stood trial for murder. Although their storytracks cross, the lives of Strehlow and Willshire did not. Willshire wrote very little about his own role in these events. In an appended section that concludes his *A Thrilling Tale*, he presents a collection of newspaper items that supported him and that report his acquittal. Furthermore, Willshire was deeply embittered by being brought to trial and often reflected on the injustice of it. Perhaps his most stirring statement on this matter is his comparison of himself with his contemporary, the British journalist and African explorer Henry Morton Stanley:

> Stanley saw Africa; he had his fellow white men, and the enjoyment of social intercourse was thus maintained unbroken.
>
> What that means let those who have suffered its deprivation say. Stanley was welcomed back to civilization with the acclamations of the world, praised by princes, made the familiar of kings, idolized in the drawing-room of savants, and for the time was exalted as the greatest hero of the nineteenth century.
>
> All honor to the indomitable pluck and energy which characterized Stanley's work. But in this fair land of Australia, the pioneer, the explorer, the officer of the Government goes forth with one aim only—to do his duty. He anticipates no princely reception on the completion of his arduous work, and though the laurel of well-earned victory be denied him, he is content in the calm consciousness of having done the right, and successfully accomplishing that which was demanded by his country from him.
>
> Well, Oleara's work was performed in the execution of duty as a public officer; that, and that alone was his guiding star, and faithfully did he follow it. It will come as a staggerer to the reader, to know that Oleara met with no such gratifying reception, at the hands of his country. The flattering address took the form of a warrant on the charge of murder.[62]

Some points of interest in these events can be gleaned from Willshire's writing. Strehlow believed that Willshire's motives for the killings at Tempe Downs in February 1891 were connected with the killing of Nameia at Boggy Hole in January 1890. The trial hinged on the motivation for these killings. The jury was convinced that the trackers had lied to Gillen in his investigation by indicating that they were ordered by Willshire to do the killing when, as they testified, they were acting on their own behalf—carrying out cultural practices of revenge by killing the murderers of Nameia, who was their relative.[63] In all of Willshire's writings about Central Australia, he rarely mentions killings. One reference, however, is relevant:

> His [Willshire's] camp was attacked by a mob of wild blacks from the westward on the 9th of January 1890. They managed to drive one long spear right through the body of one of the natives at the camp, named Peter, who was kept there to carry wood and water as required. His viscera protruded through the wound, and he died on the following afternoon. The spear was thrown into one of the wurleys with the intention of killing one of the active native constables. In this they failed. When daylight broke, their tracks, or rather the impressions of their feet, were plainly seen on the soft ground. Every one of them was identified by the native constables, who, as they examined the footprints, called out the names of the natives to whom they belonged.[64]

Willshire states that his trackers pursued and finally sighted these men, but they were unable to arrest them because they took refuge in deep gorges and the trackers had insufficient supplies for the time needed to ferret them out.[65]

In his writings, Willshire did not connect this event with the Tempe Downs killings. It must be recalled that Theodor Strehlow, indicating his source as a police report, named Namea as the man killed. Many aborigines had English names along with their aboriginal names, so it is possible that Peter is a name by which Nameia was called, but Willshire does not make the connection. Importantly, from his account published in the year in which he stood trial, Willshire appears ignorant of the storytrack of ritual crime, punishment, revenge, and counterrevenge that stemmed from Irbmangkara, yet the issue of revenge was clearly present during the trial and the storytrack is central to Strehlow's presentation.[66] Willshire appears to have believed that the motivation for the killing in his camp was directed at one of his native constables. He does not identify Peter as the father of one of his trackers but rather as a camp laborer.

In light of Willshire's storytrack, Theodor Strehlow's account of the murders at Tempe Downs and the events leading up to them are seen anew. From Strehlow's track, Willshire directed the killings, based on a double motivation: "The intelligence that Nameia had been the father of his native constable Aremala was undoubtedly a very welcome discovery to Willshire. Even better, this had been a Matuntara raid executed upon a Southern Aranda camp, and the white officer felt that it would for this very reason deeply offend his other Aranda native constables as well."[67]

Strehlow's portrayal of Willshire is interesting. Willshire is a killer, welcoming any excuse to murder aborigines, and he is a sensitive shepherd and defender of his Arrernte constables. Concerning Willshire's role in the killings at Tempe Downs, Strehlow appears to know Willshire's deepest motivations:

> The execution of Nameia by a hand of Matuntara men early in 1890 hence seemed to afford an excellent excuse for Willshire's punishing the dark cattle-killers in the usual way—by rifle fire. But because of the recent investigation, Willshire decided to be rather more circumspect on the coming occasion: the shooting would be done by his four Aranda native constables, who would be given arms and ammunition and ordered to kill the murderers of Nameia. To Willshire's surprise, none of his Aranda subordinates were in the least enthusiastic about his well-thought-out plan. To pursue a blood feud according to the age-old tribal norms and to kill the victim by spear and boomerang was one

> thing; but for dark men to carry out a white police officer's orders in a matter that was no concern of his, and to use white man's fire-arms against men of their own race, was an entirely different thing. It was an act of treachery against the dark race, designed to advance mainly the cause of the white usurpers of the aboriginal lands. But in the end, the four trackers could not refuse to carry out their orders; for they had good reasons for fearing their white master even more than any of their dark enemies.[68]

Strehlow has remarkable capabilities: he knows Willshire's inner motivations, he knows the trackers' inner struggles, and he is able to find a mid-twentieth-century aboriginal political sensitivity among late nineteenth-century police trackers. Further, he is able to excuse aboriginal police constables of the job they voluntarily choose: the tracking, confining, and sometimes killing (obviously with rifles) of other aborigines for acts (considered only by nonaborigines to be criminal) against the property of nonaboriginal Australians. Had they the political agenda Strehlow discovers in them, they would have been unable to perform the least of their responsibilities as native constables. And Strehlow was able to obtain all of this information decades after the deaths of all involved.

Strehlow's portrayal of these events dismisses the evidence presented at Willshire's trial in Port Augusta, evidence that convinced a jury of Willshire's innocence. The crown solicitor, J. M. Stuart, as prosecutor, established the issues: "It was said that the two victims were concerned with the murder of a native named Nimi, father of one of the troopers, in some Aboriginal vendetta. That would have to be shown. There was no doubt that cattle stealing and killing by Aborigines was prevalent in the district, but that Donkey and Roger [the victims] were delinquents was not provided." The trial, which called fourteen witnesses, established that rather than ordering the native constables to shoot the Matuntara men, Willshire had ordered them arrested and chained for return to Boggy Waterhole.

Although Strehlow does not indicate that he thought the trial was flawed, his knowledge of court proceedings conducted in aboriginal English would have given him reason to hold this suspicion.[69] A couple of excerpts from the trial show its potential for a miscarriage of justice. An aboriginal tracker who went by the name of Jacky[70] testified in aboriginal English: "Thomas, Larry and Archie were at Tempe Downs besides me. Mr Willshire told us to go to Tempe Downs, and went with us. Mr Willshire tell me 'shoot him Roger and Donkey'. He told us you go longa camp; Larry and Archie longa creek; Thomas stop longa bush. Larry shootum Donkey. Roger get away longa Thomas, who shoot him. Me shoot Roger in leg when him lying down."[71] The court upheld Sir John Downer's objection that the crown solicitor should engage someone accustomed to communicating with aborigines, and Downer proceeded to his cross-examination of Jacky: "Did you tell white fellow on camel Mr Willshire say you catchem Roger, put on handcuffs, no shootum?" Jacky replied: "Yes." Archie supported this view, indicating that he had told Gillen that Willshire had told them: "No you shootum. Put on neckchains and handcuff and takeum Boggy Water."[72]

Evidence was given that Donkey and Roger were not so unsuspecting as Strehlow presented them—they threw spears at the native constables—and that

Willshire was knocked down by a digging stick while attempting to place a neckchain on Donkey before he was killed. Despite this evidence, Strehlow might very well have made the point that Downer's style of questioning was leading the witness because aborigines commonly responded in the affirmative to any question asked by European-Australians. Thus the crucial point established by Downer's questions—that Willshire was not responsible for the killings—may have been established through inappropriate methods of questioning. Willshire's defense was supported by the contradictory nature of the testimony of the native constables. Downer summarized Willshire's case to the jury: "Here was a man of high character and responsible position performing arduous and dangerous duties, practically carrying his life in his own hands, an officer of noted integrity and ability, brought down from the far interior, hurled into gaol and put into dock to answer on peril of his life a charge of murder because he had thoroughly performed a difficult work entrusted to him. There was no proof whatever that Willshire killed the blacks. But he was put to risk of hanging on the testimony of two self-convicted murderers whose statements were of the most extraordinary contradictory character."[73] Strehlow might have held that the contradictions in the testimony of the native constables was introduced by Downer's form of questioning and by the fact that they had to communicate to the court in aboriginal English.

Though Strehlow could have made these arguments, he did not. Rather he wrote in a way perhaps even more leading than Downer's style of questioning: he convicted Willshire as murderer, against the evidence of his trial and without opportunity for defense. Such portrayals of Willshire by Strehlow, as well as by Baldwin Spencer, have led to an image of Willshire, broadly held by the late twentieth century, as a vicious killer of aborigines.[74]

Summary and Conclusion

Many storytracks run through Irbmangkara. From each one, the world and all other tracks are assessed and responded to with confidence and assurance. Yet as we shift from track to track, Willshire shifts from upstanding literate and literary public official, doing his duty for his country, to wanton aboriginal-killing monster. The Hermannsburg Lutherans shift between being the selfless defenders of aborigines and being narrow-minded and insensitive Christianizers of aborigines that they have cruelly held captive. Francis Gillen shifts between being the heroic defender of aboriginal justice, who had the courage to accuse a police official, a man of his own race, of murder, and being a meddlesome justice of the peace who overstepped his authority and was misled by the aborigines' propensity to fabricate. Theodor Strehlow shifts between being a highly respected, Arrernte-speaking academic authority and being a writer capable of complete fabrications in service to the defamation of a man he never met. Theodor Strehlow shifts between being the trusted friend and receiver of aboriginal wisdom and being an arrogant man so self-involved as to consider himself the spokesperson for all aborigines. The Arrernte residents of Irbmangkara shift between being ritual criminals and being innocent victims of a horrible massacre. The story of Kalejika is to some a malicious lie, while to others it is just cause to kill a whole community. Some Arrernte are connected to Irbmangkara through duck ancestors; yet to some Matuntara it is the snake ancestors that make the place significant.

Hearing all of these storytracks, we may shift our allegiance among the various parties as we connect more or less strongly with some storytracks than with others. We may shift between the hopelessness and despair—upon discovering that "the truth" in this situation seems impossible—and the freedom of realizing that when it comes to human history and culture, there is no truth apart from storytrack, that rights and wrongs (truths and falsehoods) depend on where one stands and that, after all, one must stand somewhere. On the one hand, we may be annoyed by the illegitimacy of presenting history from a single storytrack, while on the other hand, we may find greater satisfaction in representing more than one point of view. By acknowledging storytracks, we may find that in the way we look at others we are reflected ourselves, as in a mirror. Self-knowledge is always revealed in our inquiries into the stories of others. We may find it obvious that all studies of history are in some ways subjective—we may or may not welcome this realization.

5

Altjira

May it [a British flag raised on Mount Stuart in Central Australia in 1860] be a sign to the natives that the dawn of liberty, civilization, and Christianity is about to break upon them.

John McDouall Stuart

According to the tradition of the ancestors there is a being, called *Altjira*, who embodies the highest good (*mara*). This being is eternal (*ngambakula*).

Carl Strehlow

Twenty years ago a man named Kempe, one of the first missionaries, seized upon the word Altjira and adopted it as the word for 'God.' . . . Now after these twenty years . . . of endeavor to teach the poor natives that Altjira means 'God,' Strehlow comes forward with the momentous discovery that in the Aranta '*there is a Being of the highest order called Altjira.*'

Baldwin Spencer

As indicating a past period of a very vague and, it seemed to us, "dreamy" nature we adopted, to express as nearly as possible the meaning of the word *alcheringa* . . . the term "dream times."

Francis Gillen and Baldwin Spencer

Spencer and Gillen tell the following story of Numbakulla, whose name means "always existing" or "out of nothing."

Mircea Eliade

Hermannsburg Mission and the Christianization of the Aborigines

The Kempe Era

In Bethany, a German community in the Barossa Valley northeast of Adelaide, the children of the day school sang "Jesus, Lead Thou On" as A. H. Kempe and W. F. Schwarz departed on October 23, 1875, for their mission post in Central Australia. The 1,500-mile trip was to take them nearly two years.

The establishment of the mission station had been long in planning and preparation. It was the consequence of the 1862 challenge delivered by J. F. Meischel to the Evangelical Lutheran Church in Australia to "carry on mission work among those heathen in whose land she dwells."[1] The Australian government granted 900 square miles in an area 90 miles west of Alice Springs for the Finke River Mission. Kempe and Schwarz were chosen by the Hermannsburg Mission Institute in Germany for Australian mission service and arrived at Glenelg (the harbor at Adelaide) on September 16, 1875. Livestock that had been established on the Bethesda Mission station in South Australia was inventoried, with the plan of sending two-thirds of it to the new Finke River station.

Although trained as missionaries, Kempe and Schwarz were not prepared to be bushmen. They experienced constant problems as they traveled into Central Australia, not the least of which was the unbearable summer heat. They managed to cross 500 miles by November 29, when Kempe, ignorant of the still greater travail before him, wrote, "Often I have been almost tempted to exclaim in the words of the prophet: 'It is enough; now, O Lord, take away my life,' for I am sick at heart."[2]

Pastor G. Heidenreich, superintendent of the Finke River Mission, followed Kempe and Schwarz, leaving November 29 and moving more rapidly because he was unincumbered by herds of livestock. Their progress seemed promising, so he returned to Bethany to conduct services and to develop more support for the mission effort. In late January, Heidenreich again left Bethany for Central Australia. When, in February, he intercepted Kempe and Schwarz at Finniss Springs, near the southern end of Lake Eyre, he found "Kempe, Schwarz and Nitzschke suffering complete exhaustion. Nitzschke himself in desperation left the party to return south. Kempe and Schwarz were physically, mentally and spiritually exhausted."[3] The party had divided into five groups strung across a landscape. All were beaten by the heat and drought conditions of summer, which Kempe described: "It is dreadful, shocking, to travel here in summer. Nobody could imagine things to be as bad, and having any conception of what this journey entails."[4] After traversing 50- to 80-mile waterless stretches, on May 29 the party finally reached Dalhousie Springs, still more than 300 miles short of their land grant. They were forced to stop to await the arrival of supplies from the south, a stop that lasted over ten months but afforded a needed rest. During this interval, Heidenreich and Kempe took a party on to explore the Finke River station.

Rains finally fell, and on April 9, 1877, the party was once again on its way north. On June 4, after more than twenty-two months from the time they left Bethany, the group finally reached the mission lease. Several days later Schwarz and Kempe had decided on the location for building the Hermannsburg Mission. Attracted to a location on the Finke River, the deciding factor was the availability of fresh water when they dug in the river bed.

The first labors had to be directed to the care of the livestock. Pens for the sheep were built, especially to protect newborn lambs. Dingoes (wild dogs) were a threat to poultry, so chicken houses were built. Kennels were built for the dogs, so important to shepherding. It was weeks before dwellings for the staff could be started. But the government lease had been occupied and the Hermannsburg Mission had been established. It was only a matter of time before other missionaries would arrive and the mission work would begin in earnest.

Although at first the missionaries attended to the physical establishment of their mission station and did not attempt to contact aborigines, it was not long before a number of them visited the station. The nomadic life-style of the Western Arrernte made it difficult for the missionaries to establish a stable aboriginal community. This difficulty was partially overcome by their distribution of rations provided for the aborigines by the Australian government.

Realizing that before Christianity could be taught to the aborigines the communications barrier had to be removed, the missionaries began to learn the Arrernte language and Kempe worked on an Arrernte dictionary, which was eventually printed in Adelaide in 1888. But the translation of Christian terms into Arrernte proved difficult. As Kempe wrote:

> The difficulty of acquiring the language lies not only in the structure of the language, nor in the scarcity of concrete terms, but in the lack of abstract terms and moral ideals, of which they have no conception. We would not claim that we have mastered the language. If we wish to converse with the Natives in their language, we immediately notice our inability to arrange our ideas in the proper form of verb, noun, and adverb. The difficulty is the greater for us missionaries, since we must rely on our own scanty experience, having no helps, nor anyone to advise, assist, or correct, even if the enunciation of our Natives themselves leaves much to be desired.[5]

How to speak to the Arrernte of such an essential matter as "God"? What Arrernte term might be used so that the missionaries might speak the first word of Christianity to the Arrernte? This was the matter facing Kempe when he wrote: "They [the Arrernte] pray only to the above five gods [apparently indicating the "god of the emus," called "Merrenna"; the god of the euros, "Indira"; the god of the wallabies, "Uranama"; the god of the lake, "Tjaubutmanja"; and the "god of mankind," whose name is "Malbanga"]. All of them, the good supernatural beings, they call also 'altgiva,' [apparently an early rendering of "altjira"] as well as the firmament, with the sun, moon, and stars; also the earth, and any things specially remarkable. The word 'altgiva' signifies that these had an everlasting existence."[6]

During the missionaries' first year in Central Australia, the fiancées of Kempe and Schwarz arrived from Germany. Kempe met his bride at Dalhousie Springs, where they were married in March 1877. Kempe performed the marriage ceremony for

Schwarz in May. During the first year, Hermannsburg received a third missionary, L. G. Schulze, and his wife.

Living over a thousand miles from the people of their own culture and many thousands of miles from their German homes, these missionaries did the best they could. The first decade was a constant challenge. The labor-intensive attempts to cultivate cereal grains failed because of frequent and unpredictable droughts. Within a couple of years, the mission station was nearly surrounded by ranchers. Tensions arose. The mission operation was soon investigated by the government because of complaints about the way the missionaries used government rations directed to the aborigines. This 1879 investigation was only the first of many during the mission's first quarter century. Nor did the missionaries like the ranchers. They believed that the ranchers mistreated the aborigines, wantonly killing them to discourage cattle poaching and taking aboriginal women as sexual partners. The missionaries believed that the ranchers supported a policy of aboriginal genocide.

Despite the constant difficulties, the mission building program continued, as did the study of aboriginal languages. A building that served both as school and as church was dedicated in November 1880. Christmas celebration in the church included the singing of Christmas carols that Kempe has translated into Arrernte, and gifts were distributed to the aborigines present. Slowly aborigines were attracted to the station. There was a correlation between the weather and the aboriginal population. During severe drought, more aborigines came to the station, where they could receive government rations. They returned to their country and to hunting and gathering when the weather was less severe. In time, several aboriginal children were enrolled in school, where they were taught academic subjects, including English, as well as religious education.

In 1885 Kempe, his wife, and his son were ill and sought medical attention in Adelaide. To assist in their travel they were accompanied by two aboriginal teenage boys, Kalimala and Tekua. The journey was successful in ways beyond procuring health for the Kempe family. Along the route—especially at Herrgott Springs and the Bethesda Mission, Killalpaninna—the teenagers met Christianized aborigines, meetings that advanced their interest in becoming Christian. As Kempe wrote: "Their stay among Christian natives freed them of superstition and fear of the witch-doctor's magic. When they rejoined our party on the return journey, they told us of their spiritual experiences at the Mission, expressing the deep desire and conviction to be baptized as soon as possible."[7]

Near the end of the first decade of the Hermannsburg Mission, the first aboriginal baptisms were performed for seven teenagers, among them the two who had traveled with the Kempe family. On Easter Sunday in 1888, seventeen more aborigines were baptized, and on the day after Christmas in 1890, another five.

But times were hard for the missionaries. The experience of a decade in Central Australia was telling on every family there. By this time, everyone had challenged one's physical and psychological limits. Schwarz was the first to leave, departing in September 1889. Schulze became so weak and sick that he had to leave in early November 1891. Kempe and his wife had had seven children in the decade of their marriage; all lived at Hermannsburg. One of their four sons had died at age six. Kempe had suffered apoplexy in 1890 and had contracted typhoid fever. Shortly before Schulze left, Kempe's wife had delivered their seventh child, but she sickened and died in mid-November. Kempe found he had no choice and left Hermannsburg late in November 1891 with five of his children. He left his baby at the station with a lay worker.

A record of only a few converts and the construction of a few buildings in an isolated area seems perhaps little reward for over a decade of enormous personal sacrifice to Christian service, but Kempe's statement on this seeming failure is the measure of the character of these Lutherans: "The lack of faith of all of us is certainly the main cause of the closing chapter."[8] Perhaps Kempe's publications were to be his greatest impact on Central Australia: a twenty-one-page school primer; a fifty-four-page *Grammar and Vocabulary of the Language Spoken by the Aborigines of the MacDonnell Ranges, South Australia*; a dictionary containing 1,750 Arrernte words; and a book in Arrernte language of Christian instruction and worship, containing bible stories, psalms, hymns, and prayers.

Hermannsburg Mission was now without a pastor and began to deteriorate. Even distant church politics increased its problems when the Evangelical Lutheran Synod of Australia, who operated the mission, severed relations with the Hermannsburg Mission Society. It was several years before the mission station would once again have a pastor. A small lay staff occupied the station, and a few devoted aborigines remained.

In May 1894, a few members of the Horn Scientific Exploration Expedition to Central Australia, passed briefly through Hermannsburg. Baldwin Spencer, a member of the expedition, wrote of the conditions he observed: "The Mission at the time of our visit, was abandoned and fast falling into ruins. The few Blacks, the remnants of a larger number who were camped about the place when it was opened as a mission station, still remained, living in a squalid state in dirty whurlies. If, which is open to question, the Mission had ever done any permanent good, there was no evidence of it to be seen, either amongst these Blacks, or others whom we met with, and who had been in contact with it."[9] Spencer's next visit to Hermannsburg would coincide with the next interim period between pastors shortly after the death of Carl Strehlow in 1923.

The Strehlow Era

In 1894 the Immanuel Synod of the Lutheran Church agreed to support the mission. They appointed C. F. T. Strehlow as pastor.[10] Strehlow had been stationed at Bethesda Mission since 1892, where he had learned the Dieri language and had assisted in the first translation of the New Testament into an aboriginal language. When he arrived at Hermannsburg in October 1894, Strehlow found that the compound had deteriorated and there were no aborigines around. He threw himself into the job and soon began to realize results. By the end of the year he had attracted more than 60 aborigines to the station. The number continued to grow as he began a building program. A new church, which survives today, was dedicated in December 1897, and by 1900 the average church attendance was more than 100. Strehlow's nearly three decades at Hermannsburg were not free of controversy. In 1904 difficulties arose between Strehlow and a fellow pastor over translations.[11] The church's investigation led to the removal of the latter. In 1911, while Strehlow and his family were on furlough in Germany, an expedition into the Northern Territory passed through Hermannsburg, charged by the government to investigate the missionaries' treatment of aborigines. The leader of that expedition, Captain Barclay, filed a report that criticized the mission for unhygienic conditions, for the sale of rations to aborigines, for the diversion of income from Hermannsburg to other mission stations, for the poor quality of the clothing being given to the aborigines, for not teaching trades to aborigines, and for failing to pay wages to aborigines who worked at the station. The report was widely publicized, and the mission suffered extensive bad publicity until Mounted Constable Robert Stott of the Alice Springs police issued a generally favorable report of his inspection of Hermannsburg early in 1912.[12] Inspections subsequent to Strehlow's return in 1912 found no significant problems.

Because of a German identity, Strehlow and Hermannsburg received more unwelcome attention during World War I—being accused of teaching German to the aborigines and even of intercepting telegraph messages vital to national security and to the war.[13] Strehlow weathered these accusations and the frequent demands for the closing of Hermannsburg. He endured when his community was devastated by epidemic disease. He persisted in his writing on aboriginal cultures, motivated, at least in part, by his disagreements with the books published by Baldwin Spencer and Francis Gillen. The resulting work, published in Germany in five parts from 1907 to 1920, was *Die Aranda- und Loritja-Stämme in Zentral-Australien*. Strehlow continued, with aboriginal assistance, his studies of aboriginal languages (producing a dictionary of 8,000 words) and his efforts to translate the New Testament into native languages (the translation into Arrernte was completed in 1919). With a quarter century of his life devoted to Hermannsburg, in 1920 Strehlow requested a replacement. He expressed his patience and his interest in training his replacement. By September 1922, no replacement had been designated,[14] and because of illness, Strehlow could wait no longer. His condition grew steadily worse. Desperate efforts to procure medical help were made without result. Finally, on October 10, sick and broken like his predecessors, Strehlow left Hermannsburg with his wife and young son, Theodor. Several other Strehlow children had remained in Germany to be educated after the Strehlow's year there in 1911.[15] Strehlow suffered so much pain that he could not lie down in a wagon and was transported sitting in a chair wired to the wagon floor. In an effort to expedite the journey, the party traveled on a camel trail along the Finke River. Strehlow died at Horseshoe Bend after nine days of travel.[16]

Baldwin Spencer, by 1923 a well-established and highly respected anthropologist, was appointed by the Australian federal government to investigate the growing problem of mixed-heritage[17] aborigines, the ever-increasing product of those mixed sexual encounters the missionaries so opposed. Sixty mixed-race children lived in three corrugated iron sheds called the Bungalow in Alice Springs. Spencer extended his investigation to Hermannsburg, arriving there six months after Strehlow's death. He stayed for ten days. No missionary was in charge at the time. Spencer's report recommended that the station be taken over by the government and operated by the Salvation Army. He felt the mission should be "reorganized on such a basis that it shall provide for the moral, social, and industrial training of the Aborigines and for the maintenance of the old and infirm." And, doubtless reflecting prejudice left over from the war years, Spencer held that "it is essential that men and women of British origin and sound common sense should be in charge."[18]

Moses

One other Hermannsburg storytrack needs to be traced, although it is now nearly invisible. It is the story of Moses, whose aboriginal name was Tjalkabota.[19] Among those baptized by Kempe in 1890 was a twelve-year-old Arrernte boy who went by the Christian name of Moses. The track of Moses turns up again in the Barclay report, which indicated that during Strehlow's absence in 1911, Moses, described as blind and about forty-five years old,[20] was teaching reading and writing in the Hermannsburg school. Carl Strehlow's efforts to translate the New Testament into Arrernte, which begin in 1913, were assisted by Moses. After Strehlow's departure in 1922, the mission leadership came to rest on a lay schoolteacher, H. A. Heinrich, but Moses effectively served as pastor. He preached every Sunday and gave instruction to twenty-seven catechumens. In November, Pastor J. Riedel arrived at Hermannsburg to conduct baptisms for those prepared by Moses. Thirteen men, fifteen women, and sixteen children were baptized and one girl confirmed. Moses delivered the sermon at their baptismal service.

In July 1923, directed by their congregation, Moses and two other aboriginal Christians traveled westward from Hermannsburg, taking the Christian message to other aboriginal groups. Of this mission Moses said: "We must not idle away our time. God's command, 'Go ye and teach all nations' is also meant for this congregation, especially as we have had the Word of God for over 50 years.[21] It is now highest time that we carry the Gospel to those in darkness. If not, then God could take his Word away from us. We must be faithful with our talent."[22] Moses continued his evangelical outreach to Alice Springs and Deep Well later in the year and early in 1924. It is known that he served at the Jay Creek Mission outpost, twenty-five miles west of Alice Springs, after it was established in 1941.

In 1936, Carl Strehlow's son, Theodor, although he had received academic training, lived at Jay Creek as patrol officer for Central Australia. Later he replaced his father's Arrernte translation of the New Testament. Like his father, he called on Moses for help, and Moses was present in June 1944 when the completed manuscript was ceremoniously delivered for printing. Notably, Pastor F. W. Albrecht, the most influential figure in the Finke River Mission district from the time of his arrival in 1926 and who chronicles this event, fails to note that Moses not only assisted Strehlow in the retranslations but also that he assisted Strehlow's father in his translation thirty years earlier. Albrecht wrote: "If our Aranda New Testament is just about perfect, this is entirely due to the untiring efforts of Mr. [Theodor] Strehlow."[23]

In 1948 Moses dictated in the Arrernte language a statement to a younger Arrernte man who could read and write Arrernte. Strehlow translationed it into English. It is his account of mission history to that time from his Arrernte perspective. As a document produced entirely by Arrernte people, it is, in one sense, the first Arrernte text. Since it presents the history, as well as bears on the storytracks that intersect on the term *altjira*, it is worth quoting in full:[24]

> The preachers preached sermons year after year; but they would not believe. The old men said to the preachers—"What is this new message? We cannot believe it. We have something that is entirely different." The preachers asked them who had created the earth. The old men said—"The earth has always existed." The preachers said—"No, God created it." They did not believe any of these statements. The old men said—"Ground-paintings existed on the earth,—no other being created them. Only Malbungka [the *tjilpa* ancestor of the Western Arrernte who passed through Ltalaltuma] created all game and magically brought into life all animals." The preachers said—"You are quite mad and ignorant."[25]
>
> We children went to school, both boys and girls. When we were learning the Commandments, and when the old men heard us,—and the women too—, they were completely amazed—"What's this, Children? You are chattering away there and chirping like cicadas; you *have* learned a strange language!" They scoffed at the children—"It would be better for you to wander about with your fathers and mothers; there you will find peace" (Or, "be happy, satisfied, and without complaints").
>
> On another occasion the preachers came to them saying—"You, too, should learn [Scripture] like the children." The old men said—"But why should we learn? An abundance of different knowledge is ours,—we already have our fill." "You are utter heathens," said the preachers to them, "you are utterly ignorant and can perceive nothing," The old men asked, "What are heathens?" The preachers replied to them—"*You* are heathens." "We are not heathens; we are iliara men and not heathens,—we are men who have been initiated at ingjura festivals; we have followed in the footsteps of Kulurba [the name of the *tjilpa* ancestor associated with Ltalaaltuma *pmara kutata*, or totem site]. . . ."
>
> Again the old men heard how the children were singing and were completely amazed—"What's this, children? Is this what you 'have been given to treasure forever' [literally, "Is this what you 'have inherited to hold as your own for ever from now on'?"]?" The preachers said to them—"You too should learn hymns." The old men replied—"We are not going to learn songs like that, only children sing like that, not we; we have different songs." The preachers continued—"You too should learn hymns, also the Commandments; then you will see everything clearly." "But we have different songs; we cannot learn strange ones; we have an abundance of songs about Malbungka." The preachers said—"Malbungka is not god: this is where you are telling great lies. You heathen folk have wrong beliefs, your thoughts are utterly senseless and wrong. The true God is in the sky." That is what the preachers said. Then the old men replied—"We are a good (mara) and morally blameless (gatalarumba) people. We cannot imagine what your God is like. We are upright, we are altogether different and better [than you],—we children of the tjibulara ("tjibulara" means "brightness"). When we gaze upon the tjilpa [totemic ancestor] on his own ground, then we are performing a virtuous deed" (lit. "then this is altogether virtuous").[26]

Moses, whose birth closely coincided with the founding of the Hermannsburg Mission, did perhaps more than any other person to establish Christianity among the aborigines in Central Australia. Certainly his presence, beginning as a student in the mission school at age five, was more constant, more dependable than even the most stalwart of nonaboriginal missionaries. Still, his name and his work are remembered as little more than a footnote in the accounts of Hermannsburg told by the Lutherans.[27]

Evolutionism and Ethnography—Baldwin Spencer

The Native Tribes of Central Australia marks the fulfillment of a full cycle of development in Baldwin Spencer's life and is the convergence point, as he approached his fortieth year, for the many strands of his personal interests and abilities: artist and photographer, biologist, anthropologist, evolutionist, traveler, field worker, meticulous describer, inspiring collaborator, editor, and tireless and highly productive academic. His storytrack is a fascinating one.

Born on June 23, 1860, to Martha and Reuben Spencer, Walter Baldwin, one of thirteen children, spent the first twenty years of his life in Manchester, England. As a rising industrialist in the cotton-spinning and manufacturing business, Reuben Spencer was a civic and church leader. Upon graduating from Old Trafford School in 1878, Baldwin followed his artistic interests and entered the Manchester School of Art. Though his interests in art never ceased, he soon began to study science at Owens College in Manchester, where he studied comparative ideas in anatomy and biology. After two years, he entered London University and later Oxford University, devoted to the study of zoology. As an ardent Darwinian and agnostic, Spencer's biological views were similar to those developing in the new field of anthropology. He attended lectures delivered by Oxford's, and Britain's, first anthropologist, Edward B. Tylor. Anthropology was being developed in terms of a theory of cultural evolution, which held that culture (singular, that is, as human culture) evolved over time through distinct stages: magic followed by religion and then science.

Henry N. Moseley, Spencer's mentor, arranged for him to work closely with Tylor and others in moving a growing ethnographic collection from London to the newly constructed Pitt River Museum at Oxford. This was valuable training for Spencer's tireless collection of biological and ethnographic specimens in Australia, earning him the name, given by aborigines, "All-day-pick-'em-up-pick-'em-up."[28] At Oxford, Spencer not only studied under some of the most influential scholars of his time, but also established important and powerful relationships that would serve him well even in antipodal lands.

Upon graduating from Oxford, Spencer learned of the establishment of a chair in biology at the University of Melbourne. As a recent graduate, he doubted that he could compete successfully for the position, yet he applied. Upon his appointment on January 10, 1887, Spencer entered an Australian whirlwind that seems never to have ceased. On January 18 he married Mary Elizabeth (Lillie) Bowman, to whom he had been engaged since 1883. The newlyweds departed for Australia one month later arriving in Melbourne on March 30. On April 15, Spencer presented to the university administration plans for the establishment of the study of biology, including plans for a new laboratory building.

Spencer's skill in biology was strongest in descriptive anatomy. Between 1884 and 1886 he made eight contributions to scientific journals. These are notable for Spencer's excellent illustrations. Among his early research was the description of the eyelike conical gland, the parietal or median eye, of the reptile *Hatteria punctata* (now called *Sphenodon punctatus*). Other major work at this time was Spencer's preparation of a descriptive, illustrated atlas on the embryology of the chick.[29] In Australia, Spencer's descriptive studies began to be supplemented by field studies taken during his university vacations, on which he collected many specimens new to him. During one of his biological field trips, Spencer had his first contact with aborigines, an experience that stirred his interest in ethnography. In October 1892 he traveled to the Ebenezer Aboriginal Station on the Wimmera River near Lake Hindmarsh, in Queensland, to record and collect fauna in a mallee eucalypt environment. In the process he wrote notes on the aborigines and photographed them and the scarred trees from which they had removed the bark to make canoes. About this same time, Spencer made the acquaintance of two anthropologists, Alfred W. Howitt and Lorimer Fison, to whom he and Gillen would later dedicate *Native Tribes*. As one of the leading biologists in Australia, Spencer was beginning to expand his interest to anthropology. Given his background, the expansion was natural. As an evolutionist, Spencer was a social Darwinist. In culture, as in nature, he wanted to describe and illustrate stages in the evolutionary process. Aborigines were for him specimens of what he believed to be an early stage in the development of human culture. To record and describe these people was on a par with Spencer's descriptions of the reptilian parietal eye, the embryology of the chick, and the anatomy of the giant Gipsland earthworm (*Megascolides australis*).[30]

William Austin Horn (1841–1922) was a rugged individualist whose entrepreneurial success led him to wealth from mining fields and pastoral properties. He served a time in the South Australian parliament and aspired, though unsuccessfully, to achieve honors. Some believed that his philanthropy was gauged to these ends.[31] Whatever the case, Horn organized and funded a scientific expedition into Central Australia in 1894 that covered 2,000 miles on camel in fourteen weeks. The scientists in the party included an explorer and surveyor, anthropologist, paleontologist, ornithologist, naturalist, and taxidermist; Spencer was selected as biologist and photographer.[32] The objective was the systematic geological and mineralogical appraisal of the region, along with the description and collection of specimens of the flora and fauna, a description of the aboriginal inhabitants, and a collection of significant ethnographic objects. In his designated areas, Spencer's work was highly successful. In the area of zoology he described 398 genera (603 species) already known and 171 new species. In botany he found 8 new species, 16 others never recorded in South Australia, and 112 previously unknown to arid Australia.[33] But the significance of these achievements would eventually be overshadowed by Spencer's fortuitous meeting of Francis Gillen, the postmaster and telegraph officer in Alice Springs. Even before his arrival in Alice, Spencer had expressed much interest in aboriginal peoples, frequently sketching and photographing them. Something of the curiosity and character of Spencer was revealed by his volunteering enthusiastically to take a 330-mile side journey to Ayers Rock (now known as Uluru). This was an arduous journey, completed in twelve days. Spencer and two companions were the first scientists to visit Ayers Rock. During only thirty-six hours there, Spencer collected and recorded broadly across the spectrum of nature and culture.

This side trip was led by Police Constable Charles E. Cowle, who knew the area well. Cowle had agreed to lead this small party from Ayers Rock to Glen Helen for a rendezvous with the main group. After Ayers Rock, the party traveled to Palm Valley, where Spencer and his colleagues spent three busy days collecting and recording in this remarkable vestigial valley. The Lutheran mission station at Hermannsburg was immediately between Palm Valley and Glen Helen, and the party passed through Hermannsburg in July, when the station was without leadership. Cowle was antagonistic to the missionaries because of their attitude toward the ranchers and the police, whose job was to protect settlement interests. It is possible that Cowle's attitude toward Hermannsburg predisposed Spencer. Whatever the case, Spencer's views were highly negative.

It was mid-July when the caravan reached Alice Springs for a three-day stay. Spencer spent his days collecting zoological specimens, assisted by aborigines under the direction of Francis Gillen. Their evenings were filled with discussion about aborigines. When the expedition moved southward, Spencer remained in Alice Springs to continue his collection and his conversations. After three weeks he finally left, on August 6, hurrying to join the rest of the party.

As biologist, Spencer contributed much to the expedition, but as photographer, complemented by his growing interests in ethnography, he extended his contribution to anthropology. The task of editing the Horn expedition reports fell to Spencer. Despite the delinquency of several scientists, he persisted in the project, writing as much as half of the report himself. The results were published in 1896 in four separate volumes, perhaps the most substantial contribution to nineteenth-century Australian exploration. William Horn's gratitude to Baldwin Spencer is reflected in his son's name—Spencer.

Francis (Frank) James Gillen was born in South Australia on October 28, 1855, to Irish parents. He joined the postal department at the age of eleven and received an appointment to the Overland Telegraph in Darwin in 1875. He was later assigned to Alice Springs, where he supervised the repeater stations on the single-wire telegraph from Charlotte Waters to Tennant Creek. He was the senior South Australian public servant between Oodnadatta (north of Adelaide) and Darwin. Before Spencer's arrival in 1894, Gillen was a photographer and demonstrated interest in aborigines, although he primarily collected artifacts rather than ethnography.

Contact with Spencer ignited Gillen's enthusiasm for ethnography. During his leave from Alice Springs in the winter of 1895, Gillen spent some time with Spencer in Melbourne. Spencer introduced him to Howitt and Fison, who encouraged

Gillen by giving him the expectation for publication in journals with which they were connected. Spencer provided constant guidance from Melbourne by supplying Gillen with questions and queries. Gillen responded profusely. By the end of 1895 Spencer had received eighty-six pages of notes from Gillen in response to twenty-seven questions.[34] Gillen also began to maintain ethnographic journals.

Anticipating his upcoming summer vacation in December 1896, Spencer began to plan a biological field trip to Charlotte Waters, where he had had much success during the Horn expedition. He invited Gillen to join him there. Gillen, in his vigor for ethnographic collection, had other plans. He had arranged a performance of a large-scale initiation ceremony near the Alice Springs telegraph station for the benefit of his ethnographic collection. Gillen tempted Spencer away from Charlotte Waters and away from biology. Spencer began to realize the potential for publication of Gillen's work and suggested that Gillen consider writing a full ethnographic monograph. This prospect further fueled Gillen's interest, yet he insisted that Spencer be involved for his encouragement and scientific guidance. Gillen himself chose to remain ignorant of anthropological theory, depending on Spencer to keep abreast of it, which he did by consulting regularly with Howitt and Fison.[35]

Elder aborigines arranged the cycle of ceremonies, and groups of people began to arrive at the telegraph station in October. Gillen's provisioning of the affair was doubtless a major incentive. Spencer arrived the second week in November and spent much of his time until his departure, January 8, 1897, in a temporary shelter at the side of the ceremonial grounds where he and Gillen could observe and record the ritual events, performed at the rate of some five or six in every twenty-four-hour period. Spencer did not speak Arrernte, and Gillen's aboriginal language capabilities were limited. Much criticism has, and must, be made of this limitation to their ethnography.[36] Their interviews with elders had to rely on aboriginal English and on those aborigines who spoke it. Aborigines who spoke aboriginal English probably had limited knowledge of the more traditional aspects of their own culture. Still, Spencer recognized the importance of including native terminology and attempted to incorporate some native terms in his manuscript of *Native Tribes*. In his response to this aspect of the manuscript, Gillen wrote: "I note that you propose putting in some of the languages, is this worth while—no one seems to care much about the language of these people."[37] For Spencer and Gillen even to be able to communicate with their Arrernte consultants, they had to be assigned a classificatory relationship.[38] Gillen extended his assigned classification to Spencer by claiming that he was his younger brother. In *Native Tribes*, Spencer and Gillen indicate that they were regarded by the Arrernte as fully initiated members and thereby given unlimited access to information. Certainly they had no intention of claiming that they had undergone the long and painful initiation process, including head biting, circumcision, subincision, fasting, tooth extraction, and ordeal by fire. Yet the very process of observing and recording the ceremonials amounted to a formidable task. It was summer, and according to Spencer's field notes, it exceeded 100 degrees Fahrenheit on twenty-seven days, fell below 90 degrees only four times during his seven weeks, and once reached 114 degrees.

Spencer worked diligently to synthesize the information in Gillen's letters and journals with his own observations and records. He sent a stream of inquiries for clarification and completion to Gillen during the fall. By May he began to seek a publisher. Before Spencer had procured a publisher, he received a letter from James George Frazer, the famous author of *The Golden Bough*. This contact led quickly to Frazer's eager recommendation of Spencer and Gillen's book to Macmillan in London. But this contact also led Spencer and Gillen into the center of controversy concerning totemic models being constructed in Europe by eminent anthropological theorists, who were eagerly seeking connections with field workers from whom they might gain ethnographic support for their theories. The manuscript for *Native Tribes* was edited by Frazer and E. B. Tylor for publication in the beginning of 1899. Spencer traveled to England to deliver lectures and to be present for the publication of the work. Of the book, Frazer said: "In immortalising the native tribes of Central Australia, Spencer and Gillen have at the same time immortalised themselves."[39]

The Spencer and Gillen collaboration was widely acknowledged, and it was not long before they had begun preparation for longer field studies. In 1899 Gillen left Alice Springs to be stationed at Moonta in South Australia. The pair planned a field study that would record the tribes through a thousand-mile swath in the northern parts of Central Australia. They embarked in March 1901 on this year-long field study, culminating in the publication of *The Northern Tribes of Central Australia* (1904).

Spencer's contributions were widely honored, whereas Gillen was ignored and even passed over for promotion. Highest among his honors, Spencer was made a Companion of the Order of St. Michael and St. George in 1904. By this time Gillen had contracted amyotrophic lateral sclerosis, from which he eventually died on June 5, 1912.

Spencer returned to the field in 1913, to the Alligator River area in Arnhem Land in far northern Australia, now assisted by Paddy Cahill. This field trip produced *The Native Tribes of the Northern Territory* (1914). Again Spencer went to England to deliver the *Northern Territory* manuscript and enthralled Frazer and others with his slide lectures. Spencer was active in university administration for a number of years before his 1920 retirement, and he played an active role in the formation of federal law regarding aborigines.

It was after his retirement that the government contacted Spencer, in 1923, to enquire into the conditions of part-aboriginal children in Alice Springs. Spencer returned to Hermannsburg and once again filed a highly negative report on the institution, which was left leaderless following Carl Strehlow's death.[40] Spencer had paid his respects to Strehlow by visiting his grave at Horseshoe Bend, but he could not tolerate the institution Strehlow had worked his life to build. It was during this journey to Central Australia that Spencer began to realize the full importance of his and Gillen's anthropological achievement. He saw the enormity of the changes that had occurred in aboriginal cultures since he and Gillen did their field study in 1896. Further, Spencer was reminded that the only alternative to his and Gillen's work on the Arrernte was Carl Strehlow's work. Spencer, always antagonistic to Hermannsburg practices and policies, was unhappy with Strehlow's attempts, published in German in five volumes between 1907 and 1920, to correct and complete his and Gillen's work. During this visit, Spencer decided that he must return one final time to do field work for the revision of *Native Tribes*, paying particular attention to a response to the late Strehlow.

In 1926 Spencer was gone from Melbourne for eleven weeks, and part of his travel to Alice Springs was accomplished by automobile. He stayed with Police Constable Sergeant Robert Stott, who had replaced Gillen in 1899 as the focus of Alice Springs administration. Spencer's principal aboriginal informant was Stott's head tracker, Charlie Cooper. As police officers, neither Stott nor Cooper was respected by aborigines. Cooper was the only person Spencer found that had been involved in his 1896 field study. Spencer was particularly pleased that Cooper had, since that time, learned aboriginal English. Although Spencer indicated that he checked with a number of elders, it was Cooper's interpretation of their remarks that had to be relied on.[41]

Spencer spent six months preparing the revision of *Native Tribes*, to be entitled *The Arunta: A Study of a Stone Aged People*, which was published, again by Macmillan, in 1927. It retained the original joint Spencer and Gillen authorship and was dedicated "To Our Master Sir James George Frazer."

Spencer returned to England in June 1927, where he enjoyed the encomia for his life's work and prepared for an expedition to Tierra del Fuego among the Onas. He sailed from Newcastle in February 1929. His winter arrival and several unfortunate decisions contributed to the unfortunate end of this expedition. After a brief illness, Spencer died in a hut at Murray Narrows, Hoste Island, near Cape Horn in July 1929.[42]

Strehlow and Spencer: A Crossroads

Carl Strehlow and Baldwin Spencer never met face to face, but their storytracks often crossed. The point of one intersection can be located exactly on the Arrernte word *altjira*. On the very first page of the first volume of Carl Strehlow's *Die Aranda*, the first section is entitled "Altjira." In this section Strehlow reports Arrernte belief in "a being, called Altjira, who embodies the highest good (*mara*). This being is eternal (*ngambakula*), and is thought to be a tall, strong man with a red skin colour and long, fair hair (*gola*) which flows over his shoulders."[43] This work was published in 1907, eight years after Spencer and Gillen's *Native Tribes*. Spencer received word of Strehlow's "discovery" years before its publication. A letter written in 1901 in which Strehlow described Arrernte beliefs made its way to anthropologist Andrew Lang, presumably because he was a critic of James G. Frazer's understanding of religion. Lang used information from Strehlow's letter in his book *Social Origins* (1903). On December 1, 1903, Spencer received from Lang a copy of Strehlow's report on Altjira with a request for his explanation.[44] Spencer soon expressed his outrage to Lang and to Frazer. To Frazer he wrote (December 9, 1903):

> I have just had to write a long letter to Lang in reply to one of his enclosing a short paper by a Lutheran missionary named Strehlow stationed at the outlying Mission station in the south-west corner of Arunta land. . . . Twenty years ago a man named Kempe, one of the first missionaries, seized upon the word Altjira (= our [i.e., Spencer and Gillen's] Alcheri) and adopted it as the word for "God". He knew nothing of its significance to the natives, or of its association with the word "Alchiringa" (*Acheri* = dream; *ringa* = of, belonging to), but he saw that it had some special or sacred significance. Now after these twenty years (when the station has not been closed or the missionaries away) of endeavouring to teach the poor natives that Altjira means "God", Strehlow comes forward with the momentous discovery that in the Arunta, "*there is a Being of the highest order called Altjira or Altjira mara*" (*mara* = good); that Twanyirika [the name of one of the first two ancestors who performed circumcision] has wife and child and "is the leader of the circumcision"; that "Altjira is the highest divinity; he is the creator of the world and maker of men" (sounds rather Scriptural). The paper only occupies 1½ pp. foolscap, but has more utter misleading nonsense packed into a small space than I recollect having come across before. . . .
>
> If you see it stated that the Arunta can now be added to the long list of savage tribes who believe in an "All-Father" and "High God", you will understand what it means. The trouble is, how are people to determine what is truth and what is not?[45]

Indeed!

Upon receiving a copy of Strehlow's first volume of *Die Aranda*, Frazer wrote to Spencer requesting his remarks on the work and on Strehlow "as an anthropologist."[46] Spencer's remarks, dated March 10, 1908, reveal the level of his hostility and irritation: "I don't know what to do in regard to Strehlow. He is so uneducated that he can't write publishable German. Lang sent me his original MS., and there is no wonder that it had to be edited by an educated man; how much and in what direction it becomes changed in the process of editing of course we do not know, but that it does become changed I am sure."[47] Spencer immediately launched into a repeat of his historical explanation for Strehlow's claims and concluded that "it seems to me that he has got things muddled up in hopeless fashion."[48] Frazer took Spencer's opinion seriously and wrote him in April that he intended to make no use of Strehlow's work; he asked Spencer to publish his criticism since "the shakiness of Strehlow's facts ought to be known here in Europe."[49]

But theories of religion and culture were being rapidly spun and hotly contested in Europe, and those theorists who found support in Strehlow criticized Spencer and Gillen for what appeared to be their oversight. R. R. Marrett and T. K. Penniman, the editors of Spencer's correspondence, believed that Spencer's 1926 field study was largely motivated by his desire to show "that there was no shadow of a conception of a god among the Arunta."[50] His final statements on the matter are directed to Strehlow (by then dead), though he may have felt he was defending himself against all those who in upholding Strehlow's work had criticized him (and Gillen, by then dead for fifteen years).

The Arunta contains his final sally against Strehlow. The preface to the book contains the more personal assault and appendix D his fullest statement attacking

Strehlow's high-god discovery. Spencer warns that "it must be remembered that Mr. Strehlow's work, admirable as it is, was done entirely in the study and was based wholly on information gained from natives who had been, for at least twenty-five years, not only under the influence of the missionaries, but also dependent upon them."[51] In his appendix, entitled "The Alchera Belief and Traditions," the extent of Spencer's citations, much greater than in most of his work, reflects his long and thorough investigation of the term *altjira*.

To build greater evidence that Strehlow was discovering a belief that was itself introduced by the missionaries, Spencer turns to publications before Strehlow's time. He cites not only the early Hermannsburg missionaries Kempe and Schulze but also half a dozen others who published from 1874 to the end of the decade. He notes that Schulze, writing for 1891 publication, had described an excavation made on the sides of graves that was referred to as "*Tmara altjira*—the place where the mother of the dead person was born—that is, her altjira camp."[52] Spencer and Gillen had made a similar observation. Spencer's point was to show that the term *altjira* in Schulze's understanding was used to refer to "something associated with past times, and not the name of any person or individual."[53] Citing other uses Schulze made of the word *altjira*, Spencer found none in which it referred to a person or a god.[54]

Considering Krichauff's 1886 account, based on letters from Schulze and Kempe, Spencer holds that three of the names of the five gods attributed to the Arrernte are actually names of places, that is, ceremonial centers related to ancestors of the groups linked with these names. Spencer argues that the connection that the Arrernte would make with these place names is that they are locations "intimately associated with the far past times—the Alchera—during which the great ancestors of the tribe wandered over the country."[55]

After criticizing Strehlow's belief that there is no linguistic connection between *altjira* and *dreaming*, thus denying Spencer and Gillen's rendering of "Alcheringa" [their spelling] as "dream time," Spencer attempts to show that the genesis of Altjira as the name of a high god lies with the missionaries. He cites Kempe's grammar in rendering *Altjirala jingala etata tnema* as "God to me life gives." Finally, Spencer quotes a letter he reports having received from Kempe in 1910:

> As regards the word "Altjira" in the language of the natives of Central Australia, I beg to tell you that, so far as I know the language, it is not "God" in that sense in which we use the word—namely, as a personal being—but it has a meaning of old, very old, something that has no origin, mysterious, something that has always been so, also, always. Were *Altjira* an active being, they would have answered "*Altjirala*": the syllable "*la*" is always added when a person exercises a will (force) which influences another being or thing. We have adopted the word [*Altjira* for] "God" because we could find no better and because it comes nearest to the idea of "eternal." The people through the usage of a word often use it as a name for a person. This, according to my conviction, is the true meaning of the word *Altjira*.[56]

Finally, Spencer, having trooped out all his evidence, concludes that "there can be no doubt that *Alchera* (or *Altjira*) is not a High God, or, in fact, a name applied to any individual.[57] It is a term used in reference to everything associated with the far-past, mysterious and mythic times that 'belong to dreams,' that always existed, and in which their early ancestors, endowed with powers far greater than their descendants now possess, came into existence, lived, moved about and died, leaving behind them their spirit parts, which have since given rise to the natives of the present day."[58]

Carl Strehlow certainly describes Altjira as "a being . . . who embodies the highest good." But did he intend to proclaim that the Arrernte are among those peoples who believe in a high god? In his comments appended to the description of Altjira, Strehlow notes his inability to provide a linguistic derivation of the word *Altjira* and indicates that the aborigines assured him that "Altjira refers to him who has no beginning, who did not issue from another."[59] This, of course, would designate any of the mythic ancestral figures. He notes that Spencer and Gillen's claim that *alcheri* means "dream" is incorrect. Strehlow holds that *altjirerama* means "to dream," and it is derived from *altjira* and *rama*, in other words, "to see god." Then he writes: "It will be demonstrated later that altjira and *tukura* [the Loritja correspondent to *altjira*] in this context do not refer to the highest God in the sky but merely to a totem god which the native believes to have seen in a dream."[60] Strehlow states that the Loritja counterpart for Altjira is Tukura. In contrast with his stated intentions, he refers to this god as "the supreme being," linking the name with the Loritja concept of "the Non-created One."[61] The Western Loritja believe that Tukura has emu feet, but the Southern Loritja, according to Strehlow, believe that he has human feet. He has only one wife and one child, whereas the Arrernte's Altjira has many wives and children.

In his discussion of "the totemic conceptions of the Aranda and Loritja," Strehlow returns to the word *altjira*, which he now identifies as the totem of one's mother. He explains that although all of the children of one mother may each belong to a different totem, they all share another totem, *altjira*, which "may be viewed as their providing and protecting god, like a mother feeds and protects her children during the early years of their lives.[62] This *altjira* appears to the blacks in dreams and warns them of danger, just as he speaks of them to friends while they are sleeping."[63] Further, in his discussion of "the tjurunga of the Aranda and Loritja," Strehlow again uses *altjira* in the sense of one's mother's totem. When a boy has been circumcised, he is given a large bullroarer, which "represents the mysterious body of his maternal totem ancestor, his *altjira*. . . . [the bullroarer] is engraved with designs relating to the respective *altjira* [i.e.], . . . to his mother's totem, since his *altjiri* will accompany him from this time onward on all his journeys."[64]

Although Strehlow followed the precedent established by the missionaries before him in using *Altjira* as the best Arrernte term by which to render the name of the Christian God, based on a careful reading of his ethnographic publication, *Die Aranda*, it does not appear that he was necessarily proclaiming anything like the high god Spencer and others saw in his work. His intentions in this respect are inconclusive since Strehlow uses terms such as *highest good* for the Arrernte and *supreme being* for the Loritja. It must be remembered that Strehlow was trained as a Christian missionary and had little, if any, idea of the impact the phrases he used would elicit among those discussing anthropological theory.

Certainly Spencer's perhaps too narrow reading of Strehlow and the passion of his response are understandable. In Spencer's view of the world, as a biological and cultural evolutionist and as a protégé to Frazer, the aborigines represented a pre-religious stage in evolution, the stage of magic.[65] Spencer could not admit that there was anything religious about the aborigines. The term *religion* is not an entry in the index of any one of his books. Any report that might indicate the presence of any figure that could resemble a high god was not simply a complementary factum recorded by another ethnographer; it was also a challenge to Spencer's and Frazer's understanding of the world. The presence of a high god to whom one might pray, in contrast with mythic ancestors who were manipulated by ritual magic, was recognized as an important and distinct component of religion. The passionate emotion in Spencer's challenge, directed even at Strehlow's nationality and intelligence, was perhaps actually more a response to Strehlow's apparent ignorance of, or failure to comply with, Spencer's and Frazer's theory of cultural evolution.

Strehlow, on the other hand, as a Christian, believed in the creation of a single world by the one God, the common creation of all humans into the present full state of humanity. All the Arrernte needed was to be led into the light of Christianity. That they should believe in some gods or spiritual beings was a welcome connection and perhaps evidence of some residue of primordial religion that acknowledged God's creation. The motivation for the mission study of the Arrernte language was directed primarily toward bringing them to Christianity. The translation work still in progress by the Finke River Mission is to present Christian scripture and teachings to the Arrernte in their own language. As Kempe noted, Christianization requires a study of the Arrernte language at least partly directed toward finding suitable Arrernte terms for Christian terms expressed in German and English. Strehlow, as the other missionaries before him, frequently used the word *religion* to refer to aspects of aboriginal culture.

In Strehlow's description, Altjira has the feet of an emu and his many wives have legs like dogs. Both Altjira and his wives have skin red in color. He is tall and strong, with hair flowing over his shoulders. He lives in the sky, which has always existed. The sky is a mass of land through which runs a great river, the Milky Way.[66] In the Horn expedition report, in his article on Arrernte customs, Gillen includes under "Beliefs and Superstitions" the account of the Arrernte belief in two figures. One is Kurdaitcha, a malevolent figure, whose emu feather shoes leave no tracks. The other is Ulthaana, of whom Gillen wrote: "The sky is said to be inhabited by three persons—a gigantic man with an immense foot shaped like that of the emu, a woman, and a child who never develops beyond childhood. The man is called *Ulthaana*, meaning spirit. When a native dies, his spirit is said to ascend to the home of the great *Ulthaana*, where it remains for a short time; the *Ulthaana* then throws it into the Salt-water (sea)."[67] Strehlow did not miss the similarity of Gillen's report to his own. Noting that Gillen's description was more similar to his Loritja version than to his Arrernte version, principally because of the number of wives and children, Strehlow held that Gillen must have gotten his information from a Loritja person.[68]

It is also notable that Spencer, the editor of the Horn expedition report, seemingly never connected Gillen's record with Strehlow's descriptions.

This story of the interaction of perspectives, like all stories, has some interesting and unexpected turns. In a footnote to his discussion of Strehlow's text in *The Arunta*, which he quotes in full, Spencer comments on Strehlow's use of the term *ngambakala*: "This is the same word as *Ungambikula*, previously used by us [i.e., he and Gillen] as applied by the natives to two beings living in the western sky (*alkira aldorla*), who, according to one tradition, came down to earth and made the first men and women. . . . In the Achilpa tradition he is called *Numbakulla*."[69] Of course, the final sentence in this note refers directly to the account of Numbakulla provided by Charlie Cooper, which Spencer added to the 1927 edition of his and Gillen's work. Strehlow's use of *ngambakala* is clearly adjectival. In his footnote, as in the full account, Spencer allows the term to slip into the role of a proper noun, as when he wrote: "he is called *Numbakulla*."

It would seem a remarkable irony that in Spencer's efforts to remove any doubt at all that the Arrernte held no belief in a high god, he accomplished the opposite in the very book he so hoped would settle the controversy once and for all. By including the new chapter on Numbakulla, and even in his response to Strehlow, Spencer gave others the evidence he so hoped to quash. Certainly Eliade had no difficulty in recognizing in Spencer's account the presence of what Eliade took to be an aboriginal high god. One wonders what could have caused Spencer to be so careless. It can only be supposed that despite Spencer's agnosticism and evolutionist intellectual theories, his cultural heritage—a Christian and Western intellectual heritage—was so deep that he could not muster enough critical self-awareness to prevent what must have seemed to him the necessity for a named creator of the world and its people. There is another possibility. Much of Spencer's biological training and research focused on the use of comparative anatomy to describe a morphology, an ahistocial description of the structure of an organism. In the natural sciences, mophological patterns were given a temporal interpretation by the evolutionist hypothesis. Spencer tenaciously upheld a multiple-era schema into which he forced the classification of Arrernte mythology. Although the periods are temporally marked, they function primarily morphologically. Perhaps in applying the morphological model to mythology, Spencer had only Western religious patterns, which call for a high-god creator, to distinguish the first structural stage. By incorporating a creator into his morphological schema, Spencer undermined his evolutionary position. He indicates no awareness of the illegitimacy of this hybrid. The models and abstractions of culture and religion that Spencer inherited were apparently so real as to be beyond challenge. Thus he had to simulate Arrernte cultural details to ensure their participation in the reality of his model. It cannot be doubted that Spencer would have been rudely shocked to have seen Eliade's use and interpretation of his work. Furthermore, one wonders if Eliade would have maintained his use of "Numbakulla and the Sacred Pole" had he carefully read all of Spencer's *The Arunta*.

Origination and the Primal Crime/Primal Scene

Sigmund Freud made tracks, though from afar, on the Australian landscape by publishing his *Totem and Taboo* (1913). He tracked humankind to its psychological origins. It was in the Australian landscape, known to him only through published sources on Australian cultures, that Freud found the peoples he believed revealed evidence of the events that gave birth to humanity, civilization, and (most important for Freud) the human psyche and the history of neurosis. As so many others in the late nineteenth and early twentieth centuries who were influenced by the intellectual milieu of evolutionism, Freud sought explanation and presented theory in terms of origination. He presented the scenario of the primal crime, the "one day" event of sons killing their father, who controlled sexual access to the mother and to her daughters.

In 1929 Géza Róheim traveled to Australia to confirm through field studies Freud's primal crime theory, although by that time it had fallen into neglect, apart from being the occasional subject of residual scorn. By the late 1920s, the fervor regarding origination had passed, though Róheim, who died in 1953, continued to follow this storytrack through the balance of his academic career. His *Australian Totemism* (1925) had amassed information from published sources, but they were sorely lacking the kind of information of particular interest to psychoanalysis—dreams and accounts of sexual practices. In preparation for *Australian Totemism*, Róheim had carefully read Spencer's and Strehlow's published works, as well as much of the published ethnographic work on Australian aborigines. He claimed that aboriginal people were impressed by his extensive knowledge of their cultures, and he spent considerable time checking the accuracy of the published sources with them. The orienting and motivating forces of Róheim's storytrack are not difficult to identify, in that he was radically Freudian and his principal effort was to found the field of psychoanalytic anthropology, a field he believed would be the anthropology of the future.[70]

Numbakulla

In the Finke River area, Róheim found, as did Carl Strehlow before him, that the Tjilpa (Wildcat) totem had a major father figure named Malpunga. He also found this figure in Spencer's *The Aranda* in the section of the Tjilpa Wanderings, which Spencer collected in 1926 from Charlie Cooper, that is, the same Numbakulla account that is the crossing place for several other storytracks. In Spencer's account, Malpunga is spelled "Tmalpunga." Róheim presents an extensive but uncritical summary of Spencer's account.[71] In less than two pages, Róheim summarizes eighteen pages from Spencer. Although Róheim begins his account with a reference to Numbakulla (which he spells "Nambakalla") and in the first paragraph describes his actions, Róheim is primarily interested in the Malpunga figure (there are actually two of them), whom, as the ancestor to the wildcats, he considers to be a typical mythic father. Malpunga is extraordinarily phallic. When he runs, his penis hits his leg. His penis is so long that sometimes Malpunga carries it over his shoulder. The phallic Malpunga is, for Róheim, the prototype of all great wanderers. In the myths, he always walks behind the young men, his penis perpetually erect: "His penis is his tjurunga or his ceremonial pole, and it is with this ceremonial pole, or *tnatandja*, that he opens the road for future generations."[72] Róheim establishes an identity among walking, feet, and Malpunga's erect penis.[73]

Róheim puts his interpretation of the wildcat myth and ritual in the context of his discussion of the distinction between, yet continuity with, two Arrernte religions: the primal demon religion and the later totemic religion.[74] In this myth he found evidence of both forms of religion, although a careful comparison of his summary of Spencer's text reveals that he introduces the demon imagery without justification.

Róheim draws on Spencer's and Carl Strehlow's published materials, selectively engaging often sophisticated criticism at points of particular value to support his interest in the text. His interest is unambiguous: the demonstration of the psychoanalytic principal of utilizing the primal scene as the foundation for an interpretation and explanation derived from the Oedipal matrix. For Róheim, Numbakulla, the supposed great creator from the sky, is scarcely of interest. His attention is drawn to the great phallic father, Malpunga, who appears in the Numbakulla myths. Neither Spencer nor Strehlow was interested in the phallic character of this figure, both either suppressing this element or never eliciting it from their Arrernte informants. Róheim saw Malpunga as prototypical of the great wandering ancestors, whom he believed were also "great initiators." Their two main functions were to travel from place to place and to initiate young men.[75] Róheim postulates an original form of the ancestral wanderings myth as none other than "our old friend, the *Primal Horde Myth*."[76] Róheim holds that these "myths of transition" help young men to grow up, to "make the transition from the Oedipus situation to marriage. But the Primal Horde is *ex hypothesi* a period of transition in phylogenesis from a prehuman to a human form of society. We should not forget that the myths themselves always purport to explain the existing order of things from something that has preceded, that is, they describe a transition. The essential theme is the relation of the individual to the object-world, and libidinal cathexis as the defense used by human beings to bear the deprivations of object loss and separation."[77]

Altjira

Fully aware of the fray between Carl Strehlow and Baldwin Spencer over the term *altjira*, Róheim turns to the old Arrernte men—Moses, Renana, and Yirramba—to help him clarify the issue. The word *altjira* denotes mythical ancestors in general, not a single individual. Ngambakala[78] qualifies all *altjira*, that is, all mythic ancestors, in that they are all uncreated and indestructible. Strehlow's designation of Altjira as good (*mara*), is, in Róheim's understanding of Arrernte classification, a qualification of everything that is not a demon or monster (*erintja*), an enemy (*leltja*), violent (*aknara*), or wanton (*tnaputa*). Róheim concludes that *altjiranga mitjina* means "the eternal ones from the dream" or "the eternal people who come from dreams."[79] Eternity is understood by Róheim to be a religious concept, and he makes considerable effort to understand it as an aboriginal concept. The eternal ones of the dream are *knanaka kuta*, or "originated immortal."

Róheim contests Strehlow's classification of the figure he called Altjira by offering the story of a figure, *Altjira-iliinka*, that he heard from his informant Yirramba.

> He sits in a great hut (*ilta knarra*) in the Western Sky. The stars (*ndailpura*) are his camp-fires, his sons are little emus (*ilia kurka*), his daughters are dog-footed (*knulja-inka*); but he himself is a real man (*atua ndurpa*), except for his emu-feet. He carries a *tjimbilli* (bundle of magic sticks) under his arm, with which he kills the people whom he hates. He is a great sorcerer (*nankara*-man) and he possesses more *nankara* (magical stones) than earthly sorcerers. He is bad (*kona*) and he possesses stores of black magic (*arunkulta*). He has many wives and daughters who are also stars like his sons. The answer to the question 'Where does he come from (*iwuna knanakala*)?' was as follows: '*Antjua* (nest, i.e. the nest of the emu), that is his *knanindja* (totem or origin)'. He also has *tjurunga talkara* (stone *tjurungas*); but his most characteristic possession is his *tjimbilli* and the *nankara*-stones.[80]

Accounts of other related myths are presented not only from the Arrernte but also from other aboriginal cultures. Róheim's comparison of these stories revealed to him a "remarkable equivalence between . . . very good and very evil beings."[81] Against the background of recognizing two religions—the totemic religion, which features the *altjira mitjina*, and the primal religion of monsters and demons—Róheim reinterprets of this myth complex:

> The myth connects the Milky Way with the initiation ceremonies, which in the narrative include or are interrupted by the journey to the sky. The Milky Way is the abode of a supernatural being who is sometimes regarded as a good and helpful spirit (Yumu, Pindupi, Pitchentara), sometimes as the incarnation of all evil magic (Eastern and Northern Aranda), and who belongs more to the mythology of the demons than to that of the ancestral spirits. A striking feature is his misshapen foot and his affinity with the emu mythology. He is born from an emu nest, he has emu feet, his sons are little emus, and he hunts emus. Moreover, he appears either as a single or as a dual being. Such dual heroes are widely spread in Australia and can be seen in the sky as Magellan's clouds, or as the constellations in the neighbourhood of these clouds. . . .
>
> The sagas [including the Emu-footed *Altjira* of Strehlow's account] are concerned with a newly circumcised youth and a female demon, the pleasurable and terrifying idea of their eternal union in copulation being represented by the two pieces of wood fastened together, that is, by the *waninga*[82] cross in the Milky Way. Thus the *waninga*, perhaps even more sacred attribute of the totemic cult than the *tjurunga*, is quite clearly a representative of a copulating pair, that is, of the primal scene situation. On the other hand, however, there are no hard and fast lines between the primal scene and the projected, but not united, genitals of the two sexes. The Ngatatara call the two dark patches in the Milky Way *ngapa-tjinbis*. A *ngapa-tjinbi* is a ceremonial object made of two crossed wooden *tjurungas* wound round with thread like a *waninga*. The associated myth exactly corresponds with the Waninga myth of the couple joined in coitus.[83]

Róheim thus proposes that the Milky Way is the setting of a primal scene transported to the sky. *Altjira-iliinka*, like other parallel figures in other Central Australian cultures, is distinguished by the peculiarity of his emu feet. Róheim recalls that the equation between foot and penis is common in Central Australia. Thus he argues that the primal god is thought to be a monster or demon because he is a projection of the phallic father in the primal scene. The identification of this evil being as good is explained by Róheim as the result of the powers of sublimation, which replace negative attributes of these figures with good ones.[84]

Origination is the key element in Róheim's understanding of *altjira*, the eternal ones of the dream, for they are the ones who had no mother; they originated from themselves:

> Their immortality is a denial of separation anxiety. In their origin myths fully-formed spirit children emerge from pouches carried by the ancestors. In one sense this is a denial of fatherhood (Oedipus complex) but in another sense a denial of motherhood, with the mythical being and the pouch replacing the mother. Separation from the mother is painful; the child is represented in myth as fully formed, even before it enters the mother. The *tjurunga* from which it is born is both a phallic and a maternal symbol. The real mothers may decay, but with immortal mothers we become immortal ourselves.[85]

In his play with children, Róheim found that they played two games that sometimes merged into one. These were make-believe games. One was called Altjira (*tukurpa* in Loritja). Noting that in this context the term *altjira* means "dream," Róheim understood the game as the dramatization of daydreams. Altjira, the dream or oracle game, uses sticks and leaves to represent figures interacting with one another, according to Róheim, usually enacting coitus. In the other game, *tjitjipanga*—which means "I will do what I saw the old people doing"—children themselves enact the roles, which he identifies as scenes of parents copulating. Róheim's analysis runs thus: "The oracle or dream game is a reversal of the original situation; the player sees small objects (gum leaves) in the act of coitus, i.e. the father or mother looking at the children enjoying themselves. While the actual situation is in the reversed relation the scene represented by the game is the original one, the child seeing the married life of the adults."[86] Notably this discussion of children's games rests on the notion of the "primal scene," that is, the infant's observation of parental coitus. Róheim extended the discussion of *altjira* from children's games to adult behavior. He argued that, like children, adults play games when they are unable to gratify all their instinctual desires. Their play is called "ritual." They, too, play *altjira*, and their legendary heroes are *altjira*.[87]

At crossroads, such as Numbakulla and *altjira*, where Róheim's storytrack intersects those of others, the motivation of his interests and the framework for his interpretations are seen to be his abiding concern with origination. His identification of *altjira* with dream, myth, children's games, and adult ritual gave him an equivalency set, in that they all engage the primal scene. These Arrernte genre were also seen as being interconnected with the roots of psychoanalysis, classical Western mythology, and the evidence from clinical psychoanalysis. Róheim focused on the riddle of the sphinx to interweave all these materials into a coherent psychoanalytic, anthropological story.

The Riddle of the Sphinx

According to the story of Oedipus, after he killed Laius he hurried to Thebes. There he encountered the Sphinx, a cannibalistic monster with a woman's head, wings, and the body of a lion. Whoever could defeat the Sphinx would win the hand of Queen Jocasta and the crown of Thebes. To every passerby the monster presented a riddle. To solve the riddle was to defeat the Sphinx. To fail to do so was to provide it with dinner or its equivalent; it would spring upon the victim, strangle him, and carry him off into the air. *Sphinx* means "strangler." The riddle: what is the being that has one name, but first four feet, then two feet, and then three feet? Oedipus's answer was man, since at first he crawls on all fours, then walks upright on two legs, and in old age adds a cane to help him walk.

The riddle of the Sphinx is a focus for Róheim's consideration of the origination of religion and the human psyche. He believed that the riddle contained an "important part of the history of the human mind."[88] For analysis, he placed the Sphinx in the context of a whole class of female monsters characterized as ambiguous creatures, enticing and dangerous, who love but devour. The riddle he placed in the context of a genre of leg riddles. The psychoanalytic context is the "primal scene," that is, the event that may occur during the period of infant sexuality when the child witnesses parental coitus. Seeing the father's penis and the mother's vagina, or more properly seeing the mother as lacking genitals, evokes anxiety.

Thus Róheim argues that the riddle of the Sphinx is concerned with the primal scene, that since the Sphinx's death coincides with the solution of the riddle, it is herself the riddle's object.[89] That is, the Sphinx is the one with four legs (its body is that of a lion), then two legs (it is also woman), and then three legs (it has a penis[90]). Thus concludes Róheim: "The Sphinx herself then is the being with the indefinite number of legs, the father and mother in one person, and a representative of the two fundamental tendencies of the Oedipus situation which are awakened in the child when he observes the primal scene. In very truth only 'Swollen Foot' [i.e., Oedipus] can solve this riddle of the feet; for he is the victorious hero of the Oedipus tragedy of all mankind."[91]

From Phylogeny to Ontogeny

Róheim's mentors, Freud and Sándor Ferenczi, were interested in establishing a phylogenetic explanation for human origins and for the origin of religion. They sought the moment, the event, that marked the transition between ape and human. They correlated stages of psychological development and categories of psychoneuroses with stages of human development. For example, Róheim's mentors identified the rise of the latency period, between the end of infantile sexuality and puberty, with the Ice Age.[92] The issue, at least as Róheim saw it, was not to establish the existence of the primal horde since much existing evidence from apes was consulted as foundational. The problem was to demonstrate the transition to full humanity. Freud's resolution of this problem was to advance the primal crime hypothesis: "One day the brothers who had been driven out together, killed and devoured their father and so put an end of the patriarchal horde. United, they had the courage to do and succeed in doing what would have been impossible for them individually. (Some cultural advance, perhaps, command over some new weapon, had given them a sense of superior strength.) Cannibal savages as they were, it goes without saying that they devoured their victim as well as killing him. . . ."[93]

Róheim initially supported Freud's phylogenetic explanation. He acknowledged certain problems others raised about the approach, though he thought them unfounded. The problem, hammered by critics, had to do with Freud's understanding of time, his seeing the event as actually occurring "one day,"[94] that is, at some specifiable time. Róheim's understanding of Freud's view of time is important. He held that "the Freudian picture is intended to be a compressed and dramatic representation of the facts. 'The father' stands for generations of fathers, and 'the brothers' for generations of brothers—such, at least, is the meaning I have always attributed to these terms."[95] Róheim described Freud's primal crime hypothesis as a "story," explaining that Freud "imagined a hypothetical primal horde with a jealous leader who kept his sons from all his wives."[96] Róheim understood Freud's intent to be dealing with the period of transition between apes and humans. Róheim argued the essence of the primal horde hypothesis, in the simplest of terms. If the Oedipal complex can be accepted at all, it must have had a first appearance at some time in human history and that time must, according to the theory, have coincided with the rise of humankind. "There must have been a period when the Oedipean impulses which are now repressed by the super-ego were realized in acts; and the development of the super-ego (the introjection of the prohibiting father, the strengthening of the father identification) must have been facilitated by the absence of satisfaction expected from such deeds."[97]

The logic of this argument places priority on the demonstration of the theory in the present, in the clinic and in psychoanalytic anthropology. Róheim directs his attention first to ontogenesis, thus shifting the approach his mentors took to these anthropological materials, but remaining focused on origination. In consequence, for Róheim the primal scene is foremost that of the traumata of infantile sexuality. Only when this origination is established can one translate ontogenesis into the framework of phylogenesis. Róheim proposed, for example, the following hypothesis: "Humanity has emerged, as a human being emerges to-day, by the growth of defense mechanisms against the infantile situation, by the development of the unconscious."[98]

Arguing that the relationship between adults and children is formative, particularly interactions that produce infantile traumata, Róheim cites clinical studies to support this position. In the dual correlation between infant trauma and the pathologies of the clinic, Róheim held that every culture, particularly "primitive cultures," can be reduced to a "formula like a neurosis or a dream." For the Arrernte that formula is "a people who have repressed the '*alknarintja* [i.e., the mother sleeping on her son, thus appearing to have a penis] situation' and, for this reason, make a vagina on their penises (subincision) and decorate their *tjurungas* (penis symbol) with concentric circles (vagina symbols)."[99] Róheim argues that if one can develop an ontogenetic interpretation of culture, it should be possible to describe the origin of culture in ontogenetic terms, "that is, of deriving it from a specifically human form of childhood, from a permanent, universal, and at the same time historic, cause."[100]

Róheim's solution to the riddle of the sphinx is his insight into the primacy of ontogenesis. The solution to the riddle, as the Sphinx itself, is constructed on Róheim's concern with ontogenesis: "A human being is what he is by the elaboration of his infantile impressions (primal scene). The Sphinx (primal scene) is the riddle that has to be solved by Oedipus (mankind), and there are two solutions to this riddle, either the Sphinx-mother or Oedipus, the human child."[101] Róheim's revision, a reversal of Freud's approach, clarifies Freud's understanding of time and sidesteps the criticism directed toward Freud. Yet, it also accomplishes more.

Meaning of Primal Scene

Psychoanalysis, as Róheim understood it, depended on discerning an event or events on which to anchor the psychic history and condition of his patients. This anchoring event was commonly referred to as the primal scene. At the conclusion of his play sessions with the Arrernte and Loritja children, Róheim draws to a close his analysis of Depitarinja (a ten-year-old Arrernte boy):

> We should therefore conclude that he has seen something [Rohiem termed it the "primal scene"] which affected him deeply and in which his father played a significant part. He is showing the same thing in the language of transference, taking my place in the chair [which the boy did when Róheim was not present], identifying himself with me and imitating me. It is therefore a legitimate inference to suppose that the other mirror-scene [the mirrors in Róheim's kitchen showed traces of where the boy had been "kissing himself"] shews [*sic*] what he was imitating. The goat [a toy], that is, he himself, in the monkey's [another toy] vagina and Nyiki's [a boy] demon-lover showing her anus to Nyiki are therefore imitations of what he has observed [i.e., the primal scene] of the father cohabiting with the mother. It is in this act that the child wishes to take his father's place and love his mother. But having replaced his father he also envies his mother's happiness; and here we see Depitarinja the father kissing his reflection, i.e. Depitarinja the child.[102]

Róheim reports a similar scenario from his clinical practice. A twenty-year-old woman was suffering from melancholia after an unpleasant love affair. She often could not interact with her mother and brother except in "horror and anxiety" because of fantasies that her mother was having sexual intercourse with her brother. She also had fantasies of her father masturbating or having sexual intercourse with her. Róheim's analysis led him to the primal scene: "She had often observed her parents' intercourse until her third year, and had been so excited that she had screamed. She had repressed these strong impressions, but what was repressed had determined her whole life."[103] This analysis parallels Freud's famous analysis of the "wolf man."[104]

Róheim frequently used the term *primal scene*. He meant either an experience of infancy that although unconscious in later life[105] had a powerful influence or an event that occurred in the time of human origins. The primal scene of infancy is commonly the infant's witness of sexual acts between the father and mother; however, it could refer to any experience of infant sexuality.[106] Róheim constructs a prototypical primal scene on which he explains the development of an aboriginal "national character." This is the powerful experience of the (male) infant of having his mother sleep on top of him in the same manner in which a man lies upon a woman in coitus. In Róheim's understanding, the repression of this experience later emerges in the construction of the *alknarintja* woman, a mythic figure of a phallic female, and in the phallic mother concept.[107] Of the primal scenes associated with phylogeny, Róheim often had romantic evaluations of a Rousseauian sort. He believed that the aborigines were a happy people: "They can manage to live in a human group without giving up too much of their original aims [by which he meant "biological maleness, an inheritance of our animal ancestors"]. . . . Maybe the happy days of wish-fulfilment, the time when the eternal dream-people lived in the world, was not so very long ago after all, and we can still get a glimpse [i.e., by observing the Australian aborigines] of these bygone days."[108]

Róheim's focus on origins is parallel to what he understood as the Arrernte central concern, that is, with *knanindja* (totem or origin) and with *altjira* (the elements of the primal scene). Totemism was for him a concern of origins, a concern that for the Arrernte intertwines personal origins, which identify the totem, with group origins, which identify the ancestral models on which a totem is based.[109]

Linguistic Authority: Theodor Strehlow

Today in Alice Springs, an odd steel and concrete building with a huge, compressed earth wall houses the Strehlow Research Centre. At the end of a long ramp—which, were the display designed by Spencer, one would think of a walk backward through eons of evolutionary time—one enters a technologically sophisticated presentation of Arrernte culture. The first panels portray Arrernte concepts of creation. The display carries this explanation:

> "Before Time." Throughout the world, religions assume the existence of supernatural beings. The Aranda believed that the sky and the earth were eternal, each with its own set of supernatural beings. The Western Aranda, for example, believed the sky was inhabited by an emu-footed Great Father who, with his family, lived only on fruit and vegetables in an eternal green land. Through this celestial paradise the Milky Way flowed like a river, the stars were their campfires and life was eternal.
>
> Among the Southern Aranda they tell of a huge casuarina tree which had stood since the beginning of time in the Simpson Desert, and had touched the sky with its top branches—enabling human beings to climb the sky and eternal life.[110]

The Strehlow Research Centre honors not only the aboriginal peoples of Central Australia but also Theodor Strehlow, whose life story takes up perhaps one-third of the display area.

Theodor Strehlow was one of five children born to Carl and Frieda Strehlow at Hermannsburg Mission. During a year's furlough, the Strehlows decided to leave in Germany all their children except two-year-old Theodor, who returned to Australia with them. Until age fourteen, when the Strehlows permanently left Hermannsburg, he spent much of his time with his Arrernte friends. Carl, a severe father, required his son to study music—he played the church organ—and Latin and Greek. Theodor spoke aboriginal languages with the skill of a native speaker.[111]

Frieda resided in Adelaide after her husband's death, and Theodor attended Immanuel College and then Adelaide University, the university to which he would remain attached for the balance of his life, graduating with honors in English literature and linguistics. Shortly after graduation, he received a grant to study aboriginal culture and departed for Central Australia in May 1932.

Upon his initial arrival, Theodor Strehlow was apparently seen by some aborigines as a possible means through which to save the aspects of their cultures that were rapidly changing and in danger of extinction, principally their ritual, song, and ceremonial traditions. By the 1930s, young aborigines, attracted to Western ways, were less interested in their traditions, and the elders feared their total loss. Strehlow, though not aboriginal, not only spoke the Arrernte language but also wrote and had film equipment to make both still and motion pictures. Furthermore, he was strongly interested in recording songs, stories, and ceremonies. Although at first slightly reluctant, Strehlow soon accepted the aboriginal designation of him as a custodian of traditional knowledge and even ritual objects. He agreed that the information and objects given to him would not be shown to others as long as any one of the providing elders was living.

Strehlow traveled frequently to Central Australia to record and collect from the Arrernte. For some years in the late 1930s he served as a patrol officer in the Northern Territory, stationed at Jay Creek, some twenty-five miles west of Alice Springs. In the forty-year period spanned by his many field trips, Strehlow recorded ten kilometers of color motion picture film of aboriginal ceremonies, thousands of photographs, over 4,000 songs, and over 1,000 Arrernte and Loritja stories.[112] Strehlow took his custodianship seriously, sequestering his cultural records and artifacts in his home and refusing access to them by anyone, including Adelaide University and the Australian Institute for Aboriginal Studies, who funded much of his research.[113] At times Strehlow's possessiveness about these materials created tension. Frequently the sponsoring institutions attempted to persuade Strehlow to release his materials to them. Strehlow's biographer, Ward McNally, reports that Strehlow threatened to burn everything if required to relinquish them.[114] This collection is still Strehlow's property, inaccessible to others, and now housed at the Strehlow Research Centre in Alice Springs under the control of his second wife, Kathleen. Strehlow often waited years before he decided it was an appropriate time to publish his works. *Aranda Traditions* was assembled in three parts in 1934 but was not published until 1947. *Songs in Central Australia* was written over the years from the early 1930s until 1956, but it was not published until 1971.

After his retirement in 1973 from Adelaide University, Strehlow began to work toward the establishment of a research foundation to serve as the repository and means of control over the vast materials he had collected. This required significant funding, which was not immediately forthcoming. Eventually Strehlow attempted to sell the films and *tjurunga* collections to the Australian Institute for Aboriginal Studies (AIAS) but on the condition that he and his wife would retain exclusive use. The asking price was $300,000. The AIAS apparently offered a grant to help preserve the films from deterioration but required that a copy of them be deposited at some location other than Strehlow's home. It seems that this grant was never accepted, presumably because it required the creation of a second copy. The public offering of these materials (under the same conditions and at the same stated price) drew an angry response from aboriginal leaders, and Strehlow responded to them in the same way. It also became known to the aborigines that Strehlow was revealing to his wife, Kathleen, the materials over which he had been granted custodianship. Because aborigines deemed the materials inappropriate for women in their own culture, they believed that Strehlow had betrayed them. On his visits to Central Australia after his retirement, he was increasingly kept at a distance by the aboriginal people.

The tensest situation arose in 1978, the year of Strehlow's death, when he sold an article illustrated with color photographs to the German magazine *Stern*. Although he insisted that he had stressed to the magazine the importance of keeping the publication out of Australia, *Stern* sold secondary rights to the Australian magazine *People*, which published the article, including the photographs. The response to the publication of these secret photographs and information was severe criticism of Strehlow by aborigines, public officials, and scholars.[115]

Strehlow persisted, as he had on so many prior occasions, and plans for the research foundation continued. The formal inauguration of the Strehlow Research Foundation,[116] with an exhibition of aboriginal art and artifacts occurred in Adelaide on October 3, 1978. Strehlow missed this event, which might have been the most glorious occasion of his life; he died in his office the same afternoon, while visiting with guests.

Theodor Strehlow was a person many found difficult to get along with. McNally's biography describes numerous occasions of bitter conflict and scores of relationships that not only soured but also turned malicious. Often Strehlow chose to publicly air these personal and private conflicts. While the details of these matters are not relevant here, there is sufficient public record, without relying exclusively on Strehlow's biographer, to substantiate at least the existence of many of these unhappy situations. Strehlow often felt himself the object of persecution, and sometimes there was actual abuse. During the World War II, Strehlow, like his parents before him, received threats and accusations because of his German heritage. Late in his life, he publicly accused the Australian Broadcasting Company of attempting to ruin his reputation. Frequently he threatened legal action and made public accusations of those who used his published research without what he considered to be adequate acknowledgment. Strehlow appeared to believe that he had exclusive rights and privileges to the aboriginal materials in Central Australia. Although he elected to do a new translation of the New Testament into Arrernte, replacing that of his father, he was antagonistic to the Lutheran Church for most of his life, believing it to be responsible for his father's death.

Strehlow made extensive and frequent claims about his own distinction on the basis of being born at Hermannsburg and speaking the Arrernte language. Most scholars acknowledge his language competence and extensive personal experience as the basis for their high esteem of his scholarship and the reasons to elect his interpretations over those presented by others. But some believe that he took the authority of his birthplace too far, claiming for himself the role of custodian of traditional knowledge and ritual objects and spokesperson for the aborigines, sometimes even in opposition to the aborigines themselves. One aboriginal woman named Olga Fudge spoke to Strehlow's biographer on this point: "I knew Ted Strehlow—knew him well. Admired him in a lot of ways, too. But he spoilt himself by reminding everyone that he'd been born at Hermannsburg Mission, and had grown up with Aboriginal children, speaking their language. Fair enough, I suppose. But if a cat's born in a stable, that doesn't make it a horse, does it? Ted Strehlow's birthplace didn't make him an Aboriginal. That's just nonsense."[117]

The heavy criticism of Carl Strehlow delivered by Baldwin Spencer shortly before he died did not give Spencer the last word. Time and again Theodor Strehlow rose to his father's defense, delivering what has been for most readers the decisive and final word. Theodor Strehlow's authority rested on his knowledge of the Arrernte language. Spencer, for academic credibility and method, attempted to incorporate Arrernte terms into his ethnographies, but he was no student of the language. Gillen, despite many years in the environs of native speakers, had little patience for studying Arrernte and believed no one was interested in it. He relied mostly on aboriginal English. Carl Strehlow became fluent in Arrernte and Loritja but as second languages to German and English. Further, he had to learn these aboriginal languages with little help from former studies of the language. His son, however, was born at Hermannsburg and spoke Arrernte for a decade as a child. No other student of aboriginal cultures can claim such extensive experience and competence with Arrernte language and culture.

Although Theodor Strehlow frequently criticized Spencer and Gillen, his most sustained critique is in the introduction to his *Songs of Central Australia* (1971). Spencer and Gillen are often compared with Carl Strehlow in terms of their relative strengths and weaknesses. While Spencer and Gillen observed many aboriginal rituals, Carl Strehlow, as a missionary, never witnessed a single one. While Carl Strehlow was a student of aboriginal languages, particularly Arrernte and Loritja, in which he was fluent, Spencer and Gillen knew little of the aboriginal languages, depended on aboriginal English interpreters, and made many mistakes.[118] Another crucial area of comparison between Carl Strehlow and Spencer and Gillen concerns their informants. In the preface to *The Arunta*, Spencer accused Carl Strehlow of having gained all his information from Christianized aborigines. Theodor Strehlow considered this to be a "slur" and defended his father by a detailed description of his father's four principal informants.[119] He also defended his father against Spencer's accusation that his German was so bad it needed extensive editing: he had compared his father's handwritten manuscripts with the published accounts edited by Freiherr von Leonhardi, finding "only very occasional minor corrections."[120] He considered Spencer's statements and their impact on Frazer the reason that his father's work had been relatively neglected by anthropologists.[121] Strehlow believed that his father's informants were all initiated men, born early enough to have become fully knowledgeable of their cultures before the European and Christian presence.

Setting himself up to deeply criticize Spencer's work, Strehlow cited Frazer's praise of Spencer's work and even acknowledged its value. Then he detailed the inaccuracies, incorrect translations, and significant contradictions in Spencer's and Gillen's publications. Typical of their errors, as Strehlow presented them, is the language failure that led them to think their own totem affiliation, Udnirringita, was "witchetty grub" when, according to Strehlow, it was "caterpillar." They believed that the aborigines were "chanting songs of which they did not know the meaning" and consequently did not record any songs, whereas Carl Strehlow had recorded some 800 songs and he many more, as evident in his substantial book *Songs of Central Australia*. Strehlow criticized Spencer's and Gillen's heavy dependence on aboriginal English, showing from his own experience how inadequate it is. He criticized Spencer's dependence on Charlie Cooper in 1926. Strehlow reported that Cooper had told him that he had provided virtually all the information Spencer had gained during his field study and that Cooper's presentation of the Numbakulla story was concocted for Spencer's benefit.[122] Strehlow found that Spencer had failed to adequately divide the Northern, Southern, Eastern, and Central Arrernte sources, considering them all more or less the same; also he had failed to record any of the Western Arrernte traditions.[123]

Theodor Strehlow made some interesting comments on Spencer's criticism of his father's use of the term *altjira*. These appear in a footnote to his article "Geography and the Totemic Landscape in Central Australia" in the context of demonstrating that there was no central authoritative body, no single geographical center of authority:

> This lack of any centralized system of authority extended into the spiritual sphere as well. Each set of the multitudinous earth-born totemic ancestors exercised their power only in relatively small geographically delimited areas; and such sky dwellers as the Western Aranda or Kukatja Great Fathers exerted no influence whatever on the earth or its weather or its plants or its animals or its human inhabitants. The only myth to the contrary is that concocted for Sir Baldwin Spencer's consumption by the Alice Springs police tracker Charlie Cooper. It is ironic that Spencer, who had jeered at C. Strehlow's Western Aranda myth of "Altjira" . . . was taken in by Charlie Cooper so completely that he wrote the whole of Chapter XIII in *The Arunta* on this subject. Yet C. Strehlow's Western Aranda myth is correct as it stands, except perhaps for the two sentences in which he refers to the completely otiose Western Aranda Sky Being as being the benevolent Supreme Being of the Aranda. Spencer, however, claimed that his "great original *inkata Alchera Numbakulla*" . . . "gave rise

> to all the original Kurunas [spirits, souls], Churingas, and Knanjas [totems]." Unfortunately, the very name given to Spencer's Supreme Being shows that his informant had syncretized Aboriginal beliefs with the new doctrines of the Hermannsburg missionaries: for "*Ingkata Altjira Ngambakala*" was merely the Hermannsburg translation of a common title given to the Christian God: it means "Lord God Eternal".[124]

Elsewhere Strehlow acknowledged that the term *Altjira* had been adopted by the early Hermannsburg missionaries.[125] He rendered *altjira* as "eternal," as in his discussion of supernatural beings in *Central Australian Religion*, where he translates *altjira nditja* as "Eternal Youth."[126] Just a day or two before his death, Strehlow delivered to the editor of the *Lutheran Yearbook* an essay that recounted the history of the Hermannsburg Mission during the Strehlow years entitled "*Altjira Rega Ekalta*: Praise the Lord, the Almighty."[127] The essay is clearly a tribute to his father, Carl. The title is the same as the hymn sung at the dedication of the new mission church on Christmas day, 1897.[128]

In *Songs of Central Australia*, in the context of his discussion of "Sire Iliingka, the great Emu-footed One," Strehlow discussed the term *altjira* at some length, as well as the associated debate between his father and Spencer. Carl Strehlow wrote about the figure as "Altjira Iliinka," whereas his son's informant of 1950 referred to it as "Atua Iliingka," which could be a correct variant of the former term. Strehlow argued that his father mistakenly translated the term as "God," whereas the accurate translation would have been "the eternal." His argument is based on his claim that *Atua Iliingka* is often referred to as *altjira nditja*, that is, "the eternal youth." Strehlow went on to discuss the term *altjira*: "It is a rare word, whose root meaning appears to be 'eternal, uncreated, sprung out of itself'; and it occurs only in certain traditional phrases and collocations. . . . Then there is *altjiranga ngambakala*, which means literally 'having originated out of altjira', and is an expression used only about the earth-born supernatural beings. It can best be translated as 'having originated out of his (her, their) own eternity'. It means, in fact, that these supernatural beings have always existed and that no one created them."[129]

Nevertheless, in his *Songs of Central Australia* Strehlow remained adamant that Central Australians had no beliefs in supreme gods or high gods: "They [Iliingka and his large family] had not created the earth, nor any of its landscape features, nor any of its plants and animals, nor any of its human inhabitants. They had not brought the totemic ancestors into being, nor had they controlled any of their actions. They had no power over winds, clouds, sicknesses, dangers, or death. They were not even interested in anything that went on below them. If any crimes were committed, the evil-doers had to fear only the wrath of the totemic ancestors and the punishment of outraged human society."[130] Although Strehlow seems clear enough on *altjira* and on the absence of high gods in Central Australia, he nonetheless, though it would seem inadvertently, contributed extensively to the opposite view. In his article "Personal Monototemism in a Polytotemic Community," first published in 1964,[131] he presented a Great Father and a vital sky-earth connection. The figure is parallel to his father's Altjira:

> Throughout the Aranda-speaking area it was generally believed that both the sky and the earth were eternal, and that each of them had its own set of supernatural beings. The Western Aranda believed the sky to be inhabited by an emu-footed Great Father (*kngaritja*), who was also the Eternal Youth (*altjira nditja*). This Great Father had dog-footed wives, and many sons and daughters—all the males being emu-footed and all the females dog-footed. They lived on fruits and vegetable foods in an eternally green land, unaffected by droughts, through which the Milky Way flowed like a broad river; and the stars were their campfires. In this green land there were only trees, fruits, flowers, and birds; no game animals existed, and no meat was eaten. All of these sky dwellers were as ageless as the stars themselves, and death could not enter their home: the reddish-skinned emu-footed Great Father of the sky whose blond hair shown "like a spider web in the evening sunlight", looked as young as his own sons, and all the women who live above the stars had the grace and the full-bosomed beauty of young girls.[132]

Strehlow also recounted the story of the casuarina tree in the Simpson Desert that touched the sky. This tree had another leaning against it, providing a ladder for human beings to climb from the earth into the sky. The tree was chopped down by blood avengers, forever destroying the bridge to unending life. He told the story of the brothers who climbed up their spear into the sky and, after pronouncing a death curse on human beings, turned into clouds. These last two stories appear to account for the origin of death.[133]

Although Strehlow repeated his view "that it would be impossible to regard the emu-footed Great Father in the sky of Western Aranda mythology as a Supreme Being in any sense of the word,"[134] this strong position was overlooked, it would seem, by those who prepared the exhibit for the Strehlow Research Centre ("Before Time," as quoted above) and even by Strehlow himself. Here again we see the overwhelming influence of Western expectations regarding religion, the abstractions that precede Strehlow's simulations of the Arrernte. Strehlow qualified himself and the Arrernte in the following attempt to place the Arrernte on the world stage of religion:

> But man, helplessly subject as he is to age, decay, and death, seems always to have felt the need to look beyond his own meagre death-limited existence for some assurance that his life, unlike that of the animals, is not purely a matter of temporary physical existence in an uncertain world governed purely by blind chance, and that his purposive labours, unlike the animals, have some meaning and value even beyond his own death. One of the main purposes of religion everywhere has been to bring him into advantageous contact with supernatural Forces and Powers that are also immortal and eternal. The eternity motif may indeed be regarded as perhaps the most vital single element of the many that are blended together in any human religious system.[135]

And so it would seem, for Theodor Strehlow, that *altjira* (which according to him means "eternity") is the Arrernte personification of the "eternity motif," giving the

Arrernte a place—albeit through the back door—among religious humans, who believe in supreme beings.

Altjira and Time

Through the intersection of the storytracks of the missionaries and those of the Arrernte, there emerged the high god named Altjira. Whereas the missionaries utilized this name to present the Christian God to the Western Arrernte, from the storytracks of the aborigines—whose entire conceptual framework is so radically different from its Western counterpart—Altjira cannot possibly have conveyed to them anything approaching a Christian conception of God. The statement presented earlier in this chapter by the blind Moses, a nominal Christian aborigine throughout his life, reflects this unresolvable incongruity. *Altjira*, as a term used by Christian aborigines, refers to a new aboriginal entity, the first aboriginal deity. Interestingly, while Theodor Strehlow calculated the birthdates for various regions that would mark the division between those who were authentically traditional aborigines and those who were not,[136] virtually no academic attention[137] has been directed to the changes that aborigines have undergone under the influence of their contact with Christians and other Westerners. These changes doubtless have been more radical and rapid than the changes that occurred in the normal course of precontact aboriginal history, but they must nonetheless be in continuity with that history and they must be acknowledged as constituting authentic aboriginal history.

Carl Strehlow allowed that aborigines were fully human but suffered in not having received the light of Christianity. He saw the people as heathen and their traditions as evil. He never attended traditional cultural events, and he did not permit Christian aborigines to attend them. He promoted the abandonment of traditional culture as necessary to the introduction of Christianity. Yet, as has occurred so often among Christian missionaries the world over, to have written and published such extensive ethnographical accounts, Carl Strehlow must have found traditional aboriginal cultures inherently fascinating. His investment in studying them is far beyond the level that would be in strict service to the goals of Christianization.

Francis Gillen was identified by Spencer as the one who first rendered *Alcheringa* (*altjira*) as the "dreamtime."[138] Although "dreamtime" has certainly been challenged as an adequate rendering of the term, no alternative has escaped some strongly temporal associations.[139] Despite these challenges the term persists.[140] Now even aborigines, forced to participate in the hyperreality of the simulations made of them, use this English term, and they have developed extensive explanations to support their use of it.[141]

Baldwin Spencer believed that the aborigines represented the stage of magic in the evolution of culture. Among other reasons, he despised the mission enterprise both because it refused to allow aboriginal people to continue their practice of this magical stage of their cultural development and because it introduced religion, albeit Christianity, to them. Spencer's interest in aborigines waned in correlation to the degree in which they ceased to practice precontact cultural forms.

Géza Róheim believed that aborigines represented an early, if not the earliest, stage of human psychological development. They had no latency period, explaining their absence of civilization (Freud had identified latency as the well-spring of civilization). Róheim psychoanalyzed individual Arrernte to understand the ontogenetic correspondence with their early stage in phylogenesis. Aboriginal concepts identified with the term *altjira* were seen in light of this model of origination. *Altjira* was the intersection of the time at which the human psyche originated, the eternal ones of the dream (the ancestors), the imaginative games in which children dramatized daydreams to portray the primal scenes of their copulating parents, and the adult practice of ritual that engaged for them the primal scene.

Theodor Strehlow sought out the elders and accepted the role of custodian for the precontact cultural traditions. While he was an advocate of aboriginal rights and often went to great lengths to protect and defend them,[142] he also rudely opposed politically active, more acculturated aborigines. Although sometimes alienated from the Lutheran church, Strehlow nonetheless honored his father's work in the church and thus supported the mission's efforts. He voluntarily retranslated the New Testament into the Arrernte language. Strehlow thought himself aboriginal in a peculiar sense. He often stated that because he had been born at Hermannsburg and spoke Arrernte as a child, he thought like an aborigine, and given that he had been designated custodian of so much of the traditional knowledge and objects, he believed that he had the right to present himself as an aboriginal spokesperson.

This storytracking of Carl Strehlow, Francis Gillen, Baldwin Spencer, Géza Róheim, and Theodor Strehlow has focused on the way in which their stories intersect and interact with the Arrernte term *altjira*, showing that while they represent perspectives that initially appear to be antagonistic and contentious with one another, in some respects they are not so dissimilar after all. Based on their separate studies of the Arrernte, they all found themselves vitally engaged with explaining the term *altjira*. *Altjira* is the Arrernte term whose Arrernte meaning, when glimpsed by these men (and I think as yet it has only been glimpsed), struck to the heart of their heritage as "Western men."[143] The heritage of "Western man" gives sovereignty to time over space, and its conception of time bears a peculiar two-fold function. On the one hand, historicity and temporality are taken for granted. The constant uniform flow of natural time is thought to be utterly objective. Yet, on the other hand, time can be severed into a sequence of periods, blocks, and eras, the earliest of which is identified as a timeless realm of creators, gods, and the eternal, most evident and accessible in terms of origination. This timeless realm of origination is also accessible in dream, myth, ritual, and fantasy.[144] The interests all these men had in Australian aborigines rests firmly on their paradoxical double structure of time. It is this concept of time that enabled them to perform what appears to be a magical act: the firsthand, face-to-face encounter with the people of the primal era.

I suggest that the attention these men devoted to defining their understanding of the term *altjira* and the considerable emotion it engendered in them are due to the challenge their glimpse of the Arrernte meaning of the term presented to their identity and worldview, the world of "Western man." However tentatively and with whatever disbelief, what these men somehow confronted is that the Arrernte have neither a sense of the regular objective flow of natural time nor some notion of creation and origination. Eternity to them has nothing to do with time. All of these men whose stories cross on their common interest in *altjira* encountered the unthinkable, that is, that the aborigines' understandings of the world could not be comprehended or described in terms of the "Western man's" understanding of the world. As each encountered such a monstrosity, each engaged in his own academic magic, what in Baudrillard's terms are precessions of simulacra, to bring the aborigines into line, into time.

In tracing the storytracks of these figures, the categories—time, eternity, history, magic, religion, Christian, traditional, aboriginal, Western—seem to loose the precision of their meanings, yet it was service to these labeled categories that propelled these men along their respective tracks. When traced to their convergence at a point of common interest, it is the viability, even the sensibility, of these categories that is most in question. All that remains of the works of these men are faint traces of their journeys across the Australian landscape, mere traces that are awaiting the coherence of being rendered into story. One rendering, this storytracking, itself reliant on the ordering power of time, interconnects them by their common experience of reeling from the prospect of the downfall of "Western man."

6

The Arrernte

Baldwin Spencer and Carl Strehlow clashed over the term *Altjira*. They had significant differences over many other aspects of Arrernte culture, reflecting the major differences in their personal backgrounds and experiences. The other classical Arrernte ethnographies by Theodor Strehlow and Géza Róheim are also deeply shaped by the storytracks of these writers of culture. Although each described a culture by the name "Arrernte," in many respects the cultures appear to be different. That the ethnographer influences the ethnography by virtue of one's interests, perspectives, and field experience is nothing new. Yet authors of classical ethnographies remained largely unselfconscious about this matter, which was often made tacit to their readers and perhaps even to themselves by their objectivist assumption. The arguments among classical ethnographers focus on the relative accuracy of the works' essence. A significant portion of the ethnographic publication on the Arrernte was motivated by the desire to set straight the work of competing ethnographers. Contemporary ethnographers of Central Australian cultures, such as Diane Bell, who wrote *Daughters of the Dreaming* (1983), and Michael Jackson, who wrote *At Home in the World* (1995), are not only more fully aware of their influence on ethnography as they struggle with the accompanying issues but also attempt to take advantage of being present in the work.

While ethnographical theory has moved forward, classical ethnographies stand invariably unrevised, and the seeming authority of objectivist ethnography has established itself deeply in the history of the study of cultures because generations of scholars have depended on these works as primary sources. For so many cultures, these classical ethnographies are all that remain, especially cultures as they existed at a particular time. The criticism of classical ethnographies remains largely an evaluation of their accuracy rather than an appreciation of them as products of encounters, that is, products of intersecting storytracks.

In doing this work I have recognized that readers need to be familiar with the ethnological details that distinguish the culture referred to here as the Arrernte. The Arrernte are one of the most commonly discussed Australian aboriginal peoples; indeed, they have been presented as exemplary to or foundational for theory and proposition far and wide. At one point I was tempted to present a full picture of Arrernte culture by synthesizing the four classical ethnographies, each the product of a strong and decisive storytrack, that is, combining them in such a way as to somehow reconcile their differences. To complete this presentation, the synthesis could be filled out and homogenized with the aid of information about many other aboriginal cultures, this information itself based on the assumption that aboriginal cultures are more or less all the same. From this perspective, the Arrernte would be one version of monolithic aboriginal culture (singular). Although this approach has been taken piecemeal for occasional items in Arrernte culture, it has never been done systematically. More commonly, the Arrernte, as a religious culture, has been less interesting than the piecemeal use of these classic published sources to support global themes.

Tempting as was this synthesizing approach, I realized that it would ignore the principal position being made here: that each of these presentations is to some extent a creation, the product of intersecting storytracks. A synthesis of these several creations would constitute a creation upon a creation and would thus make even more tacit the impact these men—their dispositions, interests, histories, and approaches; in short, their storytracks—had on their descriptions and interpretations of the Arrernte. It would presume that one (me) with no Arrernte field experience or native language competence might somehow negotiate, decide, and reconcile the differences among those who did have these experiences and competencies, and at the distance of decades and a hemisphere. Such a synthesizing approach necessarily operates at a secondary level, and the result, by failing to acknowledge that all primary sources are products of storytracks, is the least desirable (most undesirable) because it pretends that the Arrernte (or whatever culture is the subject) is or even can be objectively knowable, that is, knowable apart from the creative influence of specific storytracks. This maneuver would transform subjects to objects, the complex to the simple, and the multiperspectival to the single objective view. When considering, say, Carl Strehlow's and Baldwin Spencer's works side by side, one can see that they disagree and one can appreciate each particular perspective, whereas in some synthesized account, the Arrernte would be presented—based, of course, on these highly subjective perspectives—in general, objective terms. And such synthesized presentations are usually made by persons, like me, who do not speak even aboriginal English, much less have ever seen an Arrernte or stood in their landscape (though I have done this). Considering also that some aspects of these classical ethnographies are simulations of Arrernte culture based on firmly held abstractions, and thereby have replaced the reality of Arrernte culture with constructed hyperrealities, what a novel, yet undesirable, ontology would be achieved by this attempt at synthesis, which would also probably amount to a simulation.

In this work I believe it is important to present Arrernte culture, but I feel it is necessary to make this presentation not in some homogenized form but rather in a way that retains the importance of storytracks—to make the effort to present the Arrernte as they have been separately seen and created by their principal observers. In the presentation that follows, "the Arrernte," a term that has been used by all of the principal ethnographers to designate their subject, is considered the crossing for four separate storytracks. While my presentation is itself a secondary storytracking enterprise—that is, I am in part creating the views of these observers based on the interplay of my storytrack and my experience of their works—at least the subjectivity of perspective (mine, as well as theirs) is retained; the presence of sets of lenses between the reader and the Arrernte is acknowledged.

My objective here is primarily to present outlines of Arrernte religion and culture, and to do so while acknowledging that the several descriptive accounts of the Arrernte are part of the storytracks of those who have constructed the images of this culture for us. Such a presentation could easily become an extensively detailed comparative study of several storytrack perspectives, but I will confine the presentation largely to storytrack-contextualized summary presentations. And at that, this presentation is lengthy.

A brief review of the four principal ethnographers will chart the general ethnographic landscape. Foremost, as far as its impact has been, is the work of the biologist Baldwin Spencer, a staunch cultural evolutionist, who spent only a few months observing Arrernte ritual performances and interrogating Arrernte ritualists in aboriginal English. He collaborated with Francis Gillen, an Alice Springs postmaster and telegraph operator, who shared his fascination with aboriginal peoples. Their contact was largely with the Eastern Arrernte. Much of what Spencer wrote was based on Gillen's information, also acquired primarily through aboriginal English.

Contemporary to Spencer and Gillen was Carl Strehlow, a Lutheran pastor, who spent nearly three decades at Hermannsburg as a missionary to the Western Arrernte and Loritja. He studied the Arrernte language, into which he translated scripture and other Christian works. Strehlow's Christianity required him to oppose most of the traditional practices of the culture he studied and to avoid any active participation, including the observation of ritual performances. The objective of his study was to aid in the work of Christianization and "civilization," which was inseparable from supporting the cessation of the practice of traditional Arrernte culture. He wrote a five-part work in German on Arrernte culture and religion: *Die Aranda- und Loritja-Stämme in Zentral-Australien* (1907–20) which, though translated into English, has yet to be published in that language. Carl Strehlow's contact was largely with the Western Arrernte and Loritja peoples. Given the significant differences between their perspectives, it is not surprising that there was continuing animosity between Strehlow and Spencer over their rival understandings of Arrernte culture.

The Hungarian, Géza Róheim, was an anthropologist deeply influenced by psychoanalysis. Considering Freud's *Totem and Taboo* (1913) to be the most influential book in anthropology and noting that psychoanalysis had had little if any impact on the study of anthropology, Róheim set out to establish the field of psychoanalytic anthropology, an effort at which he persisted throughout his life. He believed it was the anthropology of the future. After, as an armchair anthropologist, he wrote *Australian Totemism* (1925), which attempted to document the primal crime thesis of *Totem and Taboo*, Róheim received the resources to spend several years in field study. He devoted ten months to the study of Australian aborigines, the longest contact being with the Arrernte at the Hermannsburg Mission in 1929. Gifted at languages, Róheim quickly gained basic abilities in the Arrernte language and, as a psychoanalyst, engaged in the kinds of field investigations previously unimagined in Australia: the recording of dreams, extensive descriptions of sexual practices, attention to children at play, and discussions with elders—all of which were focused on the individual rather than the community as a whole.

Róheim went to Australia equipped with the knowledge gleaned from his careful reading of Strehlow, Spencer, and Gillen, along with many other published works on which he relied for his massive *Australian Totemism*. His preparation for field study was far greater than that of his predecessors. Róheim's many publications, which focused on or included a consideration of the Arrernte, all present the culture and the data he collected in the context of a much broader concern with psychoanalytic theories. In "Psycho-analysis of Primitive Culture Types" (1932),[1] Róheim makes the fullest statement of his field methods and criticizes those not only of ethnographers who were studying Central Australian cultures but also of ethnograpers in general, the latter criticism focused largely on the absence in most ethnography of information on sexual life. Róheim launches into the presentation of his experience with children, an interest that would emerge as sections in nearly all of his works and was central to the two-volume work, *Children of the Desert* (1974 and 1988), published as the last works in his career.[2] Published in 1934, *The Riddle of the Sphinx, or Human Origins* inquires into the origins of religion and the human psyche. Róheim's interest in ambisexuality extends beyond Freud's focus on the male. He found many examples of androgenous figures, such as the Sphinx in the Oedipus legend—the woman with a penis. *The Eternal Ones of the Dream: A Psychoanalytic Interpretation of Australian Myth and Ritual*[3] (1945) is perhaps Róheim's most overarching discussion of aboriginal religions.

It is not easy to discern a systematic presentation of the Arrernte, or Australian aborigines more broadly, in Róheim's many works. As he moved among various aspects of psychoanalytic theory, his accounts of the Arrernte shifted. His presentation of data is invariably directed by his theory. Róheim's work is regularly but sparsely cited in subsequent discussions of Australian aborigines and even in anthropological discussions in general. Róheim recognized that he was peripheral to these discussions,[4] yet his conviction about the importance of his work never wavered. Although his work on the Arrernte lacks a sustained systematic presentation and a uniform interpretation, it amounts to a remarkably complex and provocative view of these people. However much one may disagree with Róheim's assumptions, theories, and style, the psychoanalytic interpretation seen in the fullness of the many studies through which it is worked out is no less than brilliant.

Carl Strehlow's son, Theodor, took up his father's study of the Arrernte, though not as a missionary. Theodor Strehlow knew the Arrernte language almost as a native speaker—he called it a "mother tongue"—and he spent extended periods between 1932 and 1960 photographing, collecting, and witnessing cultural practices. Strehlow's work has been broadly accepted by the academic community because of his knowledge of the language and the extent of his field experience. His publications span a range from the highly detailed and technical scholarship of *Songs of Central Australia* (1971) to the vague, clichéd, and oversimplified popular presentations in *Central Australian Religion* (1978). Strehlow came to see himself as the living repository of Arrernte culture, personally charged with its maintenance and continuity. In seeing himself in this position he made claims to a position of authority not existing in traditional aboriginal cultures.

If any point must be made about the appreciation of storytracks, it is that every account of the Arrernte is the product of a storytrack, each a valued perspective and each deserving critical evaluation. Constructing accounts of any culture is an interplay between the observer's perspective, formed through one's history of experience, and the external world encountered, seemingly the world of facts. As we have seen, the constructions may be simulations with little, if any, correlation to an independent cultural reality, but to the extent that the ethnographies are legitimate interpretative presentations, none is inherently superior to any other in the sense or ensuring a more objective, true, or real account. All questions of value are necessarily framed by a specific storytrack. The Arrernte culture, in this case, is constructed (actually created) for others, by the process of encountering storytrack projects. Spencer and Gillen, Carl Strehlow, Géza Róheim, and Theodor Strehlow created the Arrernte for their readers as much as they permitted the Arrernte to present themselves in their terms through their observers' works.

Spencer's and Gillen's Arrernte

In an extensive introduction to *The Native Tribes of Central Australia* (1899), Spencer describes the land, the people, social organization, and the major customs. Then he begins a systematic, largely descriptive presentation of Arrernte ("Arunta" in Spencer and Gillen)[5] culture: social organization, marriage customs, totems, *tjurunga*, *intichiuma* (the so-called "increase" ceremonies), and male initiation rites (including the *engwura)*. The description of the *engwura* is extensive, undoubtedly because it is a performance of the ritual complex that Spencer and Gillen witnessed in Alice Springs in the summer of 1896. Spencer then presents traditions that deal with the origin of the *alcheringa* (ancestors), which are principally itineraries with summary accounts of the ancestral events that occurred at the locations mentioned in the itineraries. These itineraries are usually referred to as myth. Spencer concludes the work with descriptions of numerous customs: tooth extraction, nose boring, bloodletting, childbirth, food restrictions, cannibalism, avenge and revenge, burial and mourning, medicine practices, ways of obtaining a wife, stories regarding celestial bodies, aspects of material culture, and naming practices.

Spencer acknowledges that not only are there many aboriginal cultures but there are also significant variances among groups of Arrernte, and his descriptions often systematically present these variations. However, the bulk and the core of his descriptions are based almost wholly on the sources at hand near Alice Springs. The following description of the Arrernte, presented in a number of subsections, is based primarily on Spencer and Gillen's *Native Tribes* and *The Arunta*.[6]

The People and the Landscape

The Arrernte are divided into a large number of small groups, each occupying and identified with a specific area of land. The name of the local group is the same as the name of the locality each occupies. Further identity of the local group is that of a plant or animal, with whom many, but not all, of the group are associated. Although local groups do not designate anyone as political leader, each has a head man (*alatunja*, though Spencer notes other terms used by groups throughout the region) whose principal function is to oversee the ritual object storehouse (*ertnatulunga*) and direct the ritual process of the increase ceremonies (*intichiuma*). The office of head man is hereditary, yet it holds no power except when the officeholder has wisdom and ability. The age of the head man is not a significant factor.[7]

A number of local groups who are living in a common district are spoken of collectively by one name.[8] Several groups within a district might have the same local group designation, in which case the distinctiveness of the groups is retained by reference to the direction, designated by named cardinal or semicardinal points, within the district to which their locality corresponds. The Arrernte language distinguishes numbers only to four, though those at Alice Springs use their fingers to count to five. Quantities beyond four are designated as "great" or "much." Time is reckoned by "sleeps" or "moons" or phases of the moon. Several terms designate such temporal distinctions as summer and winter, morning, evening, yesterday, day before yesterday, tomorrow, day after tomorrow, and so on. There are names for all the birds and animals in the region.[9]

Social Organization

The Arrernte are divided into two exogamous intermarrying groups, or moieties. Each moiety is named: Nakrakia and Mulyanuka. Each is divided into two classes: Nakrakia into Panunga and Bulthara; Mulyanuka into Purula and Kumara. The marriage rules dictate that one marries outside of one's own moiety; in the other moiety, one is restricted to one of the two subclasses.[10] Descent is patrilineal, but a child receives the designation of the complementary class of his or her father's moiety designation. This arrangement can be graphically presented (as did Spencer) in the following chart, in which double arrows indicate marriages and single arrows indicate the class of the child of that marriage.

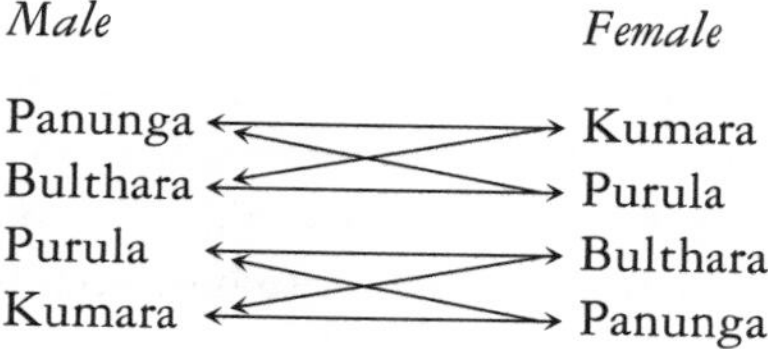

Each class is further divided into two subclasses. In cultures to the north of the Arrernte, these divisions have names; thus in those cultures there is effectively an eight-subclass system. For the Arrernte, the designations are relative to marriage eligibility. For a man of one subclass, which is one division of one of the four classes, women in only one subclass in the paired class are eligible mates. Thus, women are designated according to subclass as *unawa*, "eligible," and *unkulla*, "ineligible." All women of the same class and subclass call each other "sister," using terms that also distinguish age relative to the speaker, that is, an older sister or younger sister; males use the same system. The term that designates a man's wife is also used to designate all of her subclass "sisters." Each class has two subclasses, which designate both male and female members. Because a man calls all the women of his wife's subclass by the term "wife," Spencer posited that this system suggests evidence of earlier group marriage.

Totems

Every Arrernte person is born into a totem, that is, into a group, each member of which bears the name of and is associated with some natural object, usually a plant or animal. The Arrernte totem designations constitute a system separate from social structure. Thus, every person has his or her totem name. No totem is confined to the members of a moiety, class, or subclass. An individual's totem is determined by the place in the landscape where one's mother was when she acknowledged her pregnancy. The totem therefore provides connection with a specific geographical area and with others who share these connections, and the distinctiveness of a specific locality is expressed in terms of its setting for ancestral events, that is, for the mythic events of the *alcheringa*. Thus, a child's totem has no necessary relationship to the totem identification of either parent, and marriage rules do not restrict totem identifications.[11] Nonetheless, since a local group tends to inhabit a specific locality, the predominant totem of that locality is often found to predominate in one moiety.[12]

Alcheringa and Totemic Rites

Spencer believed that the entire history of the Arrernte is bound up with the totemic ceremonies. Each totemic rite portrays the actions of a particular "mythic ancestor," who according to Spencer's reckoning, lived in the "dim past." He called these ancestors *alcheringa*, and he used the same term to refer to the time period, "the first or earliest time." According to Spencer, in the *alcheringa,* semihuman creatures, who collected into groups that identified with a common natural object or feature, traveled about the land, stopping at specific locations where they performed particular actions. The content and subject of totemic rites are distinguised by the specific totem ancestor and locality. Arrernte individuals, who identify themselves by totem and locality, were believed by Spencer to be descendants or reincarnations of these ancestral figures.[13]

Tjurunga (Churinga)

Each of the *alcheringa* ancestors carried about a *tjurunga,* which Spencer understood to be associated with the spirit part of that ancestor. At the conclusion of the actions of each ancestral figure, he or she usually died and/or went into the ground, the body becoming identified with some natural feature in the landscape. The natural feature is considered a spirit abode (*nanja*) for that ancestor. According to Spencer, the spirit part of the figure remained in the *tjurunga,* most commonly, elongated flat, oval-shaped stone (mica) or wooden (mulga) objects that are usually incised with a significant design. Some are in the shape of, and used as, bullroarers. At local totem centers, *pmara kutata* (*oknanikilla*), *tjurunga* objects are collected and retained in a secret storehouse (*ertnatalunga*). There are ritual occasions when men observe and examine these *tjurungas,* which are regarded as representations of the ancestors, but women may never see them or approach an *ertnatalunga*, on pain of death.[14] Other activities, such as hunting, are not permitted in the area surrounding such storehouses. Spencer speculated that *ertnatalunga* suggests the rudiment of a city or house of refuge.[15] In light of his understanding that every Arrernte is a reincarnation of an ancestor, Spencer concluded that *tjurungas* are evidence of a "primitive belief in a substantive soul."[16] *Tjurungas* are the most cherished Arrernte possessions.

Increase Rites (*Intichiuma*)

Increase rites, according to Spencer, are associated with totems, the object of which is to increase the plant or animal that gives its name to the totem. He recognized these rites as probably the most important to the Arrernte, but he found no "traditions" that related their origin. The rites for each totem are distinctive. The head man decides when and where the rites are to be performed. Spencer noted that they usually occur at a time associated with the breeding of particular animals or with the flowering of particular plants identified as totems.

To demonstrate the character of the increase rites, Spencer chose to describe several: Witchetty grub near Alice Springs, Emu of the Strangeways Range, and so on. Encouraged by James G. Frazer and eager for evidence to place the Arrernte in his cultural evolution schema, Spencer was attentive to restrictions on the eating of the totem item by members of the totem group. He found that generally there is no restriction on eating one's totem animal or plant. One is usually obliged to eat small portions of the totem, lest the supply fail. Eating the totem is a requirement for the performance of the rites. The only exception is the *tjilpa* (Achilpa), or wildcat totem, the eating of which is restricted not only to a very small portion but also to the very old. This restriction extends beyond the *tjilpa* totem group to the whole culture. Spencer noted in this context that the Arrernte regard the totem as the same thing as oneself; that is, he held to the notion that each person is a reincarnation of a totem ancestor.

Spencer found significant evidence in mythic accounts for the free eating of the totem by members of the totem group. Since the mythic accounts differ from the somewhat restrictive ritual practice, Spencer pondered an explanation, positing a historical or developmental one. He thought that the mythic accounts reflect the practice of an earlier time. He noted that this explanation contrasts with Frazer's view that eating the totem at all is evidence of lessening respect for the totem. Spencer also noted that the Arrernte totem practices vary significantly from the totemic systems of other aboriginal cultures, in which the social functions, as in the regulation of marriage, are more developed. Spencer's emphasis on the religious functions of the Arrernte totem system is notable since he rarely acknowledged anything in Arrernte culture as being religious.[17]

Male Initiation Rites

Believing that Arrernte rites, in all respects, differ from those of other aboriginal cultures, Spencer provided an extensive and detailed description of the male initiation rites. It is only as an aside while discussing the male rites of subincision that Spencer mentioned female initiatory rites. In this regard Spencer noted that the first female-specific rite occurs when the girl begins to develop breasts. The rite involves rubbing the girl's breasts with fat and ocher. The second rite mentioned is described only as an operation performed to open the vagina. This rite is comparable, in Spencer's view, to the male rite of subincision. Females do not receive a series of classificatory name changes, as do the males. They are known as *quiai* until the onset of menstruation, after which they are known as *wunpa*. After developing pendulant breasts, they are known as *arakutja*.[18]

The male initiation rites commence around the age of ten and may not be fully concluded until the age of twenty-five or thirty. There are at least four named rites that must be performed in sequence, and the sequence of the stages of initiation are marked by the bestowal of a series of social classificatory names on the initiates in progress. The specific ritual process varies from totem to totem. Rather than presenting a generic description, Spencer described the rite as performed by the groups that lived along the Finke River and then noted variations in the procedures of other groups.

Throwing the Boy up in the Air (alkirakiwuma, from *alkira,* which means "sky," and *iwuma,* which means "to throw")

The first initiatory rite begins when each of the selected boys is taken one by one and tossed up in the air and caught several times by the men. The women dance around, swinging their arms and shouting. The boys' chests and backs are then painted with designs unrelated to their totem identifications. The rites, according to Spencer and Gillen's understanding, are associated with growth and manhood. They mark a social change in that following the rite, the boys may no longer play with nor camp near females. Before the rite they are called *ambaquerka*; after the rite, *ulpmerka*. Shortly after the rite their nasal septa are bored and they begin to wear nose bones.

Circumcision (lartna)

Circumcision is a rite that spans many days, and some elements are distinctive to the specific totem group that is performing the rite. The initiates are seized and carried to the ceremonial ground (*apulla*), where they are prepared for the occasion. While the men sing songs about their ancestral figures, the women dance with shields, as did the ancestors. The initiates' bodies are painted, and they receive the new classificatory name, *wurtja*. The initiates are required to squat behind a brake (brush pile) built near the end of the ceremonial ground and to avoid looking at what the men are doing. To enforce the demands made of them, the initiates are warned that violation of secrecy will result in their being carried off by the spirit, Twanyirika, whose voice they hear. Unbeknownst to the initiates, the sound identified as Twanyirika's voice is made by whirling bullroarers. For days the initiates remain secluded, other than being present, though often blindfolded, while the men perform rites that enact the deeds of the ancestors. Some of these rites may relate to the ancestral performances of circumcision rites.

On the seventh day, the initiates are taught the songs and rites and are permitted, for the first time, to see the ritual performances. The circumciser for each initiate is selected. The eighth day is filled with rites, culminating with the circumcision of the initiates. Each boy is laid on his back on the back of a man resting on his hands and knees. The bullroarers are whirled loudly nearby, indicating the voice of Twanyirika. An assistant pulls the foreskin of his penis out as far as possible and the circumciser cuts it off. The boy is congratulated if he does not cry out. Taken behind a brake, they are given a shield in which to collect the blood dripping from their wounds. Here bullroarers are brought and pressed on the wounds. The initiates are told that it is these objects, not Twanyirika, that made the sound. They are told that the bullroarers are *tjurungas* and warned against mentioning them to the women. They are given these *tjurungas* and told that they are Twanyirika and that they will help them heal. Once circumcised, the initiates receive yet a new classificatory name, *arakurta*, being *wurtja* for only the brief time of the circumcision rite.

The initiates are isolated during the period of healing. While the initiates are isolated in the bush, men may visit them, at which time the men bite the initiates' scalps or perhaps their chins as hard as they can, making them bleed. This act is associated with making the initiates' hair grow strongly.[19]

Subincision (ariltha)

Five or six weeks after circumcision, the rites of subincision are performed. Men gather at the ceremonial ground and perform rites that reenact ancestral rites. The particular ones described by Spencer are concerned with the bandicoot totem. The initiates are present at, yet shielded from, these events and required to participate. The initiates are required to embrace a ritual pole (*nurtunja*), and while doing so they are informed that they are about to be operated on but that embracing the pole will prevent the operation from being painful. Two men volunteer to form the platform for the operation. The first lies stomach down on the ground, the second on top of him. Each initiate is laid full length on these men; another man sits astride the initiate and, grasping his penis, stretches it fully to expose the urethra. Another man quickly approaches the initiate and, with a stone knife, cuts open the urethra the full length of the penis. The operation complete, the initiate is led to one side, where he squats over a shield to collect the blood from his wound. Pubic tassels are tied on, and the initiates are told that they are now fully initiated men, that is, *ertwa-kurka*. The newly initiated man is given food restrictions, and several rites, performed over the following few days, serve to present them to the women of the community. Spencer concludes his presentation of subincision with a discussion of the variances in these practices among Arrernte groups and other aboriginal cultures. He also dispels any idea that the Arrernte instituted the practice of subincision as a method of birth control.

The final phase of the male initiation rites, which Spencer termed the "fire ceremony," occurs as the concluding event, *engwura*, of the grand ceremonial complex. Doubtless because Spencer had observed a major portion of this ritual complex at Alice Springs in 1896, he has much to report. Notably, he presented his description of this ritual complex under the initiation rubric, thus casting its significance primarily in male initiatory terms. That there are many other perspectives must be kept in mind as we follow Spencer's description, in which he equates *engwura* with the final initiatory rite, the fire ceremony.

Engwura

Gillen arranged a performance of the great *engwura* ceremony of Imanda, a totem center seventy miles south of Alice Springs on the Hugh River, to be held, not at Imanda, but near the telegraph station at Alice Springs. It was performed in 1896 for his and Spencer's convenience in observing and recording the events.

According to Spencer's description, it appears that the ritual complex functions principally to accomplish the final stage in the male initiation ritual process. Its purpose is to bring the young men under the control of the old men, teaching self-restraint to the young men and revealing to them the *tjurunga* and totem secrets. Beyond its initiatory functions, Spencer noted that this ceremony offers the occasion for old men from all parts of the culture to meet in council, which they did every day. Broader concerns are implied by Spencer's description of a great many totem-locality rites,[20] five or six of which are performed during most twenty-four-hour periods, often without focus on the initiates or even performed in their presence.

Spencer divided the ceremonial complex into five phases. The first phase is preparatory. Messengers, bearing a *tjurunga* wrapped in emu feathers, are sent out to invite people to the ceremony. Guests travel from as far as 200 miles to attend. Although the host and place of the ceremony, as is the ceremony itself, are identified with a totem, guests of all totems and both moieties are invited. Meanwhile the ceremonial ground is chosen and prepared, as are *tjurunga* storage areas. Representing a particular tract of country, a mound (*parra*) thirty feet long and two feet wide is prepared on the ceremonial ground and ornamented with a row of small gum trees. A single head man, the head man for the totem group identified with the place where the ceremony is occurring (or in the case Spencer and Gillen observed, where it is supposed to occur), directs the entire ceremonial performance. Once the guests arrive, many nights are devoted to dancing festivals, in which the women play as active a role as the men. Other rites are performed exclusively by men. Upon invitation by the head man, each performed rite is identified by both totem and geographical location. These rites are owned, being inherited or developed according to revelation, that is, as the result of the communication with *iruntarinja*, or spirits. Performances may involve one or two men or a sizable group. The performers need not belong to either the totem group or even to the moiety of the owner of the rite. At the close of this phase, the young men, that is, those completing their initiations, are separated from the women and placed under the control of the older men. These young men now hunt during the days and spend their nights near the ceremonial grounds.[21]

The performance of the rites associated with totem and geographic location is the principal action of the second phase, which in 1896 lasted five weeks. Spencer described the events of the last eight days, the only days in which he was in attendance. In general terms, preparation for these rites requires the decoration of the performers' bodies with either paint or down and the assembly of ritual objects such as a ritual pole (*nurtunja*) or *waninga*, a bannerlike object constructed on a pole that is emblematic of a totemic plant or animal. The rites are danced to the accompaniment of songs. Spencer did little to record the songs, of which he wrote in regard to one rite: "Men sang a monotonous chant, the words of which were merely a constant repetition of some such simple refrain as, 'Paint it around with rings and rings.' . . . Every now and again they burst out into loud singing, starting on a high note and gradually descending, the singing dying away as the notes got lower and lower, producing the effect of music dying away in the distance."[22] The technique, style, and form of the dancing were mostly not described by Spencer. Many of these rites enact events of the ancestors (*alcheringa*), and Spencer provides extensive photographic documentation for these rites. During this phase of the ceremony, evenings are spent "singing the ground" (i.e., country), with the men occupying the ceremonial ground near the *parra*, the mound. Several evenings are occasions for bringing *tjurungas* to the ceremonial ground for examination.

Spencer's primary focus on the initiatory process is the basis for distinguishing at this point in the ritual process a phase transition. Late one night, the older men congregate at the mound. Surrounded by the younger men, that is, those completing their initiation process, the men sing for two hours swaying back and forth. Around midnight they sit down but continue their singing for another hour or so. Then the younger men are decorated with twigs and leaves, which they wear through the remainder of the *engwura*. Certain restrictions are placed on the communication between the younger and the older men who are their sponsors; the initiates are, from this point on, collectively called *illpongwurra*, meaning "not smeared with grease or colour."[23]

The third phase in every other respect simply continues the second. The rites associated with totem and place are regularly performed at the rate of five or six per twenty-four-hour period. A couple of these rites are associated with *oruncha*, commonly referred to as "devil men." Spencer discussed his understanding of the *oruncha*, who are the subject of jest in the daytime but of fear at night. He suggested that these figures had been invented as a means of social constraint on women and children. Spencer's analysis of the headdresses of the *oruncha* of one rite inspired the interpretation of the horns, widely associated with the devil, as originally pointing sticks, that is, as sticks that cause mischief when pointed at something.[24]

Notably, Spencer's descriptions of the totem rites are founded on the correlation between ritual acts and elements and events of the *alcheringa*, that is, the mythic ancestral events. Song lyrics elaborate ancentral events. Since Spencer recorded none of the songs that accompany the ritual process, he must have been dependent on explanations of the rites offered by his Arrernte informants. Much more attention is given by Spencer to costume and body decoration than to song, dance, or ritual procedures. Photographs of virtually every one of these rites illustrate the appearance of the performers.[25]

The fourth phase has a marked division when seen from Spencer's perspective in that it focuses on the initiatory process. This phase is identified with the ordeals that must be suffered by the initiates to demonstrate that they are worthy of being *uliara*, that is, fully initiated men. At sunrise one morning, the *illpongwurra* are collected at the *parra*. A group of older men, whirling bullroarers and carrying shields, spears, and boomerangs, drive the young men out of camp to hunt. During this phase the young men hunt, but because they are fasting, do not eat any of their catch. Spencer noticed that the women's camp is enlivened during the day. Toward the end of the day, the women gather outside of camp, divided into two groups according to moiety. At sunset the *illpongwurra* return from hunting and deposit their game, and the older men escort them toward the gathered women. The women, having started two fires, are prepared for the arrival of the men. As the men approach, the young men are driven by the older ones toward one, then the other, group of women. The women set fire to tufts of grass and sticks, which they throw at the men's heads. The men shield themselves. Other men, with bullroarers spinning, encircle the groups. The women chase the men away and the men return to the ceremonial ground, where they run several times around the *parra*, shouting. The young men then sit and finally lie on their backs on one side of the *parra* with their heads resting on it. Through the night the men arouse the *illpongwurra* to witness totem-locality rites.[26]

During the succeeding days, the *illpongwurra* leave camp daily to hunt, returning in the evening. On many, but not all, of these departures and returns, the young men pass by the women's camp, where the women throw fire sticks over their heads. The older men continue regular performances of totem-locality rites; now, however, one or more are prepared for the benefit of the young men when they return from their hunt.

After a number of days, another transition occurs. Spencer, for some reason, does not mark it as a change in phase. An evening of silence is observed as preparations are made. The seemingly conjoined rites that follow include the young men, who are armed with fire sticks and rush at the women and old men and throw the firebrands over their heads. Spencer describes this scene as a highly energetic and frenzied one, with whirling bullroarers accompanying this running, shouting, and throwing affair. The *illpongwurra* return to spend the night in silence, with their heads resting on the *parra*. Three older men spend a full eight-hour night, raising and lowering a special *tjurunga* called *ambilyerikirra*.[27] The following morning, these three men, accompanied by the *illpongwurra* and a group of older men, take the *ambilyerikirra* and proceed toward the women's camp, where the women are waiting. The women beckon for the men to come to them. When the group arrives within a few yards of the women, the three men throw themselves on the *tjurunga* object, supposedly, in Spencer's view, to hide the object from the women. Then the *illpongwurra* all throw themselves on these three men, where they remain for several minutes. All then arise quickly and retreat to the ceremonial ground.

Spencer received little explanation from the Arrernte and thus, with stated caution, advances his own, constructed as always on the proposition of cultural evolution. Taking select clues from Arrernte statements Spencer holds that "the whole ceremony may be commemorative of a reformatory movement which must at one time have taken place in the tribe in regard to the question of cannibalism."[28] Having strongly proclaimed the secrecy and male exclusivity of *tjurungas*, Spencer found the greatest difficulty in explaining the presentation of the *tjurunga* object to the women. Finally, it seems he consoled himself by holding that, although the older women most certainly knew what they were looking at, the women in general did not actually see the *tjurunga*.[29]

The following day, the *illpongwurra* are sent from camp with the instructions not to return for two days. At the ceremonial grounds, these days are filled with ritual preparations and the performance of rites. Further, while the *illpongwurra* are away from camp and the ceremonial ground, they undergo the fire ordeal. A pit is dug in which a fire is built. When reduced to hot embers, the fire pit is covered with green bushes. The young men are required to lie covered on this platform until permitted to arise by the *uliara*, the fully initiated men. According to Spencer, this ordeal lasts four or five minutes, but in the performance he saw it was decided that the young men must repeat it. Spencer also noted that on the day of the fire ordeal he saw the thermometer register 110 degrees fahrenheit in the shade and 156 degrees in the sun. After the ordeal, the young men rest until it is time to return to camp.[30]

Meanwhile, preparations at camp are in progress. Central to these preparations are the decoration and erection of a sizable pole, *kauaua*, which must be painted with blood. Spencer describes in some detail the enormous quantities of blood men provide by opening a vein in their arms or opening their subincision. The entire pole, fifteen to twenty feet in length, is painted with blood. A large bunch of eaglehawk feathers is attached to the top, and headbands are tied around the pole under the feathers. Tail tips of the rabbit bandicoot are attached in two bunches, one on either side, and a long nose bone is attached below the headbands. Spencer noted that "in fact the decoration [is] just that of a human head."[31] Several *tjurungas* are suspended near the top. The pole is erected some six yards outward from the center of the *parra*.

The *illpongwurra* return to the ceremonial ground, where they see the erected *kauaua* for the first time and witness a totem-locality rite before lying for several hours in a row with their heads on the *parra*. Throughout the ensuing night, the bodies of all of the *illpongwurra* are elaborately decorated by their ritual sponsors. The women in their nearby camp are engaged by the men in shouted conversations through the night. Early the following morning, the head man makes a break in the middle of the *parra*. The sponsors lead the young men around the *parra* several times, finally gathering in silence at the *kauaua*, after which, hand in hand, they walk single file through the break in the *parra*. They head toward the women's camp, the women, divided according to moiety, attend two smokey fires. Singly, the *illpongwurra* are conducted to the women's fire of the moiety opposite their own, where they kneel down in the smoke. The women press down on the shoulders of the kneeling man. After every *illpongwurra* has undergone this rite, the men return to the ceremonial ground and group around the *kauaua*. This concludes the portion of the ritual that takes place on the prepared ceremonial ground. The *kauaua* is taken down and the decorations removed. It is even rubbed clean of the blood that decorated it. The ceremonial ground becomes a place forbidden to women and children for months thereafter.[32]

The final, fifth, phase is relatively brief. It begins with dancing festivals. Spencer described one in which women play a central role. Each of the young men then brings a gift of food to his sponsor, in return for which the sponsor performs a totem-locality rite that belongs to him. In a final act, the men all group together; while singing, a ritualist touches a bunch of feathers to the mouth of each man, thus breaking the ban of silence that throughout the entire ceremony has been in force between the *illpongwurra* and their respective sponsors.[33]

Traditions of Origins

From his attention to ritual, Spencer turned to traditions of origin, that is, the temporal period during which the ancestors, the *alcheringa*, existed. Spencer organized these materials into three periods, reflecting what, in his understanding, are the four periods recognized by "the tribe"[34]: "During the first of these [periods] men and women were created; in the second the rite of circumcision by means of a stone knife, in place of a fire-stick, was introduced; in the third the rite of *Ariltha* or sub-incision was introduced, and in the fourth the present organization and marriage system of the tribe were established."[35] Spencer combined the second and third periods for his tripartite categorization. Without reference to his sources, to the contexts in which he gathered these materials, or even to the form in which the materials were presented to him, Spencer described these traditions for thirty-six pages. The dominance of the initiatory theme in Spencer's categorizations ought not to go unscrutinized. While clearly Spencer used materials collected by Gillen apart from the ritual performances they observed in 1896, a likely hypothesis is that much of the information he included in this section was gleaned from the explanations offered to him about the dozens of totem-locality rites that he saw performed.

In the first period, rudimentary creatures, that is, not fully formed humans, are transformed into human beings with appropriate slices of the knives of figures known as Ungambikula. After performing this task, these figures transform themselves into lizards.[36] Spencer continued with an account of uncircumcised plum tree totem men who lived at Quiurnpa and killed *oruncha*, that is, "devil-devil men." Spencer went to some lengths to explain his inclusion of this tradition, clearly associated with a totem-locality rite. He saw the account as "a crude attempt to describe the origin of human beings out of nonhuman creatures who were of various forms."[37]

To account for the second period, dealing with the origin of circumcision and subincision, Spencer described the "wanderings" of two totem ancestral groups, the *ullakupera*, or little hawk totem, that introduced circumcision and the *tjilpa*, or wildcat totem, that introduced subincision. These accounts are primarily itineraries, tracing the many places to which the ancestral group traveled. For each camping place, an outline of their actions and interactions with others is given. While circumcision and subincision are inaugurated in these "wanderings," these introductions are minor incidents in the context of the whole journey. The *tjilpa* ancestors, indeed, are divided into four groups, the travels of each group being recounted.[38]

With his interest in cultural evolution providing the basis for the structure that Spencer recognized in these traditions, he noted that the marriage restrictions practiced by the Arrernte were not apparently practiced by those figures in the Early and Middle Wanderings. This suggested to Spencer that these stories reflect a time period prior to the introduction of marriage restrictions. He believed there was a connection between the introduction of marriage rules and the traditions of the erlia, or emu people, yet he referred to these traditions only briefly.[39]

Spencer recounted a number of other totem ancestral traditions, that is, itineraries of the movement and outlines of actions and interactions of the ancestors with whom specific totem groups identify. Curiously, he did not identify a period in which these events took place, although he focused on customs that originated as a result.[40]

Customs

The balance of *Native Tribes* is devoted to the description of the miscellany of customs about which Spencer and Gillen had collected information: food, clothing, weapons, implements, medicine, magic, death, art, avenging parties, gender crossing, soul concepts, and so on.[41]

Carl Strehlow's Arrernte

Most of the information Carl Strehlow collected from the Arrernte came from four men who lived in the northwestern and Hermannsburg areas of the Western Arrernte. Loatijira, whose date of birth is approximately 1846, was an Arrernte medicine man who, through much of his life, was opposed to Christianity. He identified his conception site as Mbultjigata, about a mile up the Finke River from Hermannsburg. It was only after Carl Strehlow's death, in 1923, that Loatijira accepted Christian baptism. Theodor Strehlow indicated that during his youth at Hermannsburg, Loatijira was undisputed as the authority on Western Arrernte traditions. Pmala, from Ndata, was born in 1860 and baptized in 1900, a time early in Carl Strehlow's studies. Tjalkabota, who became a Christian at a young age, was not certain of his conception site and considered Hermannsburg his home. Born in 1873, he was far less informed about his Arrernte traditions than the other men with whom Strehlow worked. Strehlow's source for Loritja traditions came primarily from Talku. Born in the year 1867, around the turn of the century, Talku organized raids on cattle at the Tempe Downs station. During one such raid he was wounded by police gunfire. His companions carried him to Hermannsburg, where he was given a safe haven while his leg healed. Strehlow received extensive information as Talku's demonstration of gratitude. He was ceremonial chief of the *kukatja* (yam) center at Merini.[42]

Carl Strehlow's fieldwork was done without witnessing any actual aboriginal ritual or cultural performances. He forbid Christian aborigines at Hermannsburg to participate in or attend any of these events, and he kept the prohibition himself. Rather, he studied the Arrernte and Loritja languages and made inquiries about Arrernte and Lortija cultures and religions. He collected hundreds of stories and songs in their native languages, which he then translated into German. Many of the texts were published in three forms: the native-language version, word-for-word interlinear translations, and free translations. When songs were understood to be integrated into a ritual process, Strehlow sought detailed descriptions of the latter.

The materials collected by Carl Strehlow were published in German in four volumes during the period 1907–20.[43] First to appear was "Myths, Legends and Fables of the Aranda Tribe" (1907), designated as part I of volume I. The volume was edited by Moritz Freiherr von Leonhardi, who explains in an introduction that his editing was minor; however, he notes that he withheld from publication a section on "totemic conceptions" because it was not "sufficiently researched" but promises its inclusion in another volume. The volume is largely made up of story texts, beginning with a description of a sky-dwelling god called Altjira. Information is provided on "primordial times" and on the major totem ancestors that served as teachers for the people. Strehlow included two sections on "evil beings" and briefly described the "Island of the Dead"; the balance of the volume contains sixty-eight stories of totem ancestors, four of which are described as legends.

Traditions of Origins and the *Altjirangamitjina*, or Ancestors

Whereas Spencer, the biologist and social Darwinist, began his presentation of the Arrernte with a description of the landscape and the social order, these topics would await Strehlow's forth and last volume. As a missionary, he began at the beginning, so to speak, dealing with the creator, the creation, and the origin of human beings. Altjira is described as a tall, strong man with red skin and long, fair hair. He dwells in the sky and is thought to be eternal. According to Strehlow, the Arrernte consider him "the good god"; however, they do not believe that he either cares for or involves himself with human affairs. Altjira played a part in creation, but he was not the creator. In primordial times, the earth was covered by the sea and only a few mountains were visible. These were inhabited by "beings with divine power," called *altjirangamitjina*, that is, the eternal and noncreated ones. Some of these beings ascended to Altjira's sky realm to hunt, returning laden with game to their earthly world. Altjira then forbade this action. Along the slope of one of these mountains lived many undeveloped people called *rella manerinja* ("a person grown together") because their body parts appeared to be grown together. Other undeveloped people lived in the water. One of the totem ancestors struck the waters with a stick and commanded it to "go away." The sea retreated to the north, and dry land appeared. Some hunters ignored Altjira's command and journeyed to the sky to hunt. Angered, Altjira commanded the highest peak to disappear into the ground, thus removing the exit from the sky world. The trespassers were forced to remain forever in the sky, where they live as stars. As discussed in detail in chapter 5, it must be remembered that Spencer was highly critical of Strehlow's presentation of this "high god" because he believed that the missionaries themselves originated this deity by using the term *Altjira* as the Arrernte term by which to render the Christian term *God*.

With the retreat of the water, the *altjirangamitjina* appeared everywhere, emerging from the subterranean caves in which they had been living. Most were in human form, but each had the ability to "call into being those animals whose names they bore" and they could transform themselves into those animals. Thus, Strehlow argued, they could be described as "totem gods."[44] Each totem god was associated with a locality where he or she had "lived and generated their totem animals." [45] Some but not all of these *altjirangamitjina* went on journeys, accompanied by novices. Along the way, the totem gods performed almost daily rites to instruct their novices. Here Strehlow introduced an important distinction from, and to him a correction to, Spencer and Gillen. He noted that the purpose of performing these rites is twofold. If the rites are performed to teach the tradition to the novices, they are called *intitjiuma* (Spencer and Gillen's *intichiuma*), which Strehlow understood as meaning "initiate, instruct." If the rites are performed to effect the growth and multiplication of their totems, they are called *mbatjalkaltiuma*, which Strehlow understood as meaning "place into favorable circumstances, make fertile." Spencer and Gillen's *intichiuma*, which they identified as "increase rites," thus corresponds with Strehlow's *mbatjalkaltiuma*. Throughout his work, Strehlow frequently, though usually quite gently in footnotes, called attention to what he considered Spencer and Gillen's errors, invariably due, in Strehlow's view, to their limited knowledge of the Arrernte language.

In his description of these primordial journeys of the totem gods, Strehlow foreshadowed his later description of the Arrernte beliefs about conception totems. The *tjurunga*, often taking the form of a tree or rock, left behind by the totem gods is the source for embryos that "pass into women who happened to walk by." These are minor totem places. Once the journey was completed, the bodies of the *altjamaltjerama* were changed into wood or stone objects, *tjurunga*, which Strehlow understands as meaning "one's own, secret body." While the bodies of the ancestors are transformed into objects, according to Strehlow, their "souls" enter into the earth, where they maintain a relationship with their transformed bodies. These locations of the transformed bodies of the ancestors are designated as "major totem places," *mbatjita* or *tjarutja* ("eternal place") or *takuta* ("everlasting place").[46]

After the earth's surface had dried, the *rella manerinja* ("people grown together") continued in their helpless state until the "totem god of a fly-eating lizard" (*mangarkunjerkunja*) came from the north. With a stone knife he separated the persons from each other; cut slits for their eyes; opened their ears, mouths, noses, fingers, toes, and so on. He also circumcised and subincised them. Then he showed them how to make fire and to prepare meals. He introduced to them the spear, the spearthrower, the shield, and the boomerang and gave each of them a *tjurunga*.[47] He instructed them to adhere to the initiation ceremony. *Mangarakunjerkunja* instructed the people about the marriage system, designating that the four classes of "land dwellers" were to marry corresponding classes of "water dwellers" and echoing the most fundamental binary distinction between the two.[48] He divided the land among these eight social classes. Another *mangarakunjerkunja* arrived from the north to perform similar acts for the *rella manerinja* farther to the south. When their work was done, these two figures returned to the north. Strehlow holds that the Arrernte consider these two *mangarakunjerkunja* to be their greatest benefactors.

Strehlow described various kinds of "evil beings" (*erintja*, derived from *ara*, which means "angry, evil, biting")[49] that originated from an immense cave in the earth, which is their home. They appear in many forms, such as dog, human, bird, and wind. Strehlow observed a correlation of the cardinal direction north with benevolence and south with malevolence. He also described in some detail an "island of the dead," which is located in the far north. This is the destiny of the souls of the deceased. From this island the departed souls may make various spirit journeys back to their homes to visit and communicate with still-living relatives. Ultimately the spirit is "obliterated" by lightning. Notably, Strehlow concluded his discussion of the dead with an alternative: "There is another view which speaks of the souls of 'good' people going to *Altjira* in heaven, to live there forever, and the spirits of 'bad' people ending up in the habitation of the *atua ntjikantja* [venom gland men[50]], to be consumed by them."[51] There is little doubt that this Arrernte tradition reflects missionary teaching, and it is notable that Strehlow did not acknowledge the influence.

The balance of volume I contains many "legends concerning the totem ancestors." For the most part these are not discussed as itineraries, as Spencer and Gillen presented ancestral stories. They generally are identified by the protagonist and a location. The stories, most rather short, describe a single incident related to the particular ancestor, often actions the ancestor performs.[52]

The second publication, appearing in 1908 as part II of volume I, is an exact parallel to the first volume, focused on the Loritja rather than the Arrernte. Added to this volume is Strehlow's discussion of totemic concepts and the *tjurunga*, sections now sufficiently researched to pass von Leonhardi's critical eye. The Loritja call their supreme being Tukura. He is similar to Altjira. In a footnote, Strehlow notes the discussion of the emu-footed man described by Gillen in his Horn rxpedition report and believes that the details of Gillen's account match more closely with Tukura than Altjira, leading Strehlow to conclude that Gillen must have obtained his information from a Loritja person. Strehlow obtains forty-four Loritja legends, two of which are fables. In summary statements, he presents the differences between the Loritja and the Arrernte.

Totemic Conceptions

In the same publication,[53] Strehlow added to Spencer and Gillen's information on what was to become a highly controversial issue—human procreation. At first Strehlow held that the Arrernte do not know about sexual procreation, although he later conceded that he confirmed Spencer and Gillen's claim that the Arrernte understand that sexual intercourse is a kind of preparation of the mother for conception.[54] Strehlow explained that they believe in two methods of procreation. A woman who travels near an *altjamaltjerama's mbatjita* ("major totem place") may be recognized by a *ratapa*, or embryo child, which enters the woman at her hip. The mother feels the first signs of pregnancy at this place, which she identifies as the totem place of the child she will bear. In a second method, an ancestral figure who dwells somehow in the landscape, throws his bullroarer at the woman. It enters at her hip and takes the form of a child within her. Strehlow was unable to corroborate Spencer and Gillen's claim that all children are reincarnations of the souls of totem ancestors. Only on rare occasions does an *iningukua* (the specific *altjirangamitjina* from whose metamorphosed body the *ratapa* emerges) himself enter a woman to be reborn.

Every Arrernte has a totem identification, called *ratapa*, that is associated with the place where one's mother became aware of her pregnancy and another, called *altjira*, that is the totem of one's mother. Thus one totem is obtained by birth, the other by inheritance. A person may participate in the activities of both of these totems. At burial, one is oriented to face the mother's totem location (*tmara altjirealtja*, "the camp of the mother's totem"), which, according to Strehlow, enables the spirit of the deceased to travel to the Island of the Dead.[55] A totem is regarded as an "older brother," obligated to treat one with consideration.

In response to the wide interest of European scholars to the eating of totem species, Strehlow reported that people were forbidden to eat their totem animal or plant or, at least, were allowed to eat only the least appealing parts. His explanation was interesting, however, in that he noted that this practice was at odds with the practices of the totem ancestors, as evident in their stories, who regularly gained nourishment from their totem animals and plants. Strehlow's informants told him that they believed the prohibitions stem from "the old people who want to reserve the best parts for themselves."[56] The old people warned young men of sickness and death if they violated the food restrictions. Strehlow lists 442 totems for the Arrernte and Loritja.

Tjurunga

Strehlow concluded part II of volume I with a discussion of *tjurunga*, which he translated as "one's own secret thing."[57] The term refers, above all, to stones and wooden objects, although it can also be used to refer to one's secret name or the rituals of one's totem group. *Tjurungas* are closely linked to a person's identity and kept secret. The bodies of many *altjamaltjerama* ("ancestors") were changed into *tjurungas* when their earth-surface activities were complete. After Mangarkunjerkanja transformed the incomplete creatures into human beings, he gave each a *tjurunga*, which he described as the body of the one related to it. Thus, a *tjurunga* is closely related to the totem ancestor, as well as to the individual person to whom it belongs. It may be thought of as their common body. The *tjurunga* also ties a person to the totem plant or animal. This connection gives the *tjurunga* bearer the ability to increase the totem object and "make it fat." Rubbing the *tjurunga* with ochre or fat, as is commonly done in rituals, causes creative powers to emanate from the object. This action "will cause the totem animals to leap out of it."[58] The importance of the interconnection of the totem and the person cannot be overstated. The *tjurunga* is a way of representing and effecting this relationship. Strehlow clarified that the *tjurunga* is not the place of habitation for the soul or the life force but rather is thought of as a second body of the bearer. He held that everyone has two bodies, one of flesh and one of stone or wood. The *tjurunga* provides protection and power.

A second *tjurunga*, also considered to be a second body for a person, is identified as the *papa-tjurunga* (*papa* means "staff" or "stick"). It represents the relationship one has with one's *iningukua* (the ancestor with whom one's identity is connected). Many objects considered to be transformed parts of ancestral bodies are called *tjurungas* and are stored in the ritual storehouses, for example, bullroarers. Women have *tjurungas* but, according to Strehlow, never see them. *Tjurungas*, as personal property, are inherited, going from father to oldest son or nephew. A woman's *tjurunga* is inherited by her older brother or her son. The Loritja term parallel to the Arrernten *tjurunga* is *kuntanka*.

Ritual

With the third segment of *Die Aranda* (part III of volume I), which appeared in 1910 and 1911, Strehlow turns to the "totemic cults." The major distinction between

Spencer and Gillen's and Strehlow's presentations of ritual stems from their differing field methods. Whereas Spencer and Gillen attended ritual performances, their understanding of the Arrernte language was limited. Strehlow did not attend rituals, but he knew the Arrernte language and he obtained descriptions of rituals from his knowledgeable informants, along with the lyrics of a great many songs. Whereas Spencer and Gillen contended that the aborigines "neither knew nor understood what they were singing," Strehlow demonstrated not only that the words of the songs had meaning but also that understanding the songs was fundamental to comprehending aboriginal ritual. In section 1 (1910) of this publication, he described fifty-nine Arrernten rituals with their accompanying songs; in section 2 (1911), he described twenty-one Loritja rituals.

The totemic rituals are based on ancestral actions. The ancestors traveled around the landscape, performing ceremonies at distinct locations. They did so in order to acquaint the novices with the religious customs and to increase and strengthen the totem animal or plant with which the ancestors were identified. Arrernte ritual performances replicate these ancestral ritual performances, both as part of the initiation of youth, when the rites are called *intitjiuma*, and on other occasions to increase and strengthen the totem animals and plants. On these occasions, the rites are called *mbatjalkatiuma* ("to bring about, make fertile, improve conditions of").

Mbatjalkatiuma

Strehlow's informants indicated that the increase rites are motivated by ancestral command, not by some interest in serving the larger social group. Strehlow argued that since the rites do not actually ensure an increase in the totem plants and animals and that since harmful and useless totem plants and animals are the focus for rites, increase is not their actual purpose. Strehlow's comments are worth quoting: "They are under the impression that something enormously important is being achieved by the cult, indeed, they are convinced that they serve their totem by divine serve, as Christians view their religious duties in the same light. I was assured of this by Christian as well as pagan natives. Should an actor play his role well, then the old men particularly are deeply moved. They shed tears and—since they transfer their emotions to the stomach (*tnata*) strangely enough—declare that their stomach was sad (*tnata nturknerama*) or torn by pain."[59] The rites replicate ancestral acts at the actual locations where the original acts were performed. Strehlow reported that the totem animals are hidden in these places and that they will emerge if the old men let blood flow during the rites. It seems there is also a connection between smearing the *tjurungas* with fat and ochre and calling forth the ancestors. The ancestors appear not as spirit beings but as actual animals and plants.

Procedures for *mbatjalkatiuma* are as follows.[60] The head man sets the performance date upon consultation with other elders. On the appointed day, the men arrive at the *tjurunga* storehouse in the vicinity of where the rite is to be performed. This place is called *arknanaua* ("the cleansed"). The *tjurungas* are taken from the storehouse and laid on a cushion of branches after being rubbed with fat and red ochre. The rites are performed by men either who belong to the totem concerned or whose *altjira*, mother's totem, is this totem group.

The bodies of the performers are decorated, the designs modeled on the ancestors. Headdresses are sometimes worn that represent a part of the ancestor's body. A pole (*tnatantja*) is erected at the ceremonial site for every performance. It represents the spears of the ancestors and is constructed of spears. Strehlow described in detail the performances, including the movement and song. The songs, which Strehlow referred to as "*tjurunga* songs" are believed to describe either the episodes of the ancestral journeys or the animals or plants with which the totem ancestors identify. The songs assist in attaining the purpose of the ritual, that is, in the growth and increase of the totem. Strehlow indicated that these songs are taught to the learned men by the "hidden people" (*rella ngantja*), that is, the ancestors who live in the earth. They emerge at night and implant their songs in the sleeping men. Arachic words in the songs convinced Strehlow that they date from earlier times, being passed along through many generations. Songs usually have a two-part structure, the second part expanding on, explaining, or completing the first part. While Strehlow used the term *song*, he cautioned against applying the usual expectations to the term. Rather, aboriginal singing "consists of a monotone chanting, with an alternate rising and lowering of the pitch. One could also describe it as a nasal, singing scanning. One, seldom two, short and unstressed syllable is followed by a long, stressed syllable, with no regard to the accent of the word. . . . During the chanting of the cult songs, as the pitch drops gradually, another singer takes over and continues—usually an octave higher—and others follow him."[61] All the words are combined or appear to be undistinguished in the chanting. Strehlow differed with Spencer and Gillen's report that the totem chief was required to eat a portion of the totem plant or animal. Strehlow's informants denied this, indicating that no ritual eating occurred at all.

Initiation rites

Strehlow described initiation rites in the midst of his discussion of social life, covered as part IV of volume I, section 1, which was published in 1913.[62] The initiate is known as *ulbma*, and he enters initiation eagerly since it is required of any man wishing a voice in community affairs. It is also the prerequisite for eligibility for marriage. Circumcision (*intunama*) and subincision (*araltakama*) are considered the most important aspects of the rites and believed, at least by Strehlow's informants, to be of great antiquity, having been introduced by Mangarkunjerkunja (the fly-eating lizard ancestor). Strehlow considered these ritual surgical procedures "peculiar and cruel," yet he discussed their significance. Rejecting the hypothesis that the procedures are related to conception, Strehlow reported his informants' views that the rituals teach boys obedience to the elders, which Strehlow noted "has a wholesome influence on an unrestrained, primitive people who are not used to any kind of order."[63] Strehlow reported that circumcision is intended to restrict sexual excesses of the adolescents and that it prevents the foreskin from growing together, which would make intercourse impossible. Strehlow's informants apparently indicated that subincision makes boys more supple and able to avoid enemy spears. Finally, the old men seem to encourage the practice out of self-interest since the boys must pay tribute to their elders, mainly by giving them animals to eat.

The ritual process of initiation is divided into seven parts, according to Strehlow, much as described by Spencer and Gillen. During the circumcision rites, the day is spent conducting *intitjiuma*, that is, the totem-locality rites so extensively recorded by Spencer and Gillen. Strehlow stated that these rites performed in this context are not intended to increase or enhance the growth of the totem animals or plants. Rather, they are to acquaint the initiates with the secrets of their totem group. Strehlow provided the words to many of the songs and ritual speeches performed throughout the initiation sequence. He also provided an extensive presentation of *ankatja kerintja*, the secret language, that the initiates must learn and use while on their several-week exile and when associating with initiated men. Subincision occurs, according to Strehlow, who gave an extensive description, six weeks after circumcision. After another six weeks, two other ceremonies are performed, one with the intent of punishing the initiate for disobedience in his earlier life, the other to "provide his body with a more masculine appearance by browning it."[64] The first ceremony involves forcing the initiates' foreheads to powerfully hit a shield. The initiates run all night in a prescribed circle in the presence of men and women. At daybreak the women prepare a smoking fire, over which the initiates are laid to blacken their bodies. After the blackening, their bodies are decorated with red paint. A brief ritual is performed to produce the growth of a long beard.

The final ceremonial described is *injura* (Spencer and Gillen's *engwura*). The one- to two-month ceremonial is performed annually or every other year (depending on the need), usually in the months of October through December. It is a larger gathering than for any of the other initiation ceremonies since the youths initiated during the year are brought together from all the neighboring camps. Strehlow indicated its significance as "the solemn conclusion to the initiation and the public acceptance of the *iliara* (fully initiated men) into the fellowship and rank of authoritative and decision making men."[65] Hunting (done mainly by the initiates) and gathering (done by the women) occupy the daylight hours. *Intitjiuma* is performed at night. This long ceremonial is concluded with another fire ceremony in which the initiates are smoked. Strehlow provided a list of fifteen Arrernte terms and their Loritja counterparts that are used to indicate stages of development for males from "boy before initiation" to "very old man."[66]

Strehlow described female initiation, for which he uses the term "circumcision," and considered it a "consequence of the circumcision of the boys."[67] This procedure, performed without ceremony, is a vaginal incision intended to ease the process of giving birth. After the operation until her marriage, the woman must live in the women's camp. Several days after the operation, the man who performed it goes to the woman, "lifts her up and hugs her, while commanding her never to leave her future husband. Then he has intercourse with her. During the following nights, all the girl's *ankalla* and *noa* [i.e., men who are in a spousal relationship to her], who had helped with the circumcision, also have sexual relations with her, as a kind of reward for their services."[68] Another female procedure intended to encourage breast development is performed by men with somewhat more ceremony. This rite involves rubbing fat on the girl's chest and tying a string around her torso and across her chest while old men sing appropriate songs.

Customs

Other aspects of Arrernte and Loritja social life described by Strehlow include birth and name giving, games, body disfigurement, marriage customs, and the kinship system including extensive family trees. In section 2 of this work, published in 1915, Strehlow continued the presentation of Arrernte and Loritja social life, describing political and legal systems; death-related matters; revenge practices; illness and healing processes ("magic"); and a variety of language-related matters, such as terms for number and time, sign language, and the secret language of the men.

Géza Róheim's Arrernte

Géza Róheim[69] can be considered a "Freudian radical" in that his academic career amounted to a single-minded application of psychoanalytic categories to the study of culture.[70] His major contributions are largely grounded in the field studies he conducted from early 1929 to 1931. Princess George of Greece (Marie Bonaparte) financed Róheim's expedition.[71] He chose to study the Arrernte because of what he had learned of them from Spencer and Gillen and Strehlow (among others) while researching *Australian Totemism* (1924). His work, following Freud's *Totem and Taboo*, was concerned with origination. He held that the Central Australian aborigines are the "classical representatives of Totemism and the hunting mode of life," noting that Frazer has considered them "the most primitive [culture] known to us."[72] Róheim arrived in February 1929 at Hermannsburg, where he spent four months, followed by a period with the Pitjantjatjara. Carl Strehlow had died in 1922, Spencer had returned to the Alice Springs area in 1926, and Theodor Strehlow would enter Central Australia to begin his many years of field study in May 1932. Some of Róheim's informants had been known to Strehlow, though none that Róheim named were listed by the missionary as significant informants. Róheim specifically mentioned Wapiti and Old Moses as individuals known by Strehlow.[73] Róheim conducted play analysis, based on the theories developed by Melanie Klein, with a boy and a girl he had chosen from the Arrernte and Loritja cultures. He conversed with numerous men and women, whom he identified by name, from a variety of communities. He asked about dreams and discussed ritual and story. He also observed the performance of many rites.

Róheim compared his field method with those of his predecessors, Strehlow and Spencer and Gillen. He labeled Spencer and Gillen's approach an "extrovert attitude in field anthropology" because they attended the performances of ceremonials and described what they saw.[74] They failed, in Róheim's estimation, to comprehend that the rituals they saw were dramatizations of the songs; and since they did not record, indeed they were incapable of recording, the songs, they could not help but greatly miss the meaning of what they saw. He thought that Strehlow's approach, which prevented him from ever seeing a ceremonial performance, bore an "introvert attitude."[75] He deemed that the "mere *behaviorist* outlook (Spencer) is just as unsatisfactory as the lifeless study-method of Strehlow."[76]

Building on both, claiming to subsume the accomplishments of both approaches yet make major advances, Róheim presented his field method as constituting a "new anthropology." His approach not only combined those of both his predecessors—that is, he both witnessed and described cultural rites and activities and engaged in the collection of knowledge apart from cultural performance through discourse in native languages—but also complemented them by collecting and analyzing quite different and complementary kinds of data: dreams, information on sexual life, and children's activities (sexual and play). Unlike his predecessors, who relied on others to provide general information about the culture, Róheim centered his inquiry on individuals, whom he analyzed, to the best of his ability, outside of a clinical setting. The analysis of individuals, rather than directly providing information about the culture in general, provided Róheim with the clues and materials by which to construct a psychoanalytic interpretation of culture, to engage in a psychoanalytic anthropology.[77]

Róheim placed his field methods squarely in the realm of psychoanalytic theory, describing them in such clinical terms as "transference," "counter-transference," and "free association." Róheim's comments deserve quotation at length:

> Transference, of course, is the basis of all anthropological work, although the non-psycho-analytical anthropologist does not call it transference and knows nothing about its infantile origins. He gets the transference instinctively, because he likes his work and therefore also the people whom he is studying. I do not mean to say that the psycho-analyst will or should work according to a purely conscious scheme. He, too, must find the right attitude instinctively, i.e., through what has been called the dialogue of the unconscious. But, being accustomed to analyze his own actions, he will soon become conscious of what he is doing and why he is doing it. The anthropologist, on the other hand, works with an unanalyzed transference and especially, what is worse still, with an unanalyzed counter-transference. The counter-transference has not been sufficiently discussed in clinical analysis, yet it is an essential factor of therapy. By counter-transference we mean the attitude the analyst takes to his patients. It is that of a fond or a severe parent, not unmixed, as in the case of a real parent, with a tendency of identification with the child-parent. The anthropologist, although theoretically he may believe in the unity of mankind and therefore expect to find that the black or brown man has strivings, yearnings and fears like his own, is still the child of a different race and civilization. As he slowly overcomes the feeling of strangeness in his new environment, the sorcerer and cannibal becoming as commonplace acquaintances as his school friends, the pendulum will naturally swing in the opposite direction. Instead of a group of uncanny beings, he now sees an idyll of the type imagined by Rousseau. Human beings untrammeled by the cares and conventions of civilization, innocent children who lead a happy life where all is love, play and good-fellowship. He does not notice

> that he is also reacting against the opposite extreme, unmitigated racial hatred, as manifested in the opinions of the white trader with whom he comes into contact.
>
> I am afraid that some of our foremost field-workers, for instance, are idealizing the native beyond measure. It is not surprising that this should be so. For good field-work proves transference and transference again cannot be maintained without counter-transference. The same refers perhaps even in an enhanced degree to books written by missionaries who take an interest in anthropology. The missionary cannot possibly gain an influence of a spiritual nature without transference and counter-transference. As he is very far removed from an insight into his own psychic mechanisms and those of his flock, he will adopt an attitude in which, to put it in the words of one of the traders I have met, 'nothing the native can do is wrong.'[78]

The study of culture is parallel to clinical analysis of an individual patient. Róheim went to considerable lengths to compare the similarities and differences between the two enterprises. Psychoanalysis is based on a relationship—that of analyst and patient—which eventuates in the analyst's construction of a narrative of coherence. Psychoanalytic anthropology is distinguished from other forms of anthropology, not because other approaches are not based on the relationship between anthropologist and "native," but because the psychoanalytic anthropologist is self-consciously formal about the character of this relationship and has undergone analysis to reveal the character of the inevitable transference and countertransference. The perspective Róheim presents at once exposes the skewing subjective influence of the ethnographer, yet he embraces as inevitable the relational and subjective character of anthropology.

The intent of this chapter is to present the Arrernte as seen through the eyes (as reported in the writings) of those who lived among them. Róheim's *Australian Totemism* (1925), published before he went to Australia, stands in the broad academic tradition that has relied on the reports of others, primarily Strehlow and Spencer and Gillen, as the cultural foundation on which to construct and support a general theory on Australian aboriginal cultures.[79] A brief summary of *Australian Totemism* is of value as background to the approach Róheim was to take in his field studies. Appearing in 1925, *Australian Totemism* seems oddly out of step with the scholarly works of the time. It shared more with the perspectives of Tylor and Frazer than with those of Róheim's contemporaries. Róheim believed in the psychic unity of humankind, that is, that the unconscious was the same for all cultures.[80] *Australian Totemism* was written to defend and elaborate on the primal crime thesis set forth in Freud's *Totem and Taboo*, which Róheim considered to be perhaps the greatest work in anthropology.

Freud discerned four characteristics of totemism: (1) the totem animal was considered sacred by the totem clan and therefore never harmed or hunted; (2) however, the totem animal was sacrificed and eaten by the entire tribe on special ceremonial occasions; (3) the totem animal was a primal father to the members of the totem clan in that they all traced their ancestry to the animal; (4) the totem is associated with exogamy—that is, one had always to marry someone outside one's totem. Based on these factors, Freud described the primal crime that accounted for the origin of totemism. He posited a social group in which the father sexually monopolized the women. At a certain moment the sons band together in revolt, killing and eating the father. Yet, Freud held that after this act was completed, the sons had a change of mind. Rather than cohabiting with the women, thus satisfying the need that had motivated the murder, they created the first moral law, the prohibition of incest. This taboo, which corresponds with the social requirements for exogamy, became the basis for society. The reasons given for this change of mind and for the institution of these laws and practices are both the practical one of preventing war among the brothers over their own female relatives and the more important religious one, based on the love of the father. The brothers found that although they had killed their father, they had loved him after all. Their sexual denial created the libidinal basis for the clan, the cohesion of society. The guilt felt by the brothers led to the transformation of the dead father into a god, initially in human form but later in the form of the totem animal. Thus, Freud saw residuals of the primal crime in the totem meal and of the sons' remorse in the treatment of the totem animal.[81]

Róheim's *Australian Totemism* was written to defend and extend Freud's hypothesis, in which every dimension of Arrernte society was set. For example, the documented increase rites were seen as a repetition of the totem father's mourning feast.[82] Seeing the body decorations of the ritualists participating in the increase rites as the survival of the decoration that occurred at breeding season to enhance sexual attractiveness, Róheim argued that the primal crime had occurred during rutting season and that the primal murder had thus ended sexual periodicity, that is, breeding seasons. Further, he argued that humans were able to discard sexual periodicity because of the acquisition of the means of repression to cope with the demands of reality.[83]

Extending Freud, Róheim had an enduring interest in ambisexuality, a development of Freud's exaggeration of heterosexuality in the Oedipus complex. Foreshadowing what would become central to his later interpretations of the Arrernte, Róheim argued that at a more fundamental psychic level, the totem represented the mother; thus eating the totem animal amounted to an upward displacement of intercourse with the mother.[84]

In the field at Hermannsburg, Róheim wasted little time in becoming engaged as fully as possible with the Arrernte people. His considerable ability to learn languages allowed him to soon communicate in Arrernte. He visited adults and children, collecting dreams and asking for confirmations and extensions of the published ethnographies of Carl Strehlow and Spencer and Gillen. He asked extensively about their sexual behavior, beliefs, and practices. His focus was largely on the individual. His intent was to do psychoanalysis in the field, adapting clinical practice to fit the field situation. Given the brief time Róheim was actually in the field, he collected an astonishing amount of material and dealt in depth with a broad range of complex cultural and psychological issues. His field experience provided sufficient raw material to support the balance of his scholarly career. Time and again Róheim returned to his Australian data and experience to support yet another theoretically based study. Doubtless the enmeshment of his field data with his interpretive and theoretical positions, coupled with the general suspicion and disfavor of psychoanalysis, explains the neglect of Róheim's work. In many respects this is unfortunate. Clearly Róheim collected extensive materials of a kind that no other ethnographer thought to collect. He entered the controversy between Strehlow and Spencer on such matters as the meaning of the Arrernte word *altjira*, which Strehlow saw as a god and Spencer rendered as "dream."[85] Above all, distinct from the other ethnographers of the Arrernte, Róheim appreciated the influence ethnographers have on their subjects.[86]

Given the many readings that Róheim made of the Arrernte and other Australian aboriginal cultures, it is difficult to summarize while remaining fair to the extent, complexity, and variability of his views. A summary organized by themes and topics of the several works on which Róheim relied most heavily for Arrernten materials must serve here, although it should be remembered that, in addition, he wrote many articles that were published in English, German, and Hungarian.

The People and the Landscape

Róheim refuted what he understood as a common view that "primitive man is less adapted to his environment than we are."[87] Focusing on concentric circle designs in ground paintings (*ilpintira*), body paintings (*apmoara*), and *tjurungas*, Róheim found that these designs are commonly interpreted as the place or camp (*tmara*) of the totem ancestors. The interpretation of these circular designs, connected with the landscape as "womb," allowed him to conclude that the emotional values attached to environment are "derived from deflected genital libido." That the main weapon used in the struggle with the environment is the spear supports Róheim's interpretation of the aboriginal genitalization of the environment.[88]

Correlating the places designated as "womb" to the topography corresponds to the distinction of actual geographical places identified as totem centers (*tmara knarra,* "big place") from the remainder of the landscape. The landscape is thus divided between totem centers and the desert, which is the domain of demons and monsters.[89] In the discussion of totemism from the perspective of the infantile concept of "good" and "bad" objects,[90] Róheim divided the topography between places associated with good objects (totem centers) and those associated with bad objects. Aboriginal associations with the landscape follow Róheim's interpretation of totemism. Totemism (in this instance, specifically the increase rites) is a way of overcoming the anxiety that accompanies hunting. The landscape is filled with "good objects," which because they are destroyed to provide food, may turn on humans and thus become "bad objects." Human groups attempt to maintain the good attitudes of these good objects by not eating them (a form of symbolic identification). Thus aboriginal understandings of the landscape appear as nodes interconnected by tracks rather than contiguous territories separated by boundaries.[91] The religious aspect of this topographical designation is discussed by Róheim in terms of the concept of eternity (*altjira*). Totem centers are identified with the *altjiranga mitjina*, which Róheim interprets as "the eternal ones of the dream," that is, the totemic ancestors. Objects associated with the *altjiranga mitjina*, such as rock paintings and *tjurunga*, bear the concept of the eternal.[92] These objects constitute the prototype of the "good object" in that they are "a sort of inexhaustible store-house."[93]

The ancestors create the distinctive features in the landscape. As human beings, the Arrernte consider the world to be a human creation. According to Róheim, the names of places, as well as distinctive features in the landscape, are the result of ancestral activities.[94]

Social Organization

Róheim extends Spencer and others by attributing the identity of conception totems to night dreams. Rather than restricting the identity of the totem to a correlation with the place a woman is when she discovers she is pregnant, Róheim found that the totem can also be identified in a dream that correlates with a woman's discovery that she is pregnant. In analyzing these dreams, he found a typical theme, which he presented through the scenario of the woman being chased by her father, who entered her womb. This theme correlates with the beliefs reported by Róheim and others that a woman is impregnated when chased by the ancestors, who throw an object (*nankara,* "stone") into her hip. Róheim concluded from the incestuous theme of women's conception dreams that "the totem of an Aranda or Luritja is determined by a thinly-veiled incest dream of his mother's [*sic*]."[95] His analysis of several conception dreams led Róheim to conclude that the organization of aboriginal society is not based on the "primary Oedipus relation, i.e. on the love of the son for the mother, but on a secondary phase, a reprint of the original, on incest between father and daughter."[96]

Róheim also found that a child's totem may be determined by other methods. If the child's father is in possession of his *tjurunga*, a feather from the *tjurunga* bundle may get into his wife, thus impregnating her. In this case the child bears the father's totem.[97] Further, during the so-called birds' down totem rites (*andatta*), a man whose body has been decorated with birds' down[98] will have intercourse with his wife, during which the down (*wamulu*) will fly from his body into his wife's, thus conceiving a child. The child's totem, in this case, is determined not by location but by the totem identity of the rites the father was decorated to perform.[99]

Róheim found that Spencer and Gillen exaggerated the facts when they stated that the Arrernte did not know the causal relationship between coitus and conception. While in advocating the *tjurunga* complex one might even state the view that a man could give birth if the spirit child entered him, certainly it was well understood that coitus was a necessary preliminary. Róheim observed that playing children enact, in series, the whole process of coitus, conception, and childbirth. He felt that it was during the initiation process that individuals, introduced to the *tjurunga* complex, came to believe that something beyond coitus was necessary for conception.[100]

Róheim gave a careful and detailed account of the various kinship systems—two-, four-, and eight-class systems—that are found in Central Australia. He identified incest anxiety as a key motivation in the elaboration of these kinship systems. Incest rules were, in his experience, strictly enforced. The account, supposedly historical, of the violent death meted out to a man who had violated incest taboos would certainly serve to deter infractions. Róheim provided a careful and detailed psychoanalytic discussion of all of the principal social relationships, seeing the father-son relationship as by far the most important. He included discussions of avoidance customs (*kerintja*, which he translated as "shame"): mother-in-law avoidance, avoidance of the daughter by the father once the girl's breasts begin to develop, avoidance of the younger sister (though not the older sister) by the brother when her breasts begin to develop, and avoidance of the mother by the son once his pubic hair begins to appear. Common "tribal"[101] identification is stronger than identification between tribes, even though kinship classifications extend beyond tribal bounds. Other cultures are often considered to be manifestations of demons and blood avengers. Róheim's summary statement on kinship systems is this: "The maintenance and elaboration of the infantile respect and fear of the father are the factors which hold the tribe together."[102] He discussed the roles and privileges of the old men and chiefs (*inkata*) based on extensive accounts of his own experience.[103]

Children of the Desert

Róheim's work with children was fundamental to his field studies. Immediately upon arrival, he selected a group of children—Depitarinja (ten-year-old Arrernte boy), Nyiki (Loritja boy), and Wili-kutu and Aldinga (Arrernte and Loritja girls)—and began to engage them regularly in play activities. He presented them with toys during these play sessions—a monkey, a nanny goat, a snake, and a mirror—and observed how they interacted with them, asking endless questions about what they were doing and why. As the process developed, Róheim began to focus on Depitarinja, whose analysis became paramount: "The others were subordinate actors in the drama. And the plot of the drama was the love of the Snake and the Monkey, i.e., of the young Aranda boy and his mother."[104] He solicited dreams from them, which he correlated with their activities of play in complex psychological interpretations placed persistently in the frame of the Oedipus complex.

Róheim eventually separated from Freud to the degree that he shifted the arena of his interest in origination from phylogenesis to ontogenesis. Perhaps his interest in children reflected the shift. He focused on individuals, their psychic histories and developments, and from them made inferences about the culture. Children were among the most accessible and open of Róheim's informants. Róheim described birth customs, child-naming practices, infanticide, cannibalism, child discipline, and children's games and play sessions.[105]

Religion

In a bold departure from other observers of the Arrernte, Róheim held that "totemism is neither the religion of the whole tribe nor the religion of everyday life."[106] He correlated the religious modes of the people with the phases of their economic life. In times of plenty, the Arrernte live in larger groups. The youths and the women can easily provide food by hunting and gathering, allowing the adult men time to prepare "their totemic play." Thus totemism, according to Róheim, is the religion of abundance, and even then it is only the religion of the initiated men. Totemism focuses on the *altjiranga mitjina*, the "eternal dream-folk," who are always considered beautiful and well formed. In contrast, during times of drought, small bands, often comprising only a man and his wives and children, seek the necessities of life isolated from the rest of the group. Probably only the father is initiated and would know anything of the *tjurunga*. There is no totemism during this period. Rather the religion focuses on the fears related to monsters (*erintja*). These are not ancestors; they are monsters and demons of uncanny shape and man-eating giants. This religion is concerned with sorcery (pointing bones) and curing and the use of magical stones as cult objects.[107] Róheim's analysis of Arrernte religion is well supported and highly suggestive, yet it has received little attention.

Róheim collected and analyzed a number of dreams about a multitude of demons and monsters. He also analyzed a number of folktales, working on the principal that they are the equivalent of dreams.[108] Finding that the monsters are often identified with the father and mother or some relatives of the dreamer, Róheim attributed the existence of monsters to the reappearance of the repressed enjoyment of the primal scene, that is, the forbidden observation of the parents in the act of coitus.[109] The female monster figure Alknarintja (see more detail below) was a focus for Róheim's interpretation of this aspect of Arrernte religion and psychology.

Establishing that totemic religion is limited to grown men while the religion concerned with demons is common to the whole society, Róheim argued that the demon belief is "ontogenetically the earlier of the two." Demon belief is a "pretotemic religion." Its psychological sources are "associated with a sexual tension," stemming from the "primal scene."[110] Based on extensive analysis of myths, particularly the *tjilpa* wanderings, and rites, especially the puberty or initiation rites, Róheim attempted to trace how these two religions are distinct but interrelated. Key to his analysis is Tuanyarika, a figure who at once is associated with a belief in demons (he is believed to cut off the heads of those he catches) and is the figure who captures the youths to be inducted into totemic cults (where he is associated with circumcision). Róheim argued that the belief in demons and monsters begins with the anxiety reaction to the primal scene; it is an attempt to dispose of the disturbing content by projection, by the creation of monsters and demons. In the totemic religion, introjection occurs in which the boy is told that he or his double (*tjurunga*) is a Tuanyarika. In this way Tuanyarika is changed from a phallic demon that eats humans into a protecting ancestor; anxiety is replaced by reverence and identification.[111]

Magic

The religion of the demons, the world of magic, is concerned either with healing or destroying. It is, according to Róheim, the primal religion. From information gained from a number of informants, Róheim described and analyzed beliefs about disease and death and aggressive actions that involve the use of bones or sticks in the attempt to cause injury to others. All magic of this sort involves something—bone, stick, snake, stone—taken from the sorcerer's body and shot into that of the sick person. The same objects are used for healing. Relying on dream accounts, folklore, and the description of sorcery,[112] Róheim, not surprisingly, connected the magical bones and stones, as well as both aggressive and curative sorcery, with the primal scene: "The son fears to be killed by the father's 'bone.' But in these fantasies, 'to be killed' means 'to be castrated,' to play the passive role in the sexual act. Indeed, we can prove directly that the attack, which emanates from the sorcerer-father, is directed against the child's, that is, the victim's, penis."[113]

Alknarintja, *the Women who Avoid Men*

The analysis of this figure is a persistent concern in Róheim's work.[114] He discerned so many significant associations that he discussed them in terms of what he called "the *Alknarintja* concept." He saw the figure, and the accompanying concept, as key in identifying the "development of national character," as one of the most important figures in both mundane and ritual life. In his opinion, originally every totem had its own *alknarintja*. She is the original owner of the *tjurunga*, the symbolic penis. All women were once considered *alknarintja*, which represents the mother image.[115]

Analyzing the dream of an old man, as well as many other elements of culture, Róheim discussed and interpreted the *alknarintja*, or "eyes turn away" women. Although Róheim could not get a clear statement on whether the aborigines understood the figure to be real or mythic, he found that they used the term to refer to both. These women are thought to be wild, yet they avoid men. In mundane life, it appears that all girls are taught to avoid men; thus all women begin as *alknarintja*. It is a special challenge to men to attempt to attract an *alknarintja* woman by using love magic (*ilpindja*).[116] In myths, *alknarintja* is recognized by her appearance: smokey-colored hair, body decorated with red ochre, head ring with *alpita* (tassels that hang down to the ears), and arm strings.

Róheim drew on many elements to contribute to his interpretation of these women. First, he believed that patriarchal society arose to counteract the influence of the mother on child development. Then he turned to a bit of information that figured extensively in so much of his analysis: the typical way a mother sleeps is to lie on her male child, that is, in a manner similar to the male position on the female in sexual intercourse. He added the information he gained from stories of the *alknarintja* as women who had long clitorises—indeed their genitals had the appearance of three penes—and how two of these were removed with a stone knife. Róheim interpreted the *alknarintja* in the context of his belief that at the beginning of life, the primary impulse of every human is "the genital striving directed towards the mother." The *alknarintja* woman, associated with ancestral figures, is a "mother with a penis." A typical male infantile experience is that of an erection connected with the mother. This experience of the male, who is taking the part of the female in sex, is repressed, whereupon in the unconscious it is projected into the construction of the mythic female figure, the *alknarintja*, "who comes to the sleeper and sits on his penis and whom he is always trying to conquer with his magical wand." From here Róheim easily became engaged in a whole program of interpretation of Arrernte sexual behavior.[117]

Róheim traced a close association between the *alknarintja* and menstruation. The significance is complex. In that the *alknarintja* women are those who turn their eyes away from men, they are described as menstruating and thus to be avoided—it is taboo to have intercourse with a menstruating woman. However, in songs Róheim analyzed, he found that menstruation indicates sexual desire, that any genital flow—semen, vaginal fluids, or blood—is associated with sexual excitement. Menstrual blood is considered dangerous to men, while it is powerful for women. Girls are rubbed with their own menstrual blood. Stories depict the mythical *alknarintja* women as rubbing their *tnatandja* (yam stick) with menstrual blood. Thus, in Róheim's view, genital discharge symbolizes sexual tension. The men respond to the women's menstrual power by subincision. They call blood from the penis "milk," an indication that they are claiming the nourishing capacities of women in the flow of blood from their subincised penes. Women are not permitted near them while they are engaged in these bloodletting rites. Róheim concluded: "It is quite clear that the men who squirt blood forth from their subincised penes are playing the role of menstruating women."[118]

Róheim's studies of *alknarintja* led him to evidence of an aboriginal belief in "the primal superiority of women." A little bullroarer (a penis symbol) now used by men in love magic (*ilpindja*) was originally owned by the *alknarintja* women. Róheim believed that this primal superiority originated in infant sexuality, when, for a boy, the real mystery is his mother. The boy is separated from his mother when she is copulating with his father and when she is menstruating. In the initiation rites of subincision and *ngallunga* (a bloodletting rite), the boy represents the primal scene and the menstruating mother. In these rites the men invert the castration anxiety experienced by the sight of menstrual blood, and by presenting their own penes as bleeding vaginas, they fortify each other by the blood of the fathers.[119]

The *alknarintja* is also key to the psychology of women. Róheim argued that women identify a man's "mystic double" (*ngantja*) with a devil that belongs to a definite place. The *ngantja* is believed to live in a place close to a man's *tjurunga*. Thus Róheim argued: "The *tjurunga* appears to the women in its unsublimated form as the giant penis of a cannibalistic devil, and because they fear it, they develop an *alknarintja* psychology corresponding with the expectation of the men. The little girl longs for the father's giant penis and at the same time fears it, for it is a real danger to her narrow vagina. . . . Every man has a phallic double (a father with a giant penis) who, because he suggests the danger of seduction, may evoke the flight response characteristic of the *alknarintja*."[120]

Totemism

Writing at a time when totemism had ceased to be of interest to anthropology, Róheim still made little effort to justify his interest in it. He accepted Frazer's classical definition as "a group of human beings regarding themselves as related to an animal species (sometimes a species of plant or natural object) and deriving their names from that species."[121] Róheim, who felt there was no question that totemism was important to the Arrernte, argued for its phallic origin. A totem is called *knanindja*, which he understood to mean "origin." It is connected with the mythology of conception, that is, the fundamental denial of the sexual activity of the father by believing that a child is not begotten by his father but emanates from his totem. Despite the complexity and multiplicity of the mythology of the wandering ancestors, Róheim held:

> [There is] really only one rite, the *alknantama* [ritual quivering], which is carried out for different places. The corresponding element in the myth is either the ancestral *alknantama* (which produced the germs of children[122]) or the metamorphosis into *tjurungas*, that is, the coitus of the ancestors, was represented (*alknantama*). The present complicated structure is formed by adding the migration theme, the latent meaning of which is again the sexual act. On the one hand, actual historic wanderings have been introduced into the myth, and, on the other, names of places which, owing to some local peculiarity, determine the content and the amalgamation of the various saga themes.[123]

The chief performer of the totemic rites decorates his body with eaglehawk down and makes the quivering movement, *alknantama*. The trembling is referred to as *kuntanka nguampa*, which means, according to Róheim, "like a *tjurunga*" or "as in the ritual." However, Róheim suggests that this motion dramatizes the metamorphosis of a sorcerer into a demon and thus derives from the magical pretotemic period. He presents an elaborate argument to ground the movement in the primal situation.[124]

Tjurunga. Róheim held that everything the Arrernte do is based on the model of the ancestors, "the eternal ones of the dream," established "at the dawn of the world." The ancestors left *tjurungas* wherever they camped. They became *tjurungas* at the end of their journey.[125] Because the ancestors became *tjurungas* when they died, *tjurunga* means death; but it means more than that because "new life sprouts forth from these sticks and stones, and it is from these that the *ratapa* (unborn babies) swarm forth and enter the wombs of the women."[126] The wanderings of the ancestors were thus inseparable from begetting. The old men told Róheim that "the original rites always produced *ratapas* (children)."[127] The *tjurunga* is thus the material symbol of the totem idea. The term *knanakala*—which Róheim said means "became, born, arose"—is used in the same sense as the word *tjurungeraka*, that is, turned into *tjurunga*. Thus the metamorphosis into *tjurunga*, which the ancestors always did, is the real becoming, and it symbolizes coitus.[128]

Associated with the *tjurunga* complex is the belief in a hidden person (*ngantija*), which Róheim described in some detail under the heading of narcissism. The model for the *ngantija* is apparently the transformation into a *tjurunga* of the ancestor upon death. The *ngantija* is immortal and always in close association with *tjurunga* and with generation. In Róheim's understanding, "We love ourselves too dearly to comprehend or admit the possibility that our body is not everlasting, we desire and therefore believe in the existence of a hidden likeness of ourselves in a shape that cannot perish, eternal like a rock and full of the germs of life."[129]

Róheim gave both a phallic and a vaginal interpretation of *tjurunga*. A stone *tjurunga* was seen as an "indestructible penis," thus a penis like that of the ancestors.[130] A broader interpretation, that the *tjurunga* is symbolic of the body image, was quickly collapsed by Róheim into the first by noting that narcissism is "crystallized around the penis."[131] But the *tjurunga* is a phallus covered with circular designs, symbolizing the womb or vagina. Thus, for Róheim, the *tjurunga* is the symbol of "woman held at bay." It is associated with "a repression of the original gratification—no women are wanted, the men will enjoy themselves without them," and "it means a repetition of the primal situation, a *churunga* [*tjurunga*] covered with *tmara* marks is the boy's penis in the mother's vagina." An aboriginal man told Róheim that "the vagina is very hot, it is fire . . . and each time the penis goes in, it dies."[132] Thus, Róheim sheds light on the exclusion of women from the presence of *tjurunga*.[133]

Bullroarers (*namatuna*, Arrernte; *mandagi*, Loritja) were considered by Róheim to be *tjurungas* with holes in them. They were first owned by women. He understood their significance primarily in the context of *ilpindja*, or love magic. There is extensive documentation on the practice of love magic,[134] which usually involves the use of bullroarers, understood to be the principal instrument that "brings the woman in." In Róheim's interpretation the bullroarer, as a *tjurunga*, is a penis symbol.[135]

Totemic Mythology. One of the few extant discussions of the mythic process is presented by Róheim.[136] He emphasized both the monotony and the variability that he thought would impress a Western observer. Róheim held firm to the close interconnection between myth and song and ritual. The myths are itineraries of place names traveled to by totem ancestors. He held that the place names often correlate with the events that occurred there. Each place is the location at which ancestors performed specific actions, actions replicated in the rites that are performed by aboriginal people who have connections with the totem and the place. Thus the variability that may occur in mythic recitation correlates with the knowledge of the storyteller, as well as his personal experience with places named in the itinerary of the story. If a storyteller is initiated and has participated in the performance of the totem-location rites of a named place, that section of the myth associated with the place may be greatly expanded.

Róheim discussed various hypotheses to explain the origin of totem mythology, concluding that "the myths arose in the dim past either on the basis of real history or of ontogenetic material of the individual ancestry. This simply means that somebody in the past with an urge to communicate, first told a daydream, probably interwoven with real dream elements. Generations have been reelaborating this story in fantasy, and generations have been rehistoricizing these fantasy products in actual practice."[137] Noting that the basic structure of mythology is a movement across the landscape, often termed "wandering," Róheim engaged a fascinating discussion about the wandering connected with the famed aboriginal practice of "walk about" (*ndullabuma*). He understood that to sustain living on the land in Central Australia requires constant movement to find adequate food and water. The named sites of ancestral wanderings correlate with places where either food or water can be obtained.

In the stories, the ancestors perform ceremonies and leave "spirit children" behind at these places. Thus Róheim concluded that the "wandering is *libidinized*," by which he meant that the wandering was dealt with as if it were a sexual activity.[138] He made his point by discussions of the phallic elements in the wandering stories: the ancestors' large, erect penes; the phallic identity of feet; and the inseparable connection between wandering and initiation.

Róheim coined the term *mythe de passage*, or "transition myth," to explain the nature of totemic mythology. The structure is strictly Freudian: "The period of life which conditions the transition from mother to wife, from old to new love object, is dramatized: *the penis becomes the hero of this drama*. It is subject to operations, it is represented in symbols. The boys hear and see the story of the wandering phallic ancestors and they themselves become wanderers in space and time."[139] Yet Róheim held that this wandering only appears to be a wandering away from the mother. His analysis of myth indicates that it is actually a wandering toward her. In the end of all these ancestral wanderings, the heroes all end by becoming *tjurunga*. He cites the formula with which so many ancestral journeys end: *borkeraka tjurungeraka*; that is, they became tired, became *tjurunga*. The *tjurunga*, however, is, for Róheim, the penis. Dying is represented by the moment when the body becomes completely genitalized. Thus the ending is not an end but a beginning. The dead hero is the penis from which a new generation will arise.[140]

Róheim analyzed his collection of dual hero stories in terms of his concept of dual unity to describe the relationship between mother and child. Before birth they are one, but birth separates them into a duality. The nursing infant regains the unity with the mother. In other words, what invariably characterized the dual heroes in the myths as Róheim analyzed them is their dual unity. The heroes are phallic. Róheim argued that initiation accomplishes the final severance of the dual unity relationship between boys and their mothers. Upon initiation the boys are taken from their mothers and cannot return. In light of this loss, the stories of dual heroes, themselves presenting a dual unity, replaces the loss of the maternal relationship with these phallic myths. The boy is able to see that he no longer needs his mother, which is to say he no longer needs her nipple, because he can get pleasure from his own penis. As Róheim summarized the argument: "The body alone represents the unity of mother and son; the separation from the body (circumcision) represents a symbolic repetition of the primal trauma, the infant torn from its mother. The myth restores, by its own means (duality of heroes), the dual unity that has been broken. But it also keeps repeating the initial trauma in the attempt to master it."[141]

Totemic Ritual. According to Róheim's reckoning, there are four main types of totemic ritual:

- Corroboree (Róheim is using a term from what he called "bush English"): rites performed by men for women (*itata*) or women for men (*wuljankura*), concluding by an "exchange of women." These dances are classified as totemic because they are connected with a specific totem and location.

- *Andatta* or *tjurunga andatta*: a rite in which an episode from the totemic ancestral myths is acted for the benefit of the young men.
- Initiation ceremonies.[142]
- *Mbatjalkatiuma* (incorrectly, according to Róheim, who is supporting Carl Strehlow, called *intichiuma* by Spencer and Gillen): ritual aimed at the increase or multiplication of the totemic species. *Mbatjalkatiuma* means, according to Róheim, "to make or to throw up marks or footprints in the sand," thus refreshing an image of the ancestors in the minds of the young.[143] His informant Jirramaba told him that *mbatjalkatiuma* means "to renew the footsteps of the ancestors, that is, revive their memories, as a result of which the totemic species will multiply."[144]

Róheim recognized that totemic ceremonies cannot adequately be identified by the totem species but require the additional identification of place because totemic ritual is based on ancestral travel, as told in mythology. In totem ritual there is a necessary correlation among myth, rite, and song, and Róheim criticized Spencer for failing to grasp this most fundamental point.[145] To demonstrate this correspondence, Róheim presented a number of totem rituals in three columns: ceremony, myth, and song.[146] He discussed initiation and increase rites (*mbatjalkatiuma*) in some detail, each presentation shaped by his psychological perspective.

Initiation

Róheim focused his discussion of initiation on a bloodletting rite called *ngallunga.* Totem rites are connected either with initiation or with multiplying the totem species. Róheim documented a kind of rite, called *ngallunga*, that is performed by the Loritja, which he believed had a parallel in one performed by the tjilpa of the Arrernte (*tjoananga* in Arrernte).[147] These rites were responsible for introducing circumcision and subincision. Róheim was told that if a boy was not initiated, he might become a devil (*erintja*) and fly up in the air and kill and eat the old men of the tribe.[148] The initiation rite prevents this from happening. By "going as near to castrating the boy as may well be imagined (circumcision and subincision)," a basis is created for the identification of the boy with the men: "It is a libido identification based on the penis; father and son both in erection, the mother absent." The identification is also based on the common castration anxiety shared by fathers and sons. The *ngallunga* (which means "we two are friends"), performed as a rite of initiation, constructs a friendship based on the common experience of circumcision and subincision. In this rite, the subincision hole is called the vagina (*kuna*), thus identifying the men with both genders. *Ngallunga* therefore functions to displace the castration anxiety from the female to the male: "The boys must always have been afraid of the castrating vagina; now the fathers have this powerful weapon."[149]

Initiation may also be understood in terms of separation anxiety. As the youths are taken from their mothers, all men reexperience the trauma of separation and their defense fantasies. Through *ngallunga*, the fathers and sons proclaim: "We two are one."[150] Thus, Róheim could complete his interpretation of the initiation rituals:

> It is as if the fathers were telling the sons: it is true that the women cannot be present, that you cannot have the mother; but instead of that we offer a substitute ourselves, we have both a penis and a vagina; you too will be like we are with a penis and a vagina. Like a boomerang we return to our starting-point: *ambi-sexuality is the cure that is prescribed against the Oedipus complex. A stream that rushes like a torrent to its goal is rendered harmless by a canal into which part of its waters flow; what remains can go on flowing without threatening the stability of its shores. . . .*
>
> Since imemorial [*sic*] time, the process has been going on. Libido has been diverted from its direct incestuous and genital aim into new channels. *The genito-fugal libido thus reinforcing the narcissistic cathexis of the ego, it has become possible for many males to live together in a horde* and for humanity to fight a more effective battle against the world in general.[151]

According to Róheim, the general trend of ritual is to transform direct hetero-sexual libido into deflected homosexual libido. For blood is taken from the penis and smeared all over the body; that is, libido is withdrawn from the genital organ and used as a secondary reinforcement of the narcissistic cathexis of the whole body. To obtain this blood from the penis, the men masturbate in a group, but only in order to procure an erection, not an ejaculation. In other words, the most primitive mechanism for stabilizing society is the genitofugal trend of the libido; instead of women and instead of ejaculation, there is a ceremony in which the men perform together, having transformed their whole body into a penis. The body is smeared with blood taken from the penis and covered with the fertilizing *andatta*, that is, feathers, and the body performs the *alknantama*, the quivering, which is evidently an imitation of the movements of the penis in the vagina. Two men quivering together, and the others as onlookers, transcribe the primal scene by replacing the direct libidinal aim by a deflected one, the heterosexual object by a homosexual, and object-cathexis by identification.[152]

Increase Rites

According to Róheim, the totemic rites that focus on the increase of the totem species are difficult to distinguish from and are derived from the initiation rites.[153] Still, he offered extensive interpretive comments based not only on Central Australian cultures but also on the comparative studies of aboriginal cultures throughout Australia. He framed his discussion of the increase rites in an understanding of totemism as "essentially a cult of food animals. The natives are, in the ceremonies, 'making' the animals they have been destroying."[154] Upon discussing the treatment of ritual objects used in these rites, ritual speech and gesture, and the restrictions and practices associated with eating totemic species, Róheim offered the interpretation of totemism as "a system of reassurance against archaic destructive tendencies." Because the aborigines suffer a natural anxiety as the result of destroying the animals they hunt for food, this ritual reviving of the animals, effected through the repainting of *tjurungas* that represent the animals and the dramatic enactment of the animals, amounts to "a denial of their own aggressive tendencies or the reparation phase that follows destruction."[155] Róheim demonstrated through careful comparative analysis of myth, song, and ritual action that the aborigines present themselves as having eaten too much of the totem animal, and he conjectures that the rites include a kind of punishment for this trangression.[156] Róheim sought the broadest psychological understanding of increase rites, seeing them as atonement for the primal anxieties of object loss by retaining the image of the object in such forms as rock drawings, ground paintings, decorated *tjurungas*, and decorated ritualists. The men who enact the rites not only create a "good object" (see discussion below) but also treat it like a child by petting and rubbing it, or they may use it to symbolize coitus and rebirth. Thus, they replace the bad, corruptible, decaying object with a new good and indestructible one.[157]

Object Relations and the Primacy of the Mother

Róheim named Melanie Klein as an influence on his play analysis with children. Although he failed to cite her or to present the theoretical background in detail, it is clear that he was also influenced by Klein's "object relations theory."[158] This Klinean influence is most remarkable in Róheim's *The Eternal Ones of the Dream* (1945). His discussion of object relations is one of the most interesting examples of the power and sophistication of his work. The understanding of the "good" object rests for Róheim on the primacy of the mother. The infant comes to know "good" as opposed to "bad" in terms of the mother's breast. The presence of the nursing nipple is "good"; its absence is "bad." Róheim's use of object relations theory made two important advances. It complemented Freud's work, which focused more on drives or instincts than on relations. It also suggested the possible primacy of the female, the mother, rather than, as Freud insisted, the male, the father. Although time and again throughout his work, Róheim advanced the primacy of the father-son relationship, he nonetheless broke through that aspect, especially in *Eternal Ones of the Dream*, with the insight that even this relationship was formed in response to the more fundamental, more primary experience of the infant's relationship to the mother.

Róheim based his interpretation of increase rites on the primacy of the mother. The "good" object is the object that affords nourishment, that is, the milk-producing breast. Yet the good object can turn bad: the nipple may be withdrawn. In extension of this foundational experience, nature is found to be full of good and bad objects, which are often the same objects. Just as the nipple may be removed, animals that provide nourishment may turn against humans because of the aggression shown toward them. Here, perhaps, Róheim is reflecting Klein's notion of infantile aggression, first expressed by biting the breast that provides nourishment. Thus, Róheim argued that during increase rites, abstaining from eating the totem species is a gesture that demonstrates the avoidance of aggression toward the totem species. In this way the people guarantee the good attitude of the good object. Róheim extended this set of valued relationships to his understanding of the aboriginal conception of and relationship with their landscape and environment. On the one hand, the totem centers are "good" places in that they offer nourishment in the presence of the totem species and are the place of the florescence of *ratapa*, or potential children. On the other hand, the desert territory between totem centers is the domain of demons and monsters, that is, "bad objects." Since the primary experience through which one learns the good-bad object distinction is that of the infant-mother relationship, this relationship is basic in understanding aboriginal concepts of and relationships to the land.[159]

Róheim came to understand wandering mythology not as a wandering away from the mother but as a wandering toward her.[160] In the comparison of several myths, Róheim concluded that in becoming a *tjurunga* at death, one is accomplishing the longed-for return to the mother. The *tjurunga* as phallus returns to the ground, the earth, at the conclusion of the wanderings. This death then becomes a regenerative act in that it is the coitus, an action of male-female relationship, that provides the eternal renewal of life. Castration anxiety is generalized as the anxiety of the lost "good" object through the separation from the mother. All ritual and mythological action can then be understood as being driven by this fundamental loss.

In 1945 Róheim anticipated some of the feminist issues that emerged in the 1970s.[161] Despite the dogmatism of his Freudian agenda, Róheim anticipated the multiperspectivality of storytracking in his openness to and fascination with the ambiguity and multiplicity of possible interpretations. He saw the vaginal overlays on the phallus. He saw the phallic aspects of the sphinx, which he correlated with the Arrernte figure *alknarintja*. He saw the primacy of the mother, as well as that of the father.

Róheim's understanding and construction of the Arrernte is the most distinctive of the classic ethnographies. The storytrack from which he comprehended what he experienced and which forged his relationship with people of the culture was well defined and self-consciously held. Given my concerns about the multiperspectivality of storytracking, to me one of the most fascinating aspects of Róheim's presentations of the Arrernte is how greatly they differ from the other ethnographic accounts while still being extensively documented. The Arrernte showed Róheim a very distinctive profile.

Theodor Strehlow's Arrernte

Although Strehlow[162] believed that anthropologists had generally overemphasized the difference between Australian aborigines and "ourselves," he paid careful attention to the differences from area to area even among the Arrernte. He considered the Arrernte subdivisions as "almost completely independent tribal units."[163] From the perspective of dialect groupings, there was strife and ill feelings between groups. Linkages on a hospitable basis were forged only by totem and kinship connections, links the Arrernte believed were forged by the ancestors.[164] Even the kinship system from region to region varies significantly. For example, among the Southern Arrernte, Strehlow found a gradual merging of the patrilineal system, which characterizes the other Arrernte groups, with the matrilineal system, which characterizes cultures farther to the south.[165]

Field Methods

Strehlow makes much of his ability to speak and "to think" Arrernte in describing his field methods.[166] He collected the materials in their native languages and translated them into English. He described how complex the Arrernte language is and how broadly it differs from English and thus how difficult his translation work was. Angrily, he chastised those who depended on aboriginal English.[167]

The People and the Landscape

In Strehlow's view, the Arrernte believe that in the beginning there were only the sky and the formless, lifeless earth.[168] The present shape of the landscape is the result of ancestral activities as recounted in the myths and songs. The places where the ancestors arose from the earth and departed back into it are marked in a way distinctive to the specific ancestors. The mythology of the Northern Arrernte, according to Strehlow, attributes the gaps, chasms, and gorges in the MacDonnell Ranges to the ancestral wielding of the *tnatantja*, presently represented in ritual by a pole. Stories that tell of the theft and dragging of this pole account for riverbeds throughout the country. In Strehlow's experience, there is no expanse of land that is free of mythological sites. The stories about these sites appear to come from a long tradition. Storytellers did not tell new stories created from their imagination, nor were they much prone even to tell stories about historical events that occurred at distinct locations. Their stories included no human heroes or historical settings.[169]

According to Strehlow, the Arrernte do not consider the features in the landscape that are identified with the ancestors as "monumental mounds or signposts which 'mark the spot' where the important events" took place. Rather these features are the actual works or remains of the ancestors.[170] There is no logical problem in the Arrernte in identifying a number of landscape features with the same ancestor since, according to Strehlow, the ancestor may be simultaneously present at all of these places. The love and affection so commonly expressed by aborigines for their birthplaces and for the whole countryside is not difficult to understand. Strehlow held that the landscape is an "age-old family tree," that the country itself tells the story of the "handiwork of the ancestors from whom he himself [an Arrernte] has descended," the ancestors from whom each Arrernte is a descendant.[171]

Thus the geography of Central Australia takes the form of a "totemic landscape," a concept that ensures stability among different language groups, ensures the distribution of interlocking and intermarrying subgroups, and is a basis for authority.[172] One's totem identity is determined by the "conception site," that is, the place where one's mother is when she first realizes she is pregnant (see also Reincarnation and the Doctrine of Two Souls later in this chapter). If, at the time, she is near a feature in the land that is identified with an ancestor, the unborn child's totem is that of the identified ancestor. If no obvious determination can be made, the woman's husband consults with the elders, who search the mythology for some ancestor who traveled nearest to where the woman was. The agency of impregnation is either a bullroarer thrown by the ancestor, which enters the woman at her hip, or the entrance of the ancestor himself into the woman's body. Either a *tjurunga* or some article of clothing or body decoration belonging to the ancestor is believed to be the source of this vitalizing force.[173] The Southern Arrernte consider conception to be possible from foods eaten by young women. These are actually *tjurunga* objects left in the land by ancestors that are mistaken by the women as yams or other food items. Strehlow understood human birth in terms of the reincarnation of the ancestors. A person is considered to have two "deathless bodies," the *tjurunga* from which he or she arose—often a large immovable feature of the landscape—and at least among the Northern and Western Arrernte, a *tjurunga* determined by the old men soon after a person's birth, an object found or fashioned of wood or stone and engraved with the appropriate totem designs, rubbed with ochre and fat, and placed in the totemic storehouse.[174]

With hundreds of totem groups holding claim to geographic areas, one wonders how such small groups are able to conduct the extensive rites and activities required. The distinctiveness and land-connectedness of the individual are clear. However, how any sense of unity is achieved in the context of such diversity is an issue that requires explanation. Strehlow addressed this problem in the terms of "personal monototemism in a polytotemic society."[175] He described the functioning of the *njinanga*, or totemic clan social organization, and the *pmara kutata*, or totemic clan center. The doctrine of the conception totem exerts a disruptive effect on society because every member of a given family may belong to a different totem group. However, this disruptive effect is counterbalanced by a strong emphasis on the unifying ties to a totem clan ceremonial center and by membership obligations to the local *njinanga* organization. In any broad geographical area, a totem site serves as the intersection of many totem ancestral stories. This *pmara kutata* thus links together members of many totem groups. The leadership of this totemic clan group belongs to the members of the predominant totem associated with the place. The clan membership is an organization of fathers and their sons. Strehlow borrowed for general use the Northern Arrernte term for such an organization, *njinanga*. It is at these great totem centers, under the leadership of the *njinanga*, that all initiatory rites, all *ingkura*, are performed. Most of the *tjurungas* of the totem groups in this area are kept in the storehouse associated with the *pmara kutata*. Two or more *pmara kutata* in different areas may be connected with each other through interlinking ancestral stories and the regulated interchange of marriage partners.[176]

Social Organization

Strehlow based his discussion of social organization[177] on what he termed the *njinanga* section. He emphasized the interdependence, yet distinctiveness, of totemic and social organization. Strehlow also focused on the men of Arrernte society. He believed that women are excluded from taking part in even their own personal totemic ceremonies. While he acknowledged that the women have personal *tjurungas* and special songs, they are not allowed to see their *tjurungas* or to sing their songs. Women may be aware of some of the ritual elements of the men's ritual because at the conclusion of many male rites, the men, whose bodies are still painted with totemic designs, appear at a distance from but are observable by the women. Notably, for the women to be present when any man's song is sung was a marker for Strehlow that these songs are not "sacred."[178] While Strehlow acknowledged that women had certain rites, songs, and charms, he feared it was too late, because of the loss of traditions, to learn anything about women's religion.[179]

In the context of his discussion of "love magic," or the songs sung as love charms, Strehlow briefly discussed the eight-division social structure and gave fuller attention to what he termed the "marriage code." A man can marry women from only one of the eight social divisions. Parents often betroth a daughter when she is only an infant, usually publicly announced during the performance of a great ceremonial. An Arrernte female is considered ideal for marriage immediately upon attaining sexual maturity. A male is not considered marriageable until he has completed initiation ceremonies and after the first grey hairs have begun to show in his beard and on his head. Courting is minimal, although a young man might determine something of the interest a woman has in him by presenting her with food he has obtained in a hunt. Her acceptance indicates her interest in courtship.[180]

Reincarnation and Doctrine of Two Souls

Strehlow believed that others had broadly misunderstood the Arrernte conception beliefs. He thought that the aboriginal "belief in the reincarnation of all human individuals from supernatural totemic ancestors is undoubtedly the key to many of the special concepts found in the religious traditions of the inland tribes."[181] Late in his career, Strehlow attempted to clearly describe the Arrernte doctrine of conception, which he thought was based on a belief in two souls. Life is produced initially, for both humans and animals, by the act of sexual intercourse, which gives them one life and soul. But humans differ from animals in that the soul of an "immortal supernatural ancestor" enters an already pregnant woman at some definite point in the landscape. It is the second soul (itself immortal) that determines the totem identity and personality (even physical characteristics) of the fetus. The soul of the ancestor may enter the pregnant mother in several ways: the mother's ingestion of food impregnated with life by the ancestor, a bullroarer hurled at the mother by the ancestor, or the mother's daydream of a baby. Strehlow understood Arrernte conception as a form of ancestral reincarnation, although the ancestor also continues to "slumber" at the totem site. The second soul is believed to act as a guardian spirit for its possessor. It might even become separately visible. Dreams are accounted for by the wandering of the mortal soul. The power to increase and have influence on totem species is attributed to the soul link to the totem ancestor that is identified with the totem species.[182]

The donation of blood for the ground painting constructed during the increase rites performed by the totem group is restricted to the men who belong to the totem. Strehlow reasoned that the donated blood must be the blood of the original totemic ancestor. Only men who are considered reincarnations of the original ancestor can be considered to have the blood of the ancestor.[183]

Strehlow looked to this doctrine of reincarnation to explain the aboriginal interest in song. Given that the ancestors, not human beings, were responsible for the composition of the songs, knowing and singing the songs in the appropriate ritual setting are the means by which human aborigines, contemporary reincarnations of the ancestors, lay claim to the powers of the ancestors. The doctrine of reincarnation ensures the personal link with the ancestors.[184]

Prayer is unnecessary, given the doctrine of reincarnation, for the ancestors are always present in reincarnated form among the leaders of the totemic clans. Strehlow likened singing to prayer in that it is the repetition of words that calls forth power in the world, words created and given by the ancestors.[185] Although the songs have the power of magical charms, Strehlow argues that the Arrernte certainly do not believe that songs have the sort of compulsive power so commonly associated with magic.[186]

Authority

Perhaps because Strehlow worked so closely with elders whom he understood as authorities, he was much interested in the nature of Arrernte authority. He found that authority is associated with the totem center and totem clan, that is, with geography and religion. Although there is no central political organization, limited authority resides in councils of older men whose membership qualifications are their ability to trace lineage to an ancestor (Strehlow often considered this relationship to be the reincarnation of the ancestor, although inheritance of *tjurunga* was possible) of the site, age, and wisdom or knowledge.[187] Membership in the *njinanga* section of the totem center that controlled the area is necessary. This council of elders is responsible for the performance of all major ceremonials. Since one of the major ceremonial objectives is the increase of totemic species, the elders (sometimes the authority resides in the head man) are responsible for the "vital food-producing organization." Shortages of food are routinely blamed on the failure of the elders or the head man.[188] The elders are also responsible for ensuring accuracy and propriety in ceremonial and social actions and for punishing infringements.[189] Strehlow reported that even capital punishment for ritual crimes is common. The authoritative elders are themselves not immune from being accused and punished for ritual crimes.[190] The elders are also responsible for the storage and proper use of ritual objects. However, private disputes, although common social concerns, are of no importance to them.[191]

According to Strehlow, the way in which the youths are treated by the elders during initiation reinforces the authority of the elders. Strehlow tended to interpret initiation as a principal mechanism in supporting the system of authority.[192]

Sky-dwellers

Whereas totemic ancestors are part of the secret tradition that is the property of initiated men, the Ilingka, a tradition related to sky-dwelling beings, is known to men, women, and children. Strehlow understood the tradition, which appears to be located primarily among the Western Arrernte,[193] to be of no practical concern to human beings. This is the tradition recorded by Carl Strehlow of the figure that he identified as Altjira and understood to be God.[194] According to Theodor Strehlow's understanding, the sky is the domain of "Sire Ilingka, the great Emu-footed One, who lived there with his wives and his children." They all have bodies of handsome young men and beautiful women, but the men's feet resemble those of emus and the women's feet resemble those of dogs.[195] The sky-dwellers live beyond the stars and exert no influence whatever on anything outside the sky. They played no role in creating or shaping the earthly world or anything at all having to do with human beings. All Strehlow could finally say of the significance of these sky-dwellers to the Arrernte people is that "the Ilingka tradition undoubtedly gives expression to that hopeless longing for personal immortality and eternal untroubled happiness that must often have come over the aboriginal folk who dwelt in Central Australia."[196] The sky world of Ilingka is a paradise that a human can never hope to enter: "He could only glance at the blue sky in the day and at the starlit sky at night, and have his vision of a paradise in the sky, which was a reflex of his own Central Australian landscape when it had become reborn after heavy summer rains."[197] The lives and conditions of the sky-dwellers are thought to be in direct contrast to the totemic ancestors. No songs honor Ilingka and since he lives in the sky there is no *tjurunga* associated with him at any totemic center.[198]

Mythology

Strehlow believed that "the soul of a race is enshrined in its legend"; thus he regularly consulted Arrernte mythology to discern the elements of every aspect of culture. The landscape of Central Australia is crisscrossed with the myths of traveling totemic ancestors. These ancestral routes established the points for social contact between totemic clans and the many local groups they joined. Strehlow believed that at least some of the ancestral journeys recounted in myth are based on actual travels and historical events.[199]

The stories of the ancestors are told, in song,[200] when the members of a given totem group visit the cave in which *tjurungas* are stored. The words of the song are regrouped in the form of "chant-verses" making them unintelligible to the uninitiated. The newly initiated must have the regroupings explained to them, as well as many of the words, which are archaic or esoteric. Much of the explanation takes place in the form of sign language, and the initiates are not allowed to ask questions.[201]

Strehlow understood that the myths correspond to the chants or songs and the rites and that all of these are connected to the landscape because they describe the ancestral activities that gave it shape and meaning. So completely exhaustive are the references to any and every possible landform that Strehlow believed contemporary generations could not possibly add anything at all to these narratives. This saturation explains what he observed as a "general mental stagnation" of those he worked with.

Interpreting Arrernte mythology in the context of a concern for origination, Strehlow understood the totem ancestor as a "great father," himself uncreated, being "ever from the beginning." The great father creates only sons. When the sons reach the age of maturity, there is deep hostility between them and their "all-powerful father." The issue for Strehlow is power. The sons fear the father because of their impotence in his presence; the father distrusts his sons because he sees them as future rivals for his power. The father preys on his sons, sometimes even eating them.[202] Strehlow observes that the eating of the sons created by the great father is replicated in the ritual eating of the totem species, although many totems do not permit any such consumption. Though unacknowledged, this discussion must be influenced by Freud and Róheim, for Strehlow goes on to point out that in some myths the sons kill and eat the father. This act is usually veiled by the animal disguise of the father, but Strehlow is still able to make this interpretation, adding that by this technique "the myth-makers have been responsible for veiling the more revolting features of a crude but striking picture of life in an early primitive society."[203] Strehlow generalized on this event to comment on the function of animals, which are so fundamental to Arrernte symbolism. He believed that the use of animals in symbolic ways was motivated by the desire to veil the more primitive and highly offensive activities of a former era.

In the mythology, the ancestors are living in the same fashion as the Arrernte of Strehlow's time, although Strehlow saw the mythic era as a highly idealized time. Indeed, the stories often tell how the activities that characterize daily life—hunting and gathering, food preparation methods, and the use of specific plants and animals—originated in ancestral times.[204] The exception to this, as noted by Strehlow, is the complete lack of the "elementary conceptions of morals and virtues and ideals" that characterized the aborigines he knew. Rather the ancestors were known by their acts of violence, treachery, cruelty, and lust. Thus, Strehlow looked to myth and song to reveal an enormous range of Arrernte beliefs and practices.[205]

Song

Strehlow's most expansive and impressive work is *Songs of Central Australia*, published finally in 1971 but written over the period from 1946 to 1967, based on a collection of 5,070 aboriginal songs and more than 100 myths recorded by Strehlow in their native languages.[206] Strehlow witnessed 972 "totemic rites."[207] Beyond his knowledge of aboriginal languages, the book, which considers some 800 aboriginal songs, reflects Strehlow's training in Greek and Latin and his broad familiarity with Western classical literature, to which he constantly compares Arrernte songs. It was clearly his intent to "raise" the Arrernte songs to recognition on the stage of world literature. The subject he believed so rich had been not only ignored but also unseen, as Strehlow demonstrated by quoting passages from some of the most influential ethnographies: "While this [ritual] is in progress they are chanting songs of which they do not know the meaning" (Baldwin Spencer); "the natives are quite unable to assign any meaning to the words of these and other chants. . . . As they are uttered they form a series of recurrent rhythmical dull monotones" (E. C. Stirling); "The songs . . . are merely a collection of sounds and cannot be translated. They have no actual meaning, but are merely a means of expressing such music as there is in the native mind" (F. J. Gillen).[208]

Strehlow described songs as "traditional narrative poems . . . which are intoned according to traditional rhythmic measures."[209] All songs are associated with specific ceremonial centers and totemic ancestral beings; thus, as with all rituals, songs are identified by totem and location. Because the myths demonstrate the linkage between songs forged by the ancestral activities, which are themselves linked to travels across the landscape, the study of song must be placed in the context of the study of mythology. Strehlow's analysis is multilevel, including consideration of rhythmic and metrical form, that is, as musical compositions (part I); language and verbal structure, that is, as literature (part II); and traditional, religious, ceremonial, and social documents, that is, as the role of songs in the broader social and ritual contexts (part III).[210]

Strehlow's analysis of Central Australian songs from the perspective of music and rhythm is quite remarkable. Set often against the background of European song analysis, Strehlow describes several features of aboriginal songs. The prose lines are forced into the reshaping mold of rhythmic measure. This not only changes the speech accents but also the phonetic quality of the words. Syllables are frequently inserted to stretch words to fit the meter. Breaks between words are shifted as well, with the initial syllable sometimes being one other than the initial syllable of a word. Strehlow's analysis of this character of Arrernte songs, which he termed "word-weaving," led him to a fascinating observation: "It is an ironical reflection that it was the very variety of these native rhythmic measures and the ingenious intricacy of their word-weaving which caused highly-trained University men of the nineteenth century to find in them merely a further proof of the utter spiritual degradation and almost animal-like mental simplicity of the 'naked savages' whom they had met in Central Australia."[211] The apparent unintelligibility of song lyrics has a religious dimension. The words are thought to be composed by totemic ancestors. Because the performers who impersonate the ancestors in ritual must not show any personal features, they must use speech that does not resemble ordinary human conversation.[212]

Strehlow observed that songs that accompany ritual performances have to be constant and in exact correspondence with the actions of the performer. In other words, during a ritual performance a song has to be repeated without any break as many times as necessary until the performance is completed. There are nonspeech signals by which singers and dancers communicate. When the rite is over, the song is stopped abruptly.[213]

The Arrernte do not have a term that corresponds to the English *song*, but they do have a term that corresponds with the portion of song that is its most basic unit, the couplet. This term is *tjurunga retnja* which Strehlow rendered as "*tjurunga* name." The Arrernte believe that their songs were composed by the totemic ancestors: "The ancestors saw animals, trees, birds, flowers, and fellow ancestors, and gave 'names' to all of them—each 'name' being a complete descriptive couplet. They also handed down their own 'names' for the benefit of posterity. No man must nowadays touch their eternal bodies, the sacred tjurunga, without uttering the 'names' that they first gave to themselves."[214] Names, then, are brief descriptions that gain their fullest significance when they recall actions associated with them. Initiated Arrernte men are experienced in associating the names with the full ancestral identities revealed through myth and ritual. Thus, the names serve as tags, with significant powers of suggestion for the knowledgeable person.[215] In Strehlow's analysis, the Arrernte terms that refer to the composition of verse all relate to the notion of names and naming. This connection helped Strehlow to comprehend the apparent disjointedness between couplets collected together as songs. Since each couplet is a name coined by an ancestor, the song is a series of names.[216] By naming the objects and living things encountered, the ancestors gained "magical control" over them. To be effective and powerful, the repetition of the names through the singing of the couplets must be accompanied by the correct actions of the ancestors when they introduced the names through song. The description of these actions is maintained in the mythology, which Strehlow describes as "connected narratives of action."[217] Strehlow revealed the interdependence of song and myth: "There is little sustained narrative or lyric verse—in our sense of the term—to be found in the Central Australian songs. The gaps between the clusters of the *tjurunga retnja*, secret names of the objects that the native seeks to control, generally have to be filled in by prose passages taken from the myths; and many of the cryptic verses themselves need a considerable amount of traditional elucidatory prose commentary to make their significance clear beyond all doubt."[218]

Analyzing the language of the aboriginal songs, Strehlow articulated a number of their common themes. Songs describe and celebrate the landscape, particularly the totemic connections one has to specific places, such as the *pmara kutata* that gives identity to the totem clans.[219] Songs are often sung to prevent or to inflict injury or sickness. Such songs may be sung in the aboriginal rites of sorcery, commonly called "bone-pointing,"[220] or they may be part of the system of vengeance, which is the most common motivation for violence. The singing of some songs is believed to have the power to revive someone violently killed.[221] One of the most extensive and powerful song genres comprises those songs sung during performances of increase rites.[222] Strehlow argued that one of the principal reasons for singing is to honor the totemic ancestors. Increase rites may be performed when there is no need to increase the totem species. These performances are predominantly for purposes of worship; they commemorate the ancestors.[223] Some songs have the power of charms, to bring about changes in the weather,[224] for example, or to attract a person of the opposite sex.[225] Songs certainly are considered powerful and efficacious. The singing of songs related to the sun, usually thought of as an ancient enemy, may, if done inappropriately, cause the sun to burn up the land.[226] Many songs are, of course, directed toward initiating the youths.[227]

Initiation

Strehlow understood the privileges of adulthood (strictly speaking, for him, "manhood") to be inseparable from *tjurunga* ownership. Through the *tjurunga*, one gains independence, authority, and magical power. Such ownership is gained through rites of initiation,[228] the performance of which spans a period between the ages of fourteen and sixteen. Initiation focuses primarily on the rites of circumcision, head biting, and subincision, all performed against a background of showing the initiates the totem rites, never seen by them before, and teaching them the chants.[229] The *ingkura* festival is the set of events that completes the initiation process and entitles the initiate to a place in society. Such festivals are performed at the most important totemic sites in a given geographical area. It is not necessary for all of the initiates to be of the totem associated with that location. All the youths of the area have access to these major totem centers through membership in the "totemic clan." The *ingkura* is a major intergroup event for visitors from other local groups and from non-Arrernte groups whose *pmara kutata* are linked by myth.

Strehlow believed that by increasing its totem species, each group associated with a totem center performs an invaluable economic service for the whole region.[230] Day after day, sometimes for months, the totem-locality rites are performed by the elders, invariably involving the display and use of appropriate *tjurungas*. Sometimes, but not always, the youths are permitted to see these rites. The chants are often taught to the initiates, as well as to other visiting men. A variety of ritual paraphernalia—*tnatantja*, body decoration, and the layout of the *ingkura* ground—are used in support of the ritual performances. The final ceremony focuses on an elaborately decorated pole, identified by Strehlow as *kauaua*, erected on the ceremonial ground during the final night. The newly initiated surround the pole, considering it symbolic of the *rala parra*, the greatest of all *tjurungas*. Strehlow believed that to the initiates, it symbolizes the cause of the torment they have suffered throughout the festival. They seize the pole, lifting it up and down horizontally. With the pole on their shoulders, they dance fervently about the earthen mound on the ceremonial ground. The intent is to weary the pole and exhaust its strength. Finally, they strip it of its decorations and rudely throw it away. The initiates then shuffle about the ceremonial ground in single file, breaking through the earthen mound. Strehlow interpreted: "The great *tjurunga* has been shattered; its spell has been broken; its power is no more. The first rays of light run in thin tongues over the initiation ground: it is sunrise."[231] As usual, Strehlow emphasized the regional variations of all these procedures.

Tjurunga

According to Strehlow, all ethnographic accounts of the Arrernte by other authors restricted the term *tjurunga* to stone and wooden objects. His understanding of this term is distinguished by including not only these objects but also "ceremonies, legends, chants, and myths." This latter reference corresponds with the common Arrernte usage. Strehlow observed that the term may also refer to *tnatantja* and *waninga*, indeed, to any ritual object.[232] In his extensive analysis of *tjurunga* ownership, he restricted the term to the customary usage, that is, wooden and stone ritual objects.

Through his analysis of mythology, Strehlow concluded that the significance of *tjurunga* is the complete identification of the *tjurunga* with the totem species (witchetty grub or euro, for example) and the "sons" of the great father, the totem ancestor. The ancestor is considered to be the "sum total of the living essence" of the totem species, both animal and human. The ancestor, as the source of all life, is immortal, and the deaths of ancestors as described in the myths are more accurately transformations into a form that will "weather all the assaults of time, change, and decay." In other words, the ancestors become *tjurungas*, which are abiding. The ancestors are the unending source of future life of the natural forms of their species and "reincarnations" in human form. The vehicle for this progeneration is described as the dust particles from the *tjurunga*.[233] One's *tjurunga* is then one's "own body" from which one has been "reborn." It is the true body of the ancestor, with which one is identified.[234]

Tjurunga—in the form of wooden and stone objects, chants, rites, and stories—are the few forms of property that may be legitimately owned by an individual in Central Australia. One of these objects is an individual's personal *tjurunga*. Provided the individual is male, the *tjurunga* fashioned for him at birth will be kept in the storehouse of his totemic clan. Upon initiation, he will have the privilege of examining his personal *tjurunga* and learning the secrets and stories associated with it.[235] The *tjurungas* kept in the totemic clan storehouse and identified with the totem ancestors are the property of the head man of the clan. In advanced age, he passes them to a younger man in his totem who belongs to the same social subsection. Personal *tjurungas* are passed from father to son, exemplifying and effecting the unbreakable bond that exists between a father and his own son. *Tjurungas* may be lent by one totemic clan to another, thus forging bonds between groups attached to linked totem centers.[236]

Strehlow recognized that *tjurungas* also have destructive power. In mythology it is often the *tjurunga* that is used as a weapon to kill demons or enemies, and they are even used as a hunting weapon.[237] The *tjurunga* appears to be the force behind the suffering of the youths during their initiation. *Tjurungas* as personal possessions are dangerous, capable of causing death if their owners treat them carelessly or with contempt.[238]

Strehlow carefully described the regional differences in beliefs and practices regarding *tjurungas*.[239] For example, *tjurungas* appeared far less frequently among the Southern Arrernte, and those known in that area were all made of mulga wood, none of stone. In some areas, seashells took the place of *tjurungas* in initiation rites and were believed to be the source of children.[240]

In Strehlow's view, knowledge and ownership of *tjurungas* are strictly forbidden to women and children. Women are associated with *tjurunga* by virtue of their totem group memberships, but Strehlow believed that all the knowledge of *tjurungas* was carefully hidden from them. He acknowledged that women have traditions, chants, and exclusive property but that "far too little research has been made into this fascinating treasure of native folk-lore."[241]

Ritual

Strehlow identified a number of objectives for the performance of rites enacted by the men he considered to be reincarnations of totem ancestors. One motivation is the increase of the totem species; another is simply the "reverent commemoration of the supernational personages;" yet another is the initiation of youths. Whatever the motivation, ritual performance is fitted into the context of monototemism; that is, the totem clan of the local totem center serves as the organizing principle of all ritual performance. All ritual performances are tied to a specific ceremonial site and the totem with which it is identified.[242]

Commemorative ceremonies—called *andata* or *tjurunga andata*—are among the most common ritual performances, according to Strehlow. Their purpose is to bring before the people the totemic ancestors so that they might be worshiped and honored in song and dance.[243] Such rites commonly require extensive body decoration, using birds' down; the preparation of a ground painting; and the use of decorated ritual objects. During the performance, the actor carries out from time to time a traditional form of movement that involves a violent quivering of the body and chest, causing tufts of down to fly off his body. Even in a commemorative ceremony, this down is understood to turn into the animals and plants of the totem. [244] The performance is accompanied by the constant singing of commemorative songs. Each rite is carefully identified with a specific geographical locality.[245]

Strehlow sketched two types of rites among the Northern Arrente. One is the dance performance by one or two men whose bodies are adorned with designs. The main actor, who represents an ancestor, wears on his head a wooden *tjurunga* covered with down and tipped with bird feathers. In the other type of rite, the main actor carries a ceremonial pole, *tnatantja*, on his back. These rites also feature a ground painting that invariably represents the place from which the ancestor first arose.[246]

In the rituals of the Southern Arrernte, less importance is placed on ritual objects, such as *tnatantja* and *waninga*, and more on the mimetic action of the ritual performances. Strehlow believed that a Western observer would find the Southern Arrernte ritual performances "much more interesting and spectacular" than those of the other Arrernte groups. In these ceremonies, "one feels that glimpses may be detected of the first beginnings of proper religious drama."[247]

Strehlow extensively described the Southern Arrernte *ilkilajabia* ceremonies, which compare with the Northern and Western *ingkura* ceremonies, both considered primarily male initiation rites by Strehlow. It was Strehlow's opinion that the *ilkilajabia* ceremonies characterized Southern Arrernte religion. Apparently these ceremonies were no longer practiced when Strehlow investigated them, but he pieced together a description from "a few poor, scattered fragments of traditional folk-lore."[248] These rites, as Strehlow reconstructed them, were evidence of an earlier matrilineal perspective, which had been supplanted by the influence of the patrilineal system from the Northern Arrente groups. These ceremonies featured two ancestors identified as snakes (*ilbaralea*), who had originated from two Ntjikantja brothers, ancestors of the snake (*ilbaralea*) totem. Contrary to all Arrernte traditions, when these brothers ended their days on earth, they ascended into the sky by climbing up a tall spear. Strehlow held, though his reasoning is far from clear, that this sky ascent indicates "almost certainly a relic from older legends, a last remnant of half-forgotten traditions which had originated in a society of the older, matrilineal order."[249] In his reconstruction of the *ilkilajabia* rites, Strehlow stated that they lasted many months and featured a major trial for the initiates, which required them to hold aloft a burning torch throughout an entire night. They were told that should they fail to hold up the torch, they would most certainly die at the hands of the Ntjikantja brothers.

In the context of increase rites, Strehlow offered an interpretation of the extensive flow of blood that commonly is required in ritual performance. New life, that is, the life of the totem species, can only come out of the ground if "some of the 'life' of the original totemic ancestors had been poured down upon it."[250] The blood flowing from the arm of the ritualist, himself the reincarnation of the ancestor, is considered a representation of this "life." The magic of fertilization, so central to increase rites, is also achieved by the impersonation of totemic ancestors, who bring the ancestral phallus (in the form of a pole) to the ground painting. Songs function during the increase rites as charms to attract the ancestors and their fertilizing powers.[251]

Tnatantja

Tnatantja is the Southern Arrernte term for the pole often erected on ceremonial grounds. The Northern Arrernte term is *akauaua*; the Western Arrernte term is *tingara*.[252] Strehlow observed that the pole has creative and destructive capacities. In mythology it is used as a weapon with magical force and as a tool to cleave the gaps in the mountain ridges, thus permitting easier travel by the ancestors.[253] Frequently in mythology the *tnatantja* is considered to be a living thing. The Northern Arrernte identify the *tnatantja* as a great phallic symbol, a living being from which they are descended.[254] The Southern Arrernte appear not to use the *tnatantja* in their rituals.[255]

Waninga

Waninga is a wooden framework of spears or sticks tied together in the form of a cross or double cross and covered with hair string, on which totemic pattern designs are rendered in birds' down. Strehlow identified the *waninga* as the most common ritual emblem of the Western Arrernte and Loritja. The object does not appear to be used by the Southern Arrernte.[256] The ceremonies in which the *waninga* is used parallel the ceremonies of the Northern Arrernte, which use the *tnatantja*.[257]

Death

The ancestors' deaths as told in mythology are, in Strehlow's interpretation, not so much deaths as transformations into an abiding form. The ancestors remain after death a wellspring for future life, whereas human death is final and irrevocable. For humans there is no further existence after death.[258] Because every person possesses the eternal soul of the ancestor of whom he or she is a reincarnation, the Arrernte believe that every person possesses the eternal in his or her own lifetime. Strehlow cast this in strongly Western theological terms, indicating that an Arrernte "felt no need of waiting for a future union with a supernatural being in a life after death."[259] It is in the present that one lives in union with eternity. Death resolves this union. The mortal soul turns into the departed spirit or ghost (*ltana*) and hovers around the place where the body died, where it takes comfort from the sorrow shown by relatives and friends, who express themselves by loud lamentations and self-inflicted wounds. This soul ceases to exist after some months, said sometimes to be destroyed by lightning. The immortal soul returns to the dead person's conception site, where it is reabsorbed into the totemic ancestor, "taken up once more by the eternal landscape."[260] The Ilingka tradition (see above), which describes eternal sky-dwellers, presents a Western Arrernte image of an unattainable paradise, in Strehlow's view, paralleled in other Arrernte areas by similar mythology about sky-dwelling beings who live eternally in or near the sky. Strehlow thought that the traditions of sky-dwellers communicated the belief in the finality of death for human beings.[261]

At death, the *atua njalatja*, the spirit double or other self of the deceased, severs its connection with its relatives. The *tjurunga* of the deceased is usually removed from the storehouse and given to a relative in a distant location to keep for a number of years. Since in this distant location the people are not required to sing the songs associated with the *tjurunga*, the name of the deceased need not be uttered. It is considered a serious offence to utter either the common or secret name of the deceased. When the *tjurunga* of the deceased is finally returned, its songs, which include the name of the deceased, might be sung again, but the deceased's name is never again spoken in conversation.

When possible, the dying are attended by relatives. The moment of death is accompanied by the beginning of extensive mourning, including wailing and frantic crying. Mourning women may hit their own heads with stones or sharp sticks until their blood flows freely. Men may cut their shoulders or perform mourning incisions. Active mourning may last for weeks. A grave is dug and the deceased buried. The face of the deceased when interred is directed toward the mother's conception site, considered to be the *pmara altjira*, or the "eternal home."[262]

Death is not thought to be a natural event. After a death, considerable attention is directed toward determining its cause. Murder is often suspected, and various divination methods are used to determine the murderer. Once determined, the murder is avenged. Such actions often result in bitter blood feuds.[263]

Ethnography and Culture

This chapter is long, but this approach is necessary to establish several points fundamental to my stroytracking thesis. Much of the attention paid to the Arrernte by Western scholars has, as shown by the storytracking analyses, been more concerned with establishing proposed academic theories than with understanding or interacting with the actual peoples who live in Australia. Although my own efforts continue this hierarchy of values, I believe that the only way to avoid the negative aspects of solipsism or of an illegitimately projective method of argumentation is to comprehend and appreciate the interpreter-independent reality, that is, as imagined here, the Arrernte. Thus, I have believed it necessary to present Arrernte ethnography critically and in some detail.

This endeavor reminds us of the core issues of storytracking. It is abundantly clear from the presentations of these four ethnographers of the Arrernte that their personal, intellectual, historical, and social issues are inseparably interwoven into their descriptions of the Arrernte. Ethnographers have posited a reality they have commonly called "the Arrernte," and they all have, more or less, written with the attitude that there is some objective reality to be grasped. They have argued extensively with one another over who was right, and they have often proclaimed that others have misunderstood the culture. Yet our storytracking effort has shown that to a significant degree, each saw what he wanted and needed to see. Each reported what his storytrack dictated; each supported the continuing journey down the road traveled. The very identity of the Arrernte is dependent on these accounts, and while all the accounts indicate a common subject, clearly the objects they present are not identical. From the vantage of the present, these objects—the written accounts of nineteenth- and early twentieth-century Arrernte—are all that exist. The subject has become objectified. Although each object bears the same name, that is, "the Arrernte," it is now clear that this term serves primarily as the crossing point of four quite distinct storytracks, each one producing an account of the people so labeled.

I think some general observations relevant to ethnography can be drawn from this storytracking presentation of the Arrernte. In some respects the ethnographer creates the culture by basing a narrative of coherence about it on his or her personal experience with it. Because ethnographers represent a variety of storytracks and no two ethnographers can possibly have the same experiences, each will have a different basis, different facts, on which to substantiate the construction of a culture. Even "culture" is a relatively modern Western conception,[264] and probably there is no conceptual counterpart held by the subjects studied. "Culture," designating the expectation that every group of people can be described by a set of distinctive and common behaviors and traits, is thus already to adopt a projective strategy of interpretation. There is then no alternative to seeing the narrative presentation of ethnographers as other than creative constructions. There is no alternative to acknowledging that each and every ethnography, as far as it is legitimate and coherent, is a distinctive writing or presentation of an imagined subject. Any group of people identified as a culture may show a variety of legitimate profiles to observers who stand in differing relationships to it. Róheim and Spencer present very different images and descriptions of "the Arrernte," not necessarily because one is right and the other wrong, but because their respective dispositions and interests, their storytracks, prepared them to see and to otherwise experience different profiles.

One implication of this observation is that I believe that it is increasingly difficult to speak in an objective voice about any culture, despite our deep habit of doing so. While it is not at all uncommon to note the subjective elements in ethnography, once duly noted the practice is to revert to the objective vernacular. In the model of the totem rituals, which must be designated by both place and totem, perhaps we should cease to identify cultures only by subject name and adopt the more responsible appellation that conjoins ethnographer with culture: "Spencer's Arrernte" or "Róheim's Arrernte." This practice would remind us that there is no "culture" apart from the observer, although there are people who constitute the subject independent of those who write ethnographies. This naming practice would remind us that every time we yield to the objective voice—"the Arrernte do this or that"—we are asserting power over our subjects, who happen to be real people, entirely for our own needs.

To acknowledge multiple cultures that correspond with multiple ethnographies does not, however, equate all ethnographies. There are two perspectives for valuation. Within the purview of storytracking, there is the issue of legitimacy. Spencer's use of his sources to concoct the creation narratives is not academically legitimate. His declaration that Arrernte songs have no meaning is factually wrong. There are numerous opportunities to determine, within designated frames, the legitimacy and accuracy of ethnographic presentation. Ethnography is always creative, but it is not always legitimate; it is not always adequately constrained by the ethnographer-independent reality.

The other perspective for valuation is wholly within the purview of the ethnographer's audience, that is, the readers. The criteria for this valuation may have as much to do with cultural fashion as with anything else. Whereas Freud's "primal crime" hypothesis had a sympathetic and interested audience when published, several decades later Róheim's more adequately supported writings about a later generation of the hypothesis were largely ignored. Spencer and Gillen's publications were considered more important than Carl Strehlow's, perhaps, among other reasons, because of their alliance with James Frazer and because they were available in an English-language publication. In this arena of valuation, legitimacy of argumentation in any technical sense is rarely at issue, yet conflict among ethnographers is often couched in the objective language of who is right. The criteria for this kind of valuation reflects the interests, fashion, needs, and values of the reading audience. To approach ethnographies as intersections of storytracks demonstrates that ethnographies reveal insights not only into the cultures that are the designated subjects but also into the cultures and communities who construct and read them.

Another issue with ethnography is the degree to which the models and maps the ethnographers bring to their studies push their works beyond interpretation into simulation unsupported by cultural reference. The ethnographic enterprise, it seems to me, encourages the precession of simulacra by demanding pervasive and generic theories of culture. Should the effort be made to storytrack representative samples of each of the ethnographies presented here to their referential realities (the Arrernte people), it would doubtless be shown that all are rich admixtures of interpretation and simulation. It is not only that the Arrernte have shown different profiles to different ethnographers; the ethnographers have also simulated, unconstrained by the Arrernte, profiles that appear to be Arrernten but are demanded by their ethnographic generic concepts.

Finally, it must be noted that the presentations of these four ethnographies are themselves creative constructions heavily shaped by my own interests, by what I feel is important and relevant. My presentations are also subject to issues of illegitimacy and preceding simulation.

Having presented in chapters 3 through 6 a variety of examples set in Central Australia to demonstrate the methods of storytracking, I return to a discussion of Eliade's use of the "Numbakulla and the Sacred Pole" example, the subject of chapters 1 and 2. In the first two chapters the concern of storytracking was to trace one cultural example to its source, seeking a source independent of the lineage of interpreters, and to discern the motivations for the interpretations (and illegitimate constructions) of the sources by various scholars. In chapter 7, the same example will be placed as the crossing point of yet another set of concerns, those that define an area within the academic study of religion. Rather than seeking the Arrernte source for the Numbakulla example, we will make that example the common subject for radically differing interpretations that reflect major bodies of theory within the academic study of religion. The next chapter relates to the first two chapters on the order of turning a telescope around to look through the other end, as the micro to the macro.

7

Storytracking the Academic Study of Religion

The Arrernte and "Numbakulla and the Sacred Pole" stand at the crossroads of two other storytracks, a crossroads in the academic study of religion. In returning to the Numbakulla story, we have come full circle, but now I will trace a storytrack that intersects the one developed in the first two chapters. At this crossing a number of issues are raised, such as what is meant by the term *religion*, how comparison serves the study of religion, and what constitutes the use and interpretation of texts in the study of religion.

On several occasions during the 1950s and 1960s,[1] Mircea Eliade referred to an Arrernte text he had concocted, in accordance with his generic understanding of religion, to establish explicitly that "the religious" is synonymous with "the sacred center." In 1987 Jonathan Z. Smith extensively criticized this aspect of Eliade's work, showing, first, that Eliade's principal examples—the ancient Near East, India, and the Arrernte—do not support the pattern he attempted to establish, and second, that while the "religious" is expressed and enacted in terms of "place," it is done so in a manner much more complicated and varying than Eliade allowed.

The storytracks of Eliade and Smith are two courses along which the academic study of religion has developed. To analyze their crossing on this so-called Arrernte example offers the opportunity both to further develop and clarify storytracking as theory and method (important in drawing this work to some ending, if not a conclusion) and to reflect critically on the academic study of religion.

Eliade's Storytrack

Eliade's storytrack traces patterns throughout the history of religions. The outline of these patterns and relationships is discernable in the paragraphs preceding his presentation of the "Numbakulla and the Sacred Pole" example in *Australian Religions*: "For the Australians, as well as for other primitive societies, the world is always 'their own world,' that is to say, the world in which they live and whose mythical history they know. Outside this familiar cosmos lie amorphous, unknown dangerous lands, peopled by mysterious and inimical ghosts and magicians. . . . These strange lands do not belong to their 'world' and consequently still partake of the uncreated mode of being."[2]

In Eliade's view, primitive societies and archaic peoples are exemplars of the religious life. They are the least affected by history, which Eliade often saw as "terrifying."[3] Australians, as *ab origine*, are exemplary of the religious life. Their supposed primordiality is why Eliade, along with so many others, was interested in Australian aborigines. As hunter-gatherers, though contemporary, they are acknowledged for being preagricultural, remnants of the Stone Age.[4]

For Eliade, cosmos ("world" or "home") is a religious conception. It is the real, the known, and the familiar. That domain outside of world or cosmos is chaos, uncreated and unreal. Cosmos has positive connotations: home and familiarity. The area beyond cosmos has negative connotations: dangerous, inimical, strange, uncreated, and chaotic. People know the world in which they live not only physically but also as "mythical history," that is, the story of its origination, of its first inhabitants: "Yet even the most arid and monotonous landscape[5] can become a 'home' for the tribe when it is believed to have been 'created' or, more exactly, transformed by Supernatural Beings. Giving shape to the land, the Supernatural Beings at the same time made it 'sacred.' The present countryside is the result of their work, and they themselves belong to a realm of being different from that of men."[6]

Cosmos, home, and land (more or less synonymous) are "sacred" (i.e., religious) because they are given shape and meaning by supernatural beings. Eliade's view of religion depends on the existence of separate (i.e., ontologically distinct) realms (the realm of humans and the realm of supernatural beings), separate kinds of beings (humans and supernaturals), and separate kinds of time (human time and the time of the primordium, the beginning time): "The epoch when the Supernatural Beings appeared and began to transform the world, wandering across immense territories, producing plants and animals, making man as he is today, giving him his present institutions and ceremonies—this epoch was the 'Dream Time.' . . . This mythical time is 'sacred' because it was sanctified by the real presence and the activity of the Supernatural Beings."[7] The human world is dependent on the supernatural world in that it was created, given order, and made "real" by divine action, which occurred in the beginning time. Myth, as narrative, presents the history of the actions of the supernatural beings in the beginning time. The presence and action of the supernatural beings in the beginning time are the grounding for reality, cosmos, order, and meaning—in short, for the religious.

While myths tell the history of creative actions of the supernatural beings in the remote time of creation, this time can be "reactualized" by human beings through the enactment of ritual. As Eliade wrote: "But like all other species of 'sacred time,' although definitely remote, it is not inaccessible. It can be reactualized through ritual."[8] Ritual is modeled on the creative and transformative actions of the supernatural beings. To perform ritual is to replicate the acts of the gods, and thereby it is a means of reactualizing the beginning time, the religiously most potent time: "Everything which fully *exists*—a mountain, a water place, an institution, a custom—is acknowledged as real, valid, and meaningful because it came into being *in the beginning*."[9]

Eliade builds a tightly interrelated special vocabulary: *religious, primitive, cosmos, supernatural being, in the beginning, real, meaningful, valid, myth* (i.e., sacred history), and *ritual*. Human beings are religious when they live in a world that is created, transformed, or founded by supernatural beings in a primordial time whose history is recounted in myth. Human beings act religiously when they replicate and thereby reactualize the creative acts of the gods.

While "in the beginning" denotes the religious in temporal terms, it is the center that denotes the religious in spatial terms. To make this point Eliade calls on the Arrernte example of "Numbakulla and the Sacred Pole." In the midst of this account, Eliade writes: "This pole is charged with important symbolism and plays a central role in ritual. The fact that Numbakulla disappeared into the sky after climbing it suggests that the *kauwa-auwa* is somehow an *axis mundi* which unites heaven and earth. . . . the *axis mundi* . . . actually constitutes a 'center of the world.' This implies, among other things, that it is a consecrated place from which all orientation takes place. In other words, the 'center' imparts structure to the surrounding amorphous space." [10] The center place is then the religious place. It is where human beings have access to the supernaturals who withdrew back into their world at the conclusion of their creative actions in the beginning time, and it is the place that provides orientation—and thus defines cosmos, real, and meaningful—for religious human beings. Eliade dramatizes the importance of this center by citing the instance in which the Tjilpa ancestors died when they broke their pole: "Seldom do we find a more pathetic avowal that man cannot live without a 'sacred center' which permits him both to 'cosmicize' space and to communicate with the transhuman world of heaven."[11]

Eliade's view of religion largely determines the religious in his culturally and historically specific studies; that is, only what conforms with this view is seen as religious. By the time Eliade arrives at the study of Australian religions, it appears that his understanding of religion has become for him the primary reality. The abstract and universal character of his view of religion corresponds with his view of hierophany, that is, that the truly real stands, in principal, apart from its specific historical manifestations. His understanding of religion provides a grid, a lens, by which not only to recognize the patterns and actions that define religion among cultures throughout the world but also to simulate aspects of a particular tradition so that it will adequately fit the reality. His abstract model is no longer a map of some territory; rather it engenders the territory. In his study of Australian religions, Eliade is certainly not developing and revising his theory of religion with Australian data (an accommodative process), nor is he apparently content to understand and interpret Australian culture by the instantiation of his model of religion on

Australian cultural and historical materials (a projective process). While evidence of the latter operation is present, Eliade is, to an extent, also creating an Australian aboriginal simulacrum based on his generic understanding of religion. However, this critique of Eliade's study of religion must not be confined only to his study of Australians. His approach to comparison and his essentialist understanding of religion are academically questionable in the extent to which they unite to create simulacra of religions, as in the Numbakulla text.[12]

Eliade's approach to and understanding of religion have in many respects established the academic study of religions throughout the world. His introduction of categories of place—time and space—not only assisted in the study of diverse religious traditions but also provided a language not explicitly theological at a time, the mid-1960s, when the academic study of religion was being established in state-supported American universities.[13] Much of the academic study of religion remains, to some extent, on this storytrack. Although I think it is no longer so fashionable to base an academic study of religion explicitly on Eliade's work, I believe it will be a long time before the essentialist and nonscientific[14] foundations implicit in his seemingly neutral categories and methods will be adequately acknowledged and critically engaged. But it may no longer be possible to fully realize the degree to which studies conducted in this manner have created simulacra that are now considered, indeed have become, primary realities. Storytracking may at least reveal the otherwise tacit methods. The study of religion from the perspective of Eliade's storytrack involves using the methods of comparison to recognize, in the diversity of cultures, the familiar patterns of "the religious," as he understood it, despite their being dressed in a multiplicity of culturally specific guises. The comparative task focuses on identifying, and simulating where necessary, sameness despite diversity. From Eliade's track, one sees as religious what conforms with the definitive patterns; one simulates examples to fill gaps and thereby complete the patterns. The task appears to be directed less at comprehending religion as it occurs throughout the diverse world, though this is often the stated motivation, than at establishing a particular generic view of religion as the pervasive reality.

Smith's Storytrack

Jonathan Z. Smith's storytrack critically evaluates principles, methods, theories, and approaches to the academic study of religion. For Smith, religion is a "mode of constructing worlds of meaning, worlds within which men find themselves and in which they choose to dwell. . . . It is the quest, within the bounds of the human, historical condition, for the power to manipulate and negotiate one's 'situation' so as to have 'space' in which to meaningfully dwell."[15] According to Smith, as an academic term, *religion* denotes a second-order category or idea that has existed in the human imagination only during the last few centuries. Religion, but not specific religions, "is solely the creation of the scholar's study."[16] Religion is an academic category by which to study aspects of the diversity of culture. It is not the study of a given set of phenomena that can be distinguished by being somehow religious (as Eliade's approach would have it). Smith holds that "there is no data for religion."[17] The study of religion for Smith necessarily demands being "relentlessly self-conscious. Indeed, this self-consciousness constitutes his [the religion student's] primary expertise, his foremost object of study."[18] Thus for Smith, the question of theory, of approach, is everything.

In part because of Eliade's powerful and persistent emphasis on place, whose character is relevant to the way in which people designate order and meaning, place has become a common and widely discussed religious and cultural category. In some respects, following Eliade, place has been a persistent concern of Smith's approach to the study of religion. He holds that "once an individual or culture has expressed its vision of its place, a whole language of symbols and social structures will follow."[19] Widely discussed is his articulation of place in terms of the two categories, or kinds of religious maps, that he labels "locative" and "utopian." A locative vision of the world emphasizes place, whereas a utopian vision values being in no place.[20] Numerous works within the academic study of religion have followed from Smith's discussion of these categorizations. Unfortunately, many of these studies, by taking Smith's categories as definitive, use them as a grid or a lens to see (or to simulate?) familiar patterns in specific religions. Indeed, the locative category correlates well with a centered view of the world as described by Eliade. But to my reading, Smith's discussion of place is much richer and more complicated.

What Smith describes as maps makes better sense to me if they are thought of as mapping *strategies*. Locative and utopian as categories represent the extreme positions on a continuum. Neither, in practical terms, is possible to obtain or maintain for any length of time or on any significant scale. The very impossibility of these positions indicates that they are ideals, goals, or tendencies rather than categories. Furthermore, in almost every real situation, the closer one becomes to either of these positions, the more interesting and powerful the other appears—which demonstrates that locative and utopian are interdependent, rather than separate, positions. In actual religious cultures, the interaction between these polar positions is what is almost always operative, not the realization of either position. Smith's locative and utopian categories, then, become only ways of describing religious strategies, all of which then occur as the play between the incongruities.

Smith describes a third map, or as I prefer, mapping strategy, that supports my interpretation. Perhaps because he leaves it unlabeled, I believe it has also gone unnoticed. This strategy focuses on Smith's favorite theme, incongruity, or the issue of fit. As Smith considers comparison, mapping, living, and scholarship, he acknowledges, following Paul Ricoeur, that "incongruity gives rise to thought."[21] It is the presence of difference, the lack of fit, that makes things interesting. Incongruity is the sign of vitality: "The dimension of incongruity . . . appears to belong to yet another [besides locative and utopian] map of the cosmos. These traditions are more closely akin to the joke in that they neither deny nor flee from disjunction, but allow the incongruous elements to stand. They suggest that symbolism, myth, ritual, repetition, transcendence are all incapable of overcoming disjunction. They seek, rather, to play between the incongruities and to provide an occasion for thought."[22]

Importantly, Smith believes that similar dynamics should also be present in the methods of the academic study of religion. This similarity is expressed in terms of incongruity. Of the academic enterprise, he writes: "We need to reflect on and play with the necessary incongruity of our maps before we set out on a voyage of discovery to chart the worlds of other men."[23] This correspondence will be dealt with more fully later in this chapter.

Smith's understandings of myth and ritual follow closely his views on the importance of fit in regard to place. In sharp contrast with Eliade, Smith rejects the long tradition of scholarship that upholds the distinction between the primal moment of myth and its secondary application. He believes that "there is no pristine myth; there is only application."[24] In other words, myth as narrative is used by cultures as a "strategy for dealing with a situation."[25] Smith believes that religious cultures use myth to instigate comparison between the elements in the narrative and the aspects of the lived situation to which it is applied. Myth, more than a charter, is the instigator of thoughtful comparison: "There is delight and there is play in both the fit and the incongruity of the fit between an element in the myth and this or that segment of the world or of experience which is encountered. It is this oscillation between 'fit' and 'no fit' which gives rise to thought. Myth shares with other forms of human speech such as the joke or riddle, a perception of a possible relation between two different 'things.' It delights, it gains its power, knowledge and value from the play between."[26]

In Smith's understanding of ritual, incongruity appears to play a different role. He understands ritual largely in terms of its measure of control. Smith argues that in the course of life, it is usually impossible to control what happens. Ritual solves this problem because it "*represents the creation of a controlled environment* where the variables (i.e., the accidents) of ordinary life may be displaced *precisely* because they are felt to be so overwhelmingly present and powerful."[27] Thus, for Smith, ritual resolves the incongruities that are experienced in the course of life. Unlike myth—which itself creates and plays among incongruities in the thought-provoking processes that are religious because they engage in a "mode of constructing worlds of meaning"—ritual resolves the incongruities that are a given aspect of life. Seen from another angle, Smith holds that ritual is performed in marked-off places. A ritual place "is a place of clarification (a focusing lens) where men and gods are held to be transparent to one another."[28] Consistent with his view that ritual resolves incongruity, ritual is seen as clarifying or as focusing, as the domain where those things that do not make sense outside of the ritual space are clarified and resolved.

Incongruity is key to Smith's understanding of both myth and ritual as principal components of religion. However, the respective role of incongruity for the two differs significantly. On the one hand, myth introduces incongruity in order to give rise to thought and thus stimulates and motivates the meaning-creation mode that Smith defines as religious. Ritual, on the other hand, seems to work at resolving the incongruities that are present in life outside of ritual. Here there seems to be a shift in Smith's appreciation of the provocative nature of incongruity. Ritual appears to serve the ideal, the "ought"—determined somehow outside of and prior to the respective rites—by resolving incongruity and by clarifying. In this way ritual articulates both the recognition of incongruity and its fictive resolution.

Smith's storytrack runs crosswise to Eliade's. The latter is a noncritical and non-self-reflective trajectory, bearing little if any motivation to engage Smith's track. But as a highly self-reflective approach, Smith's track gains strength and clarification in the process of criticism and comparison with other tracks. Smith is a persistent critic of Eliade. He occasionally seeks out common data precisely to criticize what he believes is Eliade's methodologically unsound reliance on familiar patterns and established concepts. He goes beyond criticism to demonstrate a more reasonable (in his view) methodology, grounded on a close reading of the common data. In one major instance, Smith takes the opportunity to criticize and compare his and Eliade's approaches by focusing on the Arrernte text "Numbakulla and the Sacred Pole."

Crossed Tracks

Smith's Critical Analysis of Eliade's Interpretation.

Smith presents an extensive criticism of Eliade's reading of the "Numbakulla and the Sacred Pole" in "In Search of Place," the first chapter of his 1987 book, *To Take Place: Toward Theory in Ritual*. In Smith's analysis, Eliade focused his interpretation on nine elements of the myth.[29] To evaluate Eliade's interpretation of the Arrernte text, Smith compares Eliade's account with its source, Spencer and Gillen's *The Arunta* (1927). Smith shows that only one of the nine elements in Eliade's interpretation "can be accepted as Eliade has proposed them." Three elements (3, 6, and 9) are rejected entirely; five elements (1, 2, 4, 5, and 8) require revision.[30] Eliade's presumed pattern of "center" forces him to "misread the text." Smith writes: "By focusing on the false causal relationship—from broken pole to corporate death—Eliade has missed the actual structure of the narrative."[31] In response to his discovery of Eliade's misreading, Smith offers "an alternative understanding of the myth."[32]

By analyzing the sources of the text,[33] Smith discovers that the first part of the text—where Numbakulla creates the world, ending with his climb up the pole—occurs only in Spencer and Gillen's *The Arunta* (1927). The second part of the text—dealing with the travels of the ancestors, the breaking of the pole, and the death of the ancestors—is published in both the 1899 and 1927 editions of Spencer and Gillen's work on the Arrernte. Corroborated by Theodor Strehlow's observation that the Numbakulla prologue was concocted for Spencer in 1926,[34] Smith concludes that this portion is "an awkward hybrid,"[35] probably "a Christianized reinterpretation of Arandan myth."[36] Smith proceeds to his alternative reading by "putting aside the misleading and extraneous prologue of the myth of Numbakulla and his ascent up the pole."[37] Thereupon Smith restricts his analysis to the incidents of the broken pole and the death of the ancestors. He reports that he examined ninety-four incidents recorded by Spencer and Gillen but ignored by Eliade[38] in order to interpret these two incidents "set within their narrative frame."[39]

In his presentation of an alternative understanding, Smith focuses on four of the ninety-four incidents that make up the ancestral travels. All four incidents are intended to illustrate Smith's conclusion that the ancestral narrative is "an itinerary: the ancestors journeyed from this place to that; something happened; for this reason, the place is called 'so and so'; a feature in the present topography either was formed by or memorializes this event; the ancestors moved on to another place."[40] In light of what Smith believes is the typical narrative structure as determined by his analysis of the broad narrative context, he argues that the incidents of the broken pole and the dying ancestors are "not extraordinary, highly dramatic events to be lifted out and focused upon as having special cosmic significance. They are commonplace happenings within the myths of ancestral times."[41] Smith contends that "Eliade has missed the actual structure of the narrative. Each incident has two parts (again, typical of ancestral narratives): event and memorial."[42] He concludes his analysis: "By dissevering the double structure of event-memorial, Eliade has missed the generative element of the myth. It is, above all, an etiology for a topographical feature in the aboriginal landscape of today. It is the memorial that has priority."[43]

Smith cites the academic literature on the Arrernte and on the Australian aborigines in general to support his extension of this alternative reading into a description of the Arrernte understanding of place: "It is anthropology, not cosmology, that is to the fore. It is the ancestral/human alteration of and objectification of the landscape that has transformed the undifferentiated primeval space during the Dreamtime into a multitude of historical places in which the ancestors, though changed, remain accessible. This is expressed in the myths."[44]

Although Smith acknowledges that there are numerous issues that might be productively considered in this myth text,[45] he centers on the "event/memorial" pattern because it "will allow us to juxtapose two quite different understandings of the Tjilpa myth and, by extension, two quite different ways of conceiving of place within the study of religion."[46] In other words, Smith selects the issue that has the most potential to engage an intersection of storytracks that define the academic study of religion.

In Smith's analysis, the establishment of Eliade's pattern of the "sacred center" depends on only the Arrernte example and the Near Eastern examples that Eliade drew on from the pan-Babylonian school. Having criticized the Arrernte example, Smith turns to the Near Eastern examples, where he determines that "there is no pattern of the 'Center' in the sense that the Pan-Babylonians and Eliade described it in the ancient Near Eastern materials."[47] This leads Smith to conclude that "the 'center' is not a secure pattern to which data may be brought as illustrative."[48]

Smith compares anew the Arrernten materials with the ancient Near Eastern materials. In contrast to Eliade's comparative style, Smith finds that it is the differences that are most illuminating and provocative. In the Arrernten view of place, he argues, topographical features are a byproduct of ancestral journeys, while the ancient Near Eastern materials reflect a strong intentionality and deliberateness concerning the construction of place.[49] When freed of the expectations concomitant to the pattern of the "Center," Smith suggests that we might "classify and compare differences with respect to place."[50]

From an academic perspective, Smith calls into question Eliade's pattern of the "Center" on the grounds that the principal examples Eliade uses to establish the pattern—Arrernten and ancient Near Eastern—do not hold up to critical evaluation. In this criticism of a major element in Eliade's tightly interwoven set of concepts that articulates his view of religion, Smith calls into question Eliade's whole theory. Smith also criticizes the academic method that is more or less synonymous with Eliade's program, that is, comparison motivated by the desire to find similarity or sameness. Since Eliade's understanding of religion is not so much theoretical as it is ontological, Smith's challenge is far more than academic.

Critical Analysis of Smith's Alternative Interpretation.

To appreciate Smith's work on the Arrernte, it is important to comprehend that he is not, strictly speaking, presenting (as he states) an alternative to Eliade's interpretation. They are not reading the same texts. Eliade concocted an Arrernten text driven by his view of religion. Thus, Eliade's intention in presenting the Arrernten text is not explanation or illustration, as Smith considers it to be. Smith divides Eliade's text presentation into two parts: a prologue, relating Numbakulla's acts of creation, and the broken pole and ancestral death incidents extracted from an ancestral narrative. Smith uses an historical argument to set aside the prologue, allowing him to focus on the ancestral narrative. His interpretation of the prologue as the product of Christian influence is presented summarily.[51]

In not following further the interpretative study of the prologue, Smith pursues the Arrernten conception of place, which he finds discernable in the ancestral narratives. He is motivated to interpret Arrernten myths by his interest in establishing a theory of ritual based on "place" and in challenging Eliade's views and academic methods. The broken pole and ancestral death incidents in Eliade's account are only two of more than ninety incidents that Smith interprets in the myth text from Spencer and Gillen's *Native Tribes*. Although Smith focuses his interpretation on these two incidents, his interest is in the whole narrative, and thus the text he interprets is technically not the same as that considered by Eliade.

The broken pole incident is within the accounts of the so-called "middle wanderings" of the Tjilpa ancestors, which were recorded by Gillen sometime between April 17 and May 15, 1897. The Arrernte raconteurs were almost certainly aboriginal-English-speaking "police trackers" or "stock boys" who worked for Gillen at Alice Springs, or perhaps they themselves were the storytellers.[52] These accounts are divided into four sections, each one confined to the one group, or "column" in Gillen's terms, of traveling Tjilpa ancestors. Spencer edited Gillen's journal for inclusion in *Native Tribes*. His revisions were significant, but compared to other examples of his editing, the published account generally reflects Gillen's journal. For *Native Tribes*, Spencer maintained the group (or column) designations, numbered from one to four, as indicated by Gillen. However, for the publication of these accounts in *The Arunta*, Spencer reorganized them. The first and fourth groups were exchanged in identification, as well as in place. Spencer added significant general commentary and several pages of new material between the first (the former fourth) group and the second.

In the attempt to confirm Smith's view of the structure of these narratives, I have analyzed the entire story in a manner similar to Smith's;[53] that is, I have divided the narrative into camps or named places.[54] I was able to identify ninety camping places,[55] mostly on the basis of place names (see Table 1). A few places are indicated but not named. For each camping place, I noted and tabulated the significant actions. Based on the analysis of these camping places, I can make a number of observations.

The narrative, as Smith indicates, is an itinerary. Camping places are almost always named and frequently their location is described, often in reference to places known to late nineteenth-century European Australians. These nonaboriginal identifications were, I suspect, developed by Gillen's informants for his benefit or added by Gillen since they would be both unnecessary and irrelevant to aborigines. Occasionally the route of travel is described, almost always with reference to waterways or mountain ranges. On two occasions, the ancestors traveled underground; on other occasions, they entered and exited the ground but did not travel.

Although not in the published text in *Native Tribes*, Gillen's journal account notes that a pole, the *kauaua* or *nurtunja*, is erected at every camp. As Smith indicates, the presence of poles is consistently significant. The length of these poles appears to be important: longer seems to be better; short poles may be cause for embarrassment.

Ritual performances are the single most common type of event at a camping place, being performed at fifty-four of the ninety places. Often the ceremony is described by Gillen as *quabara undattha*, which Spencer usually renders as "sacred ceremonies" or "Engwura." Circumcision rites (*ariltha*) are performed on twenty-one occasions, most of them in addition to other ceremonies. A long series of ceremonies called *ampurtanurra* (in *The Arunta* Spencer presents this term as *ungperta-ngarra*) and associated with the Tjilpa group is performed seven times.

A dominant narrative feature, associated with forty-six camping places, is who is present at the location when the ancestors arrive, that is, who they meet when they arrive at a camping place. Those who are met are almost invariably identified by totem group, social subclass,[56] relative age, and gender. Occasionally the people encountered at a specific location also originated there; that is, the narrative describes them as having "jumped up" there. The names of these individuals are frequently given by Gillen, indicating their importance to the Arrernte, but the names are almost never included by Spencer. Almost without exception, the narrative indicates whether or not these persons have rituals (i.e., I think, whether they own the right to ritual performance) and a pole. Sometimes, if a pole is present, its general length is indicated.

Descriptions of the interactions between the ancestors and those people found in the camping places constitute the bulk of the narratives for many camping places. The narratives usually recount whether or not ceremonies are exchanged or shared between groups.[57] Often there are ritual exchanges. On several occasions the male

Table 1. Tjilpa Ancestral Wanderings: Analysis of Events at Camping Places

	Camp Place Name	A	B	C	D	E	F	G	H	I	Memorial	Meet Others	Leave Others	Comments
	Group I													
1	Okira [Okarra]	X												
2	Therierita [Therievula]	X	X	X									Man	
3	Atymikoala [Atnymechoala]	X	X											
4	Achilp-ilthunka [Achilpa ilthuka]	X					X				Stone where man was killed & buried	Wildcat man from Salt Water country		Name means "where Tjilpa cut man to pieces"
5	Unchipera wartna [Irrimiwurra]	X												Did not see two Opposum women
6	Aurapuncha [Kalearatunimma]	X	X							X		Smelled & saw Plumtree men		Went into ground, arose as Plumtree men
7	[Unartaonunga]	X	X											
8	Erlua	X											Few at various spots	
9	[Oralta]	X	X										Two men	
10	Arwura-puncha [Awurapuncha]	X	X									Ulpmerka men from Quinurnpa	Two men	Two parties join
11	Urangunja	X	X									Two Magpie women		
12	[Ilpaletta]	X												
13	Ilchartwa-nynga [Ilchaartwanynga]	X		X							Stone on end to mark dancing place			

14	Alawalla	X	X				X				Akakia trees shed plums like flood
15	Incharlinga [Incharulinga] On to Salt Water Country [Allia]	X	X				X				
	Group II										
16	Yungurra	X									Led by men with large erect penes
17	Imanda[a]	X	X		X				Frog, Tjilpa, White Bat, Little Bat	Some men	Divided into two groups
18	Itnuna-twuna	X	X						Purula Frog woman		
19	Ooraminna	X	X	X		X			Men suffering Erkincha & Unjiamba man & woman	Three Frog men	Initiate two women
20	Urthipata [Urthipita]	X	X						Unjiamba man & woman		Seen by Witchetty Grub man Ungperta-ngarra
21	"Small hill on Emily Plain" [Atnyraungwuramu-nia]	X	X					Stone marked camp site			
22	Okirra-kulitha [Ochirakulitha]	X	X	X							
23	Irpai-chinga [Irpaichingga]	X	X						Witchetty Grub people		
24	Achilpa-interninja	X	X							One man	Man came from tjurunga
25	Okilla-la-tunga	X	X						Purula woman (Unjiamba)		

(continued)

Table 1. (*continued*)

	Camp Place Name	A	B	C	D	E	F	G	H	I	Memorial	Meet Others	Leave Others	Comments
	Group II													
26	Ulir-ulira [Urlirurtirra]	X	X				X	X			Name means "where blood flows like river"		Ungperta-ngarra	
27	Ertua [Ertoa]	X										Two women (Wild Turkey)		
28	Arapera	X	X	X				X				Purula woman (Tjilpa)	One man	Initiate woman
29	Ilchinga [Ilchingga]	X							X		Stone marked spot	Bulthara woman (Unjiamba)		Men tired
30	Ungwurna-la-warika	X	X								Name means "where bone is stuck"	Two Bulthara women (Unjiamba)	One Purula man	
31	Ilchi-lira [Ilchieleara]	X	X									Two Unjiamba men & one Unjiamba woman	One Purula man	
32	Ituka-intura	X	X	X								Large group Tjilpa men & women	Local Tjilpa	
33	Arara	X	X											
34	"Spot on Harry Creek" X [Ultundaukartwa]				X							Smelled Tjilpa man, Unjiamba woman		
35	[Inkakilla]	X										Unjiamba man		
36	Ungunja [Unchelka]	X	X									Panunga man (Unjiamba)		
37	Apunga	X	X											
38	Burt Plain [Amullalinternika]	X					X					Bandicoot men & women		

39 Ilthwarra [Ilthwara]	X	X	X									
40 Hann Range gap [Oknicocherthera]	X									Carpet-snake man		
41 Ilchinia-pinna [Ilchinjapina]	X	X										Heard bullroarers in distance
42 Utachuta	X	X	X							Bandicoot men		Place where sound had come from
43 Inta-tella-warika [Intatelawarika]	X									Old Parula man (Tjilpa)[b]		Too tired to carry pole, dragged it
Group III												
44 Yungurra	X											
45 Urapitchera	X	X		X					Tjurunga represents head	Pigeon men & women	Purula man	
46 Itnunthawarra	X	X										
47 Iruntira	X										Bulthara man	
48 Okir-okira	X											
49 Arathetta	X	X								Panunga woman (Large Beetle)		
50 Chelperla	X	X			X						Old leader	Ungperta-ngarra Rested
51 Ungapakunna	X											
52 Ningawarta	X	X										
53 Alla (the nose)	X	X					X			Purula woman (Wattle Seed)	Two Kumara men	
54 Kupingbungwa	X					X						
55 Enaininga	X		X									
56 Iranira	X		X								Purula man	
57 Okinchalanina	X	X						X			Old Purula man	Made necklets, armlets, & forehead bands

(*continued*)

Table 1. *(continued)*

Camp Place Name	A	B	C	D	E	F	G	H	I	Memorial	Meet Others	Leave Others	Comments
Group III													
58 Lilpuririka	X					X						Old Pununga man	
59 Ilartwiura	X	X			X					Hole where kauaua stood			
60 Elunjinga	X	X	X										Ungperta-ngarra
61 Alpirakircha	X	X	X								Old Kumara man Tjilpa	Same man as found	Man had nurtunja (pole)
62 Untimara	X	X									Purula & Kumara women (Tjilpa)		Women had nurtunga
63 Ungatha	X								X			Man suffering Erkincha	
64 Udnirringintwa	X	X			X				X	Tjurunga for dead; hill for parra mound			
65 Alkirra-lilima	X	X			X						Old Panunga man (Unjiamba)		Ungperta-ngarra; man had nurtunga
66 Achichinga	X			X							Old Panunga man (Unjiamba)		Tried to take pole from man
67 Appulya Parachinta	X	X	X								Old Bulthara man (Eagle Hawk)		Man without pole
68 Arrarakwa	X		X								Panunga man (Tjilpa)		Man making pole
69 Erutatna	X	X								Place on creek where pole stood		Old Bulthara man	Ungperta-ngarra; man had pole
70 Unthilil-wichika	X	X	X								Old Bulthara man (Honey Ant)	Honey Ant people	Parties mixed

71	Kurdaitcha	X	X	X						Large group Tjilpa of all classes		Parties mixed
72	Unnamed	X								Large group Water Beetle		Parties did not mix
73	Okinyumpa	X							Stone marked place where pole broke			Broke pole, “tired & sad,” did not do ceremony
74	Unjiacherta	X							Tjurunga for dead; hill for place of death	Large group of Unjiamba of all classes		
	Group IV (leaving Yungura)											
75	Erloacha [Ertoatcha]	X	X								Two men	Led by man with big penis that dragged ground
76	Yapilpa	X								Dancing woman		
77	Ulpmaltwitcha	X	X									
78	Urichipma [Uritchipma]	X							Name means “place of pichis”; stone			
79	Kurupma	X	X								Man	
80	Poara	X	X	X				X		Hawk woman	Several men	
81	Irpungartha [Irpungartna]	X	X	X						Hawk woman		
82	Al-lemma	X								Hawk woman		
83	Ariltha [Arilta]	X	X	X	X					Hawk men & women		Leader had big penis
84	place near Lake Macdonald	X	X							Hawk men & women	One man	
85	Irincha	X								Fish man		Ungperta-ngarra

(*continued*)

Table 1. *(continued)*

Camp Place Name	A	B	C	D	E	F	G	H	I	Memorial	Meet Others	Leave Others	Comments
Group IV													
86 Alknalilika	X						X				Quail women		
87 Inkuraru	X		X							Stone marks spot where ariltha done			Tjurunga deposted
88 Irti-ipma [Irliipma]	X	X										One man	
89 Unnamed	X										Bulldog Ant woman		
90 Kuntitcha	X		X								Bandicoot men like Inapertwa	One man	Killed men
Then went north to Salt Water													
Totals	90	54	21	4	6	5	5	2	5	14	46	27	

[a]At this point in the intinerary of Spencer and Gillen's *The Arunta*, there are many extra stories.

[b]This old man opened a vein and blood flooded the country and drowned the Achilpa men.
The drowned men went into the ground.

Source is Spencer and Gillen, *Native Tribes*, pp. 402–417, and Gillen's unpublished journals. Camping places are numbered and named.
The square bracketed names indicate where Gillen's journal differs from the published account.

A = Pole erected.

B = Ceremonies performed.

C = Circumcision performed.

D = Changed language.

E = *Erkincha* (sexual disease) present.

F = Blood drunk; usually young men give arm blood to thirsty elders.

G = Sexual intercourse performed.

H = Bodies painted by men.

I = Travel underground.

ancestors have sex with a woman met in a camp. In one incident much is made of the fact that this sexual act is in violation of the ancestors' ritual law. The spread of a sexually transmitted disease called *Erkincha* is considered the result of this ritual violation. The Tjilpa ancestors observed another group performing cannibalistic acts. Sometimes, because those encountered at named camping places owned ceremonies, they were able to avoid the traveling ancestors, even to avoid sexual intercourse with them. This suggests the power or potency of owning rites. A minor but significant narrative element is that, unbeknown to the traveling party, they are sometimes seen by others as they pass a given location, or others are in the vicinity of a place but the traveling party does not see them.

Another significant inclusion (twenty-seven instances) is whether a person or persons are left at the camp when the ancestral group moves on. Who they are—number, class, totem identity, name, gender, and age—is usually given, as sometimes is the reason for their being left. Commonly, the narrative notes that a descendant of a person left behind by the ancestors presently lives at that place.

There are several minor themes of significance identifiable in these "wandering" incidents. Memorials are indicated for fourteen of the camps. Typically these are stones or hills that arise at a camping place to memorialize some event, sometimes just that the place is a campsite. Three of these memorials are unnamed places, with simple descriptions of a geological feature, indicating where the pole was erected at the camp. Two of these are *tjurungas* that are kept in storehouses, each representing a deceased ancestor. One group of stones marks the burial place of a man the traveling ancestors killed for his offensive sexual conduct. A group of stones arose to mark a dancing place. Two memorials are hills that arose to mark the place of a significant event—one where a group of ancestors died, the other where a ritual mound had been formed. One group of stones marks where a group of ancestors were drowned and entered the ground.

Only six places (and two of these can only be discerned from Gillen's journals) have place names connected in any way—at least in any clear way to a non-Arrernte speaker[58]—with the distinctive appearance or character of the physical place they designate.[59] At six of the camps groups of men either contracted or died from the disease named *Erkincha*.[60] Two of the memorials are associated with the death of ancestors due to this disease: one records the appearance of a group of *tjurungas* and the other the appearance of a large hill to mark the spot where they died.

At four camps the ancestors changed their language, and at four camps the old men who had grown tired were refreshed when the young men cut their arms and gave the old men large drinks of their blood. At one camp the young men drank their own blood.

The ancestral leaders of these groups have very long, erect penes, which are so cumbersome that they threaten the progress of the groups. On one occasion, an ancestor's penis digs a furrow in the ground as it is dragged along. These descriptions of genitalia occur only in Gillen's journals, although occasionally Spencer attempts a highly euphemistic reference.

According to Smith's understanding, "ancestral narratives," as widely distributed in Australia, have the structure of an "itinerary," which he describes in terms of five elements:

1. the ancestors journeyed from this place to that
2. something happened
3. for this reason, the place is called "so and so"
4. a feature in the present topography either was formed by or memorializes this event
5. the ancestors moved on to another place.[61]

Smith illustrates this pattern by presenting two incidents from the Tjilpa "wanderings" narratives. The first one accounts for the name Uritchimpa, meaning "the place of the pitchis," and the second selection accounts for the name Ulirulira, meaning "the place where blood flowed like a creek." However, from the preceding analysis we now know that of the ninety places only six are in any way, at least explicitly in the text, connected with the etiology of the place or place name, and for only one of these is there a relatively clear association of the place name with the events the narrative describes as occurring in that place. Smith emphasizes element number 4, the event/memorial structure, as that which most characterizes the actual structure of the whole itinerary. Yet at only fourteen out of ninety camping places is there any mention of a memorial, and only four of these memorials are landscape features that correspond with significant ancestral events described in the narrative.

Thus, in Smith's analysis of the five elements, numbers 3 and 4 are not only atypical but actually quite exceptional. This leaves only structural elements number 1, the ancestors journeyed from this place to that; number 2, something happened; and number 5, the ancestors moved on to another place. Elements 1 and 5 are effectively the same, the coincidence of point of origin and terminus; thus there remains only the rather indistinctive iterative structure of elements 1 and 2: the ancestors travel to a series of places, at each of which something happens.

Smith continues his analysis by showing that the Tjilpa narratives are consistent with the general pattern he has described: "The Tjilpa ancestors come to a place. They meet an individual or another group that has a sacred pole and/or other sacred objects. (Indeed, the lack of a pole is thought worthy of notice.) These objects are shown to the Tjilpa. Some mode of social interaction transpires between the wandering Tjilpa and the indigenous inhabitants—most usually a ceremony, but sometimes acts of violence or sexual intercourse. The Tjilpa ancestors then move on."[62] This sets the context in which Smith focuses directly on the two incidents of interest to Eliade: the broken pole and the resulting ancestral death.[63] Smith's analysis is intended to demonstrate the "event/memorial" structure of these two incidents and to show that Eliade did not see this structure.

Certainly, as far as Smith's alternative explanation of the "broken pole" incident is concerned, his emphasis on "event/memorial" identifies structural elements that appear in at least these two episodes of the "wandering" narratives, although, at least according to my analysis, he overstates his evidence by calling them "typical narrative units."[64] More significantly, Smith's alternative explanation that "the generative element of the myth . . . is . . . an etiology for a topographical feature in the aboriginal landscape of today"[65] cannot be supported by the text he analyzed.[66] The narrative clearly assumes the prior existence of every one of the camping places and almost all of the features of the landscape. In only a few cases, such as those in which a hill or stones arose as a memorial, does the landscape become transformed as a result of the presence of the ancestors, and these hills remain unnamed. In only one incident is it relatively clear that the name of the place is the result of events recounted in the narrative. Although some attention is directed in the narratives to the location of named camping places, every one of them existed before the ancestors visited them, as did the waterways and mountains. The prior existence of these places is emphasized in that for over half of them, people are present when the group arrives and the names of places are given to identify travel destinations.

Although Smith holds that "an alternative understanding of the myth [i.e., the Arrernten myth presented by Eliade] must be proposed,"[67] the effect of his approach is to partially reconstruct the myth, presenting isolated exceptional incidents as typical, to support an alternative understanding. But Smith and Eliade are not "reading" the same text. Smith's alternative amounts to another reconstruction of a text drawn from elements selected from the Spencer and Gillen published sources.

The Academic Study of Religion

Storytracking is a method by which to construct and compare narratives of coherence that present various interpretive perspectives about a given subject. In the preceding sections I have constructed partial storytracks for Mircea Eliade and Jonathan Z. Smith. I chose to focus on these two scholars because of the measure of their contribution to the academic study of religion. In constructing these tracks I have attempted to examine some basic principles underlying their work. I have constructed each narrative in anticipation of, and in hopes of, illuminating the crossing of these tracks. In the previous section, the crossing of these tracks was concretized by focusing on the "Numbakulla and the Sacred Pole" materials. Storytracking provides the frame for comparison, in which each perspective accounted for may in turn be occupied as the position from which to evaluate other intersecting storytrack perspectives. Storytracking prepares us to first take up Smith's position to evaluate that of Eliade and then to stand in Eliade's to evaluate Smith.

Thus, for example, from the perspective of Smith's track, Eliade is undone—he is wrong and is replaced. Eliade's view of religion, his understanding of the comparative enterprise, his treatment of the Arrernte—all are "wrong," at least in some respects; minimally Eliade's claims are overstated. His views and positions are to be replaced, decidedly with those presented by Smith. Yet, from the perspective of Eliade's storytrack, it might be said that Smith has been too narrow; he has not looked broadly enough to Arrernten and other Australian aboriginal materials. What of the emu-footed man? What of the casuarina tree that serves as a ladder to the sky?[68] What of the broad ritual use of poles? And so on. Do these not function in some ways as center places? Do they not designate religious importance? What of the aboriginal conjunction of the present with mythic time? Are not all aboriginal acts somehow repetitions of the acts of the mythic ancestors? And, most important of all, Smith surely cannot deny that this understanding of religion fits so many cultures other than the Arrernte, so many, in fact, that it is impractical even to attempt to recite them all. Given this, how could the Arrernte not also fit?

Any of dozens of points of comparison could easily be pursued in this fashion. However, a more powerful frame of comparison is offered by storytracking when the comparative vantage is apart from any of the storytracks traced. Here storytracking is a method of critically evaluating and extending the purposes and interests of the various stories tracked. In this case, the crossing of Smith's and Eliade's storytracks gives me the opportunity to comprehend and attempt to advance issues and approaches related to the academic study of religion. By comparing Smith and Eliade on the basis of my own interests and concerns, I am able to more fully understand them, but I am also able to more fully understand and meaningfully engage in the academic study of religion. I will not only place Eliade and Smith in the context of issues I select; I will also attempt to show how the storytracking approach suggests meaningful development of these issues.

Religion

What is meant by *religion*? For decades it has been a term widely discussed and controversially defined. Most religion scholars have grown weary of the effort and have lost interest in the discussion despite the widely accepted principle that a word that cannot be defined is a word of limited academic value. Such a conundrum as the title by which the field—the academic study of *religion*—is identified is no small reason for broadly felt discomfort and embarrassment.

Eliade's understanding of the term *religion* is based on an a priori belief about what it means to be human. Although he seemed uninterested in its academic history, he unhesitatingly used the term to identify the human perception of that which has impetus and origin beyond human agency, most frequently termed "the sacred." It is synonymous with the real and the true. Religion, that is, the human apprehension of and response to the sacred, is grounded in that which is received, revealed, and discovered. The sacred breaks into the human world from other-than-human realms and in doing so gives the human world meaning. Although the sacred is itself ineffable, it nonetheless manifests itself in distinctively religious patterns that make up a category of phenomena. With respect to their origin and structure those things that are religious are sui generis, that is, unique. Eliade held that the study of the religious for nonreligious interests, such as sociology and anthropology, is reductive and misses the religiousness of the subject. Religion is adequately comprehensible only to those who know the distinctive patterns of manifestation and appreciate that they are manifestations of "the sacred." It seems that the fundamental premise for this view is outside of the academic purview. Eliade's is an essentialist view of religion. Yet it must not be forgotten that, as shown in chapter 2, this essentialism, in practice, becomes a pervasive relativism.

Eliade understood human history as only a stream of unrepeatable events and accidents, having no meaning. Seemingly overwhelmed by the meaninglessness of history, he sought to ground whatever meaning was found in history in extrahistorical reality. Meaning arises in the experience of history, or to cast it more in Eliade's mood, "suffering becomes intelligible and hence tolerable"[69] only when seen in the light of the extrahistorical, which Eliade identified as evidenced in myth ("sacred history"), the accounts of the actions of supernaturals. History makes sense only in light of the story of the gods. The historically concrete is secondary to the extrahistorical because it is on the basis of the extrahistorical that the historically concrete can be comprehended as meaningful. Eliade's abstract generic understanding of religion correlates with the extrahistorical grounding of meaning. It makes it possible for him to identify as meaningful the otherwise random and unrelated concrete elements of diverse cultures through time. Eliade's generic understanding of religion functions in the study of religion as the extrahistorical does in the history of religion. His understanding of religion is more real, more dependable, than any of its historical and geographical manifestations. Apart from the meaning bestowed on history and culture by his model, the concrete historical and cultural materials are meaningless and random.

Jonathan Smith's understanding runs counter to Eliade's view. For Smith, religion is a mode of human creativity. It is always historical and cultural. Religion owns no particular set of data; it is a category invented only a few centuries ago to facilitate a peculiarly Western and academic effort to make sense of a diverse human world. The term is significant primarily within the academic community that invented it, and it is not a term that arises from or is somehow part of the identities of those subjects that are designated by its use. Smith directs the understanding of religion to a "mode of constructing worlds of meaning." For Smith, religion is human-based and this-worldly. He reinjects history and human historical actions as the ontological basis for comprehension and meaning. The unique,[70] the extrahistorical, are in themselves incomprehensible realities, if indeed they exist, unsuitable for academic study because no reference can be made to them other than the historically and culturally specific.

To Smith, religion and its many constituent subdivisions are always propositional, always in the process of development and refinement. It remains at least possible that the academic constructions termed *religion* can be deconstructed, rejected, or replaced. History (encompassing the cultural), for Smith, is the realm of greater reality when compared with academic constructs. It is the absence of fit, the gap between academic construct and the subject reality that vitalizes the academic process, which is always negotiable.

The storytracking perspective offers insight into Eliade's and Smith's strategies of defining religion. The technical difficulty faced in the definition of religion is that many of the subjects that students of religion want to include make absolute claims. The claims are routinely described as being based on a spiritual, nonobservable, and ineffable reality. Taken individually, these claims are seen as uncompromisable, unconditional. For example, religions commonly make claims about the creation of the world, the existence of world-creating gods, the foundation of truth, and the destiny of human beings and the entire world. The problems arise in the attempt to comprehend and affirm these unconditional, often mutually exclusive and unverifiable claims, both individually and collectively. The very character of the academic enterprise, demanding verifiable sources and a rational argumentation, seems to oppose the subject studied. I believe that both Eliade's and Smith's definitional strategies have been developed in the attempt to resolve this confounding problem.

To define religion as the ineffable or based on the ineffable, as Eliade often seems to do, allows the acceptance of multiple unconditional claims. All such statements fall equally within the domain of the unexplainable. The price paid by this strategy, at least as an academic strategy, is high. Given an interactionist approach to interpretation and given that interpretation is the work of the study of religion, the subject reality must have a structure that constrains instantiations of theory made upon it. The ineffable or the incomprehensible has no graspable or identifiable structure; thus it will allow any arbitrary interpretations made of it. Studies of religion based on this kind of nondefinition are "religious" in character; that is, they are conducted on the basis of nonpublic experiences defined and described within a single identifiable religious perspective. To hold that all religion is founded on the incomprehensible is to negate the particularity and distinctiveness of religions in any terms other than the diversity of human responses to the unfathomable. This approach mystifies religion beyond the reach of academic study. Directed toward the study of the history of religions, this approach focuses on apprehending "the sacred" in its diversity of historical and cultural manifestations, based on the unquestioned premise that the sacred manifests itself as "the center" and "in the beginning." This approach, when presenting itself as the *academic* study of religion, has been an insufferable admixture of religiously and academically motivated studies, interpretations, and preceding simulations, reflected oddly in the commonly used field name "religious studies." To the extent to which the study of religions is understood as being inseparable from apprehending the ineffable, or even the study of patterns of manifestation based on an a priori unverifiable assumption, the field falls short of being academic, though it may serve the beliefs of religious scholars. The difficulty with this understanding of religion is that the study of religion must become, in part, the manufacture of simulacra, bearing only the flavor or terminology of various historical and geographical specificity so as to appear real. Unchecked, this approach may becomes a weightless system, a self-referential hyperreality, unmoored from any reality outside itself and making reference to nothing that it has not itself constructed.

Smith's strategy, meanwhile, shifts the grounds to the "lookers," the academics. Religion is an affair of the academy. In this strategy, religion is an academic category used to investigate how a variety of human cultures engages in the business of making the world meaningful. Truth claims, statements of belief, and so on are seen in this perspective as methods by which cultures make life meaningful. This approach "saves" religion as a legitimate and possible subject for academic study. Yet, from the perspectives of those subjects that are identified as religious, this view may appear to dilute and even to deny what they consider singular and unconditional claims, to ignore that ineffable source that is most fundamental. From the perspective of some, indeed most, specific traditions, the academic study of religion, understood in these definitional terms, may seem uncaring and hostile. Furthermore, when religion is defined so broadly and vaguely as a "mode of constructing worlds of meaning," few human actions are immediately excluded as potentially religious.

Despite these problems, Smith's views must be developed if there is to be hope for an academic study of religion. Storytracking suggests ways to contribute. It suggests, following Smith, that *religion* is a term that makes sense only when seen in a ludic frame—the frame of metaphor, irony, and joke. Religion, in this light, is seen as not only embracing the mutually exclusive, the logically incompatible, but also thriving on the insights offered by such a double or multiple perspective. Current metaphor theory, that, for example, presented by Lakoff and Johnson,[71] holds that metaphors are preconceptual; that is, they are the materials from which concept networks are constructed. Metaphors are powerful precisely for the reason that they not only conjoin but also equate two things that clearly are not even in the same category. To appreciate its power, religion must be seen in similar terms.

By permitting perspectives in conflict and by embracing perspectives that are mutually exclusive, storytracking enriches the academic understanding of religion. By inviting multiple and conflicting truths and objective perspectives, storytracking qualifies truth and relativizes objectivity, yet qualified truth and relative objectivity are oxymoronic. Indeed, a storytracking approach to the academic study of religion, as it appears in this second frame of comparing perspectives from the outside, participates in the realm of such structures as oxymoron, metaphor, joke, and play. This approach to the academic study of religion must be appreciated as engaging that frame of mind in which one may both accept objectivity and truth in the radical sense of singularity and, at another phase of the oscillation, qualify and relativize such positions. A storytracking approach both appreciates the distinctiveness, authority, and groundedness of each subject perspective and acknowledges that, when compared, the perspectives may conflict with one another, be mutually exclusive, or claim to be based in realms beyond academic purview.

There are correspondences between this storytracking view of religion and Smith's discussion of a third, unnamed map. In this map, people allow incongruities to stand, seeking "rather, to play between the incongruities and to provide an occasion for thought."[72] According to this view, in practical terms, all religious actions, all that we would term *religion*, exist in the middle territory of negotiating differences, playing among incongruities. Indeed, these are the key dynamics and operations Smith identifies as religious. Religions, then, are vital on precisely the same terms as they are foundational to the academic study of religion. The name I would suggest for Smith's unnamed, third map—or as I prefer to understand it, mapping strategy—would be "religion."

Category theory is another related perspective from which to consider the definition of religion. The strategy by which the academic study of religion has attempted the definitional task has been to use what George Lakoff has called a classical theory of category.[73] Classical category theory is an objectivist theory in which a category is seen in set theoretical terms. The feature that distinguishes any member of the set must distinguish all members of the set. Certainly a review of definitions of religion confirms that this key distinctive feature is invariably sought. The most common distinction of religion has been the belief in god. This is the definitional criterion, but it also functions in studies of religion even when definitions are not explicit. For example, the late nineteenth- and early twentieth-century studies of small-scale cultures, then called "primitives," centered on "high gods" because their presence was the distinctive feature that marked the existence of religion.

Lakoff's analysis of classical theory shows that it is inseparable from a set of "familiar ideas": (1) Meaning is based on truth and reference; it concerns the relationship between symbols and things in the world. (2) Biological species are natural kinds, defined by common essential properties. (3) The mind is separate from and independent of the body. (4) Emotion has no conceptual content. (5) Grammar is a matter of pure form. (6) Reason is transcendental in that it transcends—goes beyond—the way human beings, or any other kinds of beings, happen to think. It concerns the inferential relationships among all possible concepts in this universe or any other. Mathematics is a form of transcendental reason. (7) There is a correct, God's-eye view of the world, a single correct way of understanding what is and is not true. (8) All people think by using the same conceptual system.[74] Lakoff's analysis has, it seems to me, remarkable implications for the issue of defining religion. It appears that no matter how religion is defined, the definition will be constrained by the familiar ideas wedded to the operative category theory, in this case the classical theory. Not only are these ideas central to Western thought, but also many of them are fundamental to Judeo-Christian thought. Defining religion is then doubly grounded in classical category theory and the Western religious view.

Lakoff shows that while classical category theory and its assumptions have been espoused, categories generally function more in the terms of his proposed prototype theory of category. Although the theory is complex and cannot be considered fully here, we can immediately appreciate the significance of developing categories, and thus definitions, on the basis of prototypes, or "best examples." Once a best example is generalized as a category, other examples may be included by principles of extension. Lakoff's view illuminates the existing practice of defining religion, as well as the difficulty experienced in attempting to state definitions. Although I have not made a full study of definitions of religion, it seems clear that in most of them Christianity, or more broadly Abrahamic traditions, has served as the "best example" of religion.[75] Other "religions" have been incorporated in the category by some principle of extension. For example, some traditions feature belief in more than one god. While the prototype calls for belief in a single god, multiple gods may be included by a principle of extension. Other principles have functioned. For example, rendering the Western religious ideas of a belief in God in terms of the generic "ultimate concern" allows the religion category to include even traditions that are nontheistic as long as they seem to hold some principles or beliefs as being beyond question. Chains of extensions serve to increase the category still centered on the best example.

Even these simple extensions of category make utterly complicated, if not impossible, the statement of a distinctive defining feature demanded by classical category theory.

While religion, as a modern academic category, has developed more on the order Lakoff describes as a prototype theory, it has carried out its definitional task in classical theoretical terms, and it has attempted to support the underlying assumptions of the theory. Definitions of religion are never open in the sense of being negotiated in light of the diversity of experiences one may encounter geographically and historically because the tacit assumptions doubly bind us. Hidden to the definitional process is the prototypical role of Western monotheistic traditions, and it hides the favorite ideas that are implied by the operative classical category theory. Doubly bound by tacit elements, the definition of religion can never be more than the production of a precession of simulacra, asserting itself as a colonist map that engenders a world in denial of all incongruous territory.

It is often noted that Eliade's understanding of religion was most influenced by his studies and personal experiences of Indian mysticism. However, it cannot be doubted that his discourse about religion and his studies of the history of religions rest firmly on distinctively Western assumptions of classical category theory.

Of Smith's understanding of religion in light of this discussion, more can now also be said. By emphasizing map rather than mapping strategy, it seems to me that Smith reveals a residual classical category theory. He wants containers in which to put examples of things that share the same set of distinctive properties. He names the locative and utopian map categories. He discusses their distinctive characteristics and offers examples that fit into these categories. By doing so, he encourages others who perhaps unwittingly hold a classical category theory to use these categories as models for other analyses. Thus, his third, unnamed, fuzzy category remains entirely overlooked. However, I believe that Smith, through his persistent attention to difference and incongruity, broadly challenges classical category theory and the ideas that accompany it. Furthermore, it almost goes without saying that Smith's view of religion—at least, what I have teased out of his third, unnamed mapping strategy—would displace Christianity or Abrahamic traditions as necessarily the "best example" of religion. Or at least it would demand these traditions to be seen anew. Should the implications of classical category theory be recognized as concerns in the academic study of religion, Smith's many studies that emphasize incongruity would provide a productive point from which to begin a reexamination and revision. The results would be a radical transformation of the discipline.[76]

Comparison

Comparison[77] is a focal issue in Smith's critique of Eliade. Eliade's understanding of comparison is to use familiar patterns as a grid or measure against which to comprehend the common patterns or structures among the disparate data of diverse cultures and to thereby apprehend the presence of "the sacred." The cultural elements that match the given patterns are recognized as religious or as aspects of religion.

Eliade's method is a morphological style of comparison that shares much with comparative anatomy, which served historically as its source. Morphological comparison is structural, ahistorical, and phenomenological. Even the developmental implications of such terms as *primitive* and *archaic* were not seen by Eliade as growth, progress, or development in time. Demanding historical and cultural needs have motivated this understanding of comparison. Eliade's work in religion responded to the conditions that arose in the late nineteenth century with the explosion of knowledge about thousands of cultures the world over, which was a byproduct of Western colonialism and a product of the rise of modern anthropology. This expansion was accompanied by a shift in the use of the term *culture* from the singular form of the word, which denotes the extent of development of a people, to the plural, *cultures*, which denotes the set of traits, practices, and patterns that distinguish every group from all other groups of people. In the face of such diversity, every effort had to be made to discover common bases—categories and patterns—by which the diverse peoples of the world might be interconnected. Eliade's program served this need in the area of religion. It served to define the religious for all cultures, no matter how exotic or different.

However, as the twentieth century progressed, it became apparent that the continued use of this comparative method tended to diminish, even deny, the differences that distinguish one culture from another. The success of this morphological comparative method had the effect of finding, or simulating if not present, the same patterns in every culture, no matter how otherwise diverse. For example, Eliade's discussion of the sacred center drew on ancient Near Eastern, Indian, and contemporary Australian aboriginal cultures to represent the same religious pattern. Cultural and historical particularity and distinction were overlooked in the quest for universality.

Jonathan Smith challenged this comparative method, demonstrating that when materials are carefully presented in their historical and cultural particularities, they do not so precisely fit the familiar patterns. He showed that it is the distinctiveness, the incongruities, raised by comparison that are the more interesting. Differences give rise to thought; they demand the refinement of theory and method. Smith presented a model of comparison motivated by the discovery or illumination of difference. The gain is a fuller appreciation of the historically and culturally specific. Eliade's approach to Arrernte culture not only filtered out much but also concocted what did not exist. It allowed to survive only highly select passages in the Arrernten source texts, and these were severely transformed into simulacra. The surviving passages were the structural elements that matched, or at least suggested, the comparative grid Eliade used. Only the items that confirmed or suggested the "sacred center" and its associated premises were seen. When correlate items were not found, they were concocted. This process amounts to the deterritorialization of the Arrernte. Smith's approach, in contrast, placed the items that were of interest to him and Eliade in their broader cultural and historical Arrernten and aboriginal contexts in order to more carefully evaluate them, especially from the point of view of the culture concerned. His interpretive efforts were focused on and motivated by the differences that were revealed in this kind of comparative operation. As Smith describes the process: "A comparison is a disciplined exaggeration in the service of knowledge. It lifts out and strongly marks certain features within difference as being of possible intellectual significance, expressed in the rhetoric of their being 'like' in some stipulated fashion. Comparison provides the means by which *we* 're-vision' phenomena as *our* data in order to solve *our* theoretical problems."[78]

The storytracking approach engages at least two comparative frames. One type of comparative operation is framed within the subject field, determined by the various intersecting storytrack perspectives. Each storytrack is a valued perspective. The sum of storytracks that have a common intersection makes up the subject. In series, each storytrack provides a place from which to comparatively evaluate all other perspectives at play in the subject. Another type of comparison, consistent with Smith's approach, arises in being relentlessly self-conscious as the one constructing and comparing the storytracks within a cultural and historical situation. The frame, the category of sameness in which differences are examined, is of the scholar's choosing. Smith insists that the scholar must be relentlessly self-conscious in selecting theory and method or in choosing issue and subject, for these choices shape all that follows. The storytracking approach affirms the importance of this self-consciousness while acknowledging the enormous complexity and problematicity of comparison. This second frame raises, and must somehow address even if temporarily, the issue of comparison itself, which as Smith described it is this: "How am I to apply what the one thing shows me to the case of two things?"[79] Or as Jacques Derrida wrote in his characteristic style: "We must first try to conceive of the common ground, and the *différence* of the irreducible difference."[80]

Storytracking focuses on the issue of comparison by problematizing the relationship between and among the items compared, expressed effectively through the metaphors of *gap* and *play*. Storytracking follows Smith's lead in this respect: "Comparison requires . . . a methodological manipulation of difference, a playing across the 'gap' in the service of some useful end."[81] Also: "Comparison . . . is an active, at times even a playful, enterprise of deconstruction and reconstruction which, kaleidoscope-like, gives the scholar a shifting set of characteristics with which to negotiate the relations between his or her theoretical interests and data stipulated as exemplary."[82]

Storytracking attempts a self-consciousness in two frames at once. That is, it attempts to recognize at once two kinds of gaps—the gaps among the proposed perspectives that constitute the drama of the subject and the gap that exists between the scholar (the storytracker or the comparer) and the field of the subject. Storytracking holds that comparison is possible only through the interaction of these two frames.[83]

Certainly comparison may occur in a serial fashion by indwelling any one or more of the perspectives represented as the complex subject. This comparison is facilitated or made possible by the identification, however fortuitously,[84] of the point of intersecting tracks. In the present example, we have shown that it is possible to compare Eliade to Smith and Smith to Eliade. The terms of the comparison are grounded at the crossing of their tracks, the identification of sameness or an arena of relatedness. Such comparison might be motivated to find either similarities or differences, but it can never be legitimately performed without conceiving of common ground. The common ground is always, in some sense, a category. The category frames the comparison. It determines the terms of the comparison. It assumes that the subjects to be compared have at least some representation in the category that controls the comparison; otherwise comparison would be impossible. Comparison is considerably enriched if a prototype theory of category is self-consciously employed.[85]

A second kind of comparison (theoretically inseparable from the first because it precedes and shapes it) arises in the acknowledgment that the storytracker (the scholar, "the looker") has perspectives entirely separate from those of the subject studied. It is this perspective that shapes the vocabulary, the limitations, the type of category theory, and the extent of the storytracks charted within the chosen subject of study. It is this perspective that determines the terms of the comparison, accomplished largely by the selection of the intersection points of two or more storytracks. The academic operation that facilitates self-consciousness of this influence is itself comparative. The academic's storytrack, though often more tacit than the tracks of the subjects, also intersects them. The academic operations that are required to maintain legitimacy of the interpretations of the subject studied are comparative. The results of an academically framed comparison are on the order of constructing a gestalt, that is, some view of the whole that is different from the sum of its particulars.

Comparison represents the academic field of play. As the academic establishes the terms of comparison by designating storytracks and crossing places, this person creates and constructs domains of interplay between the motivating interests and needs of an academic study and the elements of the subject studied. The terms of comparison and the comparative analysis are the tools the academic wields or, to maintain the metaphor, the equipment or toys or moves by which the academic plays. The interplay may be infinitely creative, yet it is subject to the rules and boundaries that ensure the legitimacy of interpretations and the demonstration that interpretations created by comparison are adequately constrained by the structures of the subject reality.

Interpretation

Interpretation, I argue, is the principal academic operation. All description, presentation, translation, and explanation imply interpretation. All comparison supports interpretation. Interpretation is motivated by the perceived condition of incongruity, incredulity, and incoherence. Interpretation is motivated by the emotional force of surprise or confusion. Interpretation is directed toward overcoming the gap, filling the chasm, by the creation and discovery of coherence. Certainly, coherence must be seen as a temporary and local achievement, serving issues external to the subject. Incongruity or incoherence is always a condition of particular relationships with a given subject, not a condition inherent to the subject. Coherence must be won through the application of local and temporary criteria of order and meaning. The interactionist approach to interpretation, to my understanding, is necessary.

In the case examined, Eliade did not appear to interpret his subject at all. Rather he presented the Arrernten example of "Numbakulla and the Sacred Pole" as illustration or exemplification of patterns apparently already won. But, the storytracking analysis showed that even these apparent presentations were not without elements of interpretation, although tacit. In an interactionist model, Eliade used a projective method, that is, he kept his theory of religion invariant and reconstructed his subject, although beyond legitimate limits, to cohere with his theory. But from another point of view, both more satisfying and disturbing, it has been shown that, at least in this case, Eliade was not so much interpreting Arrernte culture as simulating how religion—the generic and universal religion he held to be the foundation of reality—ought to manifest in this culturally specific aboriginal setting.

Smith presented an alternate interpretation to Eliade's, which Smith had, through criticism, deemed to be erroneous. His treatment of his sources was for the most part overt and clear. The style of Smith's presentation suggests an openness to the interplay between an accommodative style of interpretation, that is, where theories are adjusted in light of the subject, and a projective style of interpretation, that is, where theories are held invariant and instantiated on the subject. However, his interpretation that the structure of the ancestral narratives coheres on the principal of "event/memorial" engaged in a projective method of interpretation that, like Eliade's, overstepped the limits of legitimacy. Further, but at a different level, it may be suggested that Smith, rather than interpreting the Arrernte, was simulating a difference dressed in Arrernte garments to serve the terms of his preceding conviction about the importance of difference in comparison in order to criticize Eliade and to establish his own position.

Notably, both Piaget and Erikson, who developed the models of accommodation and projection, saw them as interdependent, interactive, and oscillatory.[86] While it is possible to analyze human development into stages at which one or the other process is dominant, both are necessary to psychologically healthy human development. Either strategy practiced exclusively eventually constitutes pathology. Both psychologists represented the interaction and interdependence of these methods in the terms of play, that is, an oscillatory interplay of accommodation and projection. Academic studies can find inspiration and direction in these studies. Interpretation may be analyzable in terms of the distinctive interpretive methods: accommodation and projection. Yet in practice both must, in principal, be present. One is dependent on and interactive with the other. Each realizes its potential in terms of the force and constraining effect of the other.

Academic methods are often seen as linear and progressive, perhaps not unrelated to theories of human development. Accommodation is a process of theory formation. Theories are subject to alteration and development initiated by a response to the incompatibility of theory with data. However, as theory is refined, it attains a less negotiable status. Once this status seems clear, argumentation is replaced by exemplification, and eventually simulation replaces interpretation. Yet, this process and the implied logical sequence, are misunderstandings of theory and interpretation. Theory is of interest only as long as a "maybe not" accompanies the "maybe." Theory is only one element in the required pairing that results in the construction of meaning. Theory and subject are always two sides of a chasm that must be in an interactive process of negotiation. While it may be possible to isolate and identify an instance of a projective method of interpretation, all instances should have some residual awareness that accommodation is also necessary. When theory is firmly established, exemplification becomes simply a covert practice of projective interpretation. Interpretation is always a process.

Simulation, which differs from exemplification in not having to be immediately constrained by subject reality, is in itself not illegitimate. However, it runs the high risk of being immediately devoured as real. In the absence of the real, simulacra, though hyperreal, are usually not distinguished from the real. Reality devours simulation. The tendency is toward pure simulacra.

The storytracking approach firmly confirms the importance of the interpretative process. It is not a neutral or higher perspective from which to choose among other approaches. Rather it is a method of exercising responsibility in a situation in which the scholar accepts the creative freedom of interpreting the subject studied. A multiperspectival approach concedes at the outset that it is not possible to choose a single perspective, a single paradigm or model, that will produce truth or full satisfaction.[87] Storytracking rejects monism, pursues the multiperspectival, and requires that critical self-consciousness be present throughout the entire interpretive process.

The storytracking approach requires the oscillation or play between two concerns or two methods of interpretation, that is, accommodation and projection, and two logical frames, that is, the subject frame, which is autonomous to any attempt to study it, and the frame that conjoins the subject to the perspectives and processes by which it is studied. The second frame is defined as enabling the interactive interpretative enterprise that conjoins theory and subject, interpreter and interpreted. It affirms the absolute chasm between the interpreter and the subject interpreted by demanding that the construction work of interpretation, which attempts to temporarily bridge the chasm, be done self-consciously and self-critically.

The storytracking approach acknowledges as necessary and unavoidable the impact of the "lookers" on those who are being "looked at." It affirms their inevitable interdependence while, at the same time, it depends on the absolute autonomy and independent existence of the "looked at." The storytracking approach willingly accepts that subjects can never be wholly known; indeed, to be wholly or fully known makes little sense, given that meaning and knowledge are products of an ongoing, interactionist interpretive process. Storytracking celebrates the creative and constructive roles of explanation and interpretation without shirking the responsibility to strictly discipline such creativity. It accepts that the whole explanatory enterprise is as thoroughly motivated by the explainer's quest for self-knowledge as by any neutral, merely academic, or humane interest in the subject. The storytracking approach demands, in Sartrian terms, an openness to freedom and the accompanying acceptance of responsibility in the spirit of play.[88]

Style

The criticism of academic work rarely includes elements of style. Although style might be informally noticed, it is rarely considered to have more than incidental impact on the importance, acceptability, and influence of an academic work. I suspect we miss much by ignoring academic style—by which I include rhetorical, interpretive, presentational, and argumentational, as well as literary, styles. The comparative consideration of Eliade and Smith is revealing.

Whereas Eliade performed interpretation, if this be our critical perspective, as a covert operation, held tacit by the terms of a particular rhetorical style, Smith presents his interpretation openly, clearly, and almost formally. The differences in style are of considerable interest. Smith's critical rational style appears to engage not only Eliade's reading of a specific text but also Eliade's whole program; some might feel that Smith is critical even of Eliade himself. The precision and force of Smith's criticism may be mistaken for a sharpness of tone. Interestingly, whereas Smith makes his case on the basis of attention to detail and on the criticism of another scholar's work, the resulting impression may be (ironic, it would seem to me) that Smith has more personal involvement (in the sense of an ax to grind) than the less formal, less self-conscious style used by Eliade, which masks his creative and constructive operations, thus making them difficult to evaluate in something like self-evident knowing. Furthermore, in light of the style of Smith's factually detailed criticism of Eliade, evidence (such as that which I have presented) that suggests that Smith inadequately presented his sources may appear, in comparison to Eliade, unproportionately damaging to the influence of his work.

Eliade's style, when seen in the framework of simulation, is immediately recognized as consistent with his understanding of reality. His style expresses the strength of and confidence in his conviction about the reality and truth of his understanding of religion, expressible both in his generic essentialist terms and in the specific terms of any culture whatsoever. Eliade's style of presentation, uncomplicated by the seemingly qualifying character of theorization and argumentation, capitalizes on the power of the real to devour simulation. Thus Eliade's style understandably may have a more highly persuasive effect on his readers than Smith's more scientific style. Traditional academic style is facing an increasing challenge from the mounting pervasiveness of the elements of style that accompany simulacra. The generation of reality by the abstract and generic has the effect of appearing self-evident, a condition accomplished because it is self-referential. Indeed, as the territory of modernity, or should I say postmodernity, becomes the hyperrealities of simulation, it seems to me that the academic enterprise—at least as I have characterized it, as being distinguished by interpretation—is faced with a potentially fatal threat.

On the one hand, academically explicit styles of presentation are often criticized and may be dismissed by nonacademics out of hand because of their density of argument, self-consciousness, and seemingly endless diversions. Academics, on the other hand, often distinguish the success of an academic work in the terms of standards of style of presentation and dismiss as unacademic works that fail to meet these criteria. Rigid, yet largely tacit, assumptions about academic presentation sorely need to be challenged. I find myself particularly irritated by the implications of the common and rather ubiquitous distinction between "academic" and "creative."

Storytracking as a method of constructing narratives of coherence serves as a perspective or means by which to examine and include elements of style in the evaluation of academic works, as well as other literary subjects. Style contributes powerfully to the achievement of a sense of coherence, to the advancement of persuasiveness, and to the impact realized by many works.

Loss of Subject

The comparison of Smith's and Eliade's studies of Australian aboriginal religions in terms of how these studies represent and are based on actual Australian peoples is revealing. Despite the fact that these scholars represent two of the most influential approaches to the academic study of religion, neither is primarily interested in any Arrernte reality.[89] Neither scholar did field study; neither knew the Arrernte language; neither went to Australia. Neither Eliade nor Smith demanded that his published sources or his own interpretations of these sources be evaluated in terms of the extent to which they represent or misrepresent Arrernte realities. Neither consulted archival materials. The published sources on which Eliade depended for his presentation of the Arrernte are highly limited. Smith consulted more sources, but he was far from thorough.

In this study I have shown that as a result of academic studies, the real Arrernte are lost, hidden by overpowering academic interests and the overwhelming ideas implicit in the academic theories and methods. I have also shown that the Arrernte is an academic construction, a hyperreality that has to some extent destroyed and engulfed real people.

It is ironic that the only book that attempts a broad presentation of Australian aboriginal religions is Eliade's *Australian Religions*, a book written by a scholar who never visited the country, who spoke none of the languages, who probably never met an aborigine, who was uncritical of his sources, and who in the final analysis was interested in the Australians largely to demonstrate the reality of his generic understanding of religion. It is doubly ironic—though it demonstrates how efficiently reality devours simulation—that an important cultural example that Eliade presented as representing *ab origine* can be shown to owe its existence to Western and Christian influence as borne by the Lutheran missionaries and others on the Arrernte, as well as to the constructions of the Arrernte by such Western figures as Frank Gillen and Baldwin Spencer. The simulated soon act in accordance with their hyperreality.

Should the seminal studies in many areas in the academic study of religion and other academic disciplines be subjected to the kind of storytracking method presented in this work, I would not be surprised if it were found that many of these studies have less interest in the subject named than in theoretical and academic issues and with the scholar's own cultural, historical, and even personal needs. It is possible that whole fields of study are made up of floating simulacra, almost wholly self-referential.

It is the proposition of this book that academic agenda are unavoidable for all academic studies. The issue is not to rid these perspectives from academic studies but to develop methods, such as storytracking, by which to maintain a clearer and more complete understanding of the extent and character of the influence of these perspectives on the subject studied. Doubtless in the process of gaining self-understanding and understanding of the world, the most common method any community has had available is the comparison of itself with other communities. The comparisons done by the academic community, I propose, are different from those performed by all other communities, perhaps only with respect to a necessary, relentless self-consciousness and by the insistence that the named subject must be required to be the actual subject presented in academic reports.

8

End Game

I approach the last chapter, mindful of one of the clearest things I have learned from this work and to which I alluded near the end of chapter 2: we usually achieve something different from, and quite often the opposite of, what we seek. This invites me to engage in some logic play, but there are remarks I must also make.

Origination and Storytrack Crossings

There is a kinship between concerns with origination and the crossings of storytracks. The search for the absolute grounding of origins serves as a deterrent to the knowledge that no such grounding is possible. Jean Baudrillard argues that at the point when it is acknowledged that there is "no longer a God to renounce his own, no longer a Last Judgment to separate the false from the true," there arises a nostalgia for the real. When this nostalgia assumes full meaning, "there is a plethora of myths of origin and of signs of reality—a plethora of truth, of secondary objectivity, and authenticity . . . [a] panic-stricken production of the real."[1] The late nineteenth century was, of course, when "being presence" was first broadly questioned, and it was no accident that this challenge corresponded with the rise of the modern social and natural sciences.

In seeking origins, Freud and Róheim were attempting to locate a point in time when they could engage in an exchange between the many otherwise incompatible genres and concerns with which they were interested: dream, mythology, and clinical science; psychology and anthropology; phylogenesis and ontogenesis; the primal crime scene and the primal scene in infant sexuality; the normal objective flow of time and the timeless time that allows one to meet the people of the origin (aborigines) face to face. It is in positing the origin that they attempted to locate a convergence of these many disparate genres and concerns. Seeking origins is one way to construct the joining of these many ill-fitting and incompatible concerns into an explanatory narrative of coherence.

The quest for origins in these terms remains viable despite the scorn shown to this endeavor today.[2] However, because of the temporal location of the origin, the approach is severely restricted to simulation without reference beyond the model. Origins are never real; they are always simulacra. What is needed is a means of locating, without impossible spatial or temporal restriction, a temporary place of exchange among ontologies, categories, worldviews, and perspectives, while at the same time requiring the self-conscious evaluation of the impact on the subjects studied through the selected academic constructs. Storytrack crossings are intended to be such temporary places of exchange, places that demand relentless self-consciousness. Storytrack crossings function something like "the origin" without the universalist, finalist expectations; without the implication of singularity; and without the nostalgia for full meaning. A storytrack crossing can occur in any space or time and even without a single definite spatiotemporal location. The stories whose interactions define the crossing place may extend in any combination of directions in space and time, real or metaphorical. It is at these crossings that we can negotiate exchanges, do comparisons, deconstruct and reconstruct categories, critique and create interpretations, and engage the self and the other. The crossings are themselves constructs; they do not exist independent of storytracking.[3]

Objectivism and Subjectivism

Things are often the opposite of what they appear. In this work I have found that what appears to be objectivism—ethnography and essentialism—is often anything but objective. One can argue that the multiperspectivality of storytracking—as relativistic and arbitrary as it is—achieves something approaching objectivity.[4] Yet this objectivism is deceptive in that the subjectivity of the storytracker is hidden by the storytracking process. This disappearance of the storyteller, effected by the storytelling process, is common to all modes of presentation. As we sit down to listen to a story, we are fully aware of the storyteller and the storytelling situation, but as the storyteller engages us in the story, if he or she is a good storyteller, the storyteller disappears behind the story, which by being told commands the focus of our attention. The simulation becomes real. As we enter the movie theatre, we are aware of those around us. In anticipation of giving ourselves to the storytelling, we find ourselves annoyed at the crunch of popcorn bags and the wiggling of our neighbors. But shortly after the lights dim and the credits end, we lose much of our awareness of the theatre and the flickering devices of telling the story. While experiencing the story, most of what we encounter, although only shadows on a screen, seems true and real. Those things that appear to be concocted or artificial are the things on which we focus in the full light of day during our postmortem criticism. Yet, all is concocted; nothing is literally as it appears.

These final comments must serve as a preconclusion, a closing of the book before it has ended so that its writer and readers can see it in another light. I must remind you that in this work I have been the storytracker and that I have chosen storytracks and crossings for reasons only some of which are fully known to me, only some of which are academic, and only some of which are academically justifiable. Although I have endeavored to be relentlessly self-conscious, I, too, often disappear (at least as an object to myself) in the process of story making.

This leads me to address what I have attempted to achieve: nothing more nor certainly less than doing what I do, being what I be,[5] as a person, as an academic, and as one situated in a storytrack I recognize as remarkably peculiar in human history.[6] Although I have presented storytracking in the terms of an approach (a method) to history, to comparison, to definition, and certain other academic enterprises—all exempified and grounded historically and culturally in Central Australia—I cannot recommend it without qualification as something for others to use or to attempt to apply. I have spoken of it in those terms only because that is the principal way I know how to articulate to myself and to the community with which I identify some sense of what I do to meaningfully and responsibly engage the world in which I find myself.

I have wanted to take seriously the shortcomings of a too quick and too pervasive objectivism without giving up the possibility of reading texts critically and decisively. To stand nowhere is pessimistic, if not nihilistic. I have wanted to own a subjectivism I find inevitable and personally meaningful and enjoyable. This acknowledgment is necessary to be responsible. But to hold that the place where I stand is the only real place is arrogant and indefensible.

Storytracking and the Other

We often accomplish the opposite of what we intend. There is another reason that I must object to seeing storytracking in any totalistic terms, as anything like a usable method to comprehend history, religion, and culture. Storytracking emerges from a most peculiar situation. It attempts to address issues that arise in a specific worldview and at a particular time in history. There is much irony in this position, and it demands humor. The issues emerge among those who for historical and cultural reasons (though this explanation rests on the historical and temporal assumptions that are the heritage of "Western man," the very heritage with which we struggle) find themselves attempting to make sense of a world made up of many cultures, peoples, languages, religions, histories, genders, and life-styles. It is an urgent agenda. It is a perspective that seeks to comprehend, appreciate, and understand all these perspectives in their own terms. The most commanding issue in the present is the recognition that the categories, the approaches, and the assumptions on which this seemingly selfless and humanistic endeavor has proceeded have determined, and often concocted, what we have understood and appreciated as our subjects. In conflict with our intentions, the endeavor has been characterized by dominating power and often violence toward our subjects. Often, invariably it almost seems, we have made of them what we have wanted and needed. They have been ignored, oppressed, suppressed, and destroyed by our intended generosity and magnanimity.

The contemporary response to this shocking effect has been to turn to relentless self-consciousness—to deconstruct the categories, processes, and assumptions on which our way of being (albeit one of which we are now embarrassed) depends. Presently we are at a stage no longer interested in gaining final resolution or totalization, "the method." The alternative it seems is to joyfully embrace the unresolvable, the indeterminate, and the ambiguous. In the philosophical realm (including the philosophical discussions within many academic disciplines), where these issues are most broadly addressed, this embracing of indeterminacy assumes a pervasiveness and exclusivity that is in tension with itself and with the world. That is, there are no limits to the domain of indeterminacy. Indeterminacy is the current form of totalization. Perhaps this embrace of ambiguity as our goal is fashionable, but it is self-denying and self-defeating. If we are to study culture, if we are to study history, we must stand somewhere; we must do something; we must, temporarily at least, set aside ambiguity and indeterminacy despite our knowing full well the implications and the costs of doing so. This situation reminds me of Zeno's paradox. While we may certainly choose to sit and contemplate the impossibility of ever reaching our goal of crossing the room—because we must forever span half the remaining distance to the other side, whatever distance we cover—most of us, sooner or later, need to cross the room. Most of us, sooner or later, will put the contemplation of Zeno's paradox aside, get up, and cross the room.

Furthermore, in the domain of the human sciences, the peculiarity of the view of embracing absolute indeterminacy contrasts sharply and irreconcilably with the majority, if not the totality, of the subjects of these studies. Almost all human beings, outside this peculiar contemporary group, have held and do hold views of the world that appear to contrast irreconcilably with a view of eternally embracing indeterminacy and ambiguity. Religious traditions commonly, though I believe not invariably, are characterized by a firmly objectivist worldview, as demonstrated by their beliefs in gods, ancestors, origins, creation, and eternity. I acknowledge that this belief is overwhelmingly shaped by the influence of the view of culture I criticize and seek to surpass. None of these traditions, none of these people, seeks as its principal concern the appreciation and understanding of all of the peoples, all of the perspectives, and all of the truths in the world and in the terms of those who hold these views.

To hold as our goal the achievement of this understanding by any means, including any contribution of what I term *storytracking*, is to insist on a position of hierarchical superiority to our subjects in that it implies that we can understand them, even if they cannot even imagine what we are talking about as we do so. Such a claim, to my thinking, is to fall prey once again to the ills of our heritage as "Western man." We achieve the opposite of what we seek. We prove to ourselves, once again, that we are at the apex of the process of human development. We again embrace an objectivism, albeit a godless objectivism, and the superiority that it is our present task to reject.

But we have the choice to make no claims other than to do what we—here I identify with the academic community that demands acknowledgment of the irreconcilable plurality and difference of peoples and cultures in the world—as a peculiar group of people do to be what we are: oddly self-reflective, resolutely godless, playing peculiar academic games with the cultures and histories of the world, and trying to break the cycle of achieving the opposite of what we always believe are highly laudable humane projects to help realize peace and understanding in the world.

When the issues of understanding are framed in terms of oppositional categories—objectivism/subjectivism, male/female, mind/body, abstract/concrete, public/private, sacred/profane—as they are at present and when we realize that neither pole, by itself, is at all acceptable, then we are bound by way of resolution to accept nonresolution. In a strict and narrow-minded rationalist frame, this can be the dark, nihilist option of facing meaninglessness or infinite regression. I prefer another mood, another tack. In storytracking I have attempted to embrace the vitalizing oscillatory movement between opposing positions. I have attempted to hold together, without loosing either one, and those tendencies and values at both poles of the opposition that explicitly deny one another. In storytracking I have sought to both embrace indeterminacy and, at least momentarily, to deny it. Things may be both what they appear and their opposite. The human capacity to engage in such an enigmatic operation is what we sometimes call "play."

Notes

Notes to Chapter 1

1. This is the same gap that, in distinguishing sign from signified, makes representation possible, that gives sign a stake in reality. Signs represent or refer to something that they are not. The reality of signs is on a different order than the reality to which signs refer. The gap is what constitutes the poetry of signs, the foundation of their power to signify.

2. Thomas Kuhn, *The Structure of Scientific Revolution*, 2nd ed. (Chicago: University of Chicago Press, [1962] 1970).

3. Such retrenchments are often disguised by a sort of liberal, too-quick openness to alternative ideas.

4. "Normal science" means "research firmly based upon one or more past scientific achievements, achievements that some particular scientific community acknowledges for a time as supplying the foundation for its further practice." Kuhn, *Scientific Revolution*, p. 10.

5. I choose the word *text* here because of its common use in the academic study of religion and other human and social sciences to denote the common object (and sometimes subject) of study. I suspect that the common reference to biblical authority as text has influenced the use of this word in at least the academic study of religion. The term *text* as I am using it here corresponds more closely with the term *work* as discussed by Roland Barthes, "From Work to Text," in *Textual Strategies: Perspectives in Post-structuralist Criticism,* edited by Josué V. Harari, Ithaca, N.Y.: Cornell University Press, 1979), pp. 73–81. Discussing primarily literature, Barthes charts the change taking place in our ideas about language and literature. He understands *work* to refer to the "concrete, occupying a portion of book-space" while the text "is a methodological field." *Text* then refers to aspects of literature, which Barthes describes as follows:

> 1. Text is not a defined object. It exists only as discourse. The text is experienced only in an activity, a production.

2. Text raises problems of the classification of literary genre. It always implies an experience of limits. Text is always paradoxical.
3. Text practices the infinite deferral of the signified; that is, it engages in infinite play.
4. Text achieves an irreducible plurality of meaning. Every text, is an intertext of another text; it belongs to the intertextual.

Thus, in what follows I will be suggesting for the human sciences something I call *storytrack*, which is akin to Barthes's *text*. The relationship of text to storytrack in my presentation is something on the order of work to text in Barthes.

6. Film and other media forms are sometimes considered *text*.

7. In his "'Seeking an End to the Primary Text', or 'Putting an End to the Text as Primary'" in *Beyond the Classics? Essays in Religious Studies and Liberal Education*, edited by Frank E. Reynolds and Sheryl L. Burkhalter (Atlanta: Scholars Press, 1990), pp. 41–59, Lawrence E. Sullivan discusses the extent to which the academic study of religion has restricted itself to the study of texts. He speaks out against what he calls this "tyranny of text" (p. 45), believing it "an inadequate vehicle for transporting the full cargo of religious experiences of literate peoples, including those of our own culture" (p. 47), and that the dominance of text has "narrowed this wide range of human reflection and distorted the many modes of reflection as they are found in historical cultures" (p. 47). Sullivan suggests a number of "other modalities of matter" on which the study of religion might focus: canoe making, pottery, musical performance, weeping, and so on. The problem I find with Sullivan's study appears to be an illegitimate shift in analytic frame in the midst of his argument. Certainly the academic study of religion has often restricted its attention to that set of texts ordinarily labeled primary texts. It can be rightly noted that this class of texts is in many senses restrictive of the religions from which they come. But this is no new criticism. For decades many textual studies have been set within cultural and historical contexts. This tyranny of text was challenged long ago. Sullivan proposes as a radical alternative to primary text the study of performative aspects of culture. I fail to see the novelty of this suggestion since the studies of the nonwritten elements of culture are extensive and common. If Sullivan is suggesting that such things as canoe making and pottery are the common source for scholarly discourse—that is, without the mediation of even descriptive narratives regarding canoe making or pottery—then it would seem to me that scholarship would be limited to a face-to-face discourse in the presence of these activities and objects in situ and perhaps even more severely limited somehow to the engagement of academics in these very activities themselves. I doubt that this is what Sullivan is intending since it is to be noted that in every instance in which he presents these alternatives he makes bibliographical reference to "written" accounts of these activities. What he leaves unconsidered is the additional critical issues that arise in the mediation of these performances and objects by the "written" accounts on which scholarship depends. Sullivan appears to hold that ethnography is free of interpretive issues. On this point the essays collected by James Clifford and George E. Marcus (eds.), *Writing Culture: The Poetics and Politics of Ethnography* (Berkeley: University of California Press, 1986), are insightful.

8. I use the term *interpretation* here in a general and nontechnical sense to include all those techniques and methods employed in rendering a text meaningful. Certainly there is precedent for using *interpretation* to refer to the subjective, personal, and perhaps speculative approach, distinguished from the term *explanation* to refer to the more rigorous and "scientific" methods. Should such a distinction be made, I would hold that they are in some ways

inseparable and are interactive. For a discussion of these terms and how they have been understood, see E. Thomas Lawson and Robert N. McCauley, *Rethinking Religion: Connecting Cognition and Culture* (New York: Cambridge University Press, 1990), pp. 14–31.

9. One underlying reason for selecting this text is personal and incidental, but I would not pursue this publicly if it did not eventually transcend this motivation. A brief summary, though a bit personal, is in order. In a small book on the religions of small-scale tribal cultures, I turned to Eliade's example of "Numbakulla and the Sacred Pole" to illustrate the religious importance of centers to these kinds of peoples, a principle I then thought not only valid but also centrally important. Some years after the publication of that book I received a letter from Carl W. Ernst, a professor at Pamona College, asking my views on the incredulity that the Arrernte people, whose actions of lying down to die I had presented, following Eliade, as having been observed in the late nineteenth century. Ernst had discovered that the ethnographic source, Spencer and Gillen, had presented the example as myth. He asked for my view on the impact of this difference. Almost simultaneously I read Jonathan Smith's book *To Take Place: Toward Theory in Ritual* (Chicago: University of Chicago Press, 1987). The first chapter presents a stunning text criticism of Eliade's "Numbakulla and the Sacred Pole" example. By comparing Eliade's account of the text with the source documents he cites, Smith shows that Eliade largely concocts this text. Holding the sanctity of the text inviolable, Smith uses his demonstration of Eliade's construction as the grounds to undo Eliade's key point, that is, that the center universally and necessarily designates the religious. The differences between Eliade and Smith reflect two important, though not entirely unrelated, approaches to the academic study of religion. These issues will be taken up in chapter 7.

10. *Arrernte* is the currently preferred spelling of the Australian aboriginal culture whose name has been variously spelled, most commonly *Aranda* and *Arunta*. See John Henderson and Veronica Dobson, *Eastern and Central Arrernte to English Dictionary* (Alice Springs: IAD Press, 1994).

11. Mircea Eliade, *Australian Religions: An Introduction* (Ithaca, N.Y.: Cornell University Press, 1967), p. 50.

12. Ibid, pp. 50–53.

13. Ibid, p. 53.

14. Mircea Eliade, *The Sacred and the Profane*, (New York: Harper & Row, 1959), pp. 32–33; first published in German translation, *Das Heilige und das Profane* (Hamburg: Rowohlt, 1957). The English translation was prepared from the first French edition, *Le Sacré et le profane* (Paris: Gallimard, 1965). The passage also appears in *Occultism, Witchcraft and Contemporary Fashions* (Chicago: University of Chicago Press, 1976), p. 20. See also Mircea Eliade, *Zalmoxis: The Vanishing God* (Chicago: University of Chicago Press, 1972), p. 186.

15. See Eliade, *Sacred and Profane*.

16. Jonathan Smith's study of Eliade's use of the Arrernte example, "In Search of Place," in *To Take Place*, focuses on the substantive points of Eliade's presentation Smith concludes that only one of the points was actually "verifiable without ambiguity" (p. 6) in Spencer and Gillen. Smith's conclusion is that Eliade "has misread the text" (p. 6). My assessment is that Eliade constructs his text rather than misreads it. My study compares Eliade with his cited source at the word, phrase, and sentence level. Nearly every word can be found in Spencer and Gillen, though this does not release Eliade from the accusation of sheer fabrication. What seems more interesting to me is the attempt to discern what motives he had for selecting and organizing the materials as he did.

17. *Tjilpa* is the latest spelling of the name for the wildcat group Spencer and Gillen, as well as many others, spelled it *Achilpa*.

18. See, for example, Sam Gill, *Beyond "the Primitive": The Religions of Nonliterate Peoples* (Englewood Cliffs, N.J.: Prentice Hall, 1982), pp. 19–21.

19. Theodor Strehlow provides one and the suggestion of others in *Central Australian Religion: Personal Monototemism in a Polytotemic Community* (Adelaide: Australian Association for the Study of Religions, 1978), p. 12, and in his *Aranda Traditions* (Melbourne: Melbourne University Press, 1947), p. 78.

20. Eliade, *Australian Religions*, p xviii.

21. Tony Swain notes, for example, that Eliade's book is "the most coherent general introduction to Aboriginal religions" *Aboriginal Religions in Australia: A Bibliographical Survey* (New York, Westport, Conn.: Greenwood Press, 1991), p. 19.

22. There is some ambiguity about how well Gillen knew the Arrernte language. Theodor Strehlow constantly criticized Gillen and Spencer for not knowing the language and for their frequent, serious mistranslations. Gillen was surprised that Spencer wanted to include native terms in their publications because he felt no one was interested in maintaining the language, perhaps a reflection of his own lack of interest in learning Arrernte. Nonetheless, it is difficult to believe that Gillen spent so much time among the Arrernte people and incorporated a large number of Arrerente terms in the materials he recorded without knowing something of the language. There is little doubt that this lack seriously limited his recording and research.

23. D J. Mulvaney and J. H. Calaby, *'So Much That Is New': Baldwin Spencer, 1860–1929, A Biography* (Melbourne: University of Melbourne Press, 1985); see chap. 7.

24. "Inapwerla" in the Horn expedition report, though it should have been printed *inapwerta*. The *l* probably occurred because in Gillen's cursive style he rarely crossed his *t*s. In *The Arunta* the term becomes "Inapartua." Spencer explains: "We have adopted the spelling of *atua* for man instead of *ertwa*" (p. 308, n. 1).

25. It is clear that the missionaries who established Hermannsburg in 1877—as well as Francis Gillen, who became a telegraph operator at Alice Springs and began keeping journals about the aborigines in the early 1890s—began their inquiries with expectations shaped by Christianity. What are the first questions these Christians would be likely to ask other peoples about their traditions? Surely among the first must have been this: How did the world get created? How did human beings get created? Who are your gods? All of the principal works stemming from this early period begin with accounts of gods and creation.

It can be hypothesized that the very asking of these questions, as the first questions, has extensively shaped what is known of Arrernte culture. With no linguistic competence by early missionaries and with the Arrernte people not yet knowing aboriginal English, there had to be a great deal of negotiation in these first recordings and first translations. Surely the Arrernte negotiated their language to accommodate the questions as much as the German- and English-speaking missionaries adjusted their understandings of spiritual traditions (religion was not yet even a relevant comparative category) as a category that might contain more than German Lutheranism. Both, to accommodate the other, changed their ideas of the world. It is not at all unlikely that in this early phase of negotiation the Arrernte learned what would be acceptable to the European-Australians when asked questions about gods and creation. These accounts need not have preexisted in these painful first encounters but could have been constructed in the process. People with a culture that has no story of cosmic creation may very well permit one to be constructed through the processes of negotiating with inquirers who demand such information. By the time Gillen asks these key questions of his aboriginal English-speaking Arrernte in 1894, the Arrernte had already had more than fifteen years to grow familiar with what might have come to be a new story.

While this sequence of events is hypothetical, it is nonetheless far from unlikely. Should it be correct, there would be significant irony in Eliade's (and many others') use of Arrernte stories of creation. Eliade, as so many others, sought *ab original* sources because he believed that they represented primal, if not primordial, stages in the development of human culture. How ironic it would be if these sources were the direct product of a Christian presence in Central Australia.

The creation story of the gigantic emu-footed man is also recorded in these earliest days of contact. See chapter 5 for a discussion of this figure.

26. Carl Strehlow has a similar story. He uses the term *rella manerinja* to refer to these "undeveloped people." He notes: *manerinja* means grown together, stuck together; *rella* means a person or people. In the course of his presentation Strehlow refers to the hands of these undeveloped people as being grown to their breast, a condition (presumably) he refers to by the terms *turba* or *innopúta*. In a footnote Strehlow adds: "*innopúta* presumably = *inapertwa* in Spencer and Gillen." See Strehlow, *Die Aranda- und Loritja-Stämme in Zentral-Australien*, edited by Moritz Freiherr von Leonhardi (Frankfurt am Main: Joseph Baer, 1907), vol. I, part I, p. 3 (page numbers refer to the unpublished translation by Hans D. Oberscheidt).

27. Even in the earliest missionary accounts there is a sense of the Arrernte expressing the idea that some figures in their stories were not created F. E. H. W. Krichauff, "The Customs, Religious Ceremonies, etc. of the 'Aldolinga' and 'Mbenderinga' Tribe of Aborigines in Krichauff Ranges, South Australia," *Royal Geographical Society of South Australia* 2 (1886–88): 33–37, based on letters written by J. Kempe, L. Schulze, and G. A. Heidenreich, all Lutheran pastors in Central Australia. Often this term is rendered "they jumped up of themselves."

28. These are often called totem groups.

29. For more information on Oruncha, see Spencer and Gillen, *Native Tribes*, pp 326–28 and 525–26, and Baldwin Spencer and F. J. Gillen, *Across Australia* (London: Macmillan, 1912), pp. 337f.

30. See Spencer and Gillen, *Native Tribes*, p. 388, n. 1.

31. Smith calls Ungambikula a "common corporate name," which is accurate, but it seems to me the emphasis of the term is more adjectival, that is, concerned with how they came about.

32. Such omissions may not have been Spencer's. There is evidence that James G. Frazer and Edward B. Tylor, who edited the manuscript for publication in London, debated extensively about the appropriateness of the sexual and genital matters in the work. See Mulvaney and Calaby, *'So Much That Is News,'* p. 179. It is possible that Spencer included such references only to have them removed by the editors. It must be remembered that while I am attributing the treatment of Gillen's records solely to Spencer, and I believe his influence was principal, both Frazer and Tylor (and perhaps others) may have had a hand in the final result.

33. An inquiry into the materials related in one way or another to this human creation story reveals a very complicated set of issues.

34. Spencer and Gillen, *Arunta*, pp. 306–7.

35. Ibid, p. 307.

36. Ibid, p. 307, n. 2.

37. On pp. 39 and 40 of the first volume of Gillen's unpublished journal.

38. Spencer wrote the following in the preface (pp. ix–x) to *Arunta*:

> The changes that have taken place in the tribe during recent years have been of so vital a nature that it would now be absolutely impossible for anyone, starting

> afresh, to study it adequately. Of the local group of Udnirringita people at Alice Springs, that numbered forty when we knew them in 1896, not a solitary man, woman or child remains, and this is only one of many such groups, studied by us in the early days, upon whom the same fate has fallen. There are but a few of the older, unspoilt Arunta men left anywhere, and soon there will be none, and with them will pass away all knowledge of primitive customs and beliefs. . . .
>
> My chief informant was a native who, in 1896, was old enough to act as one of the leaders in the Engwura witnessed by Mr. Gillen and myself. He had since then learnt to speak English well and was thoroughly acquainted with the beliefs and traditions of the tribe. He himself was a Purula man of the Irriakura (a plant bulb) totem. . . .

39. Aboriginal English is a pidgin language, that is, one that has never been the first language of any group of speakers. It arises as a medium for communication between different speech communities. The more powerful (or "aggressor") community supplies the basis for the lexicon. The syntax and lexicon are usually highly restricted. See John W. Harris, *Northern Territory Pidgins and the Origin of Kriol*, Pacific Linguistics Series C, no. 89, (Canberra: Australian National University, 1986), and Jakelin Troy, *Australian Aboriginal Contact with the English Language in New South Wales: 1788 to 1845*, Pacific Linguistics Series B-103 (Canberra: Australian National University, 1990).

40. Theodor Strehlow, *Songs of Central Australia* (Sydney: Angus & Robertson, 1971), p. xxviii. In another publication, *Aranda Traditions* (Melbourne: Melbourne University Press, 1947), Strehlow dramatizes the impact of rendering standard English into aboriginal English by presenting the story of Shakespeare's *Macbeth* as it would be told in aboriginal English. It begins:

> Long time ago ole feller Donkey him bin big feller boss longa country. Alright. By an' by another feller—him name ole Muckbet—bin hearem longa three feller debbil-debbil woman: them feller debbil-debbil woman bin tellem him straight out—"You'll be big feller boss yourself soon." Alright. Him bin havem lubra, ole lady Muckbet. (p. xix)

41. Spencer and Gillen, *Arunta*, p. ix.

42. Strehlow estimates that these "informants" were twenty-five to thirty-five years old. *Songs*, p. xxviii.

43. Spencer and Gillen, *Arunta*, p. x.

44. Ibid, p. 65.

45. Strehlow, *Songs*, pp. xxix–xxx.

46. See Strehlow's comments in *Songs*, p. xxix.

47. See Theodor Strehlow, "Geography and the Totemic Landscape in Central Australia," in *Australian Aboriginal Anthropology*, edited by Ronald M. Berndt (Perth: University of Western Australian Press, 1970), pp. 138–39, n. 25.

Notes to Chapter 2

1. Robert P. Crease, in *The Play of Nature: Experimentation as Performance* (Bloomington: University of Indiana Press, 1993), indicates that various interpreters see different profiles of the same object. See p. 146.

2. Immanuel Kant, *Critique of Pure Reason*, translated by Norman Kemp Smith (New York: St. Martin's Press, [1787], 1965).

3. Ernst Cassirer, *The Philosophy of Symbolic Forms*, translated by R. Manheim (New Haven, Conn.: Yale University Press, 1955), vols. 1–3; summarized in *An Essay on Man* (New Haven, Conn.: Yale University Press, 1944).

4. Nelson Goodman, *Language of Art*, 2nd ed. (Indianapolis: Hackett, 1976), and *Ways of Worldmaking* (Indianapolis: Hackett, 1978).

5. Bipin Indurkhya, *Metaphor and Cognition: An Interactionist Approach* (Dordrecht: Kluwer, 1992).

6. See Jean Piaget, *Genetic Epistemology*, translated by E. Duckworth (New York: Columbia University Press, 1970), and Jean Piaget and B. Inhelder, *The Psychology of the Child*, translated by Helen Weaver (New York: Basic Books, 1966).

7. George Lakoff and Mark Johnson, *Metaphors We Live by* (Chicago: University of Chicago Press, 1980).

8. George Lakoff, *Women, Fire, and Dangerous Things* (Chicago: University of Chicago Press, 1987).

9. See Wolfgang Köhler, *The Task of Gestalt Psychology* (Princeton, NJ.: Princeton University Press, 1969); David Katz, *Gestalt Psychology: Its Nature and Significance* (New York: Ronald Press, 1950); and George W. Hartman, *Gestalt Psychology: A Survey of Facts and Principles* (New York: Ronald Press, 1935). For important works on sensory anthropology, see David Howes (ed.), *The Varieties of Sensory Experience: A Sourcebook in the Anthropology of the Senses* (Toronto: University of Toronto Press, 1991), and Constance Classen, *Worlds of Sense: Exploring the Senses in History and across Cultures* (New York: Routledge, 1993).

10. Whorf, Benjamin L. "An American Indian Model of the Universe," in *Language, Thought and Reality: Selected Papers of Benjamin Lee Whorf*, edited by J. B. Carroll (Cambridge, Mass.: MIT Press, 1956), pp. 57–64. See also Lakoff's discussion of Whorf in *Women, Fire*, pp. 304ff.

11. Notably, this is the position, according to my reading, presented by Stephen Hawking in *A Brief History of Time: From the Big Bang to Black Holes* (New York: Bantam Books, 1988).

12. For technical terminology I will follow Indurkhya, *Metaphor and Cognition*, pp 132–33. Though it is primarily the projective-accommodative aspect of interaction cognitive theory that I will use, it remains worthwhile to present the theory in some technical detail.

13. Studies of color categories have demonstrated that they are the product of both neurophysiology and cognitive operations. See Lakoff, *Women, Fire*, pp. 21ff.

14. Piaget called this *assimilation*. I agree with Indurkhya's preference for the term *projection* in order to limit this particular operation described by Piaget from the many others to which *assimilation* has also been applied. See Indurkhya, *Metaphor and Cognition*, p. 134. It also provides a stronger description of the interpretive strategy.

15. Piaget and Erikson speak of this interaction and equilibrium between assimilation and accommodation in terms of "play."

16. Since *gestalt* means "shape," it seems an interesting idea to shift the focus from place to shape in the sense of gestalt. Place correlates rather too strongly with space and with geography. A focus on gestalt would benefit from gestalt psychological studies, as well as Lakoff's understanding of basic-level categories that arise from bodily experience that corresponds with gestalt perception.

17. The work of "writing" also reflects interpretation, as discussed from a number of perspectives with regard to ethnography in James Clifford and George E Marcus (eds.), *Writing Culture: The Poetics and Politics of Ethnography* (Berkeley: University of California Press, 1986).

18. Criteria for coherence are interesting. We think of coherence in the vague terms of *holding together* or *supported* or the slightly more technical terms of *rational* and *logical*. Practi-

cally speaking, coherence probably indicates something more likely to mean uncontested, on the one hand, and setting forth an engaging story, on the other. Some of the criteria for adequate constraint is discussed later.

19. This view of religion is summarized by Mircea Eliade in the pages immediately preceding his Numbakulla example See *Australian Religions: An Introduction* (Ithaca, N.Y.: Cornell University Press, 1967), pp. 48–49.

20. This evaluation is similar to the evaluative considerations of validity and authenticity. Validity is the measure of correspondence between the academic report and some background of theory and recorded observation. Authenticity is concerned with the provenance of the report, with whether or not it derives from the stated sources. The division that pertains in this particular case is between text reality and subject reality. The issues of evaluation rest, first, on the accurate presentation of cited text sources and, second, on the accuracy of the cultural reality purported to be presented. Technically both validity and authenticity are issues in both reality frames: the text source reality and the subject reality. Although the evaluative considerations are clearly separate, I combine them for presentation here under the terms of legitimacy. For example, technically Eliade's presentation of an interpretation based on Spencer and Gillen's *Aranta* is authentic, since it is clear that he actually consulted this source, but invalid, since there is inadequate correspondence between his source and his report. The determination of the validity and authenticity of Eliade's presentation of the Arrernte reality is more complicated since he did not directly engage the culture. While I insist that his presentation of this reality is central to our considerations, legitimacy seems more direct than does an attempt to evaluate validity and authenticity.

21. Michael Polanyi associated gestalt psychology with what he termed tacit knowing, that sense that we know more than we can tell. Key to all knowing in Polanyi's view is an internalization, or indwelling. See *The Tacit Dimension*. (Gloucester, Mass.: Peter Smith, 1983), pp. 17–18.

22. Review of *Across Australia* in *Folk Lore* 24 (1913): 278, as quoted in D. J. Mulvaney and J. H. Calaby, *'So Much That Is New': Baldwin Spencer, 1860–1929, A Biography* (Melbourne: University of Melbourne Press, 1985), pp. 395–96.

23. George Lakoff makes virtually the same point in his criticism of objectivism. He wrote: "The belief that there is a God's eye point of view and that one has access to it (that is, being a hard-and-fast objectivist) virtually precludes objectivity, since it involves a commitment to a belief that there are no alternative ways of conceptualizing that are worth considering. Interestingly enough, to be objective requires one to be a relativist of an appropriate sort." See *Women, Fire,* pp. 301–2.

24. This is a projective strategy for interpretation. See below for an analysis.

25. I suspect that this rhetorical style is not entirely independent of the use of proof texts in Judeo-Christian teaching and preaching

26. Jean Baudrillard, *Simulacra and Simulation*, translated by Sheila Faria Glaser (Ann Arbor: University of Michigan Press, 1994).

27. The exception is Jonathan Z Smith's criticism of Eliade, which will be considered in detail in chapter 7.

28. An excellent example of such disclosure of simulation is found in Diane Bell, *Daughters of the Dreaming* rev ed. (Minneapolis: University of Minnesota Press, [1983] 1993), p. 174. Bell simulates a myth where there is none and does so very self-consciously: "In extracting the story line from the ritual performances and presenting it in the form of a myth which has a beginning and an end, I am doing violence to the cultural conception. My justification for such a representation is that, short of a lifetime spent as a woman in women's

camps, it is impossible to comprehend the kaleidoscopic range of nuances, ramifications and elaborations of the bahaviour of the Dreamtime ancestors who acted out *yilpinji* myths." However, despite this warning label, it is virtually certain that the simulated myth, once presented, quickly attains the status of cultural reality rather than ethnographer's device, and future ethnographers can expect to find members of the culture who can recite the myth as their own.

29. Baudrillard's reflections (see *Simulacra and Simulation*) on how simulation characterizes so much in contemporary Western (particularly American) societies—presidential politics, Disney Land, advertising, film and television, nuclear strategies of deterrence—show the pervasiveness of simulation, which, I am arguing, also characterizes the academy.

30. Ibid, p. 7.

31. Ibid, pp. 5–6.

32. Ibid, p. 6 (Baudrillard's emphasis).

33. One might argue that it is still possible to go, as I have done, to Central Australia and have a firsthand experience with Arrernte culture However, this knowing of the Arrernte would limit the Arrernte to those members of the culture personally encountered and to the substance of the encounter. Even to ask one Arrernte about Arrernte culture is to know it through particular eyes. I am not arguing, however, that personal experience or field study is useless—quite the contrary.

34. Even our theory of category, as Lakoff has so powerfully shown, shapes all that we see and understand. See his *Women, Fire.*

35. I will engage this topic again in different terms in chapter 8.

36. See chapter 6 for further detail.

37. For a recent example, see Michael Jackson, *At Home in the World* (Durham, N.C.: Duke University Press, 1995), pp. 64–65.

38. Jonathan Z. Smith, "Map Is Not Territory," in *Map Is Not Territory: Studies in the History of Religion* (Leiden: E. J. Brill, 1978), p. 289.

39. An interesting parallel is that aborigines refer to their subclassification as "skin." Nothing in the world can be addressed except from the perspective of a specific "skin." See chapter 6 for descriptions of the classification system.

40. Such a view is dramatically presented in Samuel Eliot Morison's biography of Columbus, *Admiral of the Ocean Sea: A Life of Christopher Columbus,* vol. 1 (Boston: Little, Brown & Co. 1942), p. 308, in the statement by which he described Columbus's "discovery" of America: "Never again may mortal men hope to recapture the amazement, the wonder, the delight of those October days in 1492 when the New World gracefully yielded her virginity to the conquering Castilians." Edmundo O'Gorman has carefully analyzed the implications of this view of discovery. In a perspective consistent with the position I am advancing, O'Gorman shows that America was "invented" rather than discovered. See Edmundo O'Gorman, *The Invention of America: An Inquiry into the Historical Nature of the New World and the Meaning of Its History* (Bloomington: Indiana University Press, 1961).

41. For illustrative purposes I here speak of Arrernte as an entity, which, independent of us or even individual Arrernte speakers, it is not.

42. See M. Herzfeld, *Poetics of Manhood* (Princeton, N.J.: Princeton University Press, 1985), p. 207. See also Margaret T. Hodger, *Early Anthropology in the Sixteenth and Seventeenth Centuries* (Philadelphia: University of Pennsylvania Press, 1964). For an illuminating discussion of narrative as an ethnographic genre, see Michael Jackson, *Paths toward a Clearing: Radical Empiricism and Ethnographic Inquiry* (Bloomington: Indiana University Press, 1989), pp. 17–18. I am indebted to Jackson for the etymological information.

43. For a discussion of the visual prejudice, see Jackson, *Paths toward a Clearing*, pp. 5–7, and Howes, *Varieties of Sensory Experience*.

44. See above for a discussion of how this sort of temporary objectivity is possible.

45. It might be argued that in contrast to the expressed rejection of relativism by objectivism and essentialism, which ironically hides a certain tacit relativism, the embracing of relativism in the form of multiperspectivality achieves a measure of objectivism Lakoff, for example, defines objectivity in his experientialist perspective as "First, putting aside one's own point of view and looking at a situation from other points of view—as many others as possible. Second, being able to distinguish what is directly meaningful—basic-level and image-schematic concepts—from concepts that are indirectly meaningful" (*Women, Fire,* p. 301). Storytracking certainly accomplishes the first criteria and could well be developed more formally (though I think it does so by the example of application) to accomplish the second.

46. Michael Polanyi, "Personal Knowledge," in *Meaning*, edited by Michael Polanyi and Harry Prosch (Chicago: University of Chicago Press, 1975), pp. 22–45.

47. For an important discussion of this style of comparison, see Jonathan Z. Smith, "What a Difference a Difference Makes," in *"To See Ourselves as Others See Us": Christians, Jews, "Others" in Late Antiquity*, edited by Jacob Neusner and Ernest S. Frerichs (Chico, Calif.: Scholars Press, 1985), pp. 3–48.

48. For an interesting example of this type of comparison, see Susan L Foster, *Reading Dancing: Bodies and Subjects in Contemporary American Dance* (Berkeley: University of California Press, 1986). Foster compares four contemporary choreographers—Deborah Hay, Merce Cunningham, Martha Graham, and George Balanchine—to one another but each from the perspective of the other three (see pp. 55–56). Then she engages her set of overarching categories for developing a schema for "reading choreography."

49. The tenuous status of the academic study of religion is reflected in the constant struggle to find an appropriate name for the field The ambiguity of *religious studies* is apparent. *Religion* as a title recalls a former synonymy of religion with Christianity. In one field in the academic study of religion, scholars have struggled off and on for decades concerning whether the term that indicates the subject should be singular or plural—History of Religion or History of Religions. A commanding argument held that *religion* in the singular reflected an unacceptable essentialist or sui generis view; thus the plural form has prevailed. I am hoping to further complicate this situation by noting that religion is a recent academic invention. It is an abstract category constructed to assist in the comprehension of a multiperspectival, multicultural, highly complex world. As *religion* is a term unfamiliar to most of the subjects studied under the rubric—thus there are not independent "religions" (in these terms) in the world—the use of the singular form is a means by which to acknowledge the independence of the term and all of the implied and potential theories denoted by it, as the product of the histories and cultures that hold that academic operations are effective ways of interacting with the world and living in the world. The same may be argued for such terms as *culture,* as has been done by Roy Wagner, *The Invention of Culture* (Englewood Cliffs, N.J.: Prentice Hall, 1975).

50. A fuller discussion of storytracking as a comparative method is in chapter 7.

51. Jonathan Z. Smith, *Imagining Religion: From Babylon to Jonestown* (Chicago: University of Chicago Press, 1982), p. xi.

Notes to Chapter 3

1. See Patrick Wolfe, "On Being Woken up: The Dreamtime in Anthropology and in Australian Settler Culture," *Comparative Study of Society and History* 33 (1991): 197–224.

2. W. E. H. Stanner, "The Dreaming," in *Australian Signpost*, edited by T. A. G. Hungerford (Melbourne: F. W. Cheshire, 1956), pp. 51–65; reprinted in William A. Lessa and Evon V. Vogt (eds.), *Reader in Comparative Religion: An Anthropological Approach* (New York: Harper & Row, 1958), pp. 158–67; see p. 159.

3. It is of interest to note that in the Arrernte language there are only two ordinals: *nyinta*, "one"; *tharra*, "two." Apparently these can be used in combination to achieve the numbers 3 and 4, but this usage is rare. Other important number terms are *ntjarra*, which functions to form plural nouns; *mapa*, often rendered "mob," meaning "many"; *urrputja*, which means "a few"; and *kngarra*, meaning "much." See John Pfitzner and Joan Schmaal, *Learning Arrarnta*, 2nd rev. ed. by Hans D. Oberscheidt (Alice Springs: Finke River Mission, 1991), pp. 16–17.

4. Tony Swain, *A Place for Strangers: Towards a History of Australian Aboriginal Being* (Cambridge, Mass.: Cambridge University Press, 1993), pp. 22ff. Swain's excellent work follows Stanner to a degree, in that Stanner earlier referred to "abidingness."

5. See, for example, the map and list of place names that accompanies Theodor Strehlow's *Songs of Central Australia* (Sydney: Angus & Robertson, 1971).

6. See J. Peter White, "Prehistory: The First 99% of Aboriginal History," in *The Moving Frontier: Aspects of Aboriginal-European Interaction in Australia*, edited by Peter Stanbury (Sydney: Charterbooks, 1977), pp. 13–22.

7. Frank Clune, *Overland Telegraph: The Story of a Great Australian Achievement and the Link between Adelaide and Port Darwin* (Sydney: Angus & Robertson, 1955), pp. 37–39; Ernest Favenc, *The Explorers of Australia and Their Lifework* (Christchurch, NZ: Whitcombe & Tombs, 1908), p. 135; and Hans Minchan, *The Story of the Flinders Ranges* (Adelaide: Rigby, 1964), p. 29.

8. Clune, *Overland Telegraph*, pp. 35–36.

9. B. Threadgill, *South Australian Land Exploration*, 1856–1880 (Adelaide: Public Library, Museum and Art Gallery of South Australia, 1922).

10. Ibid, pp. 41–44.

11. Clune, *Overland Telegraph*, pp. 41–47. Patrick White's novel *Voss* (New York: Viking, 1957) is obviously inspired by Leichhardt's attempts.

12. Ibid, pp. 53–54.

13. Ibid, p. 57. See also Mincham, *Flinders Ranges*, chaps. 4 and 5; Threadgill, *South Australian Land Exploration*, chap. 1; G. W. Symes, "The Exploration and Development of the Northern Part of South Australia between 1850 and 1869 and the Early Life of John Ross," *Royal Geographical Society of Australasia, South Australian Branch, Proceedings* 58 (December 1957): 1–20.

14. For biographies of Stuart, see Mona Stuart Webster, *John McDouall Stuart* (Melbourne: Melbourne University Press, 1958), and Douglas Pike, *John McDouall Stuart* (Oxford: Oxford University Press, 1958). See also William Hardman (ed.), *The Journals of John McDouall Stuart* (London, Saunders, Otley & Co., 1864).

15. Clune, *Overland Telegraph*, pp. 63–65.

16. See M. C. Hartwig, "The Progress of White Settlement in the Alice Springs District and Its Effects upon the Aboriginal Inhabitants, 1860–1894," Ph.D. thesis, University of Adelaide, 1965, pp. 97 and 111.

17. Glenelg is the port at Adelaide.

18. See Hartwig, *White Settlement*, p. 94.

19. Clune, *Overland Telegraph*, pp. 68–71.

20. Ibid, pp. 78–80.

21. Stuart had reached 700 miles north of the border between South Australia and the Northern Territory.

22. Clune, *Overland Telegraph*, pp. 78–92.

23. Ibid, pp. 97–111.

24. See Hartwig, *White Settlement*, p. 105.

25. See Ross Duncan, *The Northern Territory Pastoral Industry, 1863–1910* (Melbourne: Melbourne University Press, 1967), p. 33.

26. See Hartwig, *White Settlement*, pp. 111–24.

27. Buyers brought suit against the South Australian Government and won 10% more than their investments.

28. See Duncan, *Northern Territory*, pp. 122–27.

29. See W. L. Manser, "The Overland Telegraph," M.A. honor's thesis, University of Adelaide, 1961, chap. 2.

30. See Hartwig, *White Settlement*, pp. 138–46.

31. Clune, *Overland Telegraph*, pp. 191–92. See also Hartwig, *White Settlement*, pp. 194–220.

32. Doris Blackwell and Douglas Lockwood, *Alice on the Line* (Adelaide: Griffin Press, [1965] 1993), pp. 47–48.

33. For the early history of the colony see Douglas H. Pike, *Paradise of Dissent: South Australia 1829–1857* (London: Longman, Green & Co., 1957).

34. See Duncan, *Northern Territory*, pp. 5–17.

35. See Hartwig, *White Settlement*, pp. 179–80.

36. Ibid, pp. 180–84.

37. Duncan, *Northern Territory*, pp. 33–34.

38. See Hartwig, *White Settlement*, p. 284.

39. Duncan, *Northern Territory*, p. 44.

40. Ibid, pp. 35–37.

41. The South Australia government spent more on developing these overland routes than it did on those that would have supported the movement of cattle from Central Australia. See Hartwig, *White Settlement*, p. 374. See also Ross, *Northern Territory*, pp. 46–49, for an account of the losses in the 1890s.

42. Because of the isolation of Central Australia, it is supposed that many of these pastoralists were fleeing the more populated areas of Australia for one reason or another, being social outcasts, convicts, or persons of questionable character. Although Hartwig, *White Settlement*, pp. 350–53, discusses this point, there apparently has never been much evidence for these suppositions.

43. A relationship called at the time "comboism."

44. These children were accepted by aboriginal communities.

45. As reported in Hartwig, *White Settlement*, pp. 344–46.

46. Ibid., pp. 347–48.

47. A fuller discussion of the early mission era is found in chapter 6, "Altjira." Basic sources for the history of the mission enterprise in Central Australia are Everard Leske (ed.), *Hermannsburg: A Vision and a Mission* (Adelaide: Lutheran Publishing House, 1977), and Hartwig, *White Settlement*, pp. 459–546. See Hartwig's extensive bibliography for the resources for mission history, pp. 656–59.

48. Quoted in Hartwig, *White Settlement*, p. 475. (*Lutheran Kirchenbote* 1/87, p. 7).

49. Ibid., p. 511 [*Hermannsburg Missions.* (Beiblatt) 3/85, p. 22].

50. Ibid., pp. 524–25.

51. Lindsay named the gorge after his wife. Today it is part of the Ruby Gap Nature Park.

52. Hartwig, *White Settlement*, pp. 549–50.

53. Ibid, pp. 551–52.

54. See Geoffrey Blainey, *The Rush That Never Ended: A History of Australian Mining* (Melbourne: Melbourne University Press, 1963), and Hartwig, *White Settlement*, pp. 547–91.

55. Hartwig, *White Settlement*, pp. 554–55.

56. Sometimes Paddy's Rockhole.

57. The stories of Willshire and the police will be told in greater detail in chapter 4, "Irbmangkara."

58. Hartwig, *White Settlement*, pp. 556–63.

59. Ibid, pp. 564–66.

60. Though not a product of mining activities and not quite of this particular time period but nonetheless still notable, in 1896 Jerome J. Murif was the first person to cross Australia from south to north on a bicycle. See J. J. Murif, *From Ocean to Ocean: A Record of a Trip across the Continent of Australia from Adelaide to Port Darwin* (Melbourne: George Robertson & Co., 1897).

61. Hartwig, *White Settlement*, p. 587.

62. See Ion L Idriess, *Lasseter's Last Ride: An Epic of Central Australian Gold Discovery* (Sydney: Angus & Robertson, 1931); Errol Coote, *Hell's Airport: The Key to Lasseter's Gold Reef* (Sydney: Peterman Press, 1934); and Hartwig, *White Settlement*, p. 552. Fittingly, an exclusive resort-hotel casino in present-day Alice Springs bears the name Lasseter's.

63. Hartwig, *White Settlement*, pp. 578–81.

64. Ibid, pp. 583–85. Notably, presently one-seventh of the Australian population has an Asian heritage.

65. Ibid, pp. 576–78. The railroad reached Alice Springs in 1929.

66. Ibid, p. 569; W. A. Horn, *Bush Echoes and Ballads on the Warrigal Pegasus* (London: H. Rees, 1901).

67. This relationship will be recounted in detail in chapter 5, "Altjira." See W. Baldwin Spencer (ed.), *Report on the Work of the Horn Scientific Expedition to Central Australia* (London: Dulau, 1896), and C. Winnecke, *Journal of the Horn Scientific Exploring Expedition, 1894* (Adelaide: C. E. Briston 1896).

68. Perhaps also aboriginal languages were difficult for European-Australians to handle. Typically, when aboriginal names are used they are significantly transformed. For example, the Arrernte name for Paddy's Hole is Annurra ntinga, which came to be rendered as Arltunga.

69. The naming of Port Darwin and later Darwin after Charles Darwin is a notable exception.

70. Notable exceptions occur in the coastal regions of the Northern Territory, the Top End. For example, the community established at Port Essington on the Gulf of Carpentaria and a major river southwest of present-day Darwin were both named Victoria in honor of the 1837 beginning of the reign of Queen Victoria. This was long before the domination of the South Australians in Central Australia.

71. Though time would convolute this perhaps a bit. Charles Todd's surname was given to the river passing through Alice Springs, the springs and later town that bore his wife's name. Today, the name Alice Springs has much greater recognition than does the Todd River.

Notes to Chapter 4

1. The word *irbmangkara* is the composite of *urbma*, meaning "pod," and *ankara*, meaning "broad"; thus it means "the broad [acacia] pod" Carl Strehlow, *The Aranda and Loritja Tribes of Central Australia* [*Die Aranda- und Loritja-Stämme in Zentral-Australien*], translated

by Hans D. Oberscheidt, (Frankfort am Maln: Joseph Baer, 1907), vol. I, Part I, p. 82, n. 3.

2. Aboriginal people living to the southwest of the Western Arrernte.

3. See Strehlow, *Aranda*, vol. I, Part I, pp. 94–96, for a full account. Theodor Strehlow, in *Journey to Horseshoe Bend* (Adelaide: Rigby, 1969), indicates that one group of duck ancestors followed "Remalarinja north-west through Western Aranda territory to Kularata, a place situated in the floodout swamps of the Dashwood River, north of Ulaterka" (p. 35).

4. The structure of each of these stories is an itinerary in which the group of ancestors moves from named place to named place, at each of which they perform ceremonies and rites. The stories here are indicated only by their origination and/or destination places, as well as their connection to Irbmangkara. Only these places are indicated by Theodor Strehlow in his sketch of the storytracks in *Journey to Horseshoe Bend* (p. 36). The fuller texts of some of these stories, such as the duck ancestors, are available in Carl Strehlow's work.

5. Mulga, also malga, is a small tree or shrub (*Acacia aneura*) The name is derived from a word in central New South Wales aboriginal languages that loosely means "the bush."

6. The name suggests another story about crayfish.

7. Strehlow, *Journey to Horseshoe Bend*, pp. 35–36.

8. Ibid, p. 36.

9. This story is recounted by Strehlow in *Journey to Horseshoe Bend*, pp. 36–48, supplemented by his accounts in "Geography and the Totemic Landscape in Central Australia: A Functional Study" in *Australian Aboriginal Anthropology: Modern Studies in the Social Anthropology of the Austrailian Aborigines*, edited by Ronald M. Berndt (Canberra: Australian Institute of Aboriginal Studies, 1970), pp. 124–26, and *Central Australian Religion: Personal Monotheism in a Polytotemic Community* (Adelaide: Australian Association for the Study of Religion, 1978), p. 37.

10. In another recounting of these events, Strehlow indicates the date as "somewhere about 1876." See *Central Australian Religion*, p. 37.

11. The German Lutherans founded Hermannsburg mission to the north of Irbmangkara in 1877, and cattle stations in the area were established soon after.

12. Strehlow considered the accusation false, at least according to his account in "Totemic Landscape," p. 124. In the same account, he describes the crime as "having given uninitiated boys blood drawn from the veins of initiated men to drink, in mockery of a particularly sacred initiatory rite" (p. 124).

13. In *Central Australian Religion*, Strehlow identifies Tnauutatara as a ceremonial center to both Southern Aranda and Matuntara groups (see p. 37).

14. Strehlow indicates that groups linked to a common totemic center had the "obligation to guard the sanctity of the various centres." Ibid, p. 63, n. 21.

15. Strehlow says that he was told that Tjinawariti was a ceremonial chief (*ingkata*) with a great reputation as a warrior and that he was assisted by Papaluru, ceremonial chief of Akaaua, an important native cat site on the Palmer River. See "Totemic Landscape," p. 125.

16. In "Totemic Landscape," Strehlow indicates that the baby was an infant boy named Kaltjirbuka (p. 125).

17. In "Totemic Landscape," Strehlow indicates that the revenge party was organized only because it was believed that Ltjabakuka and his elders were innocent of the ritual crime of which they were accused (p 126).

18. Ibid, p. 45.

19. Strehlow, *Journey to Horseshoe Bend*, pp. 7–8.

20. Ibid, p. 7.

21. As reported by Austin Stapleton in *Willshire of Alice Springs* (Carlisle, Western Australia: Hesperian Press, 1992), p. 45.

22. Ibid.

23. Strehlow, *Journey to Horseshoe Bend*, p. 39.

24. Ibid, p. 40.

25. Ibid, p. 44.

26. Ibid, p. 4.

27. Ward McNally, *Aborigines, Artefacts and Anguish* (Adelaide: Lutheran Publishing House, 1981), p. 190.

28. It is important to point out that the facts of this account vary from the story told in "Totemic Landscape" and *Central Australian Religion*. In both of these other accounts, Strehlow presents this story as an illustration for his discussion of how aborigines punish ritual crimes.

29. McNally, *Aborigines, Artifacts and Anguish*, p. 27.

30. Stapleton, *Willshire of Alice Springs*, p. ix.

31. For a history of Alice Springs and the area, see Shirley Brown, *My Alice: A Personal History of Alice Springs* (Alice Springs: Inday Printing for Shirley Brown, 1991); Doris Blackwell and Douglas Lockwood, *Alice on the Line* (Adelaide: Griffin Press, 1965); and *Telegraph Stations of Central Australia: Historical Photographs* (Northern Territory: Government Printing Office, n.d.).

32. The 1888 edition was published by D. Drysdale in Port Augusta, the 1891 edition by the South Australian Government Printer in Adelaide.

33. Published by Frearson & Brother, Adelaide.

34. What is now Australia's Northern Territory was under the control of South Australia until 1911. Willshire was posted from 1893 to November 1895 at Port Darwin, Victoria River, which was then the far northern part of South Australia.

35. Published by W. K. Thomas, Adelaide.

36. In his dedication statement in *Aborigines of Central Australia*, he wrote: "Those two admirable institutions, the Australian Natives' Association and the Geographical Society, will no doubt be pleased to see that the author, who has no pretensions to literary merit, has tried to do something for his countrymen, and has also tried to preserve the language of the aborigines" (p. 3). He reported that in 1886 he learned from an Adelaide newspaper that the "Geographical Society of Australia was anxious that all the knowledge relating to the aboriginal races that could be collected from reliable sources should be made public" (p. 6). Willshire writes in the preface to *Land of the Dawning*: "The book has been written for the purpose of supplying information to the Australian Natives' Association, also for Mr. J. G. Frazer, M.A., F.R.G.S, Trinity College, Cambridge, England, who asked, through the Commissioner of Police (Mr. W. J. Peterswald, J.P.), for such information regarding 'Uncivilized or semi-civilized peoples'" (p. 3).

37. Willshire, *Aborigines of Central Australia*, p. 6.

38. "The manners and customs, the religious or superstitious rites practiced by them, as well as their language, are matters of great interest." Ibid., p. 5.

39. The only clue to Willshire's views on religion is that he believed the aborigines to be of Jewish descent: "On rounding them up, and examining their features closely, the conclusion became almost irresistible that they were of Jewish descent." Ibid., p. 27. "I will not attempt to trace their ancestral line, or I might have to go so far back as the tribes of Israel." Willshire, *Thrilling Tale*, p. 9.

40. Willshire, *Aborigines of Central Australia*, p. 10. This sentiment is repeated (p. 26) along with a note: "They are assiduous in their care of the blacks, but they are quite aware

that the natives kill cattle, and are a source of constant trouble to all the settlers whose stations surround that of the missionaries" (p. 26).

41. Ibid, p. 12.

42. Ibid, p. 34.

43. Diane Bell's work, *Daughters of the Dreaming* rev ed. (Minneapolis: University of Minnesota Press, [1983] 1993), provides additional information from the aboriginal women that supports this claim.

44. Willshire, *Aborigines of Central*, p. 37; repeated in *Thrilling Tale*, p. 26.

45. Willshire, *Thrilling Tale*, p. 26.

46. See *Aborigines of Central Australia*, p. 28.

47. Ibid, pp. 37–38.

48. Ibid, p. 41.

49. Willshire, *Land of the Dawning*, p. 6.

50. Oleara is a name given to Willshire by Chillberta. When she met Willshire, he was making strings for camel nose pegs. Because he seemed to work so persistently with string, Chillberta called him Oleara, which means "string." *Thrilling Tale*, p. 12.

51. Ibid, p. 9.

52. Ibid, p. 16.

53. Ibid, p. 19.

54. Ibid.

55. I have dealt with the Pocahontas theme more fully in *Mother Earth: An American Story* (Chicago: University of Chicago Press, 1987), pp. 34–39.

56. Willshire, *Land of the Dawning*, p. 41. For another example of the Pocahontas theme, see *Thrilling Tale*, pp. 28–29.

57. Willshire, *Thrilling Tale*, p. 25.

58. There is evidence that Willshire, though a married man, lived with an aboriginal woman. At the time of his trial in Port Augusta, the prosecution wanted to interrogate "Willshire's lubra [i.e., woman]," but because of the objection by John Downer, she was not questioned.

59. Willshire, *Thrilling Tale*, p. 31.

60. Willshire, *Land of the Dawning*, p. 9.

61. This poem is published in Stapleton, *Willshire of Alice Springs*, pp. 1–2.

62. Willshire, *Thrilling Tale*, p. 44.

63. For an account of the trial, see ibid., pp. 56–58.

64. Willshire, *Aborigines of Central Australia*, p. 33.

65. Ibid, pp. 33–34.

66. Willshire's account of this killing appears to have been written before his accusal and trial in 1891. His response to being tried for murder was presented in an extensive addendum to his book *Thrilling Tale*, published in 1895.

67. Strehlow, *Journey to Horseshoe Bend*, p. 45.

68. Ibid, p. 46.

69. As shown more fully in chapter 1.

70. Strehlow identifies this tracker by the name Jack (or Kwalba), who along with Aremala (who was called Larry) was from the Upper Southern Arrernte area. Aremala, it is to be remembered, is identified by Strehlow as the son of Nameia.

71. As reported in Stapleton, *Willshire of Alice Springs*, p. 35.

72. Ibid.

73. Ibid, p. 36.

74. Stapleton's motivation for writing *Willshire of Alice Springs* is to combat this image of Willshire. In the preface to the book, he cites a number of examples of the denigration of Willshire's character (see p. v).

Notes to Chapter 5

1. Everard Leske, *Hermannsburg: A Vision and a Mission* (Adelaide: Lutheran Publishing House, 1977), p. 7.
2. Ibid, p. 9.
3. Ibid, p. 10.
4. Ibid, p. 11.
5. Ibid, p. 15.
6. F. E. H. W. Krichauff, "The Customs, Religious Ceremonies, etc. of the 'Aldolinga' or 'Mbenderinga' Tribe of Aborigines in Krichauff Ranges, South Australia," *Royal Geographical Society of South Australia* 2 (1886–88): 33–37; quotation on pp. 35–36. Krichauff collected, arranged, and translated from German letters from Kempe and Schulze dated July 1, 1886. Probably the *v* in *altgiva* is a misreading of Kempe's cursive *r*. See below where Spencer notes that three of these names are place names, not the names of gods.
7. Leske, *Hermannsburg*, pp. 19–20.
8. Ibid, p. 22.
9. Ibid, p. 23.
10. For other information about the Strehlow era of the mission, see Ward McNally, *Aborigines, Artifacts and Anguish* (Adelaide: Lutheran Publishing House, 1981), chap. 1.
11. See Leske, *Hermannsburg*, p. 17.
12. Ibid, p. 30.
13. Carl and Frieda Strehlow were naturalized citizens but were made to fill out alien registration forms and were not permitted to travel from their place of residence without obtaining a police permit See McNally, *Aborigines*, p. 19.
14. According to Pastor F. W. Albrecht, the records indicate that Strehlow was offered a post in South Australia one or two years before he left Hermannsburg. Theodor Strehlow said that his father stayed at Hermannsburg primarily because he wanted to disprove Baldwin Spencer's report, delivered prior to Strehlow's posting at Hermannsburg, which doubted that the mission would ever do anyone any good. See McNally, *Aborigines*, pp. 91–92.
15. Ibid., p. 17.
16. The story of this journey from Hermannsburg to Horseshoe Bend is dramatically told by Theodor Strehlow, *Journey to Horseshoe Bend* (Adelaide: Rigby, 1969).
17. Commonly termed *half caste* in the literature of that time.
18. Quoted in Leske, *Hermannsburg*, p. 34. See D. J. Mulvaney and J. H. Calaby, *'So Much That Is New': Baldwin Spencer, 1860–1929, A Biography* (Melbourne: University of Melbourne, 1985), pp. 377–81, for details about Spencer's visit and the report he filed. See McNally, *Aborigines*, pp. 93–94, especially for Theodor Strehlow's views on the harm he thought Spencer did to his father's reputation.
19. See Theodor Strehlow, "Geography and the Totemic Landscape in Central Australia: A Functional Study," in *Australian Aboriginal Anthropology: Modern Studies in the Social Anthropology of the Australian Aborigines,* edited by Ronald M. Berndt (Wedlands, Western Australia: Australia Institute of Aboriginal Studies, 1970) pp. 126–28, for a remarkable account of Moses's heritage.

20. If reports of his age at baptism are correct, he would have been more nearly thirty-five years old.

21. A slight exaggeration—the mission was established in 1877.

22. Leske, *Hermannsburg*, p. 36.

23. Ibid, p. 83. My chronicle of the life of Moses has had to depend more on his appearance in photographs than on narrative descriptions of him. I have found no biographical accounts of the man. Theodor Strehlow's biographer, Ward McNally, recounts a fascinating exchange, reported by Pastor F. W. Albrecht, between Strehlow and Moses about this translation:

> I remember Ted sitting on a blackened ghost gum stump, discussing his translation of the New Testament with a group of elders, including a wise old Aboriginal named Blind Moses. The elders were critical of his translation, claiming it was too precise for most of their people to understand it. Their argument was that he should have simplified it, so that even the young people could read it and appreciate it.
>
> But Ted ridiculed that. He told them that, when a young man had passed through his initiation rites and entered the tribe as a full man, and had something to say, the old men listened to him because they thought he now had something worthwhile to say—something that had been ignored earlier. . . .
>
> Ted fixed the sighted elders with a stony look and said that his translation had been made in terms he believed they, as mature men, could understand, and which they should explain to the young people of the tribe. And he told them that, if they couldn't understand that, they weren't mature men themselves.
>
> Old Blind Moses said it wasn't easy for the young people to become enthusiastic about church when the translation was so difficult. Ted replied sharply: "Well, explain it to them, as I've suggested. . . . That's why you're elders. To lead!" There was a moment of uncomfortable silence, then Blind Moses said: "Okay. Okay. You right. We teach!" That was the end of the argument. Ted Strehlow won again. (McNally, *Aborigines*, pp. 105–6)

24. Quoted in Theodor Strehlow, *Songs of Central Austrailia* (Sydney: Angus & Robertson, 1971), pp. 346–47. The bracketed additions are based on Strehlow's footnotes.

25. This response is especially interesting given that the notion that Malbangka is the creator of game animals is probably the product of Christian influence.

26. This account is also quite remarkable in revealing the processes by which the Arrernte elders compared themselves to their Christian counterparts.

27. In Theodor Strehlow's brief history of Hermannsburg during the Strehlow era, "Altjira Rega Ekalta: Praise to the Lord, the Almighty," *Lutheran Yearbook, 1979* (Adelaide: Lutheran Church of Australia), he mentions Moses in only one paragraph, crediting him as "one of the main language helpers to Strehlow and his predecessors in their Aranda missionary translation work" (p. 46). When he describes the baptisms of 1923, Strehlow credits only his father, although they took place more than a year after his death: "All these men and women had received baptismal instruction from [Carl] Strehlow for a number of years" (p. 47).

28. Mulvaney and Calaby, *Baldwin Spencer*, p. 377.

29. Ibid, p. 57.

30. For Spencer's contributions to biology, see ibid., chap. 8.

31. Ibid, p. 116.

32. Ibid, pp. 118–19.

33. Ibid, p. 117.

34. Ibid, pp. 170–71.

35. Ibid, pp. 170–72.

36. Most notably the criticism of Theodor Strehlow, as will be discussed below.

37. July 30, 1897, as quoted in Mulvaney and Calaby, *Baldwin Spencer*, p. 440, n. 69.

38. The necessity of anyone having to have a "skin," that is, a subclassification, is carefully described by Diane Bell in *Daughters of the Dreaming*, rev. ed. (Minneapolis: University of Minnesota Press, [1983] 1993), pp. 18–20 and app. 2.

39. James George Frazer, "Observations on Central Australian Totemism," *Journal of the Anthropological Institute of Great Britain and Ireland* 28 (1899): 281–82; quoted in Mulvaney and Calaby, *Baldwin Spencer*, p. 180.

40. Spencer's recommendations included closing Hermannsburg because of what he regarded as hopeless economic mismanagement, inadequate housing with poor hygiene, and a misguided educational policy. He drew attention to two children's dormitories, which he described as dungeons in which the children were incarcerated at night. The measure of Spencer's bias is that he overlooked a record that others would interpret positively: The mission had attracted 200 aboriginal residents to Hermannsburg because it was their "country," the birthrate exceeded the death rate, among the residents were able-bodied men and women (children made up only 44%), and they used the Arrernte language in school. Interestingly, Spencer demanded the use of English. The Lutherans, as a result of being given Spencer's report, made a number of changes, including the introduction of industrial training.

41. Mulvaney and Calaby, *Baldwin Spencer*, pp. 383–85.

42. The fascinating story of Spencer's long relationship with Jean Hamilton, thirty-one years his junior, must remain here untold other than to note that she accompanied Spencer on this last journey. Ibid., pp. 374ff.

43. Carl Strehlow, *Die Aranda Und Loritja-Stämme in Zentral Australia*, edited by Moritz Freiherr von Leonharde, translated by Hans D. Oberscheidt (Frankfurt am Main: Joseph Baer, 1907–15), vol. I, part I, p. 1.

44. According to Mulvaney and Calaby, this letter was found in Spencer's copy of Strehlow's *Die Aranda*. See *Baldwin Spencer*, p. 470, n. 52.

45. *Spencer's Scientific Correspondence with Sir J. G. Frazer and Others*, edited by R. R. Marrett and T. K. Penniman (London: Oxford University Press, 1932), pp. 95–97. The level of Spencer's irritation with Strehlow's high-god claim is found again in a letter he wrote to Frazer on March 18, 1904: "If I have not told you of it before, you will find the red-ink account of how Herr Strehlow of the Hermannsburg mission discovered the existence of a 'High God' amongst the Arunta rather interesting and instructive. It will probably be published in Germany and quoted and requoted as the evidence of one who knows the natives intimately. I cannot think how it was that I missed Schulze's paper [apparently Frazer had called this to Spencer's attention], and in some future publication must give him credit for what, so far as it goes, is a good piece of work." Spencer turns Schulze's work against Strehlow in appendix D of *The Arunta*. In a marginal note Spencer reveals to Frazer that Lang had sent the Strehlow material to him in confidence, and he asks Frazer not to use either the Strehlow material or his comments in publication. Spencer here connects the All-Father with Central Australia, though it is a figure identified more closely with aboriginal cultures in Southeast Australia. For an important study of how the concept of the All-Father arose as a response to contact, see Tony Swain, *A Place for Strangers: Towards a History of Australian Aboriginal Being* (Cambridge, Mass.: Cambridge University Press, 1993), chap. 3.

46. *Spencer's Scientific Correspondence*, pp. 106–7. The letter is dated February 5, 1908.

47. Ibid, pp. 109–10.

48. Ibid.

49. Ibid, p. 116. Letter is dated April 19, 1908.

50. Ibid, p. 126.

51. Baldwin Spencer and Francis Gillen, *The Arunta: A Study of a Stone Age People* (London: Macmillan, 1904), p. ix.

52. Ibid., p. 591, referring to Louis Schulze, "The Aborigines of the Upper and Middle Fink River [etc.]," *Transactions and Proceedings and Report of the Royal Society of South Australia* 14 (1891): 242.

53. Ibid. In focusing on time, Spencer is missing the more important point that the designation of the mother's birthplace is the identification of the country to which one has a *kurdungurlu* relationship. It is a designation of country or territory, not time.

54. Schulze makes one clear reference to the meaning of the word *altjira* that Spencer does not refer to. In describing disk-shaped *tjurunga* called *tjurunga arknanoa*, Schulze writes: "Upon these various markings are engraved, which the respective old man to whom they belong alone understands, describing the whole meaning of his *tjurunga*, as to its origin and purport. They pretend that these *tjurunga arknanoa* were *altjira*—that is, were not made—but I suspect, as they occasionally give some to white people, that the old men and sorcerers made them themselves." Schulze, "Aborigines of the Upper and Middle Finke River," pp. 210–46; quotation on p. 242. It would appear that Schulze's view of the term corresponds with Kempe's and Spencer's as referring to that which has always existed or, when they give it a temporal interpretation, that which is eternal. In the terms introduced by Stanner and developed by Swain, this would be the "abiding." Carl Strehlow seems to be at variance, indicating that there are four Arrernte words to describe the eternal: "*ngambakala*, *ngambintja*, *ngamitjina*, and *ngarra*." *Die Aranda- Und Loritja-Stämme in Zentral Australia,* edited by Moritz Freiherr von Leonhardi, translated by Hans D. Oberscheidt (Frankfurt am Main: Joseph Baer, 1907–15), vol., part I, p. 1, n. 1. In the Loritja language, Strehlow renders *kututu* as "eternal" (vol. I, part II, p. 2).

55. Spencer and Gillen, *Arunta*. p. 592.

56. Ibid, p. 596. Note the correspondence of Kempe's views with those of Schulze, as indicated in note 54. Patrick Wolfe's careful tracing of the use of *altjira* locates a German publication by H. Kempe, "Zur Sittenkunde der Centralaustralischen Schwarazen," pp. 52–56 in *Mittheilungen des Vereins für Engkunde zu Halle*, who reports that Central Australians say that Altjira gives children: "Die Kinder, sagen sie, schenkt Altjira (Gott)." Quoted in Patrick Wolfe, "On Being Woken up: The Dreamtime in Anthropology and in Australian Settler Culture," *Comparative Study of Society and History* 33 (1991): 219–20.

57. Spencer obviously contradicts his own evidence since Kempe specifically states that the Arrernte use the word *Altjira* as a name for the Christian God, or their conception of this god, to whom they have been introduced, but we understand his argument

58. Ibid, p. 596.

59. Strehlow, *Die Aranda*, vol. I, part I, p. 2.

60. Ibid.

61. Ibid., vol. I, part II, p. 1.

62. It appears that Strehlow is referring to the connection to land and totem through one's mother or maternal grandmother. This is usually referred to by the regional term *kurdungurlu*, which is a Warlpiri term. Strehlow's information suggests that *altjira* is the Arrernte term that at least in some uses, designates this maternal connection to country. To my knowledge, this use of the term has never been recognized as a possibility, yet the evidence that supports this understanding seems to be extensive.

63. Strehlow, *Die Aranda*, vol. I, part II, p. 77. Thus *tmara altjira* is the place where one's mother was conceived, and *tmara altjirealtja* is the place of the totem with which one is associated.

64. Ibid., pp. 102 and 104.

65. Two powerful statements to attest to this view are Francis Gillen, "Magic amongst the Natives of Central Australia," and James George Frazer, "On Some Ceremonies of the Central Australian Tribes," both in *Report of the Eighth Meeting of the Australasian Association for the Advancement of Science Held at Melbourne, Victoria, 1900*, edited by T. S. Hall (Melbourne: Australian Association for the Advancement of Science, 1901), pp. 109–23 and 312–21, respectively.

66. Strehlow, *Die Aranda*, vol. I, part I, pp. 1–2.

67. Francis J Gillen, "Notes on Some Manners and Customs of the Aborigines of the McDonnell Ranges Belonging to the Arunta Tribe," in *Report on the Work of the Horn Scientific Expedition to Central Australia*, edited by Baldwin Spencer (London: Dulau, 1896), part IV, pp. 162–85.

68. Strehlow, *Die Aranda*, vol. I, part II, p. 1, n. 1.

69. Spencer and Gillen, *Arunta*, p. 593, n. 2.

70. See chap. 6 for further details.

71. Géza Róheim, *The Riddle of the Sphinx, or Human Origins,* translated by R. Money-Kyrle (London: International Psycho-analytical Library, 1934), pp. 139–40.

72. Géza Róheim, *The Eternal Ones of the Dream: Psychoanalytic Interpretation of Austrailian Myth and Ritual* (New York: International Universities Press, 1945), p. 10.

73. In another focus for interpretation, Róheim considers the mythic and ritual references to *ambilia-ikura,* sacks in which pairs of *tjurunga* are carried He deftly negotiates Carl Strehlow's and Spencer's understandings of the term *ambilia-ikura*, supporting reinterpretations based on the authority of Yirramba, a man who Róheim claims was initiated during the rites witnessed by Spencer and Gillen in 1896. (This information is of interest in that Spencer claimed to have found no survivors from 1896 when he returned to the field in 1926. Perhaps Yirramba was located at Hermannsburg at that time and Spencer simply did not know this. One wonders how many other authorities, other than Charlie Cooper, Spencer might have found had he made a greater effort during his 1926 field studies.) Róheim settles on Strehlow's presentation of the term as *mbiljirkara,* which means "stuck together," referring to the *tjurungas* that are bound together in the sack. For Róheim, these paired *tjurungas* represent the primal scene of the father and mother in coitus. An alternative rendering, based on Spencer's work, is that it might mean either "uterus-hole" or "child-his," which, either way for Róheim, meant "the womb" (*Riddle of the Sphinx*, p. 143). Drawing on highly select elements of the myth and the correlating ritual as described by Spencer and Gillen, Róheim arrives at "the essence of the myth and ritual," which, not surprisingly, is focused on the "father-son relationship." Originally man and wife, as two Malpungas they became father and son. The primal aggression of the young males in the primal scene is sublimated: "The father and son are 'joined together'; heterosexual genital libido becomes aim-inhibited and homosexual"(pp. 145–46). Róheim correlates the myth interpretation with the rite in which two old men spend the whole night during the *inkura* lifting up and down the *ambilia-ikura*, that is, the *tjurunga* pair. The men represent the two Malpungas, according to Róheim. The initiates lie motionless. Should the men not be able to maintain the action, representing the maintenance of an erection, throughout the night, the initiates will die. Róheim argues that the "boy's parricidal impulses had been evoked by the erection in the primal scene"(p. 146).

74. See chap. 6 for more details.

75. Róheim, *Eternal Ones*, p. 11.

76. Ibid., p. 16.

77. Ibid., p. 17.

78. Róheim appears not to connect Ngambakala with the figure he finds in Spencer's *Aranda.*

79. Róheim, *Eternal Ones*, p. 211.

80. Róheim, *Riddle of the Sphinx*, pp. 126–27.

81. Ibid., p. 129.

82. A quadrilateral form made of two or more pieces of wood, joined at right angles, around which hairstring is wound.

83. Róheim, *Riddle of the Sphinx*, p. 131.

84. Ibid., pp. 132–33.

85. Róheim, *Eternal Ones*, p. 222.

86. Géza Róheim, "Psycho-analysis of Primitive Culture Types," *The International Journal of Psycho-Analysis* 13 (1932): 34

87. Géza Róheim, *Children of the Desert: The Western Tribes of Central Australia*, (New York: Harper & Row, 1974), p. 79.

88. Róheim, *Riddle of the Sphinx*, p. 17.

89. Ibid., p. 21.

90. This fact seems to be derived directly from Róheim's analysis of the folklore of riddles that deal with legs. He examines materials collected and analyzed by the Finnish folklorist, A. Aarne. Ibid., p. 21.

91. Ibid., p. 22.

92. Ibid., pp. 166–67. Although Róheim took this phylogenetic work of Freud for granted, it is supported by few of Freud's published works. Certainly there is *Totem and Taboo: Some Points of Agreement between the Mental Lives of Savages and Neurotics,* translated by James Strauchy (New York: Norton, 1913). Róheim cites (see *Riddle of the Sphinx*, p. 166) Freud's "Das Ich und das Es," *Gesammelte Schriften*, vi. 374. And there is an interesting manuscript that turned up in 1983 among Ferenczi's papers. Freud's note to Ferenczi on the manuscript gave him permission to "throw it away or keep it." It was published as *A Phylogenetic Fantasy: Overview of the Transference Neuroses*, edited by Ilse Grubrich-Simitis, translated by Axel Hoffer and Peter T. Hoffer (Cambridge, Mass.: Harvard University Press, 1987). The manuscript is identified as the last of twelve metapsychological papers that Freud had written in 1915, only five of which ever appeared in publication with Freud's approval. It seems possible that Ferenczi encouraged his student Róheim to give anthropological credibility to the work that in *Phylogenetic Fantasy* Freud called "nothing more than a playful comparison."

93. Freud, *Totem and Taboo*, pp. 141–42.

94. For an outstanding analysis of Freud's view of time, see Tomoko Masuzawa, *In Search of Dreamtime: The Quest for the Origin of Religion* (Chicago: University of Chicago Press, 1993), chap. 4, pp. 76–161. Freud also explained in a footnote that the vagueness of the reference "one day" was necessary because "it would be as foolish to aim at exactitude in such questions as it would be unfair to insist upon certainty" (p. 143).

95. Róheim, *Riddle of the Sphinx*, p. 202.

96. Ibid., p. 172.

97. Ibid., pp. 202–3.

98. Ibid., p. 210.

99. Ibid., p. 169.

100. Ibid., p. 173.

101. Ibid., p. 211.

102. Róheim, "Psycho-analysis," p. 31.

103. Róheim, *Riddle of the Sphinx*, p. 221.

104. Sigmund Freud, *From the History of an Infantile Neurosis. The Standard Edition of the Complete Psychological Works of Sigmund Freud*, translated by James Strauchey, no. 17 (London: Hogarth Press [for] the Institute of Psychoanalysis, 1953–74). Although Róheim does not date his clinical example, it doubtless postdates Freud's wolf man case.

105. See, for example, "Psycho-analysis," p. 55, in which Róheim describes as a primal scene the male infancy experience of genital striving, directed toward his mother in the common situation of the mother sleeping on top of her infant son.

106. In a complex interpretation of an aboriginal dream, Róheim depends on the primal scene as the basis for his interpretation. Notably, in this dream, an act of "boning," that is, a kind of projectile sorcery, killed a man by entering his breast; Róheim called on the primal scene, this time "perceived through the mirror of the sucking child's eroticism; for to enter the mother through the breast is just what the baby is trying to do." See "Psycho-analysis," pp. 89–90.

107. See chapter 6 for more details.

108. Róheim, "Psycho-analysis," p. 56.

109. See, for example, ibid., p. 57.

110. The display, which I observed in September 1993, credits Theodor Strehlow's *Central Australian Religion: Personal Monototemism in Polytotemic Society* (Adelaide: Australian Association for the Study of Religions, 1978).

111. There is much information on Theodor Strehlow's life in the biography by McNally, *Aborigines*. McNally, a friend of Strehlow in his later years, depends extensively on interviews for this work. It is a very personal biography filled with undocumented supposition, and has no formal documentation. His key interviews were with Bertha, Strehlow's first wife, whom he deserted; Theodor, Jr., his son, whom he apparently occasionally denied and frequently ignored; several Adelaide University officials; academic students of aboriginal culture such as Ronald Berndt; and several others. Notably, Strehlow's second wife, Kathleen, refused to cooperate with McNally, as he reports, when he refused to exclude Strehlow's first wife (of a thirty-three year marriage) from the biography. Needless to say, the biography is controversial; I have relied on it only for general factual information and I have used the uncorroboratable information with care, if at all.

112. Ibid., p. 149. See also Strehlow, *Songs of Central Australia*.

113. McNally reports in *Aborigines* that between 1957 and 1973 Strehlow received grants from these two institutions amounting to $273,400. Apparently, although this was generous funding for the sort of research Strehlow did, he was frequently bitter about the level of his funding, which he thought inadequate.

114. Ibid., p. 153.

115. Ibid., p. 188. This article was also published in the United States in *Discover* magazine.

116. Forerunner to the Strehlow Research Centre.

117. McNally, *Aborigines*, p. 145.

118. This criticism is made by Róheim, *Riddle of the Sphinx*, pp. 84–86, and in Strehlow, *Songs of Central Australia* pp. xv–xvi.

119. Strehlow, *Songs of Central Australia*, pp. xx–xxi. This same defense appears also in Strehlow's *Central Australian Religion*, p. 58, n. 1.

120. Strehlow, *Songs of Central Australia*, p. xxxi.

121. Strehlow quotes from Frazer's *Totemism and Exogamy*, vol. I, p. 186, in which Frazer writes: "In these circumstances it seems to me that the sources from which Mr. Strehlow has drawn his accounts are deeply tainted; and as it would be impossible for me, who have no first-hand knowledge of these tribes, to filter the native liquid clear of its alien sediment, I shall abstain from making use of Mr. Strehlow's information." Quoted in Strehlow, *Songs of Central Australia*, p. xxii, n. 7. To counter this position, Strehlow also quotes a statement by Andrew Lang, "A Theory of Arunta Totemism," *Man* 4 (1904), 67–69, who criticizes Spencer and Gillen and defends Carl Strehlow.

122. Strehlow, "Totemic Landscape," pp. 92–140; see p. 138, n. 25.

123. See Strehlow, *Songs of Central Australia*, pp. xxi–xxxii.

124. Strehlow, "Totemic Landscape," pp. 138–39, n. 25.

125. In a footnote in his *Central Australian Religion*, p. 58, n. 1, Strehlow writes: "Green [a critic of his father's work]—who . . . mistakenly claims that the word "God" had been adopted by the early Hermannsburg missionaries (actually it was the word "altjira" that they had adopted). . . ."

126. Ibid., p. 11.

127. Theodor Strehlow, "Altijira Rega Ekalta: Praise to the Lord, the Almighty," in pp. 25–49.

128. The term *Altjira* is listed as the Arrernte word for the English word "God" in the 1991 edition of the Finke River Mission's *Learning Arrarnta.* See John Pfitzner and Joan Schmaal, *Learning Arrarnta*, 2nd ed. by Hans D. Oberscheidt (Alice Springs: Finke River Mission, 1991), p. 81.

129. Strehlow, *Songs of Central Australia*, p. 614. Later he writes that "the root meaning of the Aranda word 'altjira' is 'eternal, uncreated'" (p. 694).

130. Ibid., p. 615. Also quoted in *Central Australian Religion*, p. 13.

131. It was first published in a Festschrift für Ad. E. Jensen and later as a small volume by the Australian Association for the Study of Religions, 1978.

132. Strehlow, *Central Australian Religion*, pp. 11–12.

133. Ibid., pp. 12–13.

134. Ibid., p. 13.

135. Ibid., pp. 13–14.

136. Strehlow, *Songs of Central Australia*, pp. xxxiv–xxxv.

137. An important exception to this statement is Tony Swain and Deborah B. Rose (eds.), *Aboriginal Australians and Christian Missions: Ethnographic and Historical Studies* (Adelaide: Australian Association for the Study of Religion, 1988).

138. For additional discussion of the history of the concept now commonly rendered as "dreamtime," see Swain, *Place for Strangers*, pp. 20–22, and Patrick Wolfe, "On Being Woken up," especially app. B, pp. 219–20.

139. Stanner's term *everywhen* and his attention to *abidingness* (developed extensively by Tony Swain) still have, from the view of "Western man," an unavoidable temporal dimension. Certainly Swain's discussion of the ontological difference of aboriginal worldviews in *Place for Strangers* is the most effective effort to date to actually consider how fundamental the difference in worldviews is.

140. I have focused this chapter on the Arrernte term *altjira*, intentionally avoiding the common rendering of the term as "dreamtime" because of its power and seductiveness. Most of the publications about anything related to Australian aborigines incorporates some form of "dreamtime." Wolfe's article, "On Being Woken up," is an insightful study of why these terms have been so attractive to Western audiences.

141. This is another example of Western self-fulfillment. As Spencer accused Carl Strehlow of finding Arrernte what his predecessors had introduced, we now find aborigines speaking with authority of the "dreamtime." Perhaps the irony is that this shows that they have come to understand Western perspectives in order to survive, but in doing so they may have engaged in a major ontological shift. My experience in attempting to document such a case in North America—*Mother Earth: An American Story* (Chicago: University of Chicago Press, 1987)—has been that to point out this process is often unwelcome. Interestingly, a parallel to the Native American engagement in *Mother Earth* has sprung up in aboriginal Australia. See Tony Swain, "The Mother Earth Conspiracy: An Australian Episode," *Numen* 38, no. 1 (1992): 3–26. Wolfe deals carefully and insightfully with this process in the aboriginal use of "dreamtime"; see "On Being Woken up," especially pp. 216–18.

142. An important example was Strehlow's efforts to defend an aboriginal man accused of raping and murdering a white girl named Mary Hatten in 1959. See McNally, *Aborigines*, pp. 112ff.

143. I am following here the indictment of Masuzawa, *In Search of Dreamtime*, pp. 177–79.

144. Each of these terms, interestingly, bears a paradoxical double structure parallel to that of the conception of time.

Notes to Chapter 6

1. Géza Róheim, "Psycho-analysis of Primitive Culture Types," *The International Journal of Psycho-analysis* 13 (1932): 1–223.

2. Géza Róheim, *Children of the Desert: The Western Tribes of Central Australia* (New York: Harper & Row, 1974); *Children of the Desert II: Myths and Dreams of the Aborigines of Central Australia*, Oceania Ethnographics, no. 2 (Sydney: Oceania Publications, University of Sydney, 1988).

3. Géza Róheim, *The Eternal Ones of the Dream: Psychoanalytic Interpretation of Australian Myth and Ritual* (New York: International Universities Press, 1945).

4. Paul A. Robinson, *The Freudian Left: Wilhelm Reich, Géza Róheim, Herbert Marcuse* (New York: Harper & Row, 1969), p. 145.

5. With a few exceptions—Arrernte, *tjurunga*, Loritja—native terms will be spelled as in the sources cited. Spelling variations will be noted where appropriate.

6. Although the description refers to Arrernte culture as it existed in the last decades of the nineteenth century, the present tense will be used to avoid what always seems to me a primitivist tone when using the past tense. Further, since I am attempting to show, in summary, the Arrernte through Spencer's and Gillen's eyes, we must become contemporary with them, which we may do by using the present tense.

7. W. Baldwin Spencer and Francis J., Gillen, *The Native Tribes of Central Australia*, (London: Macmillan, 1899), pp. 8–11.

8. This collection is what Theodor Strehlow later described in greater detail as "clan totem."

9. Spencer and Gillen, *Native Tribes*, p. 25.

10. In contemporary aboriginal communities, subclass is familiarly called "skin."

11. Spencer and Gillen, *Native Tribes*, pp. 112–16.

12. Ibid., p. 120. This concentration in a given area of people associated to one totem supports the collective identity that Spencer described and that Theodor Strehlow will later designate as "clan totem."

13. Ibid. Unlike most ethnographers, Tony Swain has questioned the notion of reincarnation. He finds no evidence or reason to uphold such a belief. See *A Place for Strangers: Towards a History of Australian Aboriginal Being* (Cambridge, Mass.: Cambridge University Press, 1993). p. 45.

14. Although in Spencer's experience the women neither had *tjurungas* nor knew about them, later ethnographers such as Diane Bell would observe women's *tjurungas.*

15. Spencer and Gillen, *Native Tribes*, p. 135.

16. Ibid., p. 137. Theodor Strehlow will later develop a two-soul theory.

17. Ibid., pp. 167–211, especially pp. 207–11. Spencer, upholding Frazer's view that religion is a stage in cultural evolution that follows magic and believing the Arrernte representative of the magical stage, saw the term *religion* as inappropriate. See, for example, his statement in Baldwin Spencer, "Totemism in Australia," Presidential Address to Ethnology and Anthropology Section, *Report of the Tenth Meeting of the Australasian Association for the Advancement of Science* (Dunedin: Australasian Association for the Advancement of Science, 1904), p. 404.

18. Spencer and Gillen, *Native Tribes*, p. 269. Although this description of female initiation is brief, it is remarkable that Spencer and Gillen were able to learn anything at all about women's rites. This reference to female activities, as well as a number of others, as will be evident in the following descriptions, belies the criticism so often leveled against them that they ignored and discounted women.

19. Ibid., pp. 218–251.

20. Most of the rites are identified both by totem and location, the location being one of the stopping places in the itinerary of ancestral travels that define country.

21. Spencer and Gillen, *Native Tribes*, pp. 275–82.

22. Ibid., p. 284. Spencer and Gillen's failure to record the songs that Carl and Theodor Strehlow found to be so important is probably due not simply to their lack of knowledge of Arrernte language but also to their dependence on uninitiated men for interpreters. The words of songs are broken and recombined in such a way that even uninitiated speakers of the language would not be able to comprehend the lyrics.

23. Ibid., pp. 320–22.

24. Ibid., pp. 326–336. Róheim, as will be shown, suggested that such malevolent figures were part of a religion ignored by other ethnographers. This religion, in contrast with the totem-centered religion that is practiced when large groups congregate, is the religion of the bush practiced by small groups of hunter-gatherers and centered on the threat of malevolent figures thought to populate these regions.

25. Ibid., pp. 323–47.

26. Ibid., pp. 347–52.

27. An act Róheim will see as sexually significant (see below).

28. Spencer and Gillen, *Native Tribes*, p. 368.

29. Ibid., pp. 363–69.

30. Ibid., pp. 172–73.

31. Ibid., p. 372.

32. Ibid., pp. 374–80.

33. Ibid., pp. 381–86.

34. Ibid., p. 387.

35. Ibid., pp. 387–88.

36. Ibid., pp. 388–89. See also chapter 1 for critical analysis of the sources.

37. Ibid., p. 392.

38. Ibid., pp. 394–417. These accounts are carefully analyzed in chapter 7.
39. Ibid., pp. 420–21.
40. Ibid., pp. 423–49.
41. Ibid., pp. 450–635.
42. Theodor Strehlow, *Songs of Central Australia* (Sydney: Angus & Robinson, 1971), pp. xx–xxi.
43. I have depended heavily on the unpublished English translation of Strehlow's books by Hans D Oberscheidt, completed at Hermannsburg in 1991.
44. Carl Strehlow, *Die Aranda- Und Loritja-Stämme in Zentral-Australien*, edited by Moritz Freiherr von Leonhardi (Frankfurt am Main: Joseph Baer, 1907–15), vol. I, part I, p. 4.
45. Ibid., p. 5.
46. Ibid., p. 7.
47. Ibid. This is a curious correlation to the fly-catching lizard story collected by Gillen and used by Spencer to form a creation story. See chapter 1. It seems possible that Spencer's concoction may have been accepted by the Arrernte, perhaps when Strehlow, who read it in *Native Tribes,* asked them about it. He may then have later recorded it, as did Róheim decades later. What is increasingly apparent—though beyond demonstration, given the materials available from this period—is that there was much interchange between the Arrernte and the ethnographers. Certainly Strehlow had a copy of Spencer and Gillen's *Native Tribes* since he often referred to it. It is quite possible that his dependence on Spencer's construction was the method of introducing this story of the fly-eating lizard into the tradition.
48. Ibid., p. 8.
49. Ibid., p. 13. These are Spencer and Gillen's *oruncha*.
50. Ibid., pp. 25ff.
51. Ibid., p. 19.
52. It appears that whereas Spencer and Gillen received only the outlines of broad mythologies, Strehlow received only the stories, and the correlating rites, of the ancestors at specific geographical locations. The two bodies of materials seem to complement one another.
53. Strehlow, *Aranda*, vol. I, part II, pp. 70ff.
54. Ibid., vol. I, part III, p. viii.
55. Ibid., vol. I. part II, pp. 70–80.
56. Ibid., p. 80.
57. Ibid., p. 96.
58. Ibid., p. 97.
59. Ibid., vol. 1, part III, section 1, p. 2.
60. Ibid., p. 10. Strehlow's use of the Christian idea of duty is consistent with his storytrack.
61. Ibid., p. 7.
62. Ibid., pp. 12–80.
63. Ibid., p. 14. As a German Lutheran missionary and father, obedience was highly important to Strehlow.
64. Ibid., p. 45.
65. Ibid., p. 49.
66. Ibid., p. 54.
67. Ibid., pp. 54–56.
68. Ibid., p. 54.
69. Other biographical information about Róheim can be found in Michael Balint, "Géza Róheim: 1891–1953," *International Journal of Psycho-analysis* 35 (1954): 434–36; René A Spitz, "Géza Róheim: 1891–1953," *The Psychoanalytic Quarterly* 22 (1953): 324–27; Weston LaBarre,

"Géza Róheim, 1891–1953: Psychoanalysis and Anthropology," in *Psychoanalytic Pioneers*, edited by F. Alexander, S. Eisenstein, and M. Grotjahn (New York: Basic Books, 1966), pp. 272–81; and John Morton, "Introduction: Géza Róheim's Contribution to Australian Ethnography," in Róheim's *Children of the Desert II*, pp. vii–xxx.

70. Robinson, *Freudian Left*, p 75.

71. Róheim, "Psycho-analysis," p. 2.

72. Ibid.

73. Róheim indicated that Wapiti was a main informant of Carl Strehlow, who did not name him. Wapiti told Róheim that "the information he gave Strehlow was '*gammon*', the sort of thing he would tell a missionary" (ibid., p. 13). Elements of Moses's biography are provided in chapter 5.

74. Strehlow's *Songs of Central Australia* would bear out this point.

75. Róheim, "Psycho-analysis," p. 20.

76. Ibid.

77. Ibid., p. 21.

78. Ibid., pp. 16–17.

79. To my knowledge no effort has been made to collect these works and to evaluate the significance of their dependence on aboriginal materials nor, as this study would suggest, the impact of the unauthenticity of so much of the ethnography on which these works relied. The list of authors and works that appear in this category are indeed impressive, including Émile Durkheim, *Elementary Forms of Religious Life,* translated by Joseph Ward Swain (New York: Free Press, [1915] 1965); Sigmund Freud, *Totem and Taboo: Some Points of Agreement between the Mental Lives of Savages and Neurotics* (New York: Norton, [1913] 1950); Arnold van Gennep, *Mythes et Légendes d'Australie* (Paris: Librairie Orientale et Americaine, 1906); and James George Frazer, *The Golden Bough: A Study in Magic and Religion* (London: Macmillan, 1911–15). See also D. J. Mulvaney, "Gum Leaves on the Golden Bough: Australia's Paleolithic Survivals Discovered," in *Antiquity and Man: Essays in Honor of Glyn Daniel*, edited by John D. Evans, B. Cunliffe, and C. Renfrew (London: Thames & Hudson, 1981), pp. 52–64.

80. Géza Róheim, *Psychoanalysis and Anthropology: Culture, Personality and the Unconscious* (New York: International Universities Press, 1950), pp. 435, 444.

81. Freud, *Totem and Taboo*, especially part IV.

82. Géza Róheim, *Australian Totemism: A Psycho-analytic Study in Anthropology* (London: George Allen & Unwin, 1925), p. 233.

83. Ibid., pp. 280–81.

84. Ibid., pp. 249, 285.

85. This issue was the central topic of discussion in chapter 5.

86. Róheim, "Psycho-analysis," pp. 16–17.

87. Ibid., p. 99.

88. Ibid., pp. 100–01.

89. This designation is fundamental to Róheim's hypothesis about different forms of religion in these different aboriginal conceptions of space. See Religion later in this chapter.

90. It appears that Róheim is here using the object relationship theory developed by Melanie Klein. He cites Klein as influential in his work with children. See also Object Relations and the Primacy of the Mother later in this chapter.

91. Róheim, *Eternal Ones*, pp. 149–50. See also discussion of increase rites below.

92. Tony Swain has called these "abiding events." *Place for Strangers*, pp. 13–47.

93. Róheim, *Eternal Ones*, p. 149.

94. Ibid., p. 212.

95. Róheim, "Psycho-analysis," p. 45.

96. Ibid., p. 48.

97. Ibid., p. 63.

98. Róheim holds that *andatta*, eagle-down feathers, are parallel to the *tjurunga*, in that the feathers represent the sperm of the ancestors. Géza Róheim, *The Riddle of the Sphinx, or Human Origins*, translated by R. Money-Kyle (London: International Psycho-analytic Library, 1934), pp. 121–22.

99. Róheim, "Psycho-analysis," p 64. See also Róheim, *Riddle of the Sphinx*, p. 121, and Róheim, *Eternal Ones*, p. 155. Birds' down is associated with spirit children in the performance of *alknantama,* the quivering rite that is understood to represent coitus. During the quivering movement, the down used to decorate the body of the ritual performer flies off. This is associated with the spirit children, who flew off the totem ancestors in their performance of the rites. See below for a fuller discussion of *alknantama.*

100. Róheim, "Psycho-analysis," p. 97.

101. The term *tribe*, used by Róheim, has been recently questioned about its adequacy in describing cultural distinctions.

102. Róheim, *Children of the Desert*, p. 31. See pp. 3–32 for Róheim's discussion of kinship.

103. Ibid., pp. 53–64.

104. Róheim, "Psycho-analysis," p. 25.

105. Róheim, *Children of the Desert,* pp. 65–121. Róheim described many play sessions, which were grouped on the basis of whether the play took place at the mission or in the bush (see pp. 80–121).

106. Róheim, *Riddle of the Sphinx*, p. 23.

107. Ibid., pp. 23–24.

108. Ibid., pp. 34–41.

109. Ibid., p. 30. See also Róheim, *Eternal Ones*, pp. 190ff.

110. Róheim, *Riddle of the Sphinx*, p. 40.

111. Ibid., pp. 156–57.

112. Ibid., pp. 57–83.

113. Ibid., pp. 61. See also Róheim, *Eternal Ones*, pp. 190–91, for discussion of the objects of magic in terms of the early distinction made by infants between "good object" (i.e., the nipple) and "bad object."

114. A chapter is devoted to this topic in Róheim's *Children of the Desert*, pp. 122–52.

115. Ibid., pp. 148–49.

116. Róheim collected dozens of *ilpindja* songs and related myths, which he analyzed to extend his understanding of the *alknarintja* and the sexual lives of the aborigines in Central Australia. Ibid., pp. 153–224.

117. Róheim, "Psycho-analysis," pp. 49–56, 93, and Róheim, *Riddle of the Sphinx*, pp. 32–33. See also Róheim, *Eternal Ones*, pp. 165– 66.

118. Róheim, *Eternal Ones*, p. 174. See also the following discussion of *ngallunga* rites.

119. Ibid., p. 176.

120. Róheim, *Riddle of the Sphinx*, pp. 32–33.

121. Róheim, "Psycho-analysis," p. 56.

122. See also Róheim, *Eternal Ones*, p. 155 and *Australian Totemism*, pp. 218–19.

123. Róheim, *Riddle of the Sphinx*, p. 138. It is notable that Róheim believed that mythology, the migration sagas, had been made up through the combination of a number of originally short songs and rites.

124. Ibid., p. 148. See also Róheim, *Eternal Ones*, pp. 249–50.

125. Róheim, *Riddle of the Sphinx*, pp. 105–6.

126. Róheim, "Psycho-analysis," p. 52.

127. Róheim, *Riddle of the Sphinx*, p. 106.

128. Ibid., pp. 106, 121.

129. Róheim, "Psycho-analysis," p. 105.

130. Ibid., p. 56. For a broad comparative study of *tjurungas*, see Róheim, *Eternal Ones*, pp. 84–91.

131. Róheim, *Eternal Ones*, p. 101.

132. Róheim, "Psycho-analysis," pp. 117–18.

133. But, of course, Diane Bell and others have shown that women have their own boards.

134. See Diane Bell, *Daughters of the Dreaming*, rev. ed. (Minneapolis: University of Minnesota Press, [1983] 1993), for love magic as practiced by women. Róheim and others focus on the male practice.

135. Róheim, *Eternal Ones*, pp. 83–84. See also the connection of bullroarers with *alknarintja*.

136. Ibid., chapter 1.

137. Ibid., p. 7.

138. Ibid., p. 9.

139. Ibid., p. 16.

140. Ibid., pp. 208–9.

141. Ibid., p. 67. See pp. 18–66 for examples of dual hero mythology.

142. Ibid., p. 92.

143. Ibid., p. 104.

144. Ibid., p. 130. Footsteps are key in that a person is represented by one's footsteps. Aborigines are well known for being able to identify one another by the imprint of the foot.

145. Róheim, *Riddle of the Sphinx*, pp. 84–85.

146. Ibid., pp. 88–104.

147. In "Psycho-analysis," Róheim did not have the Arrernte name. He quotes W. Baldwin Spencer and Francis J. Gillen *The Arunta: A Study of a Stone Age People* (London: Macmillan, 1927), vol. II, p. 448. They describe an Arrernte ceremony in which "all of the men stood up, opened their veins in their penes by means of sharp flakes or pointed sticks, and, standing opposite to one another, allowed the blood to spurtle out over each other's thighs" (p. 113). See also Róheim, *Eternal Ones*, pp. 155–77, and the myths in "dual heroes," pp. 18–67.

148. In *Eternal Ones,* Róheim notes that initiation serves also as a means of controlling the increasing strengths of the boy. Thus circumcision may appear as a "furious father attacking his son's penis." Róheim cites documented practices of the women, who whip the youth soon before he is initiated (pp. 74–75).

149. Ibid., p. 174.

150. Ibid., pp. 176–77.

151. Róheim, "Psycho-analysis," pp. 72–73 (Róheim's emphasis).

152. Ibid., pp. 95, 113, 119. For another statement of this argument see Róheim, *Riddle of the Sphinx*, pp. 118–19. For a full discussion of *ngallunga* rites, see Róheim, *Eternal Ones*, pp. 155–77.

153. For further discussion of totemic ritual, see Róheim, *Eternal Ones*, pp. 92–101.

154. Ibid., p. 139. Others have noted that among all animal, plant, and other phenomena identified as totems, only some are edible, while some are in fact harmful to human beings. Unfortunately, Róheim does not address this issue.

155. Ibid., p. 146.

156. Ibid., p. 140.

157. Ibid., pp. 153–54.

158. The dependence on Klein is particularly obvious since Róheim associated his discussion of "objects" in the context of a discussion that seems to assume the innateness of aggression, one of Klein's more radical theses.

159. See Róheim, *Eternal Ones*, pp. 150–51, and chapter 5.

160. Discussed above; ibid., pp. 208–9.

161. Róheim has been ignored or criticized for his Freudian views by students of aboriginal women. For example, he is included in François Dussart's review of the works on aboriginal women in her Ph.D. thesis, "Warlpiri Women's Yawulyu Ceremonies: A Forum for Socialization and Innovation," Australian National University, Canbera, 1988), p. 6; but she refers only to his "Women and Their Life in Central Australia," *Journal of the Royal Anthropological Institute* (1933): 207–65.

162. Details of Strehlow's biography are available in chapter 4.

163. Theodor Strehlow, *Aranda Traditions* (Melbourne: Melbourne University Press, 1947), pp. 51 and 69, where Strehlow explains a specific criticism Baldwin Spencer made of his father, Carl Strehlow, concerning regional differences.

164. Ibid., pp. 52–53 and 47–83, has a comparative study of three Arrernte groups designated as Central, Northern, and Western.

165. Ibid., pp. 71–72.

166. Strehlow summarized his field trips in "Aboriginal Language, Religion, and Society in Central Australia," *Australian Territories* 2, no. 1 (1962): pp. 4–11.

167. Strehlow, *Aranda Traditions*, p xviii. See also Strehlow, "Aboriginal Language, Religion, and Society," pp. 4–6.

168. In *Central Australian Religion: Personal Monotheism in a Polytotemic Community* (Adelaide: Australian Association for the Study of Religions, 1978), Strehlow recounts the emu-footed man story and the embryo story, and he mentions the Numbakulla accounts (pp. 11–14).

169. Strehlow, *Songs of Central Australia*, p. 705.

170. Strehlow, *Aranda Traditions*, p. 28.

171. Ibid., pp. 30–33.

172. Theodor Strehlow, "Geography and the Totemic Landscape in Central Australia: A Functional Study," in *Australian Aboriginal Anthropology: Modern Studies in the Social Anthropology of the Australian Aborigines*, edited by R. M. Berndt (Nedlands, Western Australia: Australian Institute of Aboriginal Studies, 1970), pp. 92, 133–35.

173. Strehlow, *Aranda Traditions*, pp. 86–91.

174. Ibid., pp. 94–95.

175. See the discussion of how unity is achieved in this situation in Strehlow's *Central Australian Religion*, pp. 39–44.

176. Strehlow, *Aranda Traditions*, pp. 139–61, and Strehlow, "Totemic Landscape," pp. 95–101. In *Songs of Central Australia*, pp. 542–93, Strehlow discusses Arrernte songs that describe and celebrate the *pmara kutata*.

177. See Strehlow, "Culture, Social Structure, and Environment in Aboriginal Central Australia," in *Aboriginal Man in Australia: Essays in Honor of Emeritus Professor A P. Elkin*, edited by Ronald M. Berndt and Catherine H. Berndt (Sydney: Angus & Robertson, 1965), pp. 121–45.

178. See, for example, Strehlow's analysis of "semi-sacred" songs in *Songs of Central Australia*, pp. 622–36.

179. Strehlow, *Central Australian Religion*, pp. 38–39. As a "digression" while discussing men's initiation rites, Strehlow made further comments on women's religion in *Songs of Central Australia*, pp. 392–95. Strehlow discussed women's songs, which he considered "a closed book" (pp. 647–53). This brief discussion amounts to a summary of all Strehlow's knowledge about women's religion.

180. Strehlow, *Songs of Central Australia*, pp. 492–94.

181. Ibid., p. 594.

182. Strehlow, *Central Australian Religion*, pp. 20–26. See also *Songs of Central Australia*, pp. 596–99 where Strehlow elaborates on the two-soul doctrine.

183. Strehlow, *Songs of Central Australia*, p. 598.

184. Ibid., p. 244.

185. Ibid., p. 332.

186. Ibid., p. 334.

187. Strehlow, "Totemic Landscape," p. 109.

188. Ibid., p. 111.

189. Strehlow was extensively interested in the punishment for ritual and social crimes. Ibid., pp. 112–21.

190. Ibid., pp. 123–28.

191. Ibid., p. 123.

192. Ibid., pp. 116–19.

193. Strehlow notes that other Arrernte areas have stories about sky-dwelling beings, such as the Sun, Moon, Evening Star, and Ntjikantja brothers. See *Songs of Central Australia*, pp. 620–21.

194. See above and chapter 5.

195. Strehlow, *Songs of Central Australia*, pp. 613–14.

196. Ibid., p. 616. Interestingly, Strehlow presented an excerpt from a tape recording made in 1949 of a conversation between two aborigines that supports his interpretation (see pp. 616–17).

197. Ibid., p. 618.

198. Ibid., p. 620.

199. Strehlow, "Totemic Landscape," p. 94.

200. Although Strehlow holds that a separate narrative is required to elucidate the lyrics of the songs. See the following section.

201. Strehlow, *Aranda Traditions*, p. 4.

202. Ibid., p. 11.

203. Ibid., p. 13. Strehlow provides examples of *tjilpa* stories that establish the acts of hostility committed by the sons against their fathers.

204. Ibid., pp. 33–35.

205. Ibid., pp. 1–46.

206. It must be remembered that Spencer and Gillen recorded no songs, probably because they did not know the Arrernte language and relied on interpreters who were not initiated men. Strehlow described their informants in *Songs of Central Australia*, p. xxxiii, n. 23.

207. Strehlow went to considerable lengths to discuss and analyze the competence and reliability of his informants, particularly as set against his severe criticism of Spencer and Gillen's informants. Ibid., pp. xxxv–xxxvii.

208. Ibid., pp. 6–9.

209. Ibid., p. xiii.

210. Ibid., p. xv.

211. Ibid., p. 65.

212. Ibid., p. 127.

213. Ibid., p. 39.

214. Ibid., p. 122.

215. Ibid., pp. 382–86.

216. Ibid., pp. 126, 382.

217. Ibid., p. 146.

218. Ibid., p. 146. Strehlow effectively demonstrated the relationship between myth and song through an extensive presentation of the Emianga myth, interwoven with its corresponding songs, and followed by a comparative analysis (see pp. 147–63).

219. Ibid., pp. 542–93.

220. Ibid., pp. 262–65.

221. Ibid., pp. 273–76.

222. Ibid., pp. 277–327.

223. Ibid., pp. 337, 349–91. Strehlow wanted to demonstrate that while the Arrernte people are commonly understood to have a culture at the evolutionary stage of magic, which he did not deny, they are also engaged in truly religious forms of action. He made his case by emphasizing their attitude of commemoration and worship. Notably, this discussion, probably constructed in the mid-twentieth century, was rather out of step with the tenor of academic beliefs.

224. Ibid., pp. 443–61, described a number of rain and other weather-related rites. Notable among these descriptions is the extent to which blood is shed in association with rain ceremonies. To Strehlow's knowledge, more blood is used—commonly streaming through a cut in an arm vein—in these rites than in any others.

225. Ibid., pp. 462–541. Interestingly, Strehlow offered extensive comment about the sexual practices of the aborigines. He believed that the interest in sexual matters by such ethnographers as Róheim encouraged the aborigines to concoct materials in order to be compensated for them. There is no restriction or secrecy about sexual matters that there is on so many other aspects of culture. Strehlow wrote: "In Dr. Róheim's case, for instance, I was assured that some of his native informants had gone to a great deal of trouble in thinking out fresh matter in order to please the Freudian tastes of their erudite investigator" (p. 464).

226. Ibid., p. 440.

227. Ibid., pp. 392–417.

228. A fascinating summary account of initiation as practiced in the Hermannsburg area through the 1960s and beyond, with comments on the impact of traditional initiation rites on the prospects for Christianity, is found in Theodor Strehlow, "Central Australian Man-making Ceremonies: With Special Reference to Hermannsburg, Northern Territory," *The Lutheran*, April 10, 1978, pp. 150–55.

229. Strehlow, *Aranda Traditions*, pp. 96–100. In *Songs of Central Austrailia*, Strehlow identified the five initiation ceremonies as *alkiraka iwuma* ("to toss up to the sky"), circumcision, subincision, head biting and smoking, and initiation on the *ingkura* ground. Some groups include nail extraction as another ceremony (see pp. 395–417 for a fuller description of these rites).

230. Strehlow, "Totemic Landscape," p. 102. Here Strehlow did not clearly distinguish between the increase rites and the initiation rites.

231. Strehlow, *Aranda Traditions*, pp. 100–11.

232. Ibid., pp. 84–86. Strehlow listed eleven referents that may be identified by the term *tjurunga*.

233. Ibid., p. 17.
234. Ibid., p. 116.
235. Ibid., pp. 119–21.
236. Ibid., pp. 160–63.
237. Ibid., p. 22.
238. Ibid., pp. 131–32.
239. Ibid., pp. 54–56.
240. Ibid., pp. 73–74.
241. Ibid., p. 93.
242. Strehlow, *Central Australian Religion*, p. 29.
243. Strehlow, *Songs of Central Austrailia*, p. 349. Strehlow analyzes commemorative songs (pp. 349–91).
244. Ibid., p. 375. Recall that this quivering rite was considered fundamental by Róheim.
245. Strehlow presented a detailed description, including the actions and song texts, of an *ilbalintja* (bandicoot) cycle he observed in 1933. It took two months to perform and included some forty separate acts. Ibid., pp. 352–78.
246. Strehlow, *Aranda Traditions*, pp. 56–58.
247. Ibid., p. 76.
248. Ibid., p. 80. Strehlow held that in 1933 at Horseshoe Bend, he had evidence that the last two men to undergo this approach to initiation—thus in his view the last incarnations of the Ntjikantja brothers—had died some years before. By that time the youths of the Southern Arrernte were initiated in the same manner as their counterparts to the north.
249. Ibid., p. 78.
250. Strehlow, *Central Australian Religion*, p. 27.
251. Strehlow, *Songs of Central Australia*, p. 315, see pp. 277–327 for an extensive analysis of increase songs.
252. Strehlow, *Aranda Traditions*, p. 77.
253. Ibid., p. 23.
254. Ibid., pp. 22–25.
255. Ibid., p. 74.
256. Ibid., p. 74.
257. Ibid., pp. 67–68.
258. Ibid., pp. 42–45.
259. Strehlow, *Central Australian Religion*, p. 35.
260. Ibid., p. 35. See also Strehlow, *Aranda Traditions*, p. 43, and Strehlow, *Songs of Central Australia*, pp. 599–621.
261. Strehlow, *Songs of Central Australia*, p. 621.
262. Ibid., pp. 601–4.
263. Ibid., pp. 607–11.
264. See Roy Wagner, *The Invention of Culture* (Englewood Cliffs, N. J.: Prentice Hall, 1975).

Notes to Chapter 7

1. See Roland Barthes, "From work to Text," in *Textual Strategies: Perspectives in Post-structuralist Criticism,* edited by Josué V. Harari (Ithaca, N.Y.: Cornell University Press, 1979), pp. 73–81.
2. Mircea Eliade, *Australian Religions: An Introduction* (Ithaca, NY: Cornell University Press, 1973), p 42.

3. See the final chapter, "The Terror of History" in Mircea Eliade, *Cosmos and History: Myth of the Eternal Return*, translated by Willard Trask (Princeton, N.J.: Princeton University Press, 1954).

4. The source Eliade cited for his Numbakulla example, W. Baldwin Spencer and Francis J. Gillen's book *The Arunta* is subtitled *A Study of a Stone Age People*. (London: Macmillan, 1927).

5. Eliade here reveals his bias about the Australian landscape that he never saw.

6. Eliade, *Australian Religions*, p 42.

7. Ibid., pp. 42–43.

8. Ibid.

9. Ibid., p. 43 (Eliade's emphasis).

10. Ibid., pp. 51–52.

11. Ibid., p. 53.

12. See chapter 2 for this critical analysis.

13. This explosive expansion of the study of religion beyond seminaries was stimulated by the U.S. Supreme Court ruling that distinguished between teaching religion and teaching *about* religion. This distinction allowed state-supported schools to legally establish departments and courses in religion. Eliade's neutral-sounding language of place offered important terminology for this nontheological teaching about religions.

14. I mean nonscientific in the sense in which conclusions arise from certain unchallenged beliefs rather than from carefully argued and negotiated hypotheses, as well as in the sense that his simulations or concoctions of religious cultures are not grounded in eventual comparisons of scholar-independent reality. Such an approach, taken in order to ensure that the meaning in the world is founded on an other-worldly reality (and Eliade's approach often appears to be grounded here), should also be characterized as "religious."

15. Jonathan Z. Smith, "Map Is Not Territory," in *Map Is Not Territory: Studies in the History of Religions* (Leiden: E. J. Brill, 1978), pp. 290–91.

16. Jonathan Z. Smith, *Imagining Religion: From Babylon to Jonestown* (Chicago: University of Chicago Press, 1982), p. xi.

17. Ibid.

18. Ibid.

19. Jonathan Z. Smith, "The Influence of Symbols on Social Change," in *Map Is Not Territory*, p. 141.

20. Smith, "Map Is Not Territory," pp 308–9.

21. Ibid., p. 294.

22. Ibid., p. 309.

23. Ibid.

24. Ibid., p. 299. For a similar statement see Jonathan Z. Smith, "Good News Is No News," Aretalogy and Gospel," *Map Is Not Territory*, pp. 205–6.

25. Jonathan Z. Smith "The Wobbling Pivot," in *Map Is Not Territory*, p. 97. Smith borrows this phrase from Kenneth Burke.

26. Smith, "Map Is Not Territory," p. 300. For a very similar passage see Smith, "Good News Is No News," pp. 205–6.

27. Jonathan Z. Smith, *To Take Place: Toward Theory in Ritual* (Chicago: University of Chicago Press, 1987), p. 63 (Smith's emphasis).

28. Jonathan Z. Smith, "The Bare Facts of Ritual," in *Imagining Religion*, p. 54.

29. Smith, *To Take Place*, p. 6, summarizes these elements as follows:

1. The pole was fashioned by Numbakulla from a gum tree.
2. After anointing the pole with blood, Numbakulla climbed up the pole and disappeared into the sky.
3. The pole is a "cosmic axis."
4. Following Numbakulla's withdrawal, the pole plays a ritual role.
5. The pole is always carried about by the ancestors in their wanderings.
6. The ancestors determine the direction in which they travel by the direction toward which the pole bends.
7. The pole is broken by accident.
8. The ancestors die because the pole has broken.
9. This is because the breaking of the pole is like "the end of the world."

30. For Smith's detailed critique, see ibid., pp. 125–27, n. 19.

31. Ibid., p. 9.

32. Ibid.

33. I am relying here on the reader's familiarity with the analysis of this text in chapter 1.

34. Smith, *To Take Place*, p. 124, n. 15.

35. Ibid., p. 5.

36. Ibid.

37. Ibid.

38. Eliade summaries these incidents in a single phrase: "seemingly endless detail of wanderings of the first Achilpa Ancestors after the disappearance of Numbakulla."

39. Smith, *To Take Place*, p. 6.

40. Ibid., p. 7.

41. Ibid., p. 8.

42. Ibid., p. 9.

43. Ibid., p. 10.

44. Ibid., p. 11.

45. Smith describes other significant themes and issues raised by his analysis of the text in an extended footnote. Ibid., pp. 128–30, n. 31.

46. Ibid., p. 10.

47. Ibid., p. 16.

48. Ibid., p. 17.

49. Ibid., p. 18.

50. Ibid., p. 22.

51. It is interesting that Smith did not make more of the information indicating that Charlie Cooper had concocted the "prologue" of this story for Spencer's benefit. Although Smith notes this (ibid., n. 15), had he taken it seriously he could have dismissed this part of the text as bogus or a joke. While the prologue might be a text, documenting "Arrernte individual practices as ethnographic informants" and, therefore, be "saved" as relevant to the study of Arrernte culture and history, this limited significance of the text should be clearly stated. What interests me is what appears to be the sacrosanctity of any text. Somehow, despite much evidence that many documents are not what they appear to be, we never seem to want to reject any text. However hyperreal or fallacious, anything presented as text makes an almost overwhelming claim to be real, as demonstrated by the attention given to the works of Casteneda and even (though I resist even mentioning her name because of the very principle I am discussing) Marlo Morgan (you will not find her in the bibliography).

52. The outline presentational form would support the latter.

53. The results of this analysis are summarized in table 1. Further, to show the relationship between Gillen's journal account and that edited by Spencer for W. Baldwin Spencer and Francis J. Gillen, *The Native Tribes of Central Australia* (London: Macmillan, 1899), I have juxtaposed both versions of the accounts related to the third group, that is, the group whose journey concludes with the broken pole and the ancestor's death.

54. My sources are Spencer and Gillen's *Native Tribes*; Spencer and Gillen's *Arunta*; and Gillen's unpublished journals, Barr Smith Library, University of Adelaide, South Australia.

55. While I made this determination on both the Spencer and Gillen published sources and Gillen's unpublished journals (the latter of which Smith did not examine), I was unable to identify ninety-four places as reported by Smith.

56. See chapter 6 for a description of the four-class social system.

57. This, of course, correlates with the principal actions of the Arrernte at these locations; it is the interactions performed by those whose totem group storytracks intersect at a specific location.

58. Since the names of places are given in the Arrernte language, it is possible that, were the meanings of the place names translated, they would correspond with significant events. Géza Róheim indicated such a correspondence in *The Eternal Ones of the Dream: Psychoanalytic Interpretation of Australian Myth and Ritual* (New York: International Universities Press, 1945), pp. 210–13. However, for this analysis it is irrelevant because no one has provided any indication of the meanings of these place names and there is no evidence, other than Róheim's study, that they correspond with events. Further, the descriptions of the events found in the outline myths in *Native Tribes* are inadequate in detail to correlate event to place.

59. Ulir-ulira means "where blood flows like a river." Ungwurna-la-warika means "where bone is struck" (Gillen has it as "where the man was struck by the bone"). Alla, according to Spencer but not so indicated in Gillen's journal, means "the nose"; Spencer writes (again without support from Gillen) that it designates "a sharply outlined hill." Okinchalanina is referred to by Gillen, though not carried to the published version by Spencer, as "the necklace." Spencer writes that Lilpuririka "means running like a creek," though Gillen did not record this. Gillen notes (Spencer did not use this information) that Unjiacherta "means the place of the Unjiamba men." Urichipma means "place of pitchis."

60. *Erkincha* is a sexually transmitted disease that is often referred to in the Tjilpa stories.

61. Smith, *To Take Place*, p. 7.

62. Ibid., p. 7.

63. Incidents 78 and 79; ibid.

64. Ibid., p. 8.

65. Ibid., p. 10.

66. It appears that on this point Smith may have been significantly influenced by Róheim, whom he quotes to corroborate the interpretation that in the Arrernten view "the environment is made out of man's activity." In *Eternal Ones of the Dream* (pp. 210–11), Róheim indicates that place names are derived from ancestral events as told in myths, and he supports this interpretation by offering examples from a number of myths. His evidence often amounts to the translations of place names that have explicit sexual and genital associations. Some examples, all of which come from myths Róheim collected are illustrative:

> In a Pitjentara wildcat myth of Kikinkura (Mulga-seed) a place is called "Inflate the nose" because an angry old man inflated his nose there; a tree marks the spot. Two stones were originally two black iguana men. A place is called "Throws it"

(Wanpurangu) because a ceremonial spear was thrown there. Where a *tingari* ceremonial spear was put up, a soakage arose. The place where a fence was made is called "Fence". . . . In a Ngatatara version of the Testicles and Semen myth, in which the heroes take out their teeth the place is called "Teeth". They put on a pubic tassel for the first time: the place is called "Pubic Tassel". They pulled their testicles out, the place is called "Testicles". Then they looked at their penes and the place is called "Penis". Where they defecated the place is called "Excrement", where they urinated it is called "Urine". (p. 212)

Róheim did not develop or replicate this correlation between action in the landscape and place names elsewhere in his work that I have found.

In materials that Smith did not cite, there is evidence for other strong correlations between myths and "names." Theodor Strehlow, *Songs of Central Australia* (Sydney: Angus & Robertson, 1971), indicates that totemic ancestors "'named' various objects and living things encountered by them in order to gain magical control over them; hence each 'name' or verse tends to be a self-contained unit. But while 'magic' of this sort can be effective only if it is combined with the real 'name' of the object, it is necessary for the member of the totemic clan concerned to know also the correct symbolic action with which the singing of the verse had originally been associated" (p. 146). Strehlow confirms Smith's interpretation of the ancestral narratives as itineraries: "It [the story] lists all the places he [the totemic ancestor] visits in his wanderings and lays down the route of his travels with high geographical accuracy" (p. 147).

Through a comparison of myth with corresponding sets of song, Strehlow illuminates much that is distinctive of myth and song. He understands that place names, which appear extensively as itineraries in myths, are so important because of the correlation between geographical location and personal identity: "Every man's genealogy has, as it were, been imprinted into the countryside; and the myth which mentions the name of his own conception site may be regarded as the birth certificate which entitles him to his share of the religious ceremonies of his group, and as one of the legal documents which define his social standing in his own community" (ibid., p. 158). Whereas myths mention place names and describe in detail the actions of the ancestors at each place, the place names rarely occur in songs; yet it is in the songs that places are described in scenic detail. "The *tjurunga retnja*, the 'secret name', of a place is very frequently a couplet which describes the scenic setting of the sacred site without actually naming it" (p. 159).

Although it has yet to be established, in Arrernten mythology there may be a significant relationship between place names and their etiology. Certainly place names are centrally important to ancestral narratives. However, Smith's statement about the generative element of myth cannot be established on the basis of evidence drawn from the myth he analyzes, and I find no evidence that the statement might be founded in any extant body of Arrernte mythology.

67. Smith, *To Take Place*, p. 6.

68. As indicated in the Strehlow Research Center exhibit in Alice Springs. See chapter 5 for this account.

69. Eliade, *Cosmos and History*, p. 98.

70. Jonathan Z. Smith offers a major critique of "the unique" in *Drudgery Divine: On the Comparison of Early Christianities and the Religions of Late Antiquity* (Chicago: University of Chicago Press, 1990), chap. 2.

71. George Lakoff and Mark Johnson, *Metaphors We Live by* (Chicago: University of Chicago Press, 1980).

72. Smith, "Map Is Not Territory," p. 309.

73. George Lakoff, *Women, Fire, and Dangerous Things* (Chicago: University of Chicago Press, 1987).

74. Ibid., p. 9.

75. If there is any doubt that Christianity has served, though occasionally tacitly, as the "best example" of religion, one need only read Walter H. Capps, *Religious Studies: The Making of a Discipline* (Minneapolis: Fortress Press, 1995). This book is remarkable in demonstrating how the academic study of religion has been almost single-mindedly Christian in its development.

76. Notably, a certain corner of the academic study of religion has recently shifted away from the traditional, more theological categories to that of "place." One might suppose that this new emphasis is a strategy designed to move away from the confines of the ideas incumbent on classical category theory. Yet, little can be gained in this endeavor unless it is seen that classical category theory is inseparable from the very ideas that scholars wish to abandon. While "place" appears less dependent on these ideas—it certainly has the appearance of theological and historical neutrality—it nonetheless serves as a way of describing containers into which sets of objects with common distinctive characteristics may be sorted. Smith's locative and utopian designations of place are such containers. Although Smith has strongly rejected the ubiquity of center as designating the religious place, the locative category corresponds closely with the ideas that accompany the center. A prototype category theory would, I believe, if acknowledged and applied in terms of the effect on assumptions, shift the academic study of religion away from place containers toward relational dynamics. The attempt to fit objects into containers would be far less interesting than appreciating how subjects interrelate. This does not at all amount to a rejection of all categories; rather, it is to see that within categories (such as religion) members of the category reveal different profiles from a variety of perspectives. From some perspectives they hide attributes seen from alternative perspectives.

77. The following is a restatement and development of the discussion of comparison in chapter 2.

78. Smith, *Drudgery Divine*, p. 52 (Smith's emphasis).

79. Jonathan Z. Smith, "In Comparison a Magic Dwells," in *Imagining Religion*, p. 35.

80. Jacques Derrida, "Structure, Sign, and Play in the Discourse of the Human Sciences," in *The Languages of Criticism and the Sciences of Man*, edited by Richard Macksey and Eugenio Donato (Baltimore: Johns Hopkins Press, 1970), p. 265.

81. Smith, "In Comparison a Magic Dwells," p. 35. See also Fritz John Porter Poole, "Metaphors and Maps: Towards Comparison in the Anthropology of Religion," *Journal of the American Academy of Religion* 54(1968): especially p. 417. Poole's essay, as one of the few technical discussions of comparison, is well worth reading carefully. He gives extensive consideration to Smith's contributions. For further discussion, Smith, *Drudgery Divine*, especially chap. 2; Jonathan Z. Smith, "*Adde Parvum Parvo Magnus Acervus Erit*," in *Map Is Not Territory*, pp. 240–64; and Jonathan Z. Smith, "What a Difference a Difference Makes," in *"To See Ourselves as Others See Us": Christians, Jews, "Others" in Late Antiquity*, edited by Jacob Neusner and Ernest S. Frerichs (Chico, Calif.: Scholars Press, 1985), pp. 3–48.

82. Smith, *Drudgery Divine*, p. 53.

83. In more technical terms, as Smith (ibid., p. 51) shows:

> The statement '*x* resembles *y*' is logically incomplete for what is being asserted is not a question of the classification of species *x* and *y* as instances of a common ge-

> nus, but rather a suppressed multi-term statement of analogy and difference capable of being properly expressed in formulations such as:
>
> '*x* resembles *y* more than *z* with respect to . . .'
>
> or
>
> '*x* resembles *y* more than *w* resembles *z* with respect to. . . .'
>
> That is to say, the statement of comparison is never dyadic, but always triadic; there is always an implicit 'more than', and there is always a 'with respect to'. In the case of an academic comparison, the 'with respect to' is most frequently the scholar's interest. . . .

Storytracking embraces the level of self-consciousness that acknowledges that the scholar determines all the elements of comparison by choosing to focus on *x*, *y*, *z*, and so on, and as Smith shows, it is the scholar's values that supply the property or value (the intersecting point) that determines the "with respect to."

84. I do not think fortuity has been adequately acknowledged. Despite the systematicity implied by the scientific methods of academia, chance is ever present. Fortunately, we can never predict what impact the aleatory aspect of the next event encountered will have on what we do. Scholarship only ceases to be vital when we inure ourselves to surprise.

85. Lakoff's prototype category theory significantly affects the potential effectiveness of comparison. One way of appreciating prototype category theory, in contrast with the assumptions underlying classical category theory, is that it enhances our understanding of the ways in which differences may occur within the set that constitutes a category.

86. See for example, Erik H. Erikson, "Play and Actuality," in *Play and Development*, edited by Maria W. Piers (New York: Norton, 1972), pp. 127–167; and Jean Piaget, "Explanation of Play," *Play, Dreams and Imitation in Childhood*, translated by C. Gattegno and F. M. Hodgson (New York: Norton, 1962), pp. 147–68.

87. Notably, however, the multiperspectivality of storytracking obtains the criteria set forth by Lakoff, *Women, Fire, and Dangerous Things*, p. 301, for a revised understanding of objectivity:

> Objectivity consists in two things:
>
> First, putting aside one's own point of view and looking at a situation from other points of view—as many as possible.
>
> Second, being able to distinguish what is directly meaningful—basic level and image-schematic concepts—from concepts that are indirectly meaningful.
>
> Being objective therefore requires:
>
> - knowing that one has a point of view, not merely a set of beliefs but a specific conceptual system in which beliefs are framed
> - knowing what one's point of view is, including what one's conceptual system is like
> - knowing other relevant points of view and being able to use the conceptual systems in which they are framed
> - being able to assess a situation from other points of view, using other conceptual systems
> - being able to distinguish concepts that are relatively stable and well-defined, given the general nature of the human organism and our environment . . . from those concepts that vary with human purposes and modes of indirect understanding.

88. Admittedly this is my creative interpretation of Sartre developed on hints about a possible "spirit of play" in his discussion of "doing" and "having" (pp. 734–65) as contrasted

with what he called the "spirit of seriousness" (p. 796). See Jean-Paul Sartre, *Being and Nothingness: A Phenomenological Essay on Ontology*, translated by Hazel E. Barnes (New York: Washington Square Press, 1956).

89. Of course, neither has this study, despite the attention given to trying to find the Arrernte. I have wanted to rectify the exclusion of the Arrernte by the extensive presentations of ethnography in chapter 6.

Notes to Chapter 8

1. Jean Baudrillard, *Simulacra and Simulation*, translated by Sheila Faria Glaser (Ann Arbor: University of Michigan Press, 1994), pp. 6–7.

2. Tomoko Masuzawa, *In Search of Dreamtime: The Quest for the Origin of Religion* (Chicago: University of Chicago Press, 1993), powerfully demonstrates this point in "recovery" analysis of the origination concerns of Durkheim, Müller, and Freud.

3. The bridge metaphor—representing the connection between interpreter and subject interpreted—with which I began this work and to which I have occasionally returned, was developed by Wendy Doniger [O'Flaherty] in *Other People's Myths: The Cave of Echoes* (New York: Macmillan, 1988). She tells the well-known story of Rabbi Isaac of Cracow, who must follow his dream of a treasure beneath a distant bridge to learn of the treasure in his own home. She believes that "myths may function as the bridges between foreign cultures." In a twist and shift of metaphors, she likens this "network of bridges" to "a roundhouse" and engages in a discussion (though based on a railroad metaphor) remarkably similar to storytracking and storytrack crossings. The roundhouse is, of course, "the place where all the tracks of a railway meet so that the trains may pass from any one track to any other. The mythical roundhouse is the place where we can move from the track of one person's reality to another's, passing through the myth that expresses them all" (p. 163). Doniger seems to believe that myth may actually and effectively bridge the gap between cultures, apparently not caring to problematize the radical separation of interpreter and subject, as I believe is necessary. Given careful self-reflectiveness, this problematization might be an implication of Doniger's further criticism and revision of essentialism:

> The people who live in the nonexistent roundhouse that they themselves construct are the exponents of a kind of absolutism or essentialism, who believe that all the myths of the world are not only somehow related (which is a belief that I share) but somehow the same myth (a belief against which I have argued in this book). The belief in the interconnection between myths is one I find acceptable only in a rather sharply modified version: there is indeed a common thread running through the great myths of the world, and it does arise out of the common experience of humankind. But the meaning of that experience, and therefore the meaning of the myth, changes constantly across the barriers of time and space. (p. 163)

Most significant is Doniger's view of the roundhouse as the place where differences in kind may be negotiated.

4. George Lakoff presents a version of this argument in *Women, Fire, and Dangerous Things*, (Chicago: University of Chicago Press, 1987), pp. 301–2.

5. I do not here intend anything like a process of seeking or achieving any sense of full being or full presence. I have more in mind the notion that each thing I do is only a supplement, in a Derridian sense, to what I am always becoming. See Jacques Derrida, "The Supple-

ment of Copula: Philosophy before Linguistics," in *Textual Strategies: Perspectives in Post-structuralist Criticism,* edited by Josué Harari (Ithaca, N.Y.: Cornell University Press, 1979), pp. 33–35.

6. That I identify myself with a community (though physically dispersed and intellectually and culturally diverse) is the principal reason for believing that these comments should be of any interest to others.

References

Balint, Michael. "Géza Róheim: 1891–1953." *International Journal of Psycho-analysis* 35 (1954): 434–36.

Barthes, Roland. "From Work to Text." In *Textual Strategies: Perspectives in Post-structuralist Criticism.* Edited by Josué V. Harari, pp. 73–81. Ithaca, N.Y.: Cornell University Press, 1979.

Baudrillard, Jean. *Simulacra and Simulation.* Translated by Sheila Faria Glaser. Ann Arbor: University of Michigan Press, 1994.

Bell, Diane. *Daughters of the Dreaming*, rev. ed. Minneapolis: University of Minnesota Press, [1983] 1993.

Blackwell, Doris, and Douglas Lockwood. *Alice on the Line.* Adelaide: Griffin Press, [1965] 1993.

Blainey, Geoffrey. *The Rush That Never Ended: A History of Australian Mining.* Melbourne: Melbourne University Press, 1963.

Brown, Shirley. *My Alice: A Personal History of Alice Springs.* Alice Springs: Inday Printing for Shirley Brown, 1991.

Capps, Walter H. *Religious Studies: The Making of a Discipline.* Minneapolis: Fortress Press, 1995.

Cassirer, Ernst. *An Essay on Man.* New Haven, Conn: Yale University Press, 1944.

_________. *The Philosophy of Symbolic Forms.* Translated by R. Manheim. New Haven, Conn.: Yale University Press, 1955.

Charlesworth, Max. "Australian Aboriginal Religion in a Comparative Context." *Sophia (Australia)* 26 (1987): 50–57.

Chodorow, Nancy. *The Reproduction of Mothering.* Berkeley: University of California Press, 1978.

Christen, Kimberly A. "'We Mob Gotta Hold Up This Country:' Warumungu Women's Ritual Responsibility. MA Thesis. University of Colorado, Boulder, 1996.

Classen, Constance. *Worlds of Sense: Exploring the Senses in History and across Cultures.* New York: Routledge, 1993.

Clifford, James, and George E. Marcus (eds.). *Writing Culture: The Poetics and Politics of Ethnography*. Berkeley: University of California Press, 1986.

Clune, Frank. *Overland Telegraph: The Story of a Great Australian Achievement and the Link between Adelaide and Port Darwin*. Sydney: Angus & Robertson, 1955.

Coote, Errol. *Hell's Airport: The Key to Lasseter's Gold Reef*. Sydney: Peterman Press, 1934.

Crease, Robert P. *The Play of Nature: Experimentation as Performance*. Bloomington: University of Indiana Press, 1993.

Derrida, Jacques "Structure, Sign, and Play in the Discourse of the Human Sciences. In *The Languages of Criticism and the Sciences of Man*. Edited by Richard Macksey and Eugenio Donato, pp. 247–65. Baltimore: Johns Hopkins Press, 1970.

________."The Supplement of Copula: Philosophy before Linguistics." In *Textual Strategies: Perspectives in Post-structuralist Criticism*. Edited by Josué Harari, pp. 82–120. Ithaca, N.Y.: Cornell University Press, 1979.

Dinnerstein, Dorothy. *The Mermaid and the Minotaur: Sexual Arrangements and Human Malaise*. New York: Harper & Row, 1976.

Doniger [O'Flaherty], Wendy. *Other Peoples' Myths: The Cave of Echoes*. New York: Macmillan, 1988.

Duncan, Ross. *The Northern Territory Pastoral Industry, 1863–1910*. Melbourne: Melbourne University Press, 1967.

Durkheim, Émile. *Elementary Forms of Religious Life*. Translated by Joseph Ward Swain. New York: Free Press, [1915] 1965.

Dussart, François. "Warlpiri Women's Yawulyu Ceremonies: A Forum for Socialization and Innovation." Ph.D. Thesis. Australian National University, Canberra, 1988.

Eliade, Mircea. *Australian Religions: An Introduction*. Ithaca, N.Y.: Cornell University Press, 1967.

________. *Cosmos and History: Myth of the Eternal Return*. Translated by Willard Track. Princeton, N.J.: Princeton University Press, 1954.

________. *Occultism, Witchcraft and Contemporary Fashions*. Chicago: University of Chicago Press, 1976.

________. *The Sacred and the Profane*. New York: Harper & Row, [1957] 1959.

________. *Zalmoxis: The Vanishing God*. Chicago: University of Chicago Press, 1972.

Elkin, A. P. *The Australian Aborigines*. Garden City, N.Y.: Doubleday, 1964.

Erikson, Erik H. "Play and Actuality." In *Play and development.* Edited by Maria W. Piers, pp. 127–67. New York: Norton, 1972.

Favenc, Ernest. *The Explorers of Australia and Their Lifework*. Christchurch, NZ: Whitcombe & Tombs, 1908.

Foster, Susan. *Reading Dancing: Bodies and Subjects in Contemporary American Dance*. Berkeley: University of California Press, 1986.

Foucault, Michel. "Nietzsche, Genealogy, History." In *The Foucault Reader*. Edited by Paul Rabinow, pp. 76–100. New York: Pantheon Books, 1984.

Frazer, James George. *The Golden Bough: A Study in Magic and Religion*. London, Macmillan 1890, vols. I–II; 2d ed., London, Macmillan 1900, vols I–III; 3d ed., London, Macmillan 1911–15, vols. I–XII.

________. "Observations on Central Australian Totemism." *Journal of the Anthropological Institute of Great Britain and Ireland* 28 (1899): 281–86.

________. "On Some Ceremonies of the Central Australian Tribes." In *Report of the Eighth Meeting of the Australiasian Association for the Advancement of Science Held at Melbourne, Victoria,*

1900. Edited by T. S. Hall, pp. 312–21. Melbourne: Australiasian Association for the Advancement of Science, 1901.

Freud, Sigmund. *From the History of an Infantile Neurosis. The Standard Edition of the Complete Psychological Works of Sigmund Freud.* Translated by James Strauchey, no. 17. London: Hogarth Press [for] the Institute of Psychoanalysis, 1953–74.

———. *A Phylogenetic Fantasy: Overview of the Transference Neuroses.* Edited by Ilse Grubrich-Simitis. Translated by Axel Hoffer and Peter T. Hoffer. Cambridge, Mass: Harvard University Press, 1987.

———. *Totem and Taboo: Some Points of Agreement between the Mental Lives of Savages and Neurotics.* Translated by James Strauchy. New York: Norton, 1913.

Gill, Sam D. *Beyond 'the Primitive': The Religions of Nonliterate Peoples.* Englewood Cliffs, N.J.: Prentice Hall, 1982.

———. *Mother Earth: An American Story.* Chicago: University of Chicago Press, 1987.

Gillen, Francis J. Unpublished journals. Barr Smith Library, University of Adelaide, South Australia.

———. "Magic amongst the Natives of Central Australia." In *Report of the Eighth Meeting of the Australiasian Association for the Advancement of Science Held at Melbourne, Victoria, 1900.* Edited by T. S. Hall, pp. 109–23. Melbourne: Australiasian Association for the Advancement of Science, 1901.

———. "Notes on Some Manners and Customs of the Aborigines of the McDonnell Ranges Belonging to the Arunta Tribe." In *Report on the Work of the Horn Scientific Expedition to Central Australia.* Edited by Baldwin Spencer, pp. 162–85. London: Dulau, 1896.

Glainey, Geoffrey. *The Rush That Never Ended: A History of Australian Mining.* Melbourne: Melbourne University Press, 1963.

Goodman, Nelson. *Language of Art.* 2nd ed. Indianapolis: Hackett, 1976.

———. *Ways of Worldmaking.* Indianapolis: Hackett, 1978.

Haitt, L. R. "Totemism Tomorrow: The Future of an Illusion." *Mankind* 7, no. 2 (1969): 83–93.

Harari, Josué V. (ed.). *Textual Strategies: Perspectives in Post-structuralist Criticism.* Ithaca, N.Y.: Cornell University Press, 1979.

Hardman, William (ed.). *The Journals of John McDouall Stuart.* London: Saunders, Otley, & Co., 1864.

Harris, John W. *Northern Territory Pidgins and the Origin of Kriol.* Pacific Linguistic Series C, no. 89. Canberra: Australian National University, 1986.

Hartman, George W. *Gestalt Psychology: A Survey of Facts and Principles.* New York: Ronald Press, 1935.

Hartwig, M. C. "The Progress of White Settlement in the Alice Springs District and Its Effects upon the Aboriginal Inhabitants, 1860–1894." Ph.D. thesis, University of Adelaide, 1965.

Hawking, Stephen. *A Brief History of Time: From the Big Bang to Black Holes.* New York: Bantam Books, 1988.

Henderson, John, and Veronica Dobson. *Eastern and Central Arrernte to English Dictionary.* Alice Springs: IAD Press, 1994.

Herzfeld, M. *Poetics of Manhood.* Princeton, N.J.: Princeton University Press, 1985.

Hodger, Margaret T. *Early Anthropology in the Sixteenth and Seventeenth Centuries.* Philadelphia: University of Pennsylvania Press, 1985.

Horn, W. A. *Bush Echoes and Ballads on the Warrigal Pegasus.* London: H. Rees, 1901.

Howes, David (ed.). *The Varieties of Sensory Experience: A Sourcebook in the Anthropology of the Senses*. Toronto: University of Toronto Press, 1991.
Idriess, Ion L. *Lasseter's Last Ride: An Epic of Central Australian Gold Discovery*. Sydney: Angus & Robertson, 1931.
Indurkhya, Bipin. *Metaphor and Cognition: An Interactionist Approach*. Dordrecht: Kluwer, 1992.
Jackson, Michael. *At Home in the World*. Durham, N.C.: Duke University Press, 1995.
________. *Paths toward a Clearing: Radical Empiricism and Ethnographic Inquiry*. Bloomington: Indiana University Press, 1989.
Kant, Immanuel. *Critique of Pure Reason*. Translated by Norman Kemp Smith. New York: St. Martin's Press, [1787] 1965.
Katz, David. *Gestalt Psychology: Its Nature and Significance*. New York: Ronald Press, 1950.
Keen, Ian. "Stanner on Aboriginal Religion." *Canberra Anthropology* 9, no. 2 (1986): 26–50.
Köhler, Wolfgang. *The Task of Gestalt Psychology*. Princeton, N.J.: Princeton University Press, 1969.
Kolig, Erich. *The Silent Revolution: The Effects of Modernization on Australian Aboriginal Religon*. Philadelphia: Institute for the Study of Human Issues, 1981.
Krichauff, F. E. H. W. "The Customs, Religious Ceremonies, etc. of the 'Aldolinga' and 'Mbenderinga' Tribe of Aborigines in Krichauff Ranges, South Australia." *Royal Geograpahical Society of South Australia* 2 (1886–88): 33–37.
Kuhn, Thomas. *The Structure of Scientific Revolution*. 2nd. ed. Chicago: University of Chicago Press, [1962] 1970.
LaBarre, Weston. "Géza Róheim, 1891–1953: Psychoanalysis and Anthropology." In *Psychoanalytic Pioneers*. Edited by F. Alexander, S. Eisenstein, and M. Grotjahn, pp. 272–81. New York: Basic Books, 1966.
Lakoff, George. *Women, Fire, and Dangerous Things*. Chicago: University of Chicago Press, 1987.
Lakoff, George and Mark Johnson. *Metaphors We Live by*. Chicago: University of Chicago Press, 1980.
Lang, Andrew. "A Theory of Arunta Totemism." *Man* 4 (1904): 67–69.
________. *Social Origins*. London: Longmans, Green & Co., 1903.
Lawson, E. Thomas, and Robert N. McCauley. *Rethinking Religion: Connecting Cognition and Culture*. New York: Cambridge University Press, 1990.
Leske, Everard (ed.). *Hermannsburg: A Vision and a Mission*. Adelaide: Lutheran Publishing House, 1977.
Lessa, William A., and Evan V. Vogt (eds.). *Reader in Comparative Religion: An Anthropological Approach*. New York: Harper & Row, 1958.
Malinowski, Bronislaw. Review of *Across Australia*, by Baldwin Spencer. In *Folk Lore* 24 (1913): 278.
Manser, W. L. "The Overland Telegraph." M.A. honors thesis, University of Adelaide, 1961.
Masuzawa, Tomoko. *In Search of Dreamtime: The Quest for the Origin of Religion*. Chicago: University of Chicago Press, 1993.
McCarthy, Cormac. *The Crossing*. New York: Vintage Books, 1994.
McNally, Ward. *Aborigines, Artifacts and Anguish*. Adelaide: Lutheran Publishing House, 1981.
Minchan, Hans. *The Story of the Flinders Ranges*. Adelaide: Rigby, 1964.
Morison, Samuel Eliot. *Admiral of the Ocean Sea: A Life of Christopher Columbus*. Boston: Little, Brown & Co., 1942.
Morphy, Howard. "The Resurrection of the Hydra: Twenty-Five Years of Research on Aboriginal Religion." In *Social Anthropology and Australian Aboriginal Studies: A Contempo-*

rary Overview. Edited by Ronald M. Berndt and R. Tonkinson, pp. 241–66. Canberra: Aboriginal Studies Press, 1988.

Morton, John. "The Effectiveness of Totemism: 'Increase Rituals' and Resource Control in Central Australia." *Man* 22 (1987): 453–74.

________. "Introduction: Géza Róheim's Contribution to Australian Ethnography." In *Children of the Desert II: Myths and Dreams of the Aborigines of Central Australia*. Oceania Ethnographics, no. 2. By Géza Róheim, pp. vii–xxx. Sydney: Oceania Publications, University of Sydney, 1988.

Mulvaney, D. J. "The Australian Aborigines 1606–1929: Opinion and Fieldwork: Part II: 1859–1929." *Historical Studies* 8, no. 31 (1958): 297–314.

________. *Encounters in Place: Outsiders and Aboriginal Australians 1606–1985*. St. Lucia: University of Queensland Press, 1989.

________. "Gum Leaves on the Golden Bough: Australia's Palaeolithic Survivals Discovered." In *Antiquity and Man: Essays in Honor of Glyn Daniel*. Edited by John D. Evans, B. Cunliffe and C. Renfrew, pp. 52–64. London: Thames & Hudson, 1981.

Mulvaney, D. J., and J. H. Calaby. *'So Much That Is New': Baldwin Spencer, 1860–1929, A Biography*. Melbourne: University of Melbourne Press, 1985.

Murif, Jerome J. *From Ocean to Ocean: A Record of a Trip across the Continent of Australia from Adelaide to Port Darwin*. Melbourne: George Robertson & Co., 1897.

O'Gorman, Edmundo. *The Invention of America: An Inquiry into the Historical Nature of the New World and the Meaning of Its History*. Bloomington: Indiana University Press, 1961.

Peterson, Nicolas. "Totemism Yesterday: Sentiment and Local Organisation among the Australian Aborigines." *Man* 7 (1972): 12–32.

Pfitzner, John, and Joan Schmaal. *Learning Arrarnta*. 2nd. rev. ed. by Hans D. Oberscheidt. Alice Springs: Fink River Mission, 1991.

Piaget, Jean. *Genetic Epistemology*. Translated by E. Duckworth. New York: Columbia University Press, 1970.

________. "Play and Actuality." In *Play and Development*. Edited by Maria W. Piers, pp. 127–67. New York: Norton, 1972.

________. *Play, Dreams and Imitation in Childhood*. Translated by C. Gattegno and F. M. Hodgson. New York: Norton, 1962.

Piaget, Jean, and B. Inhelder. *The Psychology of the Child*. Translated by Helen Weaver. New York: Basic Books, 1966.

Pike, Douglas H. *John McDouall Stuart*. Oxford: Oxford University Press, 1958.

________. *Paradise of Dissent: South Australia 1829–1857*. London: Longman, Green & Co., 1957.

Polanyi, Michael. "Personal Knowledge." In *Meaning*. Edited by Michael Polanyi and Harry Prosch, pp. 22–45. Chicago: University of Chicago Press, 1975.

________. *The Tacit Dimension*. Gloucester, Mass: Peter Smith, 1983.

Poole, Fritz John Porter. "Metaphors and Maps: Towards Comparison in the Anthropology of Religion." *Journal of the American Academy of Religion* 54 (1968): 411–57.

Robinson, Paul A. *The Freudian Left: Wilhelm Reich, Géza Róheim, Herbert Marcuse*. New York: Harper & Row, 1969.

Róheim, Géza. *Australian Totemism: A Psycho-analytic Study in Anthropology*. London: George Allen & Unwin, 1925.

________. *Children of the Desert: The Western Tribes of Central Australia*. New York: Harper & Row, 1974.

________. *Children of the Desert II: Myths and Dreams of the Aborigines of Central Australia.* Oceania Ethnographies, no. 2. Edited by John Morton and Werner Muensterberger. Sydney: Oceania Publications, University of Sydney, 1988.

________. *The Eternal Ones of the Dream: Psychoanalytic Interpretation of Australian Myth and Ritual.* New York: International Universities Press, 1945.

________. *Fire in the Dragon and Other Psychoanalytic Essays on Folklore.* Princeton, N.J.: Princeton University Press, 1992.

________. *The Gates of the Dream.* New York: International Universities Press, [1952] 1973.

________. "The Nescience of the Aranda." *The British Journal of Medical Psychology* 17 (1938): 343–74.

________. *The Origin and Function of Culture.* Nervous and Mental Disease Monographs, no. 69. New York:, 1943.

________. *The Panic of the Gods and Other Essays.* New York: Harper & Row, 1972.

________. *Psychoanalysis and Anthropology: Culture, Personality and the Unconscious.* New York: International Universities Press, 1950.

________. "Psycho-analysis of Primitive Cultural Types." *The International Journal of Psycho-analysis* 13 (1932): 1–223.

________. *The Riddle of the Sphinx, or Human Origins.* Translated by R. Money-Kyrle. London: International Psycho-analytic Library, 1934.

________. "Women and Their Life in Central Australia." *Journal of the Royal Anthropological Institute* 63 (1933): 207–65.

Sartre, Jean-Paul. *Being and Nothingness: A Phenomenological Essay on Ontology.* Translated by Hazel E. Barnes. New York: Washington Square Press, 1956.

Schulze, Louis. "The Aborigines of the Upper and Middle Finke River: Their Habits and Customs, with Introductory Notes on the Physical and Natural-History Features of the Country." *Transactions and Proceedings and Report of the Royal Society of South Australia* 14 (1890–91): 210–46.

Smith, Jonathan Z. "*Adde Parvum Parvo Magnus Acervus Erit.*" In *Map Is Not Territory: Studies in the History of Religions*, pp. 240–64. Leiden: E. J. Brill, 1978.

________. "The Bare Facts of Ritual." In *Imagining Religion: From Babylon to Jonestown*, pp. 53–65. Chicago: University of Chicago Press, 1982.

________. "In Comparison a Magic Dwells." In *Imagining Religion: From Babylon to Jonestown,* pp. 19–35. Chicago: University of Chicago Press, 1982.

________. *Drudgery Divine: On the Comparison of Early Christianities and the Religions of Late Antiquity.* Chicago: University of Chicago Press, 1990.

________. "Good News Is No News: Aretalogy and Gospel." In *Map Is Not Territory: Studies in the History of Religions*, pp. 10–207. Leiden: E. J. Brill, 1978.

________. *Imagining Religion: From Babylon to Jonestown.* Chicago: University of Chicago Press, 1982.

________. "The Influence of Symbols on Social Change." In *Map Is Not Territory: Studies in the History of Religions*, pp. 129–46. Leiden: E. J. Brill, 1978.

________. "Map Is Not Territory." In *Map Is Not Territory: Studies in the History of Religions*, pp. 289–309. Leiden: E. J. Brill, 1978.

________. *To Take Place: Toward Theory in Ritual.* Chicago: University of Chicago Press, 1987.

________. "What a Difference a Difference Makes." In *"To See Ourselves as Others See Us": Christians, Jews, "Others" in Late Antiquity.* Edited by Jacob Neusner and Ernest S. Frerichs, pp. 3–48. Chico, California: Scholars Press, 1985.

________. "The Wobbling Pivot." In *Map Is Not Territory: Studies in the History of Religion*, pp. 88–103. Leiden: E. J. Brill, 1978.

Spencer, W. Baldwin. *Spencer's Scientific Correspondence with Sir J. G. Frazer and Others*. Edited by R. R. Marett and T. K. Penniman. London: Oxford University Press, 1932.

________. "Totemism in Australia." Presidential Address to Ethnology and Anthropology Section. *Report of the Tenth Meeting of the Australasian Association for the Advancement of Science*. Dunedin: Australasian Association for the Advancement of Science, 1904.

________. Unpublished field notes and journals. Museum of Victoria, Melbourne.

Spencer, W. Baldwin (ed.). *Report on the Work of the Horn Scientific Expedition to Central Australia*. London: Dulau, 1896.

Spencer, W. Baldwin, and Francis J. Gillen. *Across Australia*. London: Macmillan, 1912.

________. *The Arunta: A Study of a Stone Age People*. London: Macmillan, 1927.

________. *The Native Tribes of Central Australia*. London: Macmillan, 1899.

________. *The Northern Tribes of Central Australia*. London: Macmillan, 1904.

________. "Some Remarks on Totemism as Applied to Australian Tribes." *Journal of the Anthropological Insitute of Great Britain and Ireland* 28 (1899): 275–80.

Spitz, René A. "Géza Róheim: 1891–1953." *The Psychoanalytic Quarterly* 22 (1953): 324–27.

Stanner, W. E. H. *After the Dreaming*. Crows Nest, New South Wales: Australian Broadcasting Corporation, [1968] 1991.

________. "The Australian Aboriginal Dreaming as an Ideological System." *Proceedings of the Ninth Pacific Science Congress, 1957* 3 (1963): 116–23.

________. "The Dreaming." In *Australian Signpost*. Edited by T. A. G. Hungerford, pp. 51–65. Melbourne: F. W.Cheshire, 1956.

________. "On Freud's Totem and Taboo." *Canberra Anthropology* 5, no. 1 (1982): 1–7.

________. "Religion, Totemism and Symbolism." In *Aboriginal Man in Australia*. Edited by Ronald M. Berndt and Catherine H. Berndt, pp. 137–72. Sydney: Angus & Robertson, 1965.

Stapleton, Austin. *Willshire of Alice Springs*. Carlisle, Western Australia: Hesperian Press, 1992.

Strehlow, Carl. *Die Aranda- Und Loritja-Stämme in Zentral-Australien* [*The Aranda and Lortija Tribes of Central Australia*] 5 vols. Edited by Moritz Freiherr von Leonhardi. Translated by Hans D. Oberscheidt (unpublished). Frankfurt am Main: Joseph Baer, 1907–15.

Strehlow, Theodor G. H. "Aboriginal Language, Religion, and Society in Central Australia." *Australian Territories* 2, no. 1 (1962): 4–11.

________. "Altjira Rega Ekalta: Praise to the Lord, the Almighty." In *Lutheran Yearbook, 1979*, pp. 25–49. Adelaide: Lutheran Church of Australia, 1979.

________. "Ankotarinja, an Aranda Myth." *Oceania* 4 (1933): 187–200.

________. *Aranda Traditions*. Melbourne: Melbourne University Press, 1947.

________. "Central Australian Man-making Ceremonies: With Special Reference to Hermannsburg, Northern Territory." *The Lutheran*, April 10, 1978, pp. 150–55.

________. *Central Australian Religion: Personal Monototemism in a Polytotemic Community*. Adelaide: Australian Association for the Study of Religion, 1978.

________. "Culture, Social Structure, and Environment in Aboriginal Central Australia." In *Aboriginal Man in Australia: Essays in Honor of Emeritus Professor A. P. Elkin*. Edited by Ronald M. Berndt and Catherine H. Berndt, pp. 121–45. Sydney: Angus & Robertson, 1965.

________. "Geography and the Totemic Landscape in Central Australia." In *Australian Aboriginal Anthropology*. Edited by Ronald M. Berndt. Perth: University of Western Australian Press, 1970.

________. "Geography and the Totemic Landscape in Central Australia: A Functional Study." In *Australian Aboriginal Anthropology: Modern Studies in the Social Anthropology of the Australian Aborigines*. Edited by Ronald M. Berndt, pp. 92–140. Wedlands, Western Australia: Australian Institute of Aboriginal Studies, 1970.

________. *Journey to Horeshoe Bend*. Adelaide: Rigby, 1969.

________. "Religion in Aboriginal Australia." *Hemisphere*, July 1963, pp. 2–8.

________. *Songs of Central Australia*. Sydney: Angus & Robertson, 1971.

________. *The Sustaining Ideals of Australian Aboriginal Socieites*. Adelaide: Aborigines Advancement League of South Australia, 1956.

Stuart, John McDouall. "McDouall Stuart's Last Expedition into the Interior of Australia." *Journal of the Royal Geographical Society* 31 (1861): 65–145.

Sullivan, Lawrence E. "'Seeking an End to the Primary Text', or 'Putting an End to the Text as Primary'." In *Beyond the Classics? Essays in Religious Studies and Liberal Education*, Edited by Frank E. Reynolds and Sheryl L. Burkhalter, pp. 41–59. Atlanta: Scholars Press, 1990.

Swain, Tony, *Aboriginal Religions in Australia: A Bibliographical Survey*. Westport, Conn.: Greenwood Press, 1991.

________. "Dreaming, Whites and the Australian Landscape: Some Popular Misconceptions." *The Journal of Religious History* 15, no. 3 (1989): 345–50.

________. "The Mother Earth Conspiracy: An Australian Episode." *Numen* 38, no. 1 (1992): 3–26.

________. *A Place for Strangers: Towards a History of Australian Aboriginal Being*. Cambridge, Mass: Cambridge University Press, 1993.

Swain, Tony, and Deborah B. Rose (eds.). *Aboriginal Australians and Christian Missions: Ethnographic and Historical Studies*. Adelaide: Australian Association for the Study of Religion, 1988.

Symes, G. W. "The Exploration and Development of the Northern Part of South Australia between 1850 and 1869 and the Early Life of John Ross." *Royal Geographical Society of Australasia, South Australia Branch, Proceedings* 58 (December 1957): 1–20.

Telegraph Stations of Central Australia: Historical Photographs. Northern Territory: Government Printing Office, n.d.

Thomas, N. W. "Alcheringa." In *Encylopedia of Religion and Ethics*. Edited by J. Hastings, vol. I, p. 298. Edinburgh: T&T Clark, Charles Scribner's Sons 1908.

Threadgill, B. *South Australian Land Exploration, 1856–1880*. Adelaide: Public Library, Museum of Art Gallery of South Australia, 1922.

Troy, Jakelin. *Australian Aboriginal Contact with the English Language in New South Wales: 1788 to 1845*. Pacific Linguistics Series B-103. Canberra: Australian National University, 1990.

van Gennep, Arnold. "'Myth and Rite' and 'the Content of the Legends', from Mythes et Legendes D'australie." In *Australian Aboriginal Mythology*, Edited by L. R. Hiatt, pp. 183–205. Canberra: Australian Institute of Aboriginal Studies, 1975.

________. *Mythes et Légendes D'Australie*. Paris: Librairie Orientale et Americaine, 1906.

Wagner, Roy. *The Invention of Culture*. Englewood Cliffs, N.J.: Prentice Hall, 1975.

Webster, Mona Stuart. *John McDouall Stuart*. Melbourne: Melbourne University Press, 1958.

White, J. Peter. "Prehistory: The First 99% of Aboriginal History." In *The Moving Frontier: Aspects of Aboriginal-European Interaction in Australia*. Edited by Peter Stanbury, pp. 13–22. Sydney: Charterbooks, 1977.

White, Patrick. *Voss*. New York: Viking, 1957.

Whorf, Benjamin L. "An American Indian Model of the Universe." In *Language, Thought and Reality: Selected Papers of Benjamin Lee Whorf*. Edited by J. B. Carroll, pp. 57–64. Cambridge, Mass: MIT Press, 1956.

Wilbur, G. B., and W. Muensterberger (eds.). *Psychoanalysis and Culture: Essays in Honor of Géza Róheim*. New York: Internataional Universitites Press, 1951.

Willshire, William H. *The Aborigines of Central Australia*. Adelaide: C. E. Bristow, [1888] 1891.

———. *The Land of the Dawning: Being Facts Gleaned from Cannibals in the Australian Stone Age*. Adelaide: W. K. Thomas, 1896.

———. *A Thrilling Tale of Real Life in the Wilds of Australia*. Adelaide: Frearson & Brother, 1895.

Winnecke, C. *Journal of the Horn Scientific Exploring Expedition, 1894*. Adelaide: C. E. Briston, 1896.

Wolfe, Patrick. "On Being Woken up: The Dreamtime in Anthropology and in Australian Settler Culture." *Comparative Study of Society and History* 33 (1991): 197–224.

Index